W9-BGW-407

Writing the Essay
Art in the World
The World Through Art

──────── **TISCH SCHOOL OF THE ARTS CORE CURRICULUM** ────────

A Collaboration between the Expository Writing Program and the Tisch School of the Arts

EDITED BY

Benjamin W. Stewart

Darlene A. Forrest

with Randy Martin

NEW YORK UNIVERSITY

2014–2015

Expository Writing Program
College of Arts and Science
Art and Public Policy
Tisch School of the Arts

Mc
Graw
Hill
Education

3 4 5 6 7 8 9 0   QVS QVS   17 16 15

ISBN-13: 978-1-259-41437-4
ISBN-10: 1-259-41437-X

Learning Solutions Consultant: Michael Finer
Project Manager: Connie Kuhl
Cover Photo Credits: © Comstock Images

Table of Contents

PROGRESSION TWO

Reckoning

• **Required Readings**

• **Selected Essays**

PROGRESSION THREE

<u>Reviewing In Contexts</u>

- **<u>Required Reading</u>**

GAIL SEGAL
A Praise of Doubt in <u>Artistic Citizenship</u> (please consult that book directly)

- **<u>Selected Essays</u>**

SECOND SEMESTER PROGRESSIONS
Reckoning and Reviewing in Contexts

- **Required Readings**

Two chapters to be selected by a teacher from *Artistic Citizenship*. Edited by Mary Schmidt Campbell and Randy Martin.

- **Selected Essays**

Creativity and Culture

- **Required Readings**

- **Selected Essays**

INTRODUCTION for STUDENTS

<u>COURSE OVERVIEW</u>

You come to the Tisch School of the Arts at New York University not only to study art but also to understand how artists, by developing strong voices, make meaningful contributions to the world. The Tisch core curriculum challenges students to consider a range of social and ethical issues that pertain to creative work. This collaboration between the Department of Art and Public Policy and the Expository Writing Program (EWP) is a year-long essay-writing course designed to engage all TSOA freshmen in a broad investigation across various artistic media. You will learn to consider specific works of art not only for their content, but also for their formal qualities and in terms of the varied contexts in which they exist.

In the Fall semester, you will attend a series of required plenary sessions that assemble the individual writing sections into a common experience that parallels the work in the writing course. In the Spring semester, you will attend a weekly lecture on a topic relevant to the work of your writing class.

Although you may learn factual material from the plenaries and the lectures, that is not their primary purpose; teaching you to think critically and creatively is. In these sessions, we will be looking closely at particular works of art to model specific interpretive approaches that you can use in your own essays. Your job in the lecture is to pay particular attention to the ways that the lecturers interpret the works of art, what critical lenses they use, and what ideas they put forth for others to consider. The lecturers provide models of the kind of work that you will be doing as you create essays. We encourage you to think flexibly, both about the lectures' purpose, and how you approach them.

Central to the freshman experience of all Tisch students is a dialogue between the art of your chosen field and the art of writing. Advancing your capacity for writing serves the aims of enhancing self-expression and of developing your public voice. The Expository Writing Program is dedicated to teaching the art of essay writing and the understanding of the essay as both an art form and a mode of public address in which thinkers articulate their ideas for others to consider. Writing artfully for a public is a form of learning that, in many ways, parallels the experience of your studio and production classes. In both places, the interpretations you develop will shape the work that you go on to produce.

Writing and Reading

Over the course of the year, you will write five essays: three in the Fall and two in the Spring. For each essay, you will complete a sequence of assignments (a Progression) designed to help you develop the skills that you will need to write the essays. The skills you learn in each essay are meant to be cumulative: the things you learn in the Fall will be foundational to the more complex, research-based work required in the Spring.

The readings are designed to facilitate the work of each of the Progressions. We have selected them to provide a variety of perspectives, frameworks, and viewpoints for you to use as you develop the ideas in each of your essays. We believe that all of these texts will challenge you both conceptually and ideologically. That is intentional.

All of these assignments are designed to help you become attuned to the relationships between artistic media and writing. In addition to developing reading, writing, and thinking skills, the core curriculum hopes to establish an ongoing basis for collaboration and interconnection among students at Tisch.

Required Texts

Besides this reader, all students must purchase *Mercer Street*, which contains exemplary student writing, and the latest edition of *The Little, Brown Essential Handbook for Writers*, both available at the bookstore. Your writing teacher may also bring in examples of writing drawn from current publications such as *The New York Times* or *The New Yorker*.

A Final Note

As you will soon discover, you have entered a community rich in artistic and intellectual resources. As an important part of that richness, you're likely to encounter work that's not to your taste and viewpoints that clash with your own. In the face of such situations, we encourage you to suspend quick judgments: on one hand, learning what you don't value (and why) is an important aspect of artistic development; on the other hand, allowing yourself to pay attention to works you don't initially like may allow you to discover new ways of seeing and new values; these may become vital resources in helping you generate your own creative work.

Throughout the year, you will be asked to make connections between the plenary, the lecture, the writing course, and your own essays. If it is not clear to you how these are connected, you should ask, either in the plenary, the lecture, or the writing class. If you are confused about how the class is being conducted, you should have a conversation with your teacher. If you still have issues or concerns, you should contact Benjamin Stewart (EWP's Director of Faculty Development), or Kathy Engel (the Director of the Department of Art and Public Policy).

POLICIES OF THE EXPOSITORY WRITING PROGRAM
NEW YORK UNIVERSITY

The following information indicates the official minimum requirements for students enrolled in *Art in the World* (EXPOS-UA5) and *The World through Art* (ASPP-UT2). Individual teachers may have more stringent requirements for the sections they teach.

Course Goals and Parameters

Students will learn to write a variety of essays, with increasingly complex requirements, as they move across the semester and into the next course. The writing courses provide a foundation for work in the university by teaching students to construct essays and arguments that reflect an ability to read critically, question evidence, make relevant connections, develop ideas, and present their own ideas in coherent, compelling essays. In our writing courses, students create essays through a progression of reading, writing, and thinking exercises that lead them to develop their own ideas and their own essays. Progressions give students practice in the skills necessary for writing the particular kind of essay they're being asked to write. Although the activities in a given Progression generate writing toward an essay draft, drafting does not mean cutting and pasting these exercises. Instead, the work of drafting an essay involves the thoughtful reworking of these pieces into one coherent text.

Classroom Decorum

The classroom should be a place where the free exchange of ideas can occur in an atmosphere of mutual trust and respect. Teachers and students are encouraged to bring serious breaches of decorum to the attention of the EWP Directors at (212) 998-8860. This includes problems such as non-performance of class obligations, disruptive or disrespectful behavior, and prejudice on the basis of gender, race, religion, or sexual orientation.

Portfolio/Grades

Students will write three essays in the first semester and two in the second. They must always submit drafts of their major papers, not just the final version. Final versions are graded. All students should receive a midterm grade, indicating how they are progressing in the course.

There should be an opportunity for students to revise one of these essays after the grade has been given; however, it is always the student's responsibility to provide substantive revision. It is the teacher's responsibility to guide revisions, but not specifically to direct them. All students should receive information about how grades are determined. Ninety percent of the grade should be based on the final essays. Students must keep all writing done in the course, including drafts, final papers, and informal writing (e.g. journal entries, in-class writing, homework assignments). This writing should be kept together as a portfolio of work (organized in a file folder or three-ring binder) and must be submitted at the end of the course or during the term upon request. Most homework assignments and all final papers must be printed from a computer.

These papers should be double-spaced, with 1" margins. Students are responsible for collecting their portfolios after course grades have been determined. Portfolios are discarded at the middle of the following semester.

Conferences

During the semester, students are expected to have at least two conferences with their writing teacher to obtain feedback on a draft. Twenty minutes is the minimum time allowed for conferences.

Attendance and Preparedness

Because much of the learning in writing courses occurs through active discussion and in-class writing rather than through lectures, it is essential that students attend class, come prepared, and participate. Students with absences or habitual lateness will have their grades lowered, even though they may have completed their required assignments. Students should explain the reason for an absence at the time it occurs. Documented medical conditions and the observance of religious holidays are legitimate excuses for absences; however, students are still responsible for completing the work they have missed. Students should understand that absence for whatever reason will impact their ability to do their best work in the course. Students with four absences of any kind may fail the course.

How to Contact Us

EWP's Directors will be happy to respond to student inquiries, questions, and concerns. You can schedule visits with them directly at 411 Lafayette, 4th Floor, or call (212) 998-8860 for an appointment. Or, visit our website at: http://ewp.cas.nyu.edu/

<h1 style="text-align:center">THE PROGRESSIONS</h1>

First Semester: Art in the World

During this semester, you will write three essays informed by a close encounter with other writings, your engagement with works of art, and your experience of the world around you.

PROGRESSION ONE: DEEPENING

Learning the Art of the Essay

In this essay you will borrow an idea from one of several essays (written by professional essayists) and deepen the reader's understanding of that idea by considering it in light of another essay and an art object. Your goal in this process is to develop your own idea, one that emerges from the relationships among the evidence you've selected to work with.

Skills and Techniques:

- Analyzing written texts as sources of ideas.
- Selecting and incorporating evidence from visual texts and written texts to substantiate ideas.
- Representing texts (whether written, visual, or performed) in ways that accurately and compellingly present them to readers.
- Practicing the art of textual incorporation.
- Practicing the art of meaningful analysis and reflection.
- Understanding the role of recursion (of returning to prior evidence, thinking, or language) as part of the process of developing a coherent idea.
- Understanding an essay as a form in which one uses evidence to develop one's own idea.

PROGRESSION TWO: RECKONING

Learning the Art of Textual Analysis and Persuasion

In the Reckoning Progression, you will closely read an assigned essay and measure the reliability of its central idea against its evidence. Your own essay will reflect your judgment of this reliability against the standards it sets for itself, against the persuasiveness of related texts, against logical standards, and against your own experience of art and culture. Your writing task here is not so much to deepen our understanding of the original idea as it is to explore the implications and consequences of that idea as a way of measuring its reliability and its worth while developing an idea of your own about art and culture.

Skills and Techniques:

- Reading and analyzing a complex written text's rhetoric and its persuasive strategies.
- Developing a conversation among a group of ideologically-related texts.

- Using that body of texts (including an art object) to generate ideas and explore their far-reaching implications.
- Learning to substantiate and clarify an idea using those texts.
- Practicing the art of reflection both to generate and strengthen ideas.
- Documenting written texts that are cited in an essay.
- Writing a clearly-organized persuasive essay that both assesses the value of the primary text and moves beyond that assessment to develop a compelling idea in a form that accommodates the needs of an intelligent, skeptical reader.

PROGRESSION THREE: REVIEWING IN CONTEXTS

Learning the Art of Contextual Analysis

In this review essay, you will analyze the meaning of a film and explore its significance via contextual analysis. Note that, although you might write this essay about a play or performance, you'll need to be able to view the piece multiple times. In writing a review essay, your job is not to tell us whether the piece is good or bad, nor is your goal to say definitively what the work means. Rather, in approaching your chosen work, you will need to consider not only its narrative properties (the story it tells) but also its formal aspects (they way this story is told). Additionally, you'll need to consider the work's relations to selected cultural contexts (whether aesthetic, historical, scientific, or theoretical). Thus, your essay's idea will emerge out of the dynamic between what those contexts teach us about your film, and what the film teaches us about the contexts.

Skills and Techniques:

- Performing a close, sustained reading of the formal properties of a selected film.
- Representing the relationship between a selected element of the film and the film as a whole (e.g., reflecting on the meaning of a compelling image in light of the entire film).
- Recognizing how narrative and form work together (and sometimes in tension) to create meaning; selecting moments from the film to use as evidence.
- Using research to situate the film in relation to genre, to more general cultural contexts, or to theoretical perspectives that shed light on the film.
- Using critical sources to substantiate an interpretation of the selected film.
- Developing an idea about the film and its cultural relevance by using evidence from the film and by putting that evidence in conversation with other texts.

Second Semester: *The World Through Art*

In writing the second semester's two essays, you will need to incorporate all of the skills and techniques that you learned in the first three Progressions. In addition, Progressions 4 and 5 develop a broader set of research skills: finding sources via scholarly databases and other Internet tools, evaluating those sources' reliability, selecting relevant sources, and synthesizing information and ideas (recognizing patterns, categorizing and clustering those patterns, and interpreting their significance).

PROGRESSION FOUR: CREATIVITY AND CULTURE

Learning to Research as a Means of Developing Ideas

In this progression, you will write a research essay about an artist of your choice. In addition to examining that artist's body of work in detail (including the creative processes involved in its making), you will explore how that work responds to, builds on, and departs from its contexts, both those that influenced its development and those that have shaped its reception.

Some questions to consider: Where does the work of art come from and how was it made? What are the contextual factors (biographical, material, intellectual, aesthetic, cultural) that may have shaped it? How is the audience anticipated in the work and how has the critical reception of the work affected its significance? Finally, what does the work disclose about its cultural setting?

There is no formula for building these various areas of inquiry into an idea, but at the most basic level, you need to do two things: first, using selected insights you've gained from your interpretations of the work, show us why your artist matters (build a case for the work's significance using the most compelling evidence you've found); second, later in the essay, you'll want to turn the tables—show us what your artist's work teaches us about the world around it. Your goal is not simply to gain some insight into the art but to use the art as a means of gaining other insights.

Skills and Techniques:

* Performing formal readings of your artist's body of work; looking for formal patterns (similarities, variations, oppositions) within the various pieces.
* Making nuanced claims about the role those formal patterns play in generating the work's significance/meaning (which will likely also involve relating your formal readings to the work's content).
* Connecting those claims to aesthetic and/or worldly contexts (e.g., artistic movements, or social histories that have affected, or that shed some light on, the work).
* Researching those contexts and employing scholarly texts to help you present them in ways that clarify the significance of the artwork under consideration.
* Weighing the reliability of information and ideas from different sources.
* Engaging with research material in ways that complicate your idea about the artist's work.
* Learning to develop an idea that makes a claim about the relations among your disparate evidence (artist's work, contexts, scholarly texts). Your idea must emerge from your interpretation of the significance of those relations.

PROGRESSION FIVE: ART AND ITS PUBLICS

Learning to Research as a Means of Generating and Developing a Topic

In this final progression, you will write a research essay investigating how at least two different artworks engage with, respond to, or become drawn into a public issue.

In this context, public issue refers to a significant matter of public concern, one whose problems and tensions have been articulated in a variety of forms—e.g., in the popular press, in web comments, in documentaries, in scholarly articles, and in works of art. As you consider these sources, you will need to think flexibly, not just about what a public issue is, but also about how works of art can become involved with or entangled in public discussions.

As a critic, your job is to consider your chosen artworks' significance within a wide public frame: What pressures do social issues put on artistic representations, and how do these issues affect what an artwork can mean? How does this meaning help us see something further about the public issue, something that might not be visible without the lens provided by a work of art?

Skills and Techniques:

- Performing formal readings of artworks as a means of identifying connections to issues of public concern.
- Identifying modes of representation in artworks and public issues: finding overlaps and divergences.
- Weighing the reliability of information and ideas from different sources.
- Discerning patterns across a variety of sources to develop an understanding of and insight into a public issue.
- Researching the discourses surrounding a public issue across a variety of media; representing contexts relevant to that issue.
- Using research as a means to delineate and define the scope of the project's inquiry.
- Learning to develop an idea that helps you organize the relations among your disparate evidence (issue, artwork, contexts, texts); more than merely finding connections among that evidence, this idea must emerge from your interpretation of the significance of those relations.

ART FOR ART'S SAKE

E. M. Forster

An address delivered before the American Academy of Arts and Letters in New York

I believe in art for art's sake. It is an unfashionable belief, and some of my statements must be of the nature of an apology. Fifty years ago I should have faced you with more confidence. A writer or a speaker who chose "Art for Art's Sake" for his theme fifty years ago could be sure of being in the swim, and could feel so confident of success that he sometimes dressed himself in esthetic costumes suitable to the occasion—in an embroidered dressing-gown, perhaps, or a blue velvet suit with a Lord Fauntleroy collar; or a toga, or a kimono, and carried a poppy or a lily or a long peacock's feather in his mediaeval hand. Times have changed. Not thus can I present either myself or my theme today. My aim rather is to ask you quietly to reconsider for a few minutes a phrase which has been much misused and much abused, but which has, I believe, great importance for us—has, indeed, eternal importance.

Now we can easily dismiss those peacock's feathers and other affectations—they are but trifles—but I want also to dismiss a more dangerous heresy, namely the silly idea that only art matters, an idea which has somehow got mixed up with the idea of art for art's sake, and has helped to discredit it. Many things, besides art, matter. It is merely one of the things that matter, and high though the claims are that I make for it, I want to keep them in proportion. No one can spend his or her life entirely in the creation or the appreciation of masterpieces. Man lives, and ought to live, in a complex world, full of conflicting claims, and if we simplified them down into the esthetic he would be sterilised. Art for art's sake does not mean that only art matters, and I would also like to rule out such phrases as "The Life of Art," "Living for Art," and "Art's High Mission." They confuse and mislead.

What does the phrase mean? Instead of generalising, let us take a specific instance—Shakespeare's *Macbeth,* for example, and pronounce the words, "*Macbeth* for *Macbeth's* sake." What does that mean? Well, the play has several aspects—it is educational, it teaches us something about legendary

Scotland, something about Jacobean England, and a good deal about human nature and its perils. We can study its origins, and study and enjoy its dramatic technique and the music of its diction. All that is true. But *Macbeth* is furthermore a world of its own, created by Shakespeare and existing in virtue of its own poetry. It is in this aspect *Macbeth* for *Macbeth's* sake, and that is what I intend by the phrase "art for art's sake." A work of art—whatever else it may be—is a self-contained entity, with a life of its own imposed on it by its creator. It has internal order. It may have external form. That is how we recognise it.

Take for another example that picture of Seurat's which I saw two years ago in Chicago—"*La Grande Jatte*." Here again there is much to study and to enjoy: the pointillism, the charming face of the seated girl, the nineteenth-century Parisian Sunday sunlight, the sense of motion in immobility. But here again there is something more; "*La Grande Jatte*" forms a world of its own, created by Seurat and existing by virtue of its own poetry: "*La Grande Jatte*" pour "*La Grande Jatte*": l'art pour l'art. Like *Macbeth* it has internal order and internal life.

It is to the conception of order that I would now turn. This is important to my argument, and I want to make a digression, and glance at order in daily life, before I come to order in art.

In the world of daily life, the world which we perforce inhabit, there is much talk about order, particularly from statesmen and politicians. They tend, however, to confuse order with orders, just as they confuse creation with regulations. Order, I suggest, is something evolved from within, not something imposed from without; it is an internal stability, a vital harmony, and in the social and political category it has never existed except for the convenience of historians. Viewed realistically, the past is really a series of *dis*orders, succeeding one another by discoverable laws, no doubt, and cer-

tainly marked by an increasing growth of human interference, but disorders all the same. So that, speaking as a writer, what I hope for today is a disorder which will be more favourable to artists than is the present one, and which will provide them with fuller inspirations and better material conditions. It will not last—nothing lasts—but there have been some advantageous disorders in the past—for instance, in ancient Athens, in Renaissance Italy, eighteenth-century France, periods in China and Persia—and we may do something to accelerate the next one. But let us not again fix our hearts where true joys are not to be found. We were promised a new order after the first world war through the League of Nations. It did not come, nor have I faith in present promises, by whomsoever endorsed. The implacable offensive of Science forbids. We cannot reach social and political stability for the reason that we continue to make scientific discoveries and to apply them, and thus to destroy the arrangements which were based on more elementary discoveries. If Science would discover rather than apply—if, in other words, men were more interested in knowledge than in power—mankind would be in a far safer position, the stability statesmen talk about would be a possibility, there could be a new order based on vital harmony, and the earthly millennium might approach. But Science shows no signs of doing this: she gave us the internal combustion engine, and before we had digested and assimilated it with terrible pains into our social system, she harnessed the atom, and destroyed any new order that seemed to be evolving. How can man get into harmony with his surroundings when he is constantly altering them? The future of our race is, in this direction, more unpleasant than we care to admit, and it has sometimes seemed to me that its best chance lies through apathy, uninventiveness, and inertia. Universal exhaustion might promote that Change of Heart which is at present so briskly recommended from a thousand pulpits. Universal exhaustion would certainly be a new experience. The human race has never undergone it, and is still too perky to admit that it may be coming and might result in a sprouting of new growth through the decay.

I must not pursue these speculations any further—they lead me too far from my terms of reference and maybe from yours. But I do want to emphasise that order in daily life and in history order in the social and political category, is unattainable under our present psychology.

Where is it attainable? Not in the astronomical category, where it was for many years enthroned. The heavens and the earth have become terribly alike since Einstein. No longer can we find a reassuring contrast to chaos in the night sky and look up with George Meredith to the stars, the army of unalterable law, or listen for the music of the spheres. Order is not there. In the entire universe there seem to be only two possibilities for it. The first of them—which again lies outside my terms of reference—is the divine order, the mystic harmony, which according to all religions is available for those who can contemplate it. We must admit its possibility, on the evidence of the adepts, and we must believe them when they say that it is attained, if attainable, by prayer. "O thou who changest not, abide with me," said one of its poets. *"Ordina questo amor, o tu che m'ami,"* said another: "Set love in order, thou who lovest me." The existence of a divine order, though it cannot be tested, has never been disproved.

The second possibility for order lies in the esthetic category, which is my subject here: the order which an artist can create in his own work, and to that we must now return. A work of art, we are all agreed, is a unique product. But why? It is unique not because it is clever or noble or beautiful or enlightened or original or sincere or idealistic or useful or educational—it may embody any of those qualities—but because it is the only material object in the universe which may possess internal harmony. All the others have been pressed into shape from outside, and when their mould is removed they collapse. The work of art stands up by itself, and nothing else does. It achieves something which has often been promised by society, but always delusively. Ancient Athens made a mess—but the *Antigone* stands up. Renaissance Rome made a mess—but the ceiling of the Sistine got painted. James I made a mess—but there was *Macbeth*. Louis XIV—but there was *Phèdre*. Art for art's sake? I should just think so, and more so than ever at the present time. It is the one orderly product which our muddling race has produced. It is the cry of a thousand sentinels, the echo from a thousand labyrinths; it is the lighthouse which cannot be hidden: *c'est le meilleur témoignage que nous puissions donner de notre dignité. Antigone* for *Antigone's* sake, *Macbeth* for *Macbeth's,* "La Grande Jatte" pour "La Grande Jatte."

If this line of argument is correct, it follows that the artist will tend to be an outsider in the society to which he has been born, and that the nineteenth-century conception of him as a Bohemian was not inaccurate. The conception erred in three particulars: it postulated an economic system where art could be a full-time job, it introduced the fallacy that only art matters, and it overstressed idiosyncrasy and waywardness—the peacock-feather aspect—rather than order. But it is a truer conception than the one which prevails in official circles on my side of the Atlantic—I don't know about yours: the conception which treats the artist as if he were a particularly bright government advertiser and encourages him to be friendly and matey with his fellow citizens, and not to give himself airs.

Estimable is mateyness, and the man who achieves it gives many a pleasant little drink to himself and to others. But it has no traceable connection with the creative impulse, and probably acts as an inhibition on it. The artist who is seduced by matey-ness may stop himself from doing the one thing which he, and he alone, can do—the making of something out of words or sounds or paint or clay or marble or steel or film which has internal harmony and presents order to a permanently disarranged planet. This seems worth doing, even at the risk of being called uppish by journalists. I have in mind an article which was published some years ago in the London *Times,* an article called "The Eclipse of the Highbrow," in which the "Average Man" was exalted, and all contemporary literature was censured if it did not toe the line, the precise position of the line being naturally known to the writer of the article. Sir Kenneth Clark, who was at that time director of our National Gallery, commented on this pernicious doctrine in a letter which cannot be too often quoted. "The poet and the artist," wrote Clark, "are important precisely because they are not average men; because in sensibility, intelligence, and power of invention they far exceed the average." These memorable words, and particularly the words "power of invention," are the Bohemian's passport. Furnished with it, he slinks about society, saluted now by a brickbat and now by a penny, and accepting either of them with equanimity. He does not consider too anxiously what his relations with society may be, for he is aware of something more important than that—namely the invitation to invent, to create order, and he believes he will be better placed for doing this if he attempts detachment. So round and round he slouches, with his hat pulled over his eyes, and maybe with a louse in his beard, and—if he really wants one—with a pea-cock's feather in his hand.

If our present society should disintegrate—and who dare prophesy that it won't?—this old-fashioned and démodé figure will become clearer: the Bohemian, the outsider, the para-site, the rat—one of those figures which have at present no function either in a warring or a peaceful world. It may not be dignified to be a rat, but many of the ships are sinking, which is not dignified either—the officials did not build them properly. Myself, I would sooner be a swimming rat than a sinking ship—at all events I can look around me for a little longer—and I remember how one of us, a rat with particu-larly bright eyes called Shelley, squeaked out, "Poets are the unacknowledged legislators of the world," before he vanished into the waters of the Mediterranean.

What laws did Shelley propose to pass? None. The legislation of the artist is never formulated at the time, though it is some-times discerned by future generations. He legislates through creating. And he creates through his sensitiveness and his power to impose form. Without form the sensitiveness vanishes. And form is as important today, when the human race is trying to ride the whirlwind, as it ever was in those less agitat-ing days of the past, when the earth seemed solid and the stars fixed, and the discoveries of science were made slowly, slowly. Form is not tradition. It alters from generation to generation. Artists always seek a new tech-nique, and will continue to do so as long as their work excites them. But form of some kind is imperative. It is the surface crust of the internal harmony, it is the outward evi-dence of order.

My remarks about society may have seemed too pessimistic, but I believe that society can only represent a fragment of the human spirit, and that another fragment can only get expressed through art. And I wanted to take this opportunity, this vantage ground, to assert not only the existence of art, but its pertinacity. Looking back into the past, it seems to me that that is all there has ever been: vantage grounds for discussion and cre-ation, little vantage grounds in the changing chaos, where bubbles have been blown and webs spun, and the desire to create order has found temporary gratification, and the sentinels have managed to utter their challenges, and the huntsmen, though lost individually, have heard each other's calls through the impenetrable wood, and the lighthouses have never ceased sweeping the thankless seas. In this pertinacity there seems to me, as I grow older, something more and more profound, something which does in fact concern people who do not care about art at all.

In conclusion, let me summarise the various categories that have laid claim to the possession of Order.

(1) The social and political category. Claim disallowed on the evidence of history and of our own experience. If man altered psychologically, order here might be attainable; not otherwise.

(2) The astronomical category. Claim allowed up to the present century, but now disallowed on the evidence of the physicists.

(3) The religious category. Claim allowed on the evidence of the mystics.

(4) The esthetic category. Claim allowed on the evidence of various works of art, and on the evidence of our own creative impulses, however weak these may be, or however imperfectly they may function. Works of art, in my opinion, are the only objects in the material universe to possess internal order, and that is why, though I don't believe that only art matters, I do believe in Art for Art's Sake.

METALOGUE: ABOUT GAMES AND BEING SERIOUS*

Gregory Bateson

*D*aughter: Daddy, are these conversations serious?

Father: Certainly they are.

D: They're not a sort of game that you play with me?

F: God forbid . . . but they are a sort of game that we play together.

D: Then they're *not* serious!

F: Suppose you tell me what you would understand by the words "serious" and a "game."

D: Well . . . if you're . . . I don't know.

F: If I am what?

D: I mean . . . the conversations are serious for me, but if you are only playing a game . . .

F: Steady now. Let's look at what is good and what is bad about "playing" and "games." First of all, I don't mind—not much—about winning or losing. When your questions put me in a tight spot, sure, I try a little harder to think straight and to say clearly what I mean. But I don't bluff and I don't set traps. There is no temptation to cheat.

D: That's just it. It's not serious to you. It's a game. People who cheat just don't know how to *play*. They treat a game as though it were serious.

F: But it *is* serious.

D: No, it isn't—not for you it isn't.

F: Because I don't even want to cheat?

D: Yes—partly that.

F: But do you want to cheat and bluff all the time?

D: No—of course not.

F: Well then?

D: Oh—Daddy—you'll *never* understand.

F: I guess I never will.

F: Look, I scored a sort of debating point just now by forcing you to admit that you don't want to cheat—and then I tied onto that admission the conclusion that therefore the conversations are not "serious" for you either. Was that a sort of cheating?

D: Yes—sort of.

F: I agree—I think it was. I'm sorry.

D: You see, Daddy—if I cheated or wanted to cheat, that would mean that I was not serious about the things we talk about. It

*This metalogue is reprinted by permission from *ETC.: A Review of General Semantics,* Vol. X, 1953.

would mean that I was only playing a game with you.

F: Yes, that makes sense.

D: But it doesn't make sense, Daddy. It's an awful muddle.

F: Yes—a muddle—but still a sort of sense.

D: How, Daddy?

F: Wait a minute. This is difficult to say. First of all—I think that we get somewhere with these conversations. I enjoy them very much and I think you do. But also, apart from that, I think that we get some ideas straight and I think that the muddles help. I mean—that if we both spoke logically all the time, we would never get anywhere. We would only parrot all the old clichés that everybody has repeated for hundreds of years.

D: What is a cliché, Daddy?

F: A cliché? It's a French word, and I think it was originally a printer's word. When they print a sentence they have to take the separate letters and put them one by one into a sort of grooved stick to spell out the sentence. But for words and sentences which people use often, the printer keeps little sticks of letters ready made up. And these ready-made sentences are called clichés.

D: But I've forgotten now what you were saying about clichés, Daddy.

F: Yes—it was about the muddles that we get into in these talks and how getting into muddles makes a sort of sense. If we didn't get into muddles, our talks would be like playing rummy without first shuffling the cards.

D: Yes, Daddy—but what about those things—the ready-made sticks of letters?

F: The clichés? Yes—it's the same thing. We all have lots of ready-made phrases and ideas, and the printer has ready-made sticks of letters, all sorted out into phrases. But if the printer wants to print something new—say, something in a new language, he will have to break up all that old sorting of the letters. In the same way, in order to think new thoughts or to say new things, we have to break up all our ready-made ideas and shuffle the pieces.

D: But, Daddy, the printer would not shuffle all the letters? Would he? He wouldn't shake them all up in a bag. He would put them one by one in their places—all the *a*'s in one box and all the *b*'s in another, and all the commas in another, and so on.

F: Yes—that's right. Otherwise he would go mad trying to find an *a* when he wanted it.

F: What are you thinking?

D: No—it's only that there are so many questions.

F: For example?

D: Well, I see what you mean about our getting into muddles. That that makes us say new sorts of things. But I am thinking about the printer. He has to keep all his little letters sorted out even though he breaks up all the ready-made phrases. And I am wondering about our muddles. Do we have to keep the little pieces of our thought in some sort of order—to keep from going mad?

F: I think so—yes—but I don't know *what* sort of order. That would be a terribly hard question to answer. I don't think we could get an answer to that question today.

F: You said there were "so many questions." Do you have another?

D: Yes—about games and being serious. That's what we started from, and I don't know how or why that led us to talk about our muddles. The way you confuse everything—it's a sort of cheating.

F: No, absolutely not.

F: You brought up two questions. And

really there are a lot more . . . We started from the question about these conversations—are they serious? Or are they a sort of game? And you felt hurt that I might be playing a game, while you were serious. It looks as though a conversation is a game if a person takes part in it with one set of emotions or ideas—but not a "game" if his ideas or emotions are different.

D: Yes, it's if your ideas about the conversation are different from mine . . .

F: If we *both* had the game idea, it would be all right?

D: Yes—of course.

F: Then it seems to be up to me to make clear what I mean by the game idea. I know that I am serious—whatever that means—about the things that we talk about. We talk about ideas. And I know that I play with the ideas in order to understand them and fit them together. It's "play" in the same sense that a small child "plays" with blocks . . . And a child with building blocks is mostly very serious about his "play."

D: But is it a *game*, Daddy? Do you play *against* me?

F: No. I think of it as you and I playing together against the building blocks— the ideas. Sometimes competing a bit— but competing as to who can get the next idea into place. And sometimes we attack each other's bit of building, or I will try to defend my built-up ideas from your criticism. But always in the end we are working together to build the ideas up so that they will stand.

D: Daddy, do our talks have *rules?* The difference between a game and just playing is that a game has rules.

F: Yes. Let me think about that. I think we do have a sort of rules . . . and I think a child playing with blocks has rules. The blocks themselves make a sort of rules. They will balance in certain positions and they will not balance in other positions. And it would be a sort of cheating if the child used glue to make the blocks stand up in a position from which they would otherwise fall.

D: But what rules do *we* have?

F: Well, the ideas that we play with bring in a sort of rules. There are rules about how ideas will stand up and support each other. And if they are wrongly put together the whole building falls down.

D: No glue, Daddy?

F: No—no glue. Only logic.

D: But you said that if we always talked logically and did not get into muddles, we could never say anything new. We could only say ready-made things. What did you call those things?

F: Clichés. Yes. Glue is what clichés are stuck together with.

D: But you said "logic," Daddy.

F: Yes, I know. We're in a muddle again. Only I don't see a way out of this particular muddle.

D: How did we get into it, Daddy?

F: All right, let's see if we can retrace our steps. We were talking about the "rules" of these conversations. And I said that the ideas that we play with have rules of logic . . .

D: Daddy! Wouldn't it be a good thing if we had a few more rules and obeyed them more carefully? Then we might not get into these dreadful muddles.

F: Yes. But wait. You mean that I get us into these muddles because I cheat against rules which we don't have. Or put it this way. That we might have rules which would stop us from getting into muddles—as long as we obeyed them.

D: Yes, Daddy, that's what the rules of a game are for.

F: Yes, but do you want to turn these conversations into *that* sort of a game? I'd rather play canasta—which is fun too.

D: Yes, that's right. We can play canasta whenever we want to. But at the moment I would rather play this game. Only I don't know what sort of a game this is. Nor what sort of rules it has.

F: And yet we have been playing for some time.

D: Yes. And it's been fun.

F: Yes.

F: Let's go back to the question which you asked and which I said was too difficult to answer today. We were talking about the printer breaking up his clichés, and you said that he would still keep some sort of order among his letters—to keep from going mad. And then you asked "What sort of order should we cling to so that when we get into a muddle we do not go mad?" It seems to me that the "rules" of the game is only another name for that sort of order.

D: Yes—and cheating is what gets us into muddles.

F: In a sense, yes. That's right. Except that the whole point of the game is that we do get into muddles, and do come out on the other side, and if there were no muddles our "game" would be like canasta or chess—and that is not how we want it to be.

D: Is it *you* that make the rules, Daddy? Is that fair?

F: That, daughter, is a dirty crack. And probably an unfair one. But let me accept it at face value. Yes, it is I who make the rules—after all, I do not want us to go mad.

D: All right. But, Daddy, do you also change the rules? Sometimes?

F: Hmm, another dirty crack. Yes, daughter, I change them constantly. Not all of them, but some of them.

D: I wish you'd tell me when you're going to change them!

F: Hmm—yes—again. I wish I could. But it isn't like that. If it were like chess or canasta, I could tell you the rules, and we could, if we wanted to, stop playing and discuss the rules. And then we could start a new game with the new rules. But what rules would hold us between the two games? While we were discussing the rules?

D: I don't understand.

F: Yes. The point is that the purpose of these conversations is to discover the "rules." It's like life—a game whose purpose is to discover the rules, which rules are always changing and always undiscoverable.

D: But I don't call that a *game*, Daddy.

F: Perhaps not. I would call it a game, or at any rate "play." But it certainly is not like chess or canasta. It's more like what kittens and puppies do. Perhaps. I don't know.

D: Daddy, why do kittens and puppies play?

F: I don't know—I don't know.

Steps Towards a Small Theory of the Visible

John Berger

When I say the first line of the Lord's Prayer: 'Our father who art in heaven . . .' I imagine this heaven as invisible, unenterable but intimately close. There is nothing baroque about it, no swirling infinite space or stunning foreshortening. To find it—if one had the grace—it would only be necessary to lift up something as small and as at hand as a pebble or a salt-cellar on the table. Perhaps Cellini knew this.

'Thy kingdom come . . .' The difference is infinite between heaven and earth, yet the distance is minimal. Simone Weil wrote concerning this sentence: 'Here our desire pierces through time to find eternity behind it and this happens when we know how to turn whatever happens, no matter what it is, into an object of desire.'

Her words might also be a prescription for the art of painting.

Today images abound everywhere. Never has so much been depicted and watched. We have glimpses at any moment of what things look like on the other side of the planet, or the other side of the moon. Appearances registered, and transmitted with lightning speed.

Yet with this, something has innocently changed. They used to be called physical appearances because they belonged to solid bodies. Now appearances are volatile. Technological innovation has made it easy to separate the apparent from the existent. And this is precisely what the present system's mythology continually needs to exploit. It turns appearances into refractions, like mirages: refractions not of light but of appetite, in fact a single appetite, the appetite for more.

Consequently—and oddly, considering the physical implications of the notion of *appetite*—the existent, the body, disappears. We live within a spectacle of empty clothes and unworn masks.

Consider any newsreader on any television channel in any country. These speakers are the mechanical epitome of the *disembodied*. It took the system many years to invent them and to teach them to talk as they do.

No bodies and no Necessity—for Necessity is the condition of the existent. It is what makes reality real. And the system's mythology requires only the not-yet-real, the virtual, the next purchase. This produces in the spectator, not, as claimed, a sense of freedom (the so called freedom of choice) but a profound isolation.

Until recently, history, all the accounts people gave of their lives, all proverbs, fables, parables, confronted the same thing: the everlasting, fearsome, and occasionally beautiful, struggle of living with Necessity, which is the enigma of existence—that which followed from the Creation, and which subsequently has always continued to sharpen the human spirit. Necessity produces both tragedy and comedy. It is what you kiss or bang your head against.

Today, in the system's spectacle, it exists no more. Consequently no experience is communicated. All that is left to share is the spectacle, the game that nobody plays and everybody can watch. As has never happened before, people have to try to place their own existence and their own pains single-handed in the vast arena of time and the universe.

I had a dream in which I was a strange dealer: a dealer in looks or appearances. I collected and distributed them. In the dream I had just discovered a secret! I discovered it on my own, without help or advice.

The secret was to get inside whatever I was looking at—a bucket of water, a cow, a city (like Toledo) seen from above, an oak tree, and, once inside, to arrange its appearances for the better. *Better* did not mean making the thing seem more beautiful or more harmonious; nor did it mean making it more typical, so that the oak tree might represent all oak trees; it simply meant making it more itself so that the cow or the city or the bucket of water became more evidently unique!

The *doing* of this gave me pleasure and I had the impression that the small changes I made from the inside gave pleasure to others.

The secret of how to get inside the object so as to rearrange how it looked was as simple as opening the door of a wardrobe. Perhaps it was merely a question of being there when the door swung open on its own. Yet when I woke up, I couldn't remember how it was done and I no longer knew how to get inside things.

The history of painting is often presented as a history of succeeding styles. In our time art dealers and promoters have used this battle of styles to make brand-names for the market. Many collectors—and museums—buy names rather than works.

Maybe it's time to ask a naive question: what does all painting from the Palaeolithic period until our century have in common? Every painted image announces: *I have seen this*, or, when the making of the image was incorporated into a tribal ritual: *We have seen this*. The *this* refers to the sight represented. Non-figurative art is no exception. A late canvas by Rothko represents an illumination or a coloured glow which derived from the painter's experience of the visible. When he was working, he judged his canvas according to something else that he *saw*.

Painting is, first, an affirmation of the visible which surrounds us and which continually appears and disappears. Without the disappearing, there would perhaps be no impulse to paint, for then the visible itself would possess the surety (the permanence) which painting strives to find. More directly than any other art, painting is an affirmation of the existent, of the physical world into which mankind has been thrown.

Animals were the first subject in painting. And right from the beginning and then continuing through Sumerian, Assyrian, Egyptian and early Greek art, the depiction of these animals was extraordinarily true.

Many millennia had to pass before an equivalent 'life-likeness' was achieved in the depiction of the human body. At the beginning, the existent was what confronted man.

The first painters were hunters whose lives, like everybody else's in the tribe, depended upon their close knowledge of animals. Yet the act of painting was not the same as the act of hunting: the relation between the two was magical.

In a number of early cave paintings there are stencil representations of the human hand beside the animals. We do not know what precise ritual this served. We do know that painting was used to confirm a magical 'companionship' between prey and hunter, or, to put it more abstractly, between the existent and human ingenuity. Painting was the means of making this companionship explicit and therefore (hopefully) permanent.

This may still be worth thinking about, long after painting has lost its herds of animals and its ritual function. I believe it tells us something about the nature of the act.

The impulse to paint comes neither from observation nor from the soul (which is probably blind) but from an encounter: the encounter between painter and model—even if the model is a mountain or a shelf of empty medicine bottles. Mont St Victoire as seen from Aix (seen from elsewhere it has a very different shape) was Cézanne's companion.

When a painting is lifeless it is the result of the painter not having the nerve to get close enough for a collaboration to start. He stays at a *copying* distance. Or, as in mannerist periods like today, he stays at an art-historical distance, playing stylistic tricks which the model knows nothing about.

To go in close means forgetting convention, reputation, reasoning, hierarchies and self. It also means risking incoherence, even madness. For it can happen that one gets too close and then the collaboration breaks down and the painter dissolves into the model. Or the animal devours or tramples the painter into the ground.

Every authentic painting demonstrates a collaboration. Look at Petrus Christus' portrait of a young girl in the Staatliche Museum of Berlin, or the stormy seascape in the Louvre by Courbet, or the mouse with an aubergine painted by Tchou-Ta in the seventeenth century, and it is impossible to deny the participation of the model. Indeed, the paintings are *not* first and foremost about a young woman, a rough sea or a mouse with a vegetable; they are about this participation. 'The brush,' wrote Shitao, the great seventeenth-century Chinese landscape painter, 'is for saving things from chaos.'

It is a strange area into which we are wandering and I'm using words strangely. A rough sea on the northern coast of France, one autumn day in 1870, *participating in being seen* by a man with a beard who, the following year, will be put in prison! Yet there is no other way of getting close to the actual practice of this silent art, which stops everything moving.

The *raison d'être* of the visible is the eye; the eye evolved and developed where there was enough light for the visible forms of life to become more and more complex and varied. Wild flowers, for example, are the colours they are in order to be seen. That an empty sky appears blue is due to the structure of our eyes and the nature of the solar system. There is a certain ontological basis for the collaboration between model and painter. Silesius, a seventeenth-century doctor of medicine in Wrocklau, wrote about the interdependence of the seen and the seeing in a mystical way:

La rose qui contemple ton oeil de chair
A fleuri de la sorte en Dieu dans l'éternel

How did you become what you visibly are? asks the painter.

I am as I am. I'm waiting, replies the mountain or the mouse or the child.

What for?

For you, if you abandon everything else.

For how long?

For as long as it takes.

There are other things in life.

Find them and be more normal.

And if I don't?

I'll give you what I've given nobody else, but it's worthless, it's simply the answer to your useless question.

Useless?

I am as I am.

No promise more than that?

None. I can wait forever.

I'd like a normal life.

Live it and don't count on me.

And if I do count on you?

Forget everything and in me you'll find—me!

The collaboration which sometimes follows is seldom based on good will: more usually on desire, rage, fear, pity or longing. The modern illusion concerning painting (which post-modernism has done nothing to correct) is that the artist is a creator. Rather he is a receiver. What seems like creation is the act of giving form to what he has received.

Bogena and Robert and his brother Witek came to spend the evening because it was the Russian new year. Sitting at the table whilst they spoke Russian, I tried to draw Bogena. Not for the first time. I always fail because her face is very mobile and I can't forget her beauty. And to draw well you have to forget that. It was long past midnight when they left. As I was doing my last drawing, Robert said: This is your last chance tonight, just draw her, John, draw her and be a man!

When they had gone, I took the least bad drawing and started working on it with colours—acrylic. Suddenly, like a weather vane swinging round because the wind has changed, the portrait began to look like something. Her 'likeness' now was in my head—and all I had to do was to draw it out, not look for it. The paper tore. I rubbed on paint sometimes as thick as ointment. At four in the morning the face began to lend itself to, to smile at, its own representation.

The next day the frail piece of paper, heavy with paint, still looked good. In the daylight there were a few nuances of tone to change. Colours applied at night sometimes tend to be too desperate—like shoes pulled off without being untied. Now it was finished.

From time to time during the day I went to look at it and I felt elated. Because I had done a small drawing I was pleased with? Scarcely. The elation came from something else. It came from the face's *appearing*—as if out of the dark. It came from the fact that Bogena's face had made a present of *what it could leave behind of itself.*

What is a likeness? When a person dies, they leave behind, for those who knew them, an emptiness, a space: the space has contours and is different for each person mourned. This space with its contours is the person's *likeness* and is what the artist searches for when making a living portrait. A likeness is something left behind invisibly.

Soutine was among the great painters of the twentieth century. It has taken fifty years for this to become clear, because his art was both traditional and uncouth, and this mixture offended all fashionable tastes. It was as if his painting had a heavy broken accent and so was considered inarticulate: at best exotic, and at worst barbarian. Now his devotion to the existent becomes more and more exemplary. Few other painters have revealed more graphically than he the collaboration, implicit in the act of painting, between model and painter. The poplars, the carcasses, the children's faces on Soutine's canvases clung to his brush.

Shitao—to quote him again—wrote:

Painting is the result of the receptivity of ink: the ink is open to the brush: the brush is open to the hand: the hand is open to the heart: all this in the same way as the sky engenders what the earth produces: everything is the result of receptivity.

It is usually said about the late work of Titian or Rembrandt or Turner that their handling of paint became *freer*. Although, in a sense, true, this may give a false impression of *wilfulness*. In fact these painters in their old age simply became more receptive, more open to the appeal of the 'model' and its strange energy. It is as if their own bodies fall away.

When once the principle of collaboration has been understood, it becomes a criterion for judging works of any style, irrespective of their freedom of handling. Or rather (because *judgement* has little to do with art) it offers us an insight for seeing more clearly why painting moves us.

Rubens painted his beloved Hélène Fourment many times. Sometimes she collaborated, sometimes not. When she didn't, she remains a painted ideal; when she did, we too wait for her. There is a painting of roses in a vase by Morandi (1949) in which the flowers wait like cats to be let into his vision. (This is very rare for most flower paintings remain pure spectacle.) There is a portrait of a man painted on wood two millennia ago, whose participation we still feel. There are dwarfs painted by Velázquez, dogs by Titian, houses by Vermeer in which we recognise, as energy, the will-to-be-seen.

More and more people go to museums to look at paintings and do not come away disappointed. What fascinates them? To answer: Art, or the history of art, or art appreciation, misses, I believe, the essential.

In art museums we come upon the visible of other periods and it offers us company. We feel less alone in face of what we ourselves see each day appearing and disappearing. So much continues to look the same: teeth, hands, the sun, women's legs, fish . . . in the realm of the visible all epochs coexist and are fraternal, whether separated by centuries or millennia. And when the painted image is not a copy but the result of a dialogue, the painted thing speaks if we listen.

In matters of seeing, Joseph Beuys was the great prophet of the second half of our century, and his life's work was a demonstration of, and an appeal for, the kind of collaboration I'm talking about. Believing that everybody is potentially an artist, he took objects and arranged them in such a way that they beg the spectator to collaborate with them, not this time by painting, but by listening to what their eyes tell them and remembering.

I know of few things more sad (sad, not tragic) than an animal who has lost its sight. Unlike humans, the animal has no supporting language left which can describe the world. If on a familiar terrain, the blind animal manages to find its way about with its nose. But it has been deprived of the existent and with this deprivation it begins to diminish until it does little but sleep, therein perhaps hunting for a dream of that which once existed.

The Marquise de Sorcy de Thélusson, painted in 1790 by David, looks at me. Who could have foreseen in her time the solitude in which people today live? A solitude confirmed daily by networks of bodiless and false images concerning the world. Yet their falseness is not an error. If the pursuit of profit is considered as the only means of salvation for mankind, turnover becomes the absolute priority, and, consequently, the existent has to be disregarded or ignored or suppressed.

Today, to try to paint the existent is an act of resistance instigating hope.

ART AND FRIENDSHIP

by Noël Carroll

*Y*asmina Reza's play *Art* is about one man, Serge, who buys a painting, and the reactions of his friends, Marc and Yvan, to his purchase.[1] Marc's response is quite volcanic; for him, Serge's purchase of the painting threatens to wreck their friendship. Yvan tries to mediate the disaffection between Serge and Marc, often at the cost of redirecting their hostilities at himself.

As the play opens, Marc addresses the audience directly. He says:

My friend Serge has bought a painting. It's a canvas about five foot by four: white. The background is white and if you screw up your eyes, you can make out some fine white diagonal lines.

Serge is one of my oldest friends.

He's done very well for himself, he's a dermatologist and he's keen on art.

On Monday, I went to see the painting; Serge had actually got hold of it on the Saturday, but he's been lusting after it for several months.

This white painting with white lines.[2]

This prelude explicitly connects the two major themes of the play—art and friendship (Serge is one of Marc's oldest friends), and the relation thereof. After this brief exposition, then, there is a flashback to the scene where Marc first sees Serge's painting, a painting by Antrios, a famous artist. At first Marc reacts warily, tentatively, but, in almost no time at all, he denounces the painting as shit, despite its whiteness. Marc tries to pass off his vituperation as humor and invites Serge to laugh along with him. But Serge finds nothing funny about the situation, which deteriorates throughout the play as everyone's nerves fray and angers mount.

The action of the play raises an immediate question. Why is Marc's reaction to the painting by Antrios so intense, so violent? Why would a painting endanger a friendship? Why do Marc and Serge seem to be willing to split apart after fifteen years over a matter of taste? Can't they just agree to disagree and leave it at that?

But Marc, at least, cannot. He says, "It's a complete mystery to me, Serge buying this painting. It's unsettled me, it's filled me with

PHILOSOPHY AND LITERATURE, © 2002, 26: 199–206

some undefinable unease." And that undefinable unease is enough to motivate Marc to attack Serge and Yvan savagely to the point where the friendship among them seems no longer possible. But what is the nature of this undefinable unease and what does its existence tell us about the relation of art to friendship?

Marc and Serge obviously see the painting very differently. Marc keeps referring to the Antrios as white, prompting Serge to correct him—pointing out that it has diagonals as well as bits of various other colors in it. Perhaps this is author Yasmina Reza's way of signaling that Serge, so to speak, sees something in the painting—sees that there's something to it—whereas for Marc, it's a blank, it's empty, it's nothing, it's worthless. Marc continues to be amazed that Serge has paid two hundred thousand francs for the painting. But it's not the money, as such, that bothers Marc; it is what the money symbolizes: that Serge sees something worthy in that which Marc finds worthless. And this threatens their friendship. Why?

One of the earliest conceptions of friendship in Western thought is Aristotle's notion of what he calls the friendship of character or character friendship. This is not the only type of friendship there is—there are also friendships based on such things as expediency—but, for Aristotle, character friendship is the highest sort. This is the type of friendship that obtains between equals—people of equal virtue and excellence.

Now you might think that people who are virtuous and excellent already should have little need of friends. They already have it all.[3] But Aristotle suggests that without friends—friends who are our equals—we have no way of objectively assessing our own qualities—no objective measure of assessing whether or not we are virtuous or excellent. Genuine self-knowledge requires an outside viewpoint to validate it. From the inside, we all seem virtuous to ourselves.

But how can we see how things really stand with us?

Aristotle's answer is ingenious in its simplicity: look at your friends. See what kind of people they are. They will reflect your character. Your character will be like their character. They are what Aristotle calls "other selves" and what we, by way of the Romans, call "alter egos." The character and values of such alter egos will mirror your character and values. You would not be friends of the relevant sort, if they did not.

Thus, you will find out who you are by looking at who they are. This is why our parents always warned us against hanging out with the wrong crowd. Who our friends are indicates who we are. They show us, as well as others, including our parents, what we value, not only in the sense that we value our friends, but also in the sense that we are friends with them because we share the same values. Moreover, who our friends are is an important ingredient of who we are, since, just as we use a mirror to correct the part in our hair or the knot in our tie, we use our friends to shape our behavior. Our friends are "mirror selves" as well as being "other selves." Friendship of the highest sort, then, according to Aristotle, is vital to our conception of ourselves—to the apprehension and construction of our character.

Now if we suppose that the friendship between Marc and Serge is of this sort, then it is easier to understand the violence of Marc's response. Serge's incomprehensible appreciation, from Marc's point of view, of the painting implies that Serge and Marc are not alter egos, and this, of course, threatens Marc's and then Serge's sense of who they are.

Yvan, who functions throughout the play as a kind of jester or Shakespearean buffoon, has told his psychoanalyst, Finkelzohn, about the dispute between Marc and Serge. And the analyst has summarized the predicament paradoxically but with comic pointedness by suggesting this conundrum:

"If . . . I am who I am because you're who you are, and if you're who you are because I'm who I am, then I'm not who I am and you're not who you are . . . ." Or to frame the idea by means of Aristotle's metaphor, the mirror relationship between Marc and Serge has been shattered. Moreover, since, at least once, Marc refers to the disputed painting as a picture, and since the association between pictures and mirrors is as longstanding as Plato, maybe we should interpret Serge's painting as a mirror that is no longer operating properly vis-à-vis Marc and Serge.

Marc tries to understand Serge's expressed fondness for the painting. But he can only come up with cynical explanations for Serge's behavior. Serge, Marc protests, is only feigning appreciation for the painting in order to enhance his upward social mobility. Serge bought the painting, Marc hypothesizes, as an investment in what Pierre Bourdieu calls social capital. Serge wants to enter a more elite circle of acquaintances, which is also why, Marc further alleges, Serge uses the pretentious but unfathomable word "deconstruction."

This is an interpretation of Serge's behavior that Marc can at least understand, even if it does not please him. But ultimately, I think, we come to see that Marc himself does not accept this cynical rationalization. The rift goes deeper. Marc realizes that Serge is moved by the painting—that there is something in Serge that is not in Marc—and this is what disturbs him. This is what threatens his sense of who he is.

But how, you might ask, can a mere painting do all this? How could an artwork come between friends in this way? It seems almost unthinkable. One can understand that a deep disjunction in values—over something like, say, the Israeli-Palestinian conflict—could destroy a friendship. But it appears unimaginable that a difference in taste could cause such a parting of the ways. But it is perhaps Yasmina Reza's staging of this possibility that

is her greatest philosophical insight, an insight, furthermore, that sheds light on the neglected or, at least, under-theorized relation of art and friendship.[4]

Philosophers of art tend to think of our relation to art in two ways: in terms of the relation of the individual to the artwork or in terms of art in relation to society as a whole. The first relation is atomistic: how does the artwork affect the experience of the individual audience member in contemplative isolation from everyone else? The second area of concern asks about the consequences of art, or certain types of art, for society at large. If the art is too violent, will society be more violent; if it is too sensational, will it contract our attention spans; and so on. Call the atomistic approach the small-range focus and the societal approach the big-range focus. Both of these perspectives are important—indeed, indispensable. However, there is, additionally, a medium-range focus which is also integral to our daily commerce with art, but which is almost never discussed.

Often when we attend a play, a concert, or a movie, we do it with friends; likewise we read novels, and exchange our opinions with each other over dinner or coffee or drinks. Art is not just a personal affair, nor is it only a force in society writ large. It is also a medium through which we forge our small-scale, face-to-face, everyday relations with others. Sharing experiences of art with others on a face-to-face basis is a way in which we explore and discover one another—discover one another's sensibility and temperament.

Art, of course, is not the only medium through which we do this. Food, sports, fashion, humor, and politics are serviceable in similar ways. But though art may not be the only way or the unique way in which we explore each other, initiating this sort of exploration of each other's sensibility, temperament, and taste is one of the central functions of art, and probably not only in our time and our culture. Art, in short, is, among other things, a vehicle by which we may discover and construct an intimate community—by which we cultivate (a pregnant metaphor here) a circle of friends. This is especially true for those for whom art—rather than, say, sports—is a primary source of socializing. For them, art functions as a kind of social cement.

Naturally, when we discuss art among our intimate circle of confreres, we do not always agree. We may differ about whether something is good, bad, or indifferent. Nevertheless, we must share certain values in common even for meaningful disagreement to proceed. Otherwise, there is simply an utter breakdown in communication. If I fail to appreciate Frank Sinatra, amity may still prevail. But if I regard all singing as shit, as Marc might say, and you come to believe that I am sincere, you will gradually come to realize that I am very unlike you in some very deep way and, to that extent, a stranger to you. You may come to suspect that I have a screw loose. But, at the very least, you cannot continue to value me as your "other self."

Sharing our tastes in art with others is sometimes a condition, sometimes a cause, and sometimes a combination of both in the process of cultivating our friendships with others. This is a mundane fact, readily confirmed at the intermission of every play. Just look around the lobby. But though the phenomenon is mundane and neglected, it is still a fact. What Yasmina Reza has done in *Art* is to bring this fact out into the open, where we can begin to scrutinize it and its ramifications.

Admittedly, the case she imagines is an extreme one. Her thought experiment is exaggerated and streamlined to make a point. But inasmuch as the situation she sketches strikes us as a psychologically plausible one, it reveals sources of value, motivation, and importance with respect to our traffic with art which, though often as ignored by us as a fish ignores water, struc-

ture our ordinary experiences of art. Art is not only social in the sense that it shapes society at large, albeit often in mysterious ways; it is also social in the sense that it has a role in the formation and enrichment of friendship; it is a locus of intimacy. Sharing taste and sharing our lives, to the extent that we do, typically go hand in hand. That is, taste in art and taste in friends are not randomly related.

Marc is in a panic over Serge's love of his painting by Antrios, because Marc cannot feel what Serge feels. Their sensibilities, then, are profoundly different. Marc can only respond to this disappearance of his other self—which he naturally experiences as existentially self-undermining—with hostility. Serge, on the other hand, is brought to a comparable predicament, since Marc's hostility shows him that Marc lacks the capacity to be moved in the deep way that abstract art can move him. It is as if Serge just discovered that the person he regarded as his alter ego has no feeling whatsoever for music. How close could you be to such a person? Could you be their lover?

The part of Serge that resonates to the painting is deep in his being; it is unpremeditated and barely cognitive; it is his sensibility. Sensibility is one of the most important things that friends share—a foundation, often, for everything else. Art, in turn, is standardly something expressly designed to engage our sensibilities. So when art divides us, it indicates a deviation in our sensibilities which, in the kind of extremely rarefied case that Yasmina Reza proposes, can have the potential to turn friends into strangers, or even embittered enemies in the wake of unrequited friendship. And though the case that she imagines is undoubtedly hyperbolic, it arguably tracks the joints of many friendships, especially those where shared sensibilities are of the utmost importance.

Throughout the play, Reza attempts dramatically to advance this theme of the concomitant breakdown of friendship and common sensibility by what, in effect, is a running analogy between art and humor. Notice how often the characters accuse each other of having lost their sense of humor. Whether people can laugh together for the right reasons becomes a constant test of whether they have changed for the worse and/or for whether they ever really had anything in common to begin with. The characters interrogate each other's laughter in terms of whether it is contemptuous or open-hearted and mutual—for example, Serge cannot laugh along with Marc at the Antrios, because Marc's laughter is dismissive and superior, whereas he will laugh with Yvan in shared astonishment at his own *l'amour fou* in paying so exorbitantly for an artwork.

Humor, of course, requires something shared—often called a sense of humor—which in many ways resembles taste. Laughter among friends is a pleasure, and one of the pleasures of friendship is the opportunity to share laughter. At the same time, laughter reveals something about who we are—our beliefs, attitudes, and emotions—and, for that reason, we are often only willing to be so open about our sensibilities around friends. We don't joke with the Pope, though we may tell jokes about the Pope to friends—to friends rather than to strangers, since we usually have no idea about their attitudes about religion. For these reasons, humor is a special ceremony among friends. And when friendships deteriorate, the feeling of a shared sense of humor often begins to dissipate proportionately. We no longer laugh together or laugh in the same way at the same things. Our former friend's sense of humor starts to seem cruder or, at least, more peculiar to us.

Reza charts the tension between Marc, Serge, and Yvan not only through their attitudes toward the painting by Antrios, but through parallel disconnects in their senses of humor. At one point, there is even a minor disagreement at a lower order of taste—Marc thinks the food at the Lyonnaise restaurant is fatty; Serge does not. And Serge reports his instinctual, almost chemical aversion to Marc's lover Paula. It is as though once their heretofore apparently shared sensibility unravels over the painting, the fabric of their entire friendship begins to tatter.

If Marc and Serge are to sustain their friendship, they must in some way re-establish a shared sensibility. Marc must come to see something of value in Serge's painting. And this, of course, happens, though through a very odd chain of events.

In order to show that he cares for the friendship, Serge encourages Marc to efface it with a felt-tip pen. Marc draws a man skiing down a slope on the white field. Later, together, they clean the painting, erasing the skier. However, now, Marc, the anti-modernist, anti-abstractionist, can see something in the painting: a man disappearing in a blinding blizzard as he skies down a whitened snowscape. Just as Arthur Danto suggests that one might see a pure red painting as pharaoh's army at the moment that the Red Sea engulfed it, Marc has transfigured Antrios's abstraction into a representation. Speaking figuratively, friendship has prompted Marc to see something in a new light, to find value where Serge does, though not exactly in the way that Serge does,[5] and this makes possible a renewal in their friendship, underscoring the potential of art not only to confirm the existence of friendship, but the potential of friendship to expand the excellence—in this case of the sensibility—of the other self.[6]

Yasmina Reza's *Art* belongs to the theater of ideas. Specifically, it is a contribution to philosophy—to the philosophy of friendship, to the philosophy of art, and to the intersection thereof. The highly contrived, though psychologically plausible confrontation, between Marc and Serge, affords an occasion to ponder the nature and dynamics of friendship by showing one, credibly, in the process of dissolution and prodding us to infer why this is happening. At the same time, it limns the importance of art to friendship, certainly one of the most overlooked facets of the importance of art to human life in general. The play discloses something neglected about the value of art in ordinary life by means of an extraordinary case—one whose very possibility disposes us to reconceive certain ordinary experiences with new and deeper understanding. In this, *Art* provides much to think and to talk about after the play, let us hope, with friends.

UNIVERSITY OF WISCONSIN

This article was first delivered as a talk for the Madison Repertory Theater on the occasion of their production of Art *in April, 2001 in Madison, Wisconsin. The author wishes to thank Elliott Sober, Norma Sober, Lorrie Moore, and Sally Banes for their comments on an earlier version of this text.*

1. Yasmina Reza, *Art*, trans. Christopher Hampton (London: Faber and Faber, 1996).

2. That Serge is a dermatologist may be a joke about his having a predilection for surfaces.

3. This is a view that Epicurus attributed to Stilbo. See Seneca, "On Philosophy and Friendship: Epistle IX," in *Other Selves: Philosophers on Friendship,* edited by Michael Pakaluk (Indianapolis: Hackett Publishing Company, 1991), p. 119.

4. One philosopher who has not neglected the relation of art and friendship is Ted Cohen. This interpretation of *Art* is deeply indebted to his penetrating investigations of, among other things, taste and humor. I doubt this essay could have been written had I not had the benefit of Ted Cohen's powerful insights on these matters.

5. Since where Serge sees modernist abstraction, Marc sees imitation, though imitation pushing at the envelope.

6. One philosopher, explicitly mentioned in the text of the play, is Seneca, who, like Aristotle, saw part of the value of friendship in its capacity to spur one on to greater excellence. It is just this sort of transformation, I conjecture, that Serge exhibits in the final lines of the play.

STILL LIFE WITH OYSTERS AND LEMON

Mark Doty

A sharp cracking cold day, the air of the Upper East Side full of rising plumes of smoke from furnaces and steaming laundries, exhaust from the tailpipes of idling taxis, flapping banners, gangs of pigeons. Here on the museum steps a flock suddenly chooses to take flight, the sound of their ascent like no other except maybe the rush of air a gas stove makes, when the oven suddenly ignites, only with the birds that sudden suck of air is followed by a rhythmic hurry of wings that trails away almost immediately as the flock moves into the air. Their ascent echoes back from the solidity of the museum's columns and heavy doors, the wide stairway where even in the cold people are smoking and shifting their chilly weight from side to side, eating pretzels, hunching over blue and white paper cups of coffee.

I have a backache, I'm travel weary, and it couldn't matter less, for this whole scene—the crowd and hustle on the museum steps, which seem alive all day with commerce and hurry, with gatherings and departures—is suffused for me with warmth, because I have fallen in love with a painting. Though that phrase doesn't seem to suffice, not really—rather it's that I have been drawn into the orbit of a painting, have allowed myself to be pulled into its sphere by casual attraction deepening to something more compelling. I have felt the energy and life of the painting's will; I have been held there, instructed. And the overall effect, the result of looking and looking into its brimming surface as long as I could look, is love, by which I mean a sense of tenderness toward experience, of being held within an intimacy with the things of the world.

That sense has remained with me as I move out through the dark stone lobby of the museum, with its huge vase of flowers looming over the information desk in the center of the room, and out into the sudden winter brightness—the gray brightness of Manhattan in January—onto the museum steps. There, stepping outside into the day, where nothing is framed or bounded as things in the museum are, suddenly the sense of intimacy and connection I've been feeling flares out, as if my painting had been a hearth, a heated and glowing place deep in the museum interior, and I'd carried the warmth of it with me out into the morning. Is it morning still? The sky's a huge crystal, cracked and alive with fractures, contrails, cloudy patches, huge distances.

But nothing seems truly remote to me, no chill too intractable. Because I have stepped from a warm suspension out into the shatteringly cold air, something of that suspension remains within me, or around me. It is the medium in which I and my fellow citizens move. We are all moving, just now, in the light that has come toward me through a canvas the size of a school notebook; we are all walking in the light of a wedge of lemon, four oysters, a half-glass of wine, a cluster of green grapes with a few curling leaves still attached to their stem. This light is enough to reveal us as we are, bound together, in the warmth and good light of habitation, in the good and fleshly aliveness of us.

How is it possible?

It's a simple painting, really, *Still Life with Oysters and Lemon,* by one Jan Davidsz de Heem, painted in Antwerp some three hundred and fifty years ago, and displayed today—after who knows what places it has been—in a glass case at the Metropolitan, lying flat, so that one bends and looks down into its bronzy, autumnal atmosphere. Half-filled *roemer* (an old Dutch drinking glass, with a knobby base) with an amber inch of wine, dewy grapes, curl of a lemon peel. Shimmery, barely solid bodies of oysters, shucked in order to allow their flesh to receive every ministration of light. It *is* an atmosphere; the light lovingly delineating these things is warm, a little fogged, encompassing, tender, ambient. As if, added to the fragrance evoked by the sharp pulp of the lemon, and the acidic wine, and the salty marsh-scent of the oysters, were some fragrance the light itself carried.

Simple, and yet so firm in its assertions. I'll try to name them.

That this is the matrix in which we are held, the generous light binding together the fragrant and flavorful productions of vineyard, marsh, and orchard—where has that lemon come from, the Levant?

That the pleasures of what can be tasted and smelled are to be represented, framed, set apart; that pleasure is to be honored.

That the world is a dialogue between degrees of transparency—globes of the grapes, the wine in the glass equally penetrated by light but ever so slightly less clear than the vessel itself, degrees of reflectivity.

That the world of reflection implicates us, as well—there, isn't that the faintest image of the painter in the base of the glass, tilted, distorted, lost in the contemplation of his little realm? Looking through things, as well, through what he's made of them, toward us?

That there can never be too much of reality; that the attempt to draw nearer to it—which will fail—will not fail entirely, as it will give us not the fact of lemons and oysters but this, which is its own fact, its own brave assay toward what is.

That description is an inexact, loving art, and a reflexive one; when we describe the world we come closer to saying what we are.

And something else, of course; there's always more, deep in art's pockets, far down in the chiaroscuro on which these foodstuffs rest: everything here has been transformed into feeling, as if by looking very hard at an object it suddenly comes that much closer to some realm where it isn't a thing at all but something just on the edge of dissolving. Into what? Tears, gladness—you've felt like this before, haven't you? Taken far inside. When? Held. Maybe that's what the darkness behind these things, that warm brown ground, is: the dark space within an embrace.

Intimacy, says the phenomenologist Gaston Bachelard, is the highest value.

[Handwritten margin notes:]
→ this idea of the emotions evoked by Art touching this guy
getting lost (in these pics)
in Juxtaposes in places w/ hot outdoors/cold this
Talks about the exact object that affects him. (Induction?) because of that I feel this
attention, treatment, help, assistance, aid, care (what?)

I resist this statement at first. What about artistic achievement, or moral courage, or heroism, or altruistic acts, or work in the cause of social change? What about wealth or accomplishment? And yet something about it rings true, finally—that what we want is to be brought into relation, to be inside, within. Perhaps it's true that nothing matters more to us than that.

But then why resist intimacy, why seem to flee it? A powerful countercurrent pulls against our drive toward connection; we also desire individuation, separateness, freedom. On one side of the balance is the need for home, for the deep solid roots of place and belonging; on the other is the desire for travel and motion, for the single separate spark of the self freely moving forward, out into time, into the great absorbing stream of the world.

A fierce internal debate, between staying moored and drifting away, between holding on and letting go. Perhaps wisdom lies in our ability to negotiate between these two poles. Necessary to us, both of them—but how to live in connection without feeling suffocated, compromised, erased? We long to connect; we fear that if we do, our freedom and individuality will disappear.

One would not expect to turn to still life for help with these questions. But I think of the familiar phrase about there being "more than meets the eye"; in these paintings, the "more" *does* meet the eye; they suggest that knowledge is visible, that it might be seen in the daily world. They think, as it were, through things.

In my Jan Davidsz de Heem, for instance, there is a spectacular spiral of lemon peel, a flourish of painterly showing-off. The rind has been sliced in a single strip, and it curls in the air, resting atop the *roemer;* one of its coils dips inside, toward the wine, so that we see it now plainly, now veiled by the slightly gray cast of the glass. Now the pebbly yellow, as it twists through air, now the white

pith that lay between that outer skin and the body of the fruit. Shadows lie in the twisting helix, in the curling hollows—like the socket of an armpit, or the hollows at the base of the neck, the twin wells of the collarbone. These are fleshy, erotic shadows, and they stand in contrast to the brilliance raking across the peel, cut so thin as to be translucent, a slice of the warmth and energy pouring into this room we'll never see.

This is by no means the only bravura lemon in Dutch painting of the seventeenth century. They are, in fact, everywhere, in pictures by Pieter de Ring, Abraham van Beyeren, Willem Kalf, Jan Jansz den Uyl, and Adriaen van Utrecht, to name just a few. These lemons seem to leap to the foreground; the stippled, textured surface of the paint—noticeably thickened beside the glazed surface used elsewhere for silver cups and pewter plates, or bowls of porcelain—gives the eye a focal point and therefore makes the peel appear closer to us.

They are, in a way, nudes, always in dishabille, partly undraped, the rind peeled away to allow our gaze further pleasure—to see the surface, and beneath that another surface. Often the pith is cut away as well, the fruit faceted so that we can see its wet translucence, a seed just beneath, and sometimes another seed or two is tossed to the side of the plate on which this odalisque rests, diminutive seeds just as precise as the fruit and its pulpy sections; nothing is too tiny for the attentive eye.

The lemons are built, in layers, out of lead tin yellow, which the Italians called *giallo di Fiandria,* a warm canary made by heating lead and tin oxides together, which was also the preferred pigment for the petals of daffodils, and out of *luteolum Neapolitanum,* or Naples yellow, and of a glowing but unstable pigment called orpiment. Often these colors are glazed with yellow glazes made of broom or berries. Alchemists' work, turning tin and arsenic and vegetable juices into golden fruit painted with a kind of showy complication and variety that suggests there must have been competition among the painters of lemons. How to paint a lemon with a freedom and inventiveness that sets it apart? Jacob von Hulsdonck specialized in citrus partially ripe, the stippled surface of the fruit blushed with that acidy green which indicates the peel's only recently yellowed. Whose half-peeled fruit could be most complexly faceted, like a gemstone, in order to reveal nuances of transparency and reflectivity, the seeds resting within the revealed sections? Who could give the coiled peel the greatest sense of heft and curve, or spiral it down from the edge of a table, with the most convincing sense of gravity's pull? In Cornelis de Heem's *The Flute of Wine,* a swoop of lemon peel occupies the very center of the picture, looping down into the space below the edge of the table and back up again to end in a flourish of curl, impossibly long, as if the little fruit had yielded an unlikely bounty of peel to serve the painter's purposes. Whose peel could be cut the thinnest, barely there at all, a translucent yellow interruption in the air?

In another canvas of Jan Davidsz de Heem's, the lavishly wealthy *Nautilus Cup with Silver Vessels,* the painter seems to strut, to take the lemon competition as far as it might reasonably go, even a little far-ther. Here a strip of peel is shown alone, detached from its fruit, at the corner of a table shrouded in a dark cloth. The peel coils intricately, impossibly—a baroque bit of ribboning made to show us exactly what this painter could do.

Lemons: all freedom, all ego, all vanity, fragrant with scent we can't help but imagine when we look at them, the little pucker in the mouth. And redolent, too, of strut and style. Yet somehow they remain intimate, every single one of them: only lemons, only that lovely, perishable, ordinary thing, held to scrutiny's light, fixed in a moment of fierce attention. As if here our desire to be unique, unmistakable, and our desire to be of a piece were reconciled. Isn't that it, to be yourself and somehow, to belong? For a moment, held in balance.

To think through things, that is the still life painter's work—and the poet's. Both sorts of artists require a tangible vocabulary, a worldly lexicon. A language of ideas is, in itself, a phantom language, lacking in the substance of worldly things, those containers of feeling and experience, memory and time. We are instructed by the objects that come to speak with us, those material presences. Why should we have been born knowing how to love the world? We require, again and again, these demonstrations.

SOULS ON ICE

Mark Doty

In the Stop 'n Shop in Orleans, Massachusetts, I was struck by the elegance of the mackerel in the fresh-fish display. They were rowed and stacked, brilliant against the white of the crushed ice; I loved how black and glistening the bands of dark scales were, and the prismed sheen of the patches between, and their shining flat eyes. I stood and looked at them for a while, just paying attention while I leaned on my cart—before I remembered where I was and realized that I was standing in someone's way.

Our metaphors go on ahead of us; they know before we do. And thank goodness for that, for if I were dependent on other ways of coming to knowledge I think I'd be a very slow study. I need something to serve as a container for emotion and idea, a vessel that can hold what's too slippery or charged or difficult to touch. Will doesn't have much to do with this; I can't choose what's going to serve as a compelling image for me. But I've learned to trust that part of my imagination that gropes forward, feeling its way toward what it needs; to watch for the signs of fascination, the sense of compelled attention (Look at me, something seems to say, closely) that indicates that there's something I need to attend to. Sometimes it

seems to me as if metaphor were the advance guard of the mind: something in us reaches out, into the landscape in front of us, looking for the right vessel, the right vehicle, for whatever will serve.

Driving home from the grocery, I found myself thinking again about the fish, and even scribbled some phrases on an envelope in the car, something about stained glass, soapbubbles, while I was driving. It wasn't long—that same day? the next?—before I was at my desk, trying simply to describe what I had seen. I almost always begin with description, as a way of focusing on that compelling image, the poem's "given." I know that what I can see is just the proverbial tip of the iceberg; if I do my work of study and examination, and if I am lucky, the image which I've been intrigued by will become a metaphor, will yield depth and meaning, will lead me to insight. The goal here is inquiry, the attempt to get at what it is that's so interesting about what's struck me. Because it isn't just beauty; the world is full of lovely things and that in itself wouldn't compel me to write. There's something else, some gravity or charge to this image that makes me need to investigate it.

Love this line — acts as a summary of Page 37

37

Exploratory description, then; I'm a scientist trying to measure and record what's seen. The first two sentences of the poem attempt sheer observation, but by the second's list of tropes (abalone, soapbubble skin, oil on a puddle) it's clear to me that these descriptive terms aren't merely there to chronicle the physical reality of the object. Like all descriptions, they reflect the psychic state of the observer; they aren't "neutral," though they might pretend to be, but instead suggest a point of view, a stance toward what is being seen. In this case one of the things suggested by these tropes is interchangeability; if you've seen one abalone shell or prismy soapbubble or psychedelic puddle, you've seen them all.

And thus my image began to unfold for me, in the evidence these terms provided, and I had a clue toward the focus my poem would take. Another day, another time in my life, the mackerel might have been metaphor for something else; they might have served as the crux for an entirely different examination. But now I began to see why they mattered for this poem, and the sentence that follows commences the poem's investigative process:

Splendor, and splendor,
and not a one in any way

distinguished from the other
—nothing about them
of individuality.

There's a terrific kind of exhilaration for me at this point in the unfolding of a poem, when a line of questioning has been launched, and the work has moved from evocation to meditation. A direction is coming clear, and it bears within it the energy that the image contained for me in the first pace. Now, I think, we're getting down to it. This élan carried me along through two more sentences, one that considers the fish as replications of the ideal, Platonic Mackerel, and one that likewise imagines them as the intricate creations of an obsessively repetitive jeweler.

Of course my process of unfolding the poem wasn't quite this neat. There were false starts, wrong turnings that I wound up throwing out when they didn't seem to lead anywhere. I can't remember now, because the poem has worked the charm of its craft on my memory; it convinces me that it is an artifact of a process of inquiry. The drama of the poem is its action of thinking through a question. Mimicking a sequence of perceptions and meditation, it tries to make us think that this feeling and thinking and knowing is taking place even as the poem is being written. Which, in a way, it is—just not this neatly or seamlessly! A poem is always a made version of experience.

Also, needless to say, my poem was full of repetitions, weak lines, unfinished phrases and extra descriptions, later trimmed; I like to work on a computer, because I can type quickly, put everything in, and still read the results later on, which isn't always true of my handwriting. I did feel early on that the poem seemed to want to be a short-lined one; I liked breaking the movement of these extended sentences over the clipped line, and the spotlight-bright focus the short line puts on individual terms felt right. "Iridescent, watery," for instance, pleased me as a line-unit, as did this stanza:

prismatics: think abálone,
the wildly rainbowed
mirror of a soapbubble sphere.

Short lines underline sonic textures, heightening tension. The short a's of prismatics and abalone ring more firmly, as do the o's of abalone, rainbowed and soapbubble. The rhyme of mirror and sphere at beginning and end of line engages me, and I'm also pleased by the way in which these short lines slow the poem down, parceling it out as it were to the reader, with the frequent pauses introduced by the stanza breaks between tercets adding lots of white space, a meditative pacing.

And there, on the jeweler's bench, my poem seemed to come to rest, though it was clear there was more to be done. Some further pressure needed to be placed on the poem's material to force it to yield its depths. I waited a while, I read it over. Again, in what I had already written, the clues contained in image pushed the poem forward.

Soul, heaven . . . The poem had already moved into the realm of theology, but the question that arose ("Suppose we could iridesce sources . . .") startled me nonetheless, because the notion of losing oneself "entirely in the universe/of shimmer" referred both to these fish and to something quite other, something overwhelmingly close to home. The poem was written some six months after my partner of a dozen years had died of AIDS, and of course everything I wrote—everything I saw—was informed by that loss, by the overpowering emotional force of it. Epidemic was the central fact of the community in which I lived. Naively, I hadn't realized that my mackerel were already of a piece with the work I'd been writing for the previous couple of years— poems that wrestled, in one way or another, with the notion of limit, with the line between being someone and no one. What did it mean to be a self, when that self would be lost? To praise the collectivity of the fish, their common identity as "flashing participants," is to make a sort of anti-elegy, to suggest that what matters is perhaps not our individual selves but our brief soldiering in the broad streaming school of humanity— which is composed of us, yes, but also goes on without us.

The one of a kind, the singular, like my dear lover, cannot last.

And yet the collective life, which is also us, shimmers on.

Once I realized the poem's subject-beneath-the-subject, the final stanzas of the poem opened swiftly out from there. The collective momentum of the fish is such that even death doesn't seem to still rob its forward movement; the singularity of each fish more or less doesn't really exist, it's "all for all," like the Three Musketeers. I could not have considered these ideas "nakedly," without the vehicle of mackerel to help me think about human identity. Nor, I think, could I have addressed these things without a certain playfulness of tone, which appeared first in the archness of "oily fabulation" and the neologism of "iridesce." It's the blessed permission distance gives that allows me to speak of such things at all; a little comedy can also help to hold terrific anxiety at bay. Thus the "rainbowed school/and its acres of brilliant classrooms" is a joke, but one that's already collapsing on itself, since what is taught there—the limits of "me"—is our hardest lesson. No verb is singular because it is the school that acts, or the tribe, the group, the species; or every verb is singular because the only I there is is a we.

The poem held one more surprise for me, which was the final statement—it came as a bit of a shock, actually, and when I'd written it I knew I was done. It's a formulation of the theory that the poem has been moving toward all along: that our glory is not our individuality (much as we long for the Romantic self and its private golden heights) but our commonness. I do not like this idea. I would rather be one fish, sparkling in my own pond, but experience does not bear this out. And so I have tried to convince myself, here, that beauty lies in the whole and that therefore death, the loss of the part, is not so bad—is, in fact, almost nothing. What does our individual disappearance mean—or our love, or our desire—when, as the Marvelettes put it, "There's too many fish in the sea . . .?"

I find this consoling, strangely, and maybe that's the best way to go think of this poem—an attempt at cheering oneself up about the mystery of being both an individual and part of a group, an attempt on the part of the speaker in the poem (me) to convince himself that losing individuality, slipping into the life of the world, could be a good thing. All attempts to console ourselves, I believe, are doomed, because the world is more complicated than we are. Our explanations will fail, but it is our human work to make them. And my beautiful fish, limited though they may be as parable, do help me; they are an image I return to in order to remember, in the face of individual erasures, the burgeoning, good, common life. Even after my work of inquiry, my metaphor may still know more than I do; the bright eyes of those fish gleam on, in memory, brighter than what I've made of them.

MARK DOTY
A Display of Mackerel

They lie in parallel rows,
on ice, head to tail,
each a foot of luminosity

barred with black bands,
which divide the scales'
radiant sections

like seams of lead
in a Tiffany window.
Iridescent, watery

prismatics: think abalone,
the wildly rainbowed
mirror of a soapbubble sphere,

think sun on gasoline.
Splendor, and splendor,
and not a one in any way

distinguished from the other
—nothing about them
of individuality. Instead

they're all exact expressions
of the one soul,
each a perfect fulfillment

of heaven's template,
mackerel essence. As if,
after a lifetime arriving

at this enameling, the jeweler's
made uncountable examples,
each as intricate

in its oily fabulation
as the one before
Suppose we could iridesce,

like these, and lose ourselves
entirely in the universe
of shimmer—would you want

to be yourself only,
unduplicatable, doomed
to be lost? They'd prefer,

plainly, to be flashing participants,
multitudinous. Even now
they seem to be bolting

forward, heedless of stasis.
They don't care they're dead
and nearly frozen,

just as, presumably,
they didn't care that they were living:
all, all for all,

the rainbowed school
and its acres of brilliant classrooms,
in which no verb is singular,

or every one is. How happy they seem,
even on ice, to be together, selfless,
which is the price of gleaming.

JOYAS VOLADORAS

Brian Doyle (b. 1956)

Consider the hummingbird for a long moment. A hummingbird's heart beats ten times a second. A hummingbird's heart is the size of a pencil eraser. A hummingbird's heart is a lot of the hummingbird. *Joyas voladoras*, flying jewels, the first white explorers in the Americas called them, and the white men had never seen such creatures, for hummingbirds came into the world only in the Americas, nowhere else in the universe, more than three hundred species of them whirring and zooming and nectaring in hummer time zones nine times removed from ours, their hearts hammering faster than we could clearly hear if we pressed our elephantine ears to their infinitesimal chests.

Each one visits a thousand flowers a day. They can dive at sixty miles an hour. They can fly backward. They can fly more than five hundred miles without pausing to rest. But when they rest they come close to death: on frigid nights, or when they are starving, they retreat into torpor, their metabolic rate slowing to a fifteenth of their normal sleep rate, their hearts sludging nearly to a halt, barely beating, and if they are no soon warmed, if they do not soon find that which is sweet, their hearts grow cold, and they cease to be. Consider for a moment those hummingbirds who did not open their eyes again today, this very day, in the Americas: bearded helmetcrests and booted racket-tails, violet-tailed sylphs and violet-capped woodnymphs, crimson topazes and purple-crowned fairies, red-tailed comets and amethyst woodstars, rainbow-bearded thornbills and glittering-bellied emeralds, velvet-purple coronets and golden-bellied star-frontlets, fiery-tailed awlbills and Andean hillstars, spatuletails and pufflegs, each the most amazing thing you have never seen, each thunderous wild heart the size of an infant's fingernail, each mad heart silent, a brilliant music stilled.

Hummingbirds, like all flying birds but more so, have incredible enormous immense ferocious metabolisms. To drive those metabolisms they have racecar hearts that eat oxygen at an eye-popping rate. Their hearts are built of thinner, leaner fibers than ours. Their arteries are stiffer and more taut. They have more mitochondria in their heart muscles—anything to gulp more oxygen. Their hearts are stripped to the skin for the war against gravity and inertia, the mad search for food, the insane idea of flight. The price of their ambition is a life closer to

41

death; they suffer more heart attacks and aneurysms and ruptures than any other living creature. It's expensive to fly. You burn out. You fry the machine. You melt the engine. Every creature on earth has approximately two billion heartbeats to spend in a lifetime. You can spend them slowly, like a tortoise, and live to be two hundred years old, or you can spend them fast like a hummingbird, and live to be two years old.

The biggest heart in the world is inside the blue whale. It weighs more than seven tons. It's as big as a room. It *is* a room, with four chambers. A child could walk around in it, head high, bending only to step through the valves. The valves are as big as the swinging doors in a saloon. This house of a heart drives a creature a hundred feet long. When this creature is born it is twenty feet long and weighs four tons. It is waaaaay bigger than your car. It drinks a hundred gallons of milk from its mama every day and gains two hundred pounds a day, and when it is seven or eight years old it endures an unimaginable puberty and then it essentially disappears from human ken, for next to nothing is known of the mating habits, travel patterns, diet, social life, language, social structure, diseases, spirituality, wars, stories, despairs, and arts of the blue whale. There are perhaps ten thousand blue whales in the world, living in every ocean on earth, and of the largest mammal who ever lived we know nearly nothing. But we know this: the animals with the largest hearts in the world generally travel in pairs, and their penetrating moaning cries, their piercing yearning tongue, can be heard underwater for miles and miles.

Mammals and birds have hearts with four chambers. Reptiles and turtles have hearts with three chambers. Fish have hearts with two chambers. Insects and mollusks have hearts with one chamber. Worms have hearts with one chamber, although they may have as many as eleven single-chambered hearts. Unicellular bacteria have no hearts at all; but even they have fluid eternally in motion, washing from one side of the cell to the other, swirling and whirling. No living being is without interior liquid motion. We all churn inside.

So much held in a heart in a lifetime. So much held in a heart in a day, an hour, a moment. We are utterly open with no one, in the end—not mother and father, not wife or husband, not lover, not child, not friend. We open windows to each but we live alone in the house of the heart. Perhaps we must. Perhaps we could not bear to be so naked, for fear of a constantly harrowed heart. When young we think there will come one person who will savor and sustain us always; when we are older we know this is the dream of a child, that all hearts finally are bruised and scarred, scored and torn, repaired by time and will, patched by force of character, yet fragile and rickety forevermore, no matter how ferocious the defense and how many bricks you bring to the wall. You can brick up your heart as stout and tight and hard and cold and impregnable as you possibly can and down it comes in an instant, felled by a woman's second glance, a child's apple breath, the shatter of glass in the road, the words "I have something to tell you," a cat with a broken spine dragging itself into the forest to die, the brush of your mother's papery ancient hand in the thicket of your hair, the memory of your father's voice early in the morning echoing from the kitchen where he is making pancakes for his children.

NOT LOOKING AT PICTURES

E. M. Forster

Pictures are not easy to look at. They generate private fantasies, they furnish material for jokes, they recall scraps of historical knowledge, they show landscapes where one would like to wander and human beings whom one would like to resemble or adore, but looking at them is another matter, yet they must have been painted to be looked at. They were intended to appeal to the eye, but almost as if it were gazing at the sun itself the eye often reacts by closing as soon as it catches sight of them. The mind takes charge instead and goes off on some alien vision. The mind has such a congenial time that it forgets what set it going. Van Gogh and Corot and Michelangelo are three different painters, but if the mind is indisciplined and uncontrolled by the eye, they may all three induce the same mood, we may take just the same course through dreamland or funland from them, each time, and never experience anything new.

I am bad at looking at pictures myself, and the late Roger Fry enjoyed going to a gallery with me now and then, for this very reason. He found it an amusing change to be with someone who scarcely ever saw what the painter had painted. "Tell me, why do you like this, why do you prefer it to that?" he would

ask, and listen agape for the ridiculous answer. One day we looked at a fifteenth-century Italian predella, where a St. George was engaged in spearing a dragon of the plesiosaurus type. I laughed. "Now, *what* is there funny in this?" pounced Fry. I readily explained. The fun was to be found in the expression upon the dragon's face. The spear had gone through its hooped-up neck once, and now startled it by arriving at a second thickness. "Oh dear, here it comes again, I hoped that was all," it was thinking. Fry laughed too, but not at the misfortunes of the dragon. He was amazed that anyone could go so completely off the lines. There was no harm in it—but really, really! He was even more amazed when our enthusiasms coincided: "I fancy we are talking about different things," he would say, and we always were; I liked the mountain-back because it reminded me of a peacock, he because it had some structural significance, though not as much as the sack of potatoes in the foreground.

Long years of wandering down miles of galleries have convinced me that there must be something rare in those coloured slabs called "pictures," something which I am incapable of detecting for myself, though glimpses of it are to be had through the eyes

of others. How much am I missing? And what? And are other modern sight-seers in the same fix? Ours is an aural rather than a visual age, we do not get so lost in the concert hall, we seem able to hear music for ourselves, and to hear it as music, but in galleries so many of us go off at once into a laugh or a sigh or an amorous day-dream. In vain does the picture recall us. "What have your obsessions got to do with me?" it complains. "I am neither a theatre of varieties nor a spring-mattress, but paint. Look at my paint." Back we go—the picture kindly standing still meanwhile, and being to that extent more obliging than music—and resume the looking-business. But something is sure to intervene—a tress of hair, the half-open door of a summer-house, a Crivelli dessert, a Bosch fish-and-fiend salad—and to draw us away.

One of the things that helps us to keep looking is composition. For many years now I have associated composition with a diagonal line, and when I find such a line I imagine I have gutted the picture's secret. Giorgione's Castelfranco Madonna has such a line in the lance of the warrior-saint, and Titian's Entombment at Venice has a very good one indeed. Five figures contribute to make up the diagonal; beginning high on the left with the statue of Moses, it passes through the heads of the Magdalene, Mary, and the dead Christ, and plunges through the body of Joseph of Arimathea into the ground. Making a right angle to it, flits the winged Genius of Burial. And to the right, apart from it, and perpendicular, balancing the Moses, towers the statue of Faith. Titian's Entombment is one of my easiest pictures. I look at photographs of it intelligently, and encourage the diagonal and the pathos to reinforce one another. I see, with more than usual vividness, the grim alcove at the back and the sinister tusked pedestals upon which the two statues stand. Stone shuts in flesh; the whole picture is a tomb. I hear sounds of lamentation, though not to the extent of shattering the general scheme; that is held together by the emphatic diagonal, which no emotion breaks. Titian was a very old man when he achieved this masterpiece; that too I realise, but not immoderately. Composition here really has been a help, and it is a composition which no one can miss; the diagonal slopes as obviously as the band on a threshing-machine, and vibrates with power.

Unfortunately, having no natural esthetic aptitude, I look for diagonals everywhere, and if I cannot find one think the composition must be at fault. It is a word which I have learnt—a solitary word in a foreign language. For instance, I was completely baffled by Velasquez's Las Meninas. Wherever was the diagonal? Then the friend I was with—Charles Mauron, the friend who, after Roger Fry, has helped me with pictures most—set to work on my behalf, and cautiously underlined the themes. There is a wave. There is a half-wave. The wave starts up on the left, with the head of the painter, and curves down and up through the heads of the three girls. The half-wave starts with the head of Isabel de Velasco, and sinks out of the canvas through the dwarfs. Responding to these great curves, or inverting them, are smaller ones on the women's dresses or elsewhere. All these waves are not merely pattern; they are doing other work too—e.g., helping to bring out the effect of depth in the room, and the effect of air. Important too is the pushing forward of objects in the extreme left and right foregrounds, the easel of the painter in the one case, the paws of a placid dog in the other. From these, the composition curves back to the central figure, the lovely child-princess. I put it more crudely than did Charles Mauron, nor do I suppose that his account would have been Velasquez's, or that Velasquez would have given any account at all. But it is an example of the way in which pictures should be tackled for the benefit of us outsiders: coolly and patiently, as if they were designs, so that we are helped at last to the appreciation of something non-mathematical. Here again, as in the case of the Entombment, the composition and the action reinforced one another. I viewed with increasing joy that adorable party, which had been surprised not only by myself but by the King and Queen of Spain. There they were in the looking-glass! Las Meninas has a snap-shot quality. The party might have been taken by Philip IV, if Philip IV had had a Kodak. It is all so casual—and yet it is all so elaborate and sophisticated, and I suppose those curves and the rest of it help to bring this out, and to evoke a vanished civilisation.

Besides composition there is colour. I look for that, too, but with even less success. Colour is visible when thrown in my face—like the two cherries in the great grey Michael Sweertz group in the National Gallery. But as a rule it is only material for dream.

On the whole, I am improving, and after all these years, I am learning to get myself out of the way a little, and to be more receptive, and my appreciation of pictures does increase. If I can make any progress at all, the average outsider should do better still. A combination of courage and modesty is what he wants. It is so unenterprising to annihilate everything that's made to a green thought, even when the thought is an exquisite one. Not looking at art leads to one goal only. Looking at it leads to so many.

THE POETIC BASIS OF MIND

James Hillman

SOUL

Anthropologists describe a condition among "primitive" peoples called "loss of soul." In this condition a man is out of himself, unable to find either the outer connection between humans or the inner connection to himself. He is unable to take part in his society, its rituals, and traditions. They are dead to him, he to them. His connection to family, totem, nature, is gone. Until he regains his soul he is not a true human. He is "not there." It is as if he had never been initiated, been given a name, come into real being. His soul may not only be lost: it may also be possessed, bewitched, ill, transposed into an object, animal, place, or another person. Without this soul, he has lost the sense of belonging and the sense of being in communion with the powers and the gods. They no longer reach him; he cannot pray, nor sacrifice, nor dance. His personal myth and his connection to the larger myth of his people, as *raison d'être,* is lost. Yet he is not sick with disease, nor is he out of his mind. He has simply lost his soul. He may even die. We become lonely. Other relevant parallels with ourselves today need not be spelled out.

One day in Burghölzli, the famous institute in Zurich where the words *schizophre-* *nia* and *complex* were born, I watched a woman being interviewed. She sat in a wheelchair because she was elderly and feeble. She said that she was dead for she had lost her heart. The psychiatrist asked her to place her hand over her breast to feel her heart beating: it must still be there if she could feel its beat. "That," she said, "is not my real heart." She and the psychiatrist looked at each other. There was nothing more to say. Like the primitive who has lost his soul, she had lost the loving courageous connection to life—and that is the real heart, not the ticker which can as well pulsate isolated in a glass bottle.

This is a different view of reality from the usual one. It is so radically different that it forms part of the syndrome of insanity. But one can have as much understanding for the woman in her psychotic depersonalization as for the view of reality of the man attempting to convince her that her heart was indeed still there. Despite the elaborate and moneyed systems of medical research and the advertisements of the health and recreation industries to prove that the real is the physical and that loss of heart and loss of soul are only in the mind, I believe the "primitive" and the woman in the hospital: we can and do lose our souls. I believe with Jung that each of us is "modern man in search of a soul."

Because symptoms lead to soul, the cure of symptoms may also cure away soul, get rid of just what is beginning to show, at first tortured and crying for help, comfort, and love, but which is the soul in the neurosis trying to make itself heard, trying to impress the stupid and stubborn mind—that impotent mule which insists on going its unchanging obstinate way. The right reaction to a symptom may as well be a welcoming rather than laments and demands for remedies, for the symptom is the first herald of an awakening psyche which will not tolerate any more abuse. Through the symptom the psyche demands attention. Attention means attending to, tending, a certain tender care of, as well as waiting, pausing, listening. It takes a span of time and a tension of patience. Precisely what each symptom needs is time and tender care and attention. Just this same attitude is what the soul needs in order to be felt and heard. So it is often little wonder that it takes a breakdown, an actual illness, for someone to report the most extraordinary experiences of, for instance, a new sense of time, of patience and waiting, and in the language of religious experience, of coming to the center, coming to oneself, letting go and coming home.

The alchemists had an excellent image for the transformation of suffering and symptom into a value of the soul. A goal of the alchemical process was the pearl of great price. The pearl starts off as a bit of grit, a neurotic symptom or complaint, a bothersome irritant in one's secret inside flesh, which no defensive shell can protect oneself from. This is coated over, worked at day in day out, until the grit one day is a pearl; yet it still must be fished up from the depths and pried loose. Then when the grit is redeemed, it is worn. It must be worn on the warm skin to keep its luster: the redeemed complex which once caused suffering is exposed to public view as a virtue. The esoteric treasure gained through occult work becomes an exoteric splendor. To get rid of the symptom means to get rid of the chance to gain what may one day be of greatest value, even if at first an unbearable irritant, lowly, and disguised.

(*Insearch*, 43–44, 55–56)

To understand *soul* we cannot turn to science for a description. Its meaning is best given by its context. The root metaphor of the analyst's point of view is that human behavior is understandable because it has an inside meaning. The inside meaning is suffered and experienced. It is understood by the analyst through sympathy and insight. All these terms are the everyday empirical language of the analyst and provide the context for and are expressions of the analyst's root metaphor. Other words long associated with the word *soul* amplify it further: mind, spirit, heart, life, warmth, humanness, personality, individuality, intentionality, essence, innermost, purpose, emotion, quality, virtue, morality, sin, wisdom, death, God. A soul is said to be "troubled," "old," "disembodied," "immortal," "lost," "innocent," "inspired." Eyes are said to be "soulful," for the eyes are "the mirror of the soul"; but one can be "soulless" by showing no mercy. Most "primitive" languages have elaborate concepts about animated principles which ethnologists have translated by *soul*. For these peoples, from ancient Egyptian to modern Eskimo, *soul* is a highly differentiated idea referring to a reality of great impact. The soul has been imaged as the inner man, and as the inner sister or spouse, the place or voice of God within, as a cosmic force in which all humans, even all things living, participate, as having been given by God and thus divine, as conscience, as a multiplicity and as a unity in diversity, as a harmony, as a fluid, as fire, as dynamic energy, and so on. One can "search one's soul" and one's soul can be "on trial." There are parables describing possession of the soul by and sale of the soul to the devil, of temptations of the soul, of the damnation and redemption of the soul, of development of the soul through spiritual disciplines, of journeys of the soul. Attempts have been made to localize the soul in specific body organs and regions, to trace its origin to sperm or egg, to divide it into animal, vegetable, and mineral components, while the search for the soul leads always into the "depths."

The terms *psyche* and *soul* can be used interchangeably, although there is a tendency to escape the ambiguity of the word *soul* by recourse to the more biological, more modern *psyche*. *Psyche* is used more as a natural concomitant to physical life, perhaps reducible to it. *Soul,* on the other hand, has metaphysical and romantic overtones. It shares frontiers with religion.

(*Suicide,* 44–45, 47)

By *soul* I mean, first of all, a perspective rather than a substance, a viewpoint toward things rather than a thing itself. This perspective is reflective; it mediates events and makes differences between ourselves and everything that happens. Between us and events, between the doer and the deed, there is a reflective moment—and soul-making means differentiating this middle ground.

It is as if consciousness rests upon a self-sustaining and imagining substrate—an inner place or deeper person or ongoing presence—that is simply there even when all our subjectivity, ego, and consciousness go into eclipse. Soul appears as a factor independent of the events in which we are immersed. Though I cannot identify soul with anything else, I also can never grasp it by itself apart from other things, perhaps because it is like a reflection in a flowing mirror, or like the moon which mediates only borrowed light. But just this peculiar and

paradoxical intervening variable gives one the sense of having or being a soul. However intangible and indefinable it is, soul carries highest importance in hierarchies of human values, frequently being identified with the principle of life and even of divinity.

In another attempt upon the idea of *soul* I suggested that the word refers to that unknown component which makes meaning possible, turns events into experiences, is communicated in love, and has a religious concern. These four qualifications I had already put forth some years ago. I had begun to use the term freely, usually interchangeably with *psyche* (from Greek) and *anima* (from Latin). Now I am adding three necessary modifications. First, *soul* refers to the *deepening* of events into experiences; second, the significance *soul* makes possible, whether in love or in religious concern, derives from its special *relation with death.* And third, by *soul* I mean the imaginative possibility in our natures, the experiencing through reflective speculation, dream, image, and *fantasy*—that mode which recognizes all realities as primarily symbolic or metaphorical.

(*Re-Visioning,* x)

ARCHETYPAL FANTASY

This first two-horned topic invites a second and equally difficult one. What is fantasy? Here I follow C. G. Jung very closely. He considered the fantasy images that run through our daydreams and night dreams, and which are present unconsciously in all our consciousness, to be the primary data of the psyche. Everything we know and feel and every statement we make are all fantasy based, that is, they derive from psychic images. These are not merely the flotsam of memory, the reproduction of perceptions, rearranged leftovers from the input of our lives.

Rather, following Jung I use the word *fantasy-image* in the poetic sense, considering images to be the basic givens of psychic life, self-originating, inventive, spontaneous, complete, and organized in archetypal patterns. Fantasy-images are both the raw materials and finished products of psyche, and they are the privileged mode of access to knowledge of soul. Nothing is more primary. Every notion in our minds, each perception of the world and sensation in ourselves must go through a psychic organization in order to "happen" at all. Every single feeling or observation occurs as a psychic event by first forming a fantasy-image.

Here I am working toward a psychology of soul that is based in a psychology of image. Here I am suggesting both a *poetic basis of mind* and a psychology that starts neither in the physiology of the brain, the structure of language, the organization of society, nor the analysis of behavior, but in the processes of imagination.

By calling upon Jung to begin with, I am partly acknowledging the fundamental debt that archetypal psychology owes him. He is the immediate ancestor in a long line that stretches back through Freud, Dilthey, Coleridge, Schelling, Vico, Ficino, Plotinus, and Plato to Heraclitus—and with even more branches which have yet to be traced. Heraclitus lies near the roots of this ancestral tree of thought, since he was the earliest to take psyche as his archetypal first principle, to imagine soul in terms of flux and to speak of its depth without measure.

Depth psychology, the modern field whose interest is in the unconscious levels of the psyche—that is, the deeper meanings of the soul—is itself no modern term. *Depth* reverberates with a significance, echoing one of the first philosophers of antiquity. All depth psychology has already been summed up by this fragment of Heraclitus: "You could not discover the limits of the soul *(psyche),* even if you traveled every road to do so; such is the depth *(bathun)* of its meaning *(logos)."* Ever since Heraclitus brought soul and depth together in one formulation, the dimension of soul is depth (not breadth or height) and the dimension of our soul travel is downward.

One more word we need to introduce is *archetype.* The curious difficulty of explaining just what archetypes are suggests something specific to them. That is, they tend to be metaphors rather than things. We find ourselves less able to say what an archetype is literally and more inclined to describe them in images. We can't seem to touch one or point to one, and rather speak of what they are like. Archetypes throw us into an imaginative style of discourse. In fact, it is precisely as metaphors that Jung—who reintroduced the ancient idea of archetype into modern psychology—writes of them, insisting upon their indefinability. To take an archetypal perspective in psychology leads us, therefore, to envision the basic nature and structure of the soul in an imaginative way and to approach the basic questions of psychology first of all by means of the imagination.

Let us then imagine archetypes as the *deepest patterns of psychic functioning,* the roots of the soul governing the perspectives we have of ourselves and the world. They are the axiomatic, self-evident images to which psychic life and our theories about it ever return. They are similar to other axiomatic first principles, the models or paradigms, that we find in other fields. For "matter," "God," "energy," "life," "health," "society," "art" are also fundamental metaphors, archetypes perhaps themselves, which hold whole worlds together and yet can never be pointed to, accounted for, or even adequately circumscribed.

All ways of speaking of archetypes are translations from one metaphor to another. Even sober operational definitions in the language of science or logic are no less metaphorical than an image which presents the archetypes as root ideas, psychic organs, figures of myth, typical styles of existence, or dominant fantasies that govern consciousness. There are many other metaphors for describing them: immaterial potentials of structure, like invisible crystals in solution or form in plants that suddenly show forth under certain conditions; patterns of instinctual behavior like those in animals that direct actions along unswerving paths: the *genres* and *topoi* in literature; the recurring typicalities in history; the basic syndromes in psychiatry; the paradigmatic thought models in science; the worldwide figures, rituals, and relationships in anthropology.

But one thing is absolutely essential to the notion of archetypes: their emotional possessive effect, their bedazzlement of consciousness so that it becomes blind to its own stance. By setting up a universe which tends to hold everything we do, see, and say in the sway of its cosmos, an archetype is best comparable with a god. And gods, religions sometimes say, are less accessible to the senses and to the intellect than they are to the imaginative vision and emotion of the soul.

The archetypal perspective offers the advantage of organizing into clusters or constellations a host of events from different areas of life. The archetype of the hero, for example, appears first in *behavior,* the drive to activity, outward exploration, response to challenge, seizing and grasping and extending. It appears second in the *images* of Hercules, Achilles, Samson (or their cinema counterparts) doing their specific tasks; and third, in a style of *consciousness,* in feelings of independence, strength, and achievement, in ideas of decisive action, coping, planning, virtue, conquest (over animality), and in psychopathologies of battle, overpowering masculinity, and single-mindedness.

(*Re-Visioning,* xi, xii–xiv)

IMAGINAL METHOD

The use of allegory as a defense continues today in the interpretations of dreams and fantasies. When images no longer surprise us, when we can expect what they mean and know what they intend, it is because we have our "symbologies" of established meanings. Dreams have been yoked to the systems which interpret them; they belong to schools—there are "Freudian dreams," "Jungian dreams," etc. If long things are penises for Freudians, dark things are shadows for Jungians. Images are turned into predefined concepts such as passivity, power, sexuality, anxiety, femininity, much like the conventions of allegorical poetry. Like such poetry, and using similar allegorical techniques, psychology too can become a defense against the psychic power of personified images.

If the mother in our dream, or the beloved, or the wise old counselor, says and does what one would expect, or if the analyst interprets these figures conventionally, they have been deprived of their authority as mythic images and persons and reduced to mere allegorical conventions and moralistic stereotypes. They have become the personified conceits of an allegory, a simple means of persuasion that forces the dream or fantasy into doctrinal compliance. The image allegorized is now the image in service of a teaching.

In contrast, archetypal psychology holds that the true iconoclast is the image itself which explodes its allegorical meanings, releasing startling new insights. Thus the most distressing images in dreams and fantasies, those we shy from for their disgusting distortion and perversion, are precisely the ones that break the allegorical frame of what we think we know about this person or that, this trait of ourselves or that. The "worst" images are thus the best, for they are the ones that restore a figure to its pristine power as a numinous person at work in the soul.

(*Re-Visioning,* 8)

There is an invisible connection within any image that is its soul. If, as Jung says, "image is psyche," then why not go on to say, "images are souls," and our job with them is to meet them on that soul level. I have spoken of this elsewhere as befriending, and elsewhere again I have spoken of images as animals. Now I am carrying these feelings further to show operationally how we can meet the soul in the image and understand it. We can actively imagine it through word play which is also a way of talking with the image and letting it talk. We watch its behavior—how the image behaves within itself. And we watch its ecology—how it interconnects, by analogies, in the fields of my life. This is indeed different from interpretation. No friend or animal wants to be interpreted, even though it may cry for understanding.

We might equally call the unfathomable depth in the image, love, or at least say we cannot get to the soul of the image without love for the image.

Our method can be done by anyone in analysis or out. It requires no special knowledge—even if knowledge of symbols can help culturally to enrichen the image, and knowledge of idioms and vocabulary can help hear further into the image. By letting the image itself speak, we are suggesting that words and their arrangements (syntax) are soul mines. But mining doesn't require modern technical tools. (If it did, no one would ever have understood a dream or an image until modern psychology came along!) What does help mining is an eye attuned to the dark. (We shall have to take up later the question of *training,* how to catch the eye to read the image, the ear to hear it.) . . .

After this we can now essay a statement about what it is that makes an image *archetypal.* We have found our axiomatic criteria—dramatic structure, symbolic universality, strong emotion—not required in our actual operations with an image. We have found instead that an archetypal quality emerges through (a) precise portrayal of the image;

(b) sticking to the image while hearing it metaphorically; (c) discovering the necessity within the image; (d) experiencing the unfathomable analogical richness of the image.

Since any image can respond to these criteria, any image can be considered archetypal. The word *archetypal* as a description of images becomes redundant. It has no descriptive function. What then does it point at?

Rather than pointing *at* something, *archetypal* points *to* something, and this is *value.* By attaching *archetypal* to an image, we ennoble or empower the image with the widest, richest, and deepest possible significance. *Archetypal,* as we use it, is a word of importance (in Whitehead's sense), a word that values.

Should we carry this conclusion over to other places where we use *archetypal,* to our psychology itself, then by *archetypal psychology* we mean a psychology of value. And our appellative move is aimed to restore psychology to its widest, richest, and deepest volume so that it would resonate with soul in its descriptions as unfathomable, multiple, prior, generative, and necessary. As all images can gain this archetypal sense, so all psychology can be archetypal when it is released from its surface and seen through to its hidden volumes. *Archetypal* here refers to a move one makes rather than a thing that is. Otherwise, archetypal psychology becomes only a psychology of archetypes.

In most contexts where we come across the word *archetypal,* especially in relation with image ("*that* is an archetypal image"), archetypal could readily be replaced by one or another of the backgrounds on which it relies: mythical, religious, institutional, instinctual, philosophical, or literary.

But there is a difference of feeling between saying "the circle is a scientific or philosophical idea" and saying, "the circle is an archetypal idea." *Archetypal* adds the further implication of basic root structure, generally human, a necessary universal with consequences. The circle is not just any scientific idea; it is basic, necessary, universal. *Archetypal* gives this kind of value.

Now if the value implication is taken literally, we begin to believe that these basic roots, these universals *are.* We have moved from a valuation adjective to a thing and invented substantialities called archetypes that can "back up" our sense of archetypal value. Then we are forced to gather literal evidence from cultures the world over and make empirical claims about what is defined to be unspeakable and irrepresentable.

We do not need to take archetypal in this literal sense. Then the implications of basic, deep, universal, necessary, all those implications carried by the word *archetypal,* add richer value to any particular image.

This re-visioning of archetypal implies that the more accurate term for our psychology in its *operational* definition is *re-visioning.* In what we do we are more re-visionists than archetypalists; or, we evoke archetypes (gods and myths) in order to re-vision psychology. The value for re-visioning psychology of a psychology of the archetypes is that it provides a metaphorical tool of widest, richest, and deepest volume. It conforms with the soul value we wish to give to and find in our work.

("Inquiry into Image." 82–85)

LANGUAGE

In the modern language games of Wittgenstein, words are the very fundamentals of conscious existence, yet they are also severed from things and from truth. They exist in a world of their own. In modern structural linguistics, words have no inherent sense, for they can be reduced, every single one of them, to basic quasi-mathematical units. The fantasy of a basic number of irreducible elements out of which all speech can be constituted is a dissecting technique of the analytic mind which applies logical atomism to *logos* itself—a suicide of the word.

Of course there is a credibility gap, since we no longer trust words of any sort as true carriers of meaning. Of course, in psychiatry, words have become schizogenetic, themselves a cause and source of mental disease. Of course we live in a world of slogan, jargon, and press releases, approximating the "newspeak" of Orwell's *1984.*

As one art and academic field after another falls into the paralyzing coils of obsession with language and communication, speech succumbs to a new semantic anxiety. Even psychotherapy, which began as a *talking cure*—the rediscovery of the oral tradition of telling one's story—is abandoning language for touch, cry, and gesture. We dare not be eloquent. To be passionate, psychotherapy now says we must be physical or primitive. Such psychotherapy promotes a new barbarism. Our semantic anxiety has made us forget that words, too, burn and become flesh as we speak.

A new angelology of words is needed so that we may once again have faith in them. Without the inherence of the angel in the word—and *angel* means originally "emissary," "message-bearer"—how can we utter anything but personal opinions, things made up in our subjective minds? How can anything of worth and soul be conveyed from one psyche to another, as in a conversation, a letter, or a book, if archetypal significances are not carried in the depths of our words?

We need to recall the angel aspect of the word, recognizing words as independent carriers of soul between people. We need to recall that we do not just make words up or learn them in school, or ever have them fully under control. Words, like angels, are powers which have invisible power over us. They are personal presences which have whole mythologies: genders, genealogies (etymologies concerning origins and creations), histories, and vogues; and their own guarding, blaspheming, creating, and annihilating effects. *For words are persons.* This aspect of the word transcends their nominalistic definitions and contexts and evokes in our souls a universal resonance.

Freud's *talking cure* is also the cure of our talk, an attempt at that most difficult of cultural tasks, the rectification of language: the right word. The overwhelming difficulty of communicating soul in talk becomes crushingly real when two persons sit in two chairs, face to face and knee to knee, as in an analysis with Jung. Then we realize what a miracle it is to find the right words, words that carry soul accurately, where thought, image, and feeling interweave. Then we realize that soul can be made on the spot simply through speech. Such talk is the most complex psychic endeavor imaginable—which says something about why Jung's psychology was a *cultural* advance over Freud's style of talking cure, free autistic associations on the couch.

All modern therapies which claim that action is more curative than words (Moreno) and which seek techniques other than talk (rather than in addition to it) are repressing the most human of all faculties—the telling of the tales of our souls. These therapies may be curative of the child in us who has not learned to speak or the animal who cannot, or a spirit daimon that is beyond words because it is beyond soul. But only continued attempts at accurate soul-speech can cure our speech of its chatter and restore it to its first function, the communication of soul.

Soul of bulk and substance can be evoked by words and expressed in words:

for myth and poetry, so altogether verbal and "fleshless," nonetheless resonate with the deepest intimacies of organic existence. A mark of imaginal man is the speech of his soul, and the range of this speech, its self-generative spontaneity, its precise subtlety and ambiguous suggestion, its capacity, as Hegel said, "to receive and reproduce every modification of our ideational faculty," can be supplanted neither by the technology of communication media, by contemplative spiritual silence, nor by physical gestures and signs. The more we hold back from the risk of speaking because of the semantic anxiety that keeps the soul in secret incommunicado, private and personal, the greater grows the credibility gap between what we are and what we say, splitting psyche and logos. The more we become tied by linguistic self-consciousness, the more we abdicate the ruling principle of psychological existence. . . . Man is half-angel because he can speak. The more we distrust speech in therapy or the capacity of speech to be therapeutic, the closer we are to an absorption into the fantasy of the archetypal subhuman, and the sooner the archetypal barbarian strides into the communication ruins of a culture that refused eloquence as a mirror of its soul.

(Re-Visioning, 8–9, 217–218)

While other nineteenth-century investigators were polluting the archaic, natural, and mythic in the outer world, psychology was doing much the same to the archaic, natural, and mythic within. Therapeutic depth psychology shares this blame, since it shares nineteenth-century attitudes. It gave names with a pathological bias to the animals of the imagination. We invented psychopathology and thereby labeled the *memoria* a madhouse. We invented the diagnoses with which we declared ourselves insane. After subtly poisoning our own imaginal potency with this language, we complain

54

of a cultural wasteland and loss of soul. The poison spreads; words continually fall "mentally ill" and are usurped by psychopathology, so that we can hardly use them without their new and polluted connotations: *immature, dissociation, rigid, withdrawn, passive, transference, fixation, sublimation, projection* (the last three notably different in alchemy), *resistance, deviate, stress, dependence, inhibition, compulsion, illusion, split, tranquilized, driven, compensation, inferiority, derange, suppression, depression, repression, confusion*—these words have been psychologized and pathologized in the past 150 years.

So Psyche requests the psychologist to remember his calling. Psychological remembrance is given by the kind of speech that carries remembrance within it. This language is both of culture and uncultured, is both of art and artless. It is a mythic, metaphoric language, a speech of ambiguities that is evocative and detailed, yet not definitive, not productive of dictionaries, textbooks, or even abstract descriptions. Rather, it is a speech that leads to participation, in the Platonic sense, in and with the thing spoken of, a speech of stories and insights which evoke, in the other who listens, new stories and new insights, the way one poem and one tune ignite another verse and another song. It is conversation, letters, tales, in which we reveal our dreams and fantasies—and our psychopathology. It evokes, calls forth, and creates psyche as it speaks. It speaks of mood: of "sadness" and "despair" before "depression"; of "rage" before "aggression"; of "fear," "panic," and "anguish" before "anxiety attacks." This speech is "not fashioned in schools," and it will be "simple and rude," as Terrullian said. It will have "corporeal similitudes." that is, body images, speaking from and reaching to the imaginal body in order to provoke the soul's movements. It must be speech that works as an "imaginative agent," stirring fantasy. Such speech has impact because it carries body in it; it is speech alive, the word itself alive, not a description about a psychic state by a psychologist, not carefully defined, but freely imagined. . . .

Such speech meets every human at the ultimate levels, beyond education, age, or region, just as the themes of our dreams, panics, and passions are common to all humanity. If the language is of the street and workshop, then psychology has already taken another step out of the consulting room. The soul's confusions and pains need words which mirror these conditions through imagination. Adequate descriptions of the soul's states will depend less upon right definition than upon accurate transmission of style.

(*Myth of Analysis,* 205–206, 208)

CONSCIOUSNESS

If "becoming conscious" has its roots in reflection and if this instinct refers to the anima archetype, then consciousness itself may more appropriately be conceived as based upon anima than upon ego.

The ego as base of consciousness has always been an anachronistic part of analytical psychology. It is a historical truth that our Western tradition has identified ego with consciousness, an identification that found formulation especially in nineteenth-century psychology and psychiatry. But this part of Jung's thought does not sit well with either his notion of psychic reality or his therapeutic goals of psychic consciousness. What brings cure is an archetypal consciousness, and this notion of consciousness is definitely not based upon ego. . . .

The "relativization of the ego," that work and that goal of the fantasy of individuation, is made possible, however, from the beginning if we shift our conception of the base of consciousness from ego to anima archetype, from I to soul. Then one realizes from the very beginning (a priori and by definition) that the ego and all its developmental fantasies were never, even at the start, the fundament of consciousness, because consciousness refers to a process more to do with images than will, with reflection rather than control, with reflective insight into, rather than manipulation of, *objective reality*. We would no longer be equating consciousness with one phase of it, the developmental period of youth and its questing heroic mythology. Then, too, while educating consciousness even in youth, the aim of nourishing anima would be no less significant than that of strengthening ego.

Instead of regarding anima from the viewpoint of ego where she becomes a poisonous mood, an inspiring weakness, or a contrasexual compensation, we might regard ego from soul's perspective where ego becomes an instrument for day-to-day coping, nothing more grandiose than a trusty janitor of the planetary houses, a servant of soul-making. This view at least gives ego a therapeutic role rather than forcing it into the antitherapeutic position, a stubborn old king to be relativized. Then, too, we might relativize the myth of the hero, or take it for what it has become today for our psyche—the myth of inflation—and not the secret key to the development of human consciousness. The hero myth tells the tale of conquest and destruction, the tale of psychology's "strong ego," its fire and sword, as well as the career of its civilization, but it tells little of the culture of its consciousness. Strange that we could still, in a psychology as subtle as Jung's, believe that this king-hero, and his ego, is the equivalent of consciousness. Images of this psychological equivalence were projected from television screens straight and live from the heroic-ego's great contemporary epic in Vietnam. Is this consciousness?

Basing consciousness upon soul accords with the Neoplatonic tradition—which we still find in Blake—where what today is called ego-consciousness would be the consciousness of the Platonic cave, a consciousness buried in the least-aware perspectives. These habits and continuities and daily organizations of personality certainly cannot encompass the definition of consciousness, a mystery that still baffles every area of research. To put it together with ego limits consciousness to the perspectives of the cave which today we would call the literalistic, personalistic, practicalistic, naturalistic, and humanistic fallacies. From the traditional psychology (of Neoplatonism), ego-consciousness does not deserve the name of consciousness at all.

Consciousness arising from anima would therefore look to myth, as it manifests in the mythologems of dreams and fantasies and the pattern of lives: whereas ego-consciousness takes its orientations from the literalisms of its perspectives, i.e., that fantasy it defines as "reality."

Because fantasy-images provide the basis of consciousness, we turn to them for basic understanding. *Becoming conscious* would now mean becoming aware of fantasies and the recognition of them *everywhere* and not merely in a "fantasy world" separate from "reality." Especially, we would want to recognize them as they play through that "mirror in which the unconscious becomes aware of its own face" (*CW* 14. §129), the ego, its thought structures and practical notions of reality. Fantasy-images now become the instrumental mode of perceiving and insighting. By means of them we realize better what Jung so often insisted upon: the psyche is the subject of our perceptions, the perceiver through fantasy, rather than the object of our perceptions. Rather than analyzing fantasies, we analyze by means of them; and translating reality into fantasy-images would better define becoming conscious than would the former notion given by ego of translating fantasy into realities. . . .

In particular, the fantasies arising from and giving insight into attachments would refer to anima consciousness. Because anima appears in our affinities, as the *fascinosum* of our attractions and obsessions, where we feel most personal, here this consciousness best mythologizes. It is a consciousness *bound to life,* both at the level of the vital, vegetative soul as it used to be called (the psychosomatic symptom as it is now called) and at the level of involvements of every kind, from petty passions, gossip, to the dilemmas of philosophy. Although consciousness based on anima is inseparable from life, nature, the feminine, as well as from fate and death, it does not follow that this consciousness is naturalistic, or fatalistic, otherworldly and morose, or particularly "feminine." It means merely in these realms it turns; these are the metaphors to which it is attached.

Attachment now becomes a more significant term in anima consciousness than do those more guilt-making, and thus ego-referent, terms like *commitment, relatedness,* and *responsibility.* In fact, the relativization of the ego means placing in abeyance such metaphors as: choice and light, problem solving and reality testing, strengthening, developing, controlling, progressing. In their place, as more adequate descriptions of consciousness and its activities, we would use metaphors long familiar to the alchemy of analytical practice: fantasy, image, reflection, insight, and, also, mirroring, holding, cooking, digesting, echoing, gossiping, deepening.

(*Anima*, 87–89, 93–97)

When myths say gods have blue hair or blue bodies, they have. The gods live in a blue place of metaphor, and they are described less with naturalistic language than with poetic "distortion." Mythical talk must be full of hyperbole; the gods live in the highs and deeps. To depict them rightly we need the expressionist's palette, not the impressionist's. Precisely this shift into mythical perception occurs with the *unio mentalis:* we now *imagine* the nature of reality, and dark blue becomes the right color to express Dionysus's hair, because it is the natural, reasonable hue for the hair of this god in this hymn, a most realistic depiction.

Although the *caelum* here, as *unio mentalis* and quintessence, is a late stage, it is sometimes (Paracelsus, Figulus) said to be the prerequisite for all alchemical operations whatsoever. The mind from the beginning must be based in the blue firmament, like the lazuli stone and sapphire throne of mysticism, the azure heaven of Boehme, *philos sophia.* The blue firmament is an image of cosmological reason; it is a mythical place that gives metaphorical support to metaphysical thinking. It is the presentation of metaphysics in image form. These upper vaults of stone confirm the solidity of invisible thought in a mythical manner and they show the mythical foundations of thought; they allow, even command, a philosophy that reaches to just such cosmological heights and depths, the full extension and glory of imagination as philosophy, philosophy as imagination, in the *terra alba* of the imaginal as described by Corbin.

If the *caelum* must be present to begin with, then to do alchemy one must be confirmed in imaginal durabilities, transcending mere psychological perspectives and metaphorical implications. The metaphorical twist that the adjective blue gives in the immense variety of its uses in vernacular speech, removing ordinary things from their ordinary sense, is only the beginning of the epistrophic return of all things to their imaginal ground. The mind itself must be drenched in blue, cosmological.

Alchemy begins before we enter the mine, the forge, or laboratory. It begins in the blue vault, the seas, in the mind's thinking in images, imagining ideationally, speculatively, silveredly, in words that are both images and ideas, in words that turn things into flashing ideas and ideas into little things that crawl, the blue power of the word itself, which locates this consciousness in the throat of the *visuddha cakra* whose dominant color is a smoky purple-blue.

The *caelum,* then, is a condition of mind. Envision it as a night sky filled with the airy bodies of the gods, those astrological constellations which are at once beasts and geometry and which participate in all things of the world as their imaginal ground. The *caelum* does not of course take place in your head, in your mind, but your mind moves in the *caelum,* touches the constellations, the thick and hairy skull opens to let in more light, their light, making possible a new idea of order, a cosmological imagination whose thought accounts for the cosmos in the forms of images.

("Blue," 44–45)

Just Walk on By: A Black Man Ponders His Power to Alter Public Space

Brent Staples

My first victim was a woman—white, well dressed, probably in her early twenties. I came upon her late one evening on a deserted street in Hyde Park, a relatively affluent neighborhood in an otherwise mean, impoverished section of Chicago. As I swung onto the avenue behind her, there seemed to be a discreet, uninflammatory distance between us. Not so. She cast back a worried glance. To her, the youngish black man—a broad six feet two inches with a beard and billowing hair, both hands shoved into the pockets of a bulky military jacket—seemed menacingly close. After a few more quick glimpses, she picked up her pace and was soon running in earnest. Within seconds she disappeared into a cross street.

That was more than a decade ago. I was twenty-two years old, a graduate student newly arrived at the University of Chicago. It was in the echo of that terrified woman's footfalls that I first began to know the unwieldy inheritance I'd come into—the abil-

ity to alter public space in ugly ways. It was clear that she thought herself the quarry of a mugger, a rapist, or worse. Suffering a bout of insomnia, however, I was stalking sleep, not defenseless wayfarers. As a softy who is scarcely able to take a knife to a raw chicken—let alone hold it to a person's throat—I was surprised, embarrassed, and dismayed all at once. Her flight made me feel like an accomplice in tyranny. It also made it clear that I was indistinguishable from the muggers who occasionally seeped into the area from the surrounding ghetto. That first encounter, and those that followed, signified that a vast, unnerving gulf lay between night-time pedestrians—particularly women—and me. And I soon gathered that being perceived as dangerous is a hazard in itself. I only needed to turn a corner into a dicey situation, or crowd some frightened, armed person in a foyer somewhere, or make an errant move after being pulled over by a policeman. Where fear and weapons meet— and they often do in urban America—there is always the possibility of death.

In that first year, my first away from my hometown, I was to become thoroughly familiar with the language of fear. At dark, shadowy intersections in Chicago, I could cross in front of a car stopped at a traffic light and elicit the *thunk, thunk, thunk* of the driver—black, white, male, or female—hammering down the door locks. On less traveled streets after dark, I grew accustomed to but never comfortable with people who crossed to the other side of the street rather than pass me. Then there were the standard unpleasantries with police, doormen, bouncers, cabdrivers, and others whose business is to screen out troublesome individuals *before* there is any nastiness.

I moved to New York nearly two years ago and I have remained an avid night walker. In central Manhattan, the near-constant crowd cover minimizes tense one-on-one street encounters. Elsewhere—visiting friends in SoHo, where sidewalks are narrow and tightly spaced buildings shut out the sky—things can get very taut indeed.

Black men have a firm place in New York mugging literature. Norman Podhoretz in his famed (or infamous) 1963 essay, "My Negro Problem—And Ours," recalls growing up in terror of black males; they "were tougher than we were, more ruthless," he writes—and as an adult on the Upper West Side of Manhattan, he continues, he cannot constrain his nervousness when he meets black men on certain streets. Similarly, a decade later, the essayist and novelist Edward Hoagland extols a New York where once "Negro bitterness bore down mainly on other Negroes." Where some see mere panhandlers, Hoagland sees "a mugger who is clearly screwing up his nerve to do more than just *ask* for money." But Hoagland has "the New Yorker's quick-hunch posture for broken-field maneuvering," and the bad guy swerves away.

I often witness that "hunch posture," from women after dark on the warren-like streets of Brooklyn where I live. They seem to set their faces on neutral and, with their purse straps strung across their chests bandolier style, they forge ahead as though bracing themselves against being tackled. I understand, of course, that the danger they perceive is not a hallucination. Women are particularly vulnerable to street violence, and young black males are drastically over-represented among the perpetrators of that violence. Yet these truths are no solace against the kind of alienation that comes of being ever the suspect, against being set apart, a fearsome entity with whom pedestrians avoid making eye contact.

It is not altogether clear to me how I reached the ripe old age of twenty-two without being conscious of the lethality night-time pedestrians attributed to me. Perhaps it was because in Chester, Pennsylvania, the small, angry industrial town where I came of age in the 1960s, I was scarcely noticeable against a backdrop of gang warfare, street knifings, and murders. I grew up one of the good boys, had perhaps a half-dozen fist-fights. In retrospect, my shyness of combat has clear sources.

Many things go into the making of a young thug. One of those things is the consummation of the male romance with the power to intimidate. An infant discovers that random flailings send the baby bottle flying out of the crib and crashing to the floor. Delighted, the joyful babe repeats those motions again and again, seeking to duplicate the feat. Just so, I recall the points at which some of my boyhood friends were finally seduced by the perception of themselves as tough guys. When a mark cowered and surrendered his money without resistance, myth and reality merged—and paid off. It is, after all, only manly to embrace the power to frighten and intimidate. We, as men, are not supposed to give an inch of our lane on the highway; we are to seize the fighter's edge in work and in play and even in love; we are to be valiant in the face of hostile forces.

Unfortunately, poor and powerless young men seem to take all this nonsense literally. As a boy, I saw countless tough guys locked away; I have since buried several, too. They were babies, really—a teenage cousin, a brother of twenty-two, a childhood friend in his midtwenties—all gone down in episodes of bravado played out in the streets. I came to doubt the virtues of intimidation early on. I chose, perhaps even unconsciously, to remain a shadow—timid, but a survivor.

The fearsomeness mistakenly attributed to me in public places often has a perilous flavor. The most frightening of these confusions occurred in the late 1970s and early 1980s when I worked as a journalist in Chicago. One day, rushing into the office of a magazine I was writing for with a deadline story in hand, I was mistaken for a burglar. The office manager called security and, with an ad hoc posse, pursued me through the labyrinthine halls, nearly to my editor's door. I had no way of proving who I was. I could only move briskly toward the company of someone who knew me.

Another time I was on assignment for a local paper and killing time before an interview. I entered a jewelry store on the city's affluent Near North Side. The proprietor excused herself and returned with an enormous red Doberman pinscher straining at the end of a leash. She stood, the dog extended toward me, silent to my questions, her eyes bulging nearly out of her head. I took a cursory look around, nodded, and bade her good night. Relatively speaking, however, I never fared as badly as another black male journalist. He went to nearby Waukegan, Illinois, a couple of summers ago to work on a story about a murderer who was born there. Mistaking the reporter for the killer, police hauled him from his car at gunpoint and but for his press credentials would probably have tried to book him. Such episodes are not uncommon. Black men trade tales like this all the time.

In "My Negro Problem—And Ours," Podhoretz writes that the hatred he feels for blacks makes itself known to him through a variety of avenues—one being his discomfort with that "special brand of paranoid touchiness" to which he says blacks are prone. No doubt he is speaking here of black men. In time, I learned to smother the rage I felt at so often being taken for a criminal. Not to do so would surely have led to madness—via that special "paranoid touchiness" that so annoyed Podhoretz at the time he wrote the essay.

I began to take precautions to make myself less threatening. I move about with care, particularly late in the evening. I give a wide berth to nervous people on subway platforms during the wee hours, particularly when I have exchanged business clothes for jeans. If I happen to be entering a building behind some people who appear skittish, I may walk by, letting them clear the lobby before I return, so as not to seem to be following them. I have been calm and extremely congenial on those rare occasions when I've been pulled over by the police.

And on late-evening constitutionals along streets less traveled by, I employ what has proved to be an excellent tension-reducing measure: I whistle melodies from Beethoven and Vivaldi and the more popular classical composers. Even steely New Yorkers hunching toward nighttime destinations seem to relax, and occasionally they even join in the tune. Virtually everybody seems to sense that a mugger wouldn't be warbling bright, sunny selections from Vivaldi's Four Seasons. It is my equivalent of the cowbell that hikers wear when they know they are in bear country.

WE JOIN SPOKES TOGETHER IN A WHEEL

by Lawrence Weschler

*S*omehow I keep coming back to Nicholas of Cusa, that late-medieval Renaissance man (1401–1464), a devout church leader and mathematical mystic who was at the same time one of the founders of modern experimental science, propagator, for example, of some of the first formal experiments in biology (proving that trees somehow absorb nourishment from the air, and that air, for that matter, has weight) and advocate, among other things, of the notion that the earth, far from being the center of the universe, might itself be in motion around the sun (this a good two generations before Copernicus)—and yet, for all that, a cautionary skeptic as to the limits of that kind of quantifiable knowledge and thus, likewise, a critic of the then-reigning Aristotelian/Thomistic worldview. No, he would regularly insist, one could never achieve knowledge of God, or, for that matter, of the wholeness of existence, through the systematic accretion of more and more factual knowledge. Picture, he would suggest, an *n*-sided equilateral polygon nested inside a circle, and now keep adding to the number of its sides: triangle, square, penta-

gon, hexagon, and so forth. The more sides you add, the closer it might seem that you will be getting to the bounding circle—and yet, he insisted, in another sense, the farther away you will in fact be becoming. Because a million-sided regular polygon, say, has *precisely* a million sides and a million angles, whereas a circle has none, or maybe at most one. No matter how many sides you add to your polygon (ten million, a hundred million), if you are ever going to achieve any true sense of the whole, at some point you will have to make the leap from the chord to the arc, a leap of faith as it were, a leap which in turn can only be accomplished in or through grace, which is to say in some significant way *gratis*, for free—beyond, that is, the *n*-sided language of mere cause and effect.

And all of that rings true to me (the ring of truth, indeed, it seems to me, being one of the ways you might know you had popped past the *n*-sided polygon and into the realm of the circle).

And yet I also find myself holding with the late Carl Sagan, who, in his 1994 book *Pale Blue Dot*, insisted that

In some respects, science has far surpassed religion in delivering awe. How is it that hardly any major religion has looked at science and concluded, "This is better than we thought! The universe is much bigger than our prophets said—grander, more subtle, more elegant. God must be even greater than we dreamed"? Instead they say, "No, no, no! My god is a little god, and I want him to stay that way." A religion, old or new, that stressed the magnificence of the universe as revealed by modern science might be able to draw forth reserves of reverence and awe hardly tapped by conventional faiths. Sooner or later, such a religion will emerge.

That, too, seems profoundly true to me, evinces the ring of truth. But can Nicholas of Cusa and Carl of Cornell both be right? Phrased another way, I suppose, is it possible to imagine a science that, while remaining true to its own principles and methods, nevertheless manages to break free of the *n*-sided polygon and toward the circle whole?

One morning, a while back, over NPR's *Morning Edition*, somebody was reporting how scientists have determined some of the mechanisms whereby staph bacilli mutate (evolve) with astonishing rapidity so as to outwit antibiotics, sharing DNA ("information") across the entire process in ever more novel ways.

It sounds almost as if staph as such is thinking, or rather maybe daydreaming, or anyway musing—letting its thoughts (all that genetic information) meander into whatever available channels present themselves (that the attempt to counter this tendency in effect is an effort "to keep" nature's "mind from wandering, where it will go—ooh—ooh—ooohhh . . . oh oh oh oh oh").

The mind/body split may constitute a misguided formulation, as for that matter in a sense may the split between the in-itself and the for-itself, between the world and consciousness.

It may not be a matter of *cogito ergo sum*—in fact, in a sense, perhaps it's that formulation's very opposite: *sum ergo cogito*. Or better yet: *esse est cogitare.*

Being is itself thinking: the world is daydreaming.

Hence the German word: *Glaube.* Faith, belief, as in *das glaube ich* (I believe this; This is what I believe). But also, *der Globus*: the globe.

The globe glaubes.

All that is, wonders—and just goes on marveling.

And then, just the other day, there was this startling image staring up at me from the pages of the science section of my morning paper and spearing me in its gaze (I momentarily felt the way I imagine some microbe might, gazing back up the barrel of a microscope—or, then again, the way Szymborska's "darling little being with its tiny beating heart inside" must have, plastered that day across the giant screen). "The crash of two gold nuclei traveling at nearly the speed of light," the picture's caption explained, "produces a shower of debris that is detected by a house-sized detector that is part of the Relativistic Heavy Ion Collider at the Brookhaven National Laboratory on Long Island." The article itself went on to note how, "according to one theoretical physicist, the collisions have even been creating a sort of tiny, short-lived black hole" (granted, "very, very tiny and very, very short-lived," lasting "less than one-10,000,000,000,000,000,000,000th of a second").

By now I suppose you know me well enough that you won't be surprised to hear how all that got me to thinking about black holes and vision, or more precisely about what comes in and what goes out when we see. The history of thinking about vision is in fact a history of a continual rejiggering of the relative importance of those two vectors: is it that light rays enter the eye through the corneal lens (whereupon they get sprayed onto a sort of tabula rasa screen at the back of the eye)—or rather, in some sense, that the brain's, or the mind's, or anyway the self's attention courses out to the world through that lens (actively grasping and even shaping what it sees, or rather looks at, or rather chooses to tend to)?

To the extent that something is going in, what is it going in *to*? Recall how Sartre characterized voracious consciousness as Being's very obverse, which is to say, Nothingness—in that sense a (perhaps not merely conceptual) mirror of the sorts of actual physical black holes cosmologists posit out there in the actual physical universe. Consider, in this context, Rilke's melancholy Panther at Paris's Jardin des Plantes, padding in his cramped circles behind those perpetual bars, its will by now almost completely paralyzed, how (in Stephen Mitchell's marvelous translation),

Only at times, the curtain of the pupils
lifts, quietly—. An image enters in,
rushes down through the tensed,
arrested muscles, plunges into the
heart and is gone.

Then again, as I say, maybe the vectors go the other way around, and mind is more like the black hole's physical obverse, the extravagantly spewing supernova, with wave-particles gushing forth at the speed of light. Which in turn raises the question of whether the outgoing attending gaze moves at the same speed as the incoming light, which is to say, the speed of light? Or faster? Or slower?

Beats me. Maybe it's some combination of all of the above. After all, as the great sixth-century B.C. Chinese master Lao-Tzu parsed things in the eleventh of the poems that make up the *Tao te Ching* (again this time in Stephen Mitchell's superb translation, with a slight tweak of my own there at the very end):

We join spokes together in a wheel,
but it is the center hole
that makes the wagon move.

We shape clay into a pot,
but it is the emptiness inside
that holds whatever we want.

We hammer wood for a house,
but it is the inner space
that makes it livable.

We work with being,
but non-being is where we live.

Maybe it just takes a circle to know a circle.

THE BIRD OF PARADISE: THE HUNTER AND THE POET

E. O. Wilson (b. 1929)

The role of science, like that of art, is to blend proximate imagery with more distant meaning, the parts we already understand with those given as new into larger patterns that are coherent enough to be acceptable as truth. Biologists know this relation by intuition during the course of fieldwork, as they struggle to make order out of the infinitely varying patterns of nature.

Picture the Huon Peninsula of New Guinea, about the size and shape of Rhode Island, a weathered horn projecting from the northeastern coast of the main island. When I was twenty-five, with a fresh Ph.D. from Harvard and dreams of physical adventure in far-off places with unpronounceable names, I gathered all the courage I had and made a difficult and uncertain trek directly across the peninsular base. My aim was to collect a sample of ants and a few other kinds of small animals up from the lowlands to the highest part of the mountains. To the best of my knowledge I was the first biologist to take this particular route. I knew that almost everything I found would be worth recording, and all the specimens collected would be welcomed into museums.

Three days' walk from a mission station near the southern Lae coast brought me to the spine of the Sarawaget range, 12,000 feet above sea level. I was above treeline, in a grassland sprinkled with cycads, squat gymnospermous plants that resemble stunted palm trees and date from the Mesozoic era; closely similar ancestral forms might have been browsed by dinosaurs 80 million years before. On a chill morning when the clouds lifted and the sun shone brightly, my Papuan guides stopped hunting alpine wallabies with dogs and arrows, I stopped putting beetles and frogs into bottles of alcohol, and together we scanned the rare panoramic view. To the north we could make out the Bismarck Sea, to the south the Markham Valley and the more distant Herzog Mountains. The primary forest covering most of this mountainous country was broken into bands of different vegetation according to elevation. The zone just below us was the cloud forest, a labyrinth of interlocking trunks and branches blanketed by a thick layer of moss, orchids, and other epiphytes that ran unbroken off the tree trunks and across the ground. To follow game trails across this high country was like crawling through a dimly illuminated cave lined with a spongy green carpet.

A thousand feet below, the vegetation opened up a bit and assumed the appearance of typical lowland rain forest, except that the trees were denser and smaller and only a few flared out into a circle of blade-thin buttresses at the base. This is the zone botanists call the mid-mountain forest. It is an enchanted world of thousands of species of birds, frogs, insects, flowering plants, and other organisms, many found nowhere else. Together they form one of the richest and most nearly pure segments of the Papuan flora and fauna. To visit the mid-mountain forest is to see life as it existed before the coming of man thousands of years ago.

The jewel of the setting is the male Emperor of Germany bird of paradise *(Paradisaea guilielmi)*, arguably the most beautiful bird in the world, certainly one of the twenty or so most striking in appearance. By moving quietly along secondary trails you might glimpse one on a lichen-encrusted branch near the treetops. Its head is shaped like that of a crow—no surprise, since the birds of paradise and crows have a close common lineage—but there the outward resemblance to any ordinary bird ends. The crown and upper breast of the bird are metallic oil-green and shine in the sunlight. The back is glossy yellow, the wings and tail deep maroon. Tufts of ivory-white plumes sprout from the flanks and sides of the breast, turning lacy in texture toward the tips. The plume rectrices continue on as wirelike appendages past the breast and tail for a distance equal to the full length of the bird. The bill is blue-gray, the eyes clear amber, the claws brown and black.

In the mating season the male joins others in leks, common courtship arenas in the upper tree branches, where they display their dazzling ornaments to the more somberly caparisoned females. The male spreads his wings and vibrates them while lifting the gossamer flank plumes. He calls loudly with bubbling and flutelike notes and turns upside down on the perch, spreading wings and tail and pointing his rectrices skyward. The dance reaches a climax as he fluffs up the green breast feathers and opens out the flank plumes until they form a brilliant white circle around his body, with only the head, tail, and wings projecting beyond. The male sways gently from side to side, causing the plumes to wave gracefully as if caught in an errant breeze. Seen from a distance, his body now resembles a spinning and slightly out-of-focus white disk.

This improbable spectacle in the Huon forest has been fashioned by thousands of generations of natural selection in which males competed and females made choices, and the accouterments of display were driven to a visual extreme. But this is only one trait, seen in physiological time and thought about at a single level of causation. Beneath its plumed surface, the Emperor of Germany bird of paradise possesses an architecture marking the culmination of an equally ancient history, with details exceeding those that can be imagined from the elaborate visible display of color and dance.

Consider one such bird analytically, as an object of biological research. Encoded within its chromosomes is the developmental program that has led to a male *Paradisaea guilielmi.* Its nervous system is a structure of fiber tracts more complex than that of any existing computer, and as challenging as all the rain forests of New Guinea surveyed on foot. Someday microscopic studies will permit us to trace the events culminating in the electric commands carried by the efferent neurons to the skeletal-muscular system and to reproduce, in part, the dance of the courting male. We will be able to dissect and understand this machinery at the level of the cell through enzymatic catalysis, microfilament configuration, and active sodium transport during electric discharge. Because biology sweeps the full range of space and time, more and more discoveries will renew our sense of wonder at each step of research. Altering the scale of perception to the micrometer and millisecond, the cellular biologist's trek parallels that of the naturalist across the land. He looks out from his own version of the mountain crest. His spirit of adventure, as well as personal history of hardship, misdirection, and triumph, is fundamentally the same.

Described this way, the bird of paradise may seem to have been turned into a metaphor of what humanists dislike most about science: that it reduces nature and is insensitive to art, that scientists are conquistadors who melt down the Inca gold. But science is not just analytic; it is also synthetic. It uses artlike intuition and imagery. True, in the early analytic stages, individual behavior can be mechanically reduced to the level of genes and neurosensory cells. But in the synthetic phase even the most elementary activity of these biological units is seen to create rich and subtle patterns at the levels of organism and society. The outer qualities of *Paradisaea guilielmi,* its plumes, dance, and daily life, are functional traits open to a deeper understanding through the exact description of their constituent parts. They can be redefined as holistic properties that alter our perception and emotion in surprising ways.

There will come a time when the bird of paradise is reconstituted through a synthesis of all the hard-won analytic information. The mind, exercising a newfound power, will journey back to the familiar world of seconds and centimeters, where once again the glittering plumage takes form and is viewed at a distance through a network of leaves and mist. Once again we see the bright eye open, the head swivel, the wings extend. But the familiar motions are now viewed across a far greater range of cause and effect. The species is understood more completely; misleading illusions have given way to more comprehensive light and wisdom. With the completion of one full cycle of intellect, the scientist's search for the true material nature of the species is partially replaced by the more enduring responses of the hunter and poet.

What are these ancient responses? The full answer is available only through a combined idiom of science and the humanities, whereby the investigation turns back into itself. The human being, like the bird of paradise, awaits our examination in the analytic-synthetic manner. Feeling and myth can be viewed at a distance through physiological time, idiosyncratically, in the manner of traditional art. But they can also be penetrated more deeply than was ever possible in the prescientific age, to their physical basis in the processes of mental development, the brain structure, and indeed the genes themselves. It may even be possible to trace them back beyond the formation of cultures to the evolutionary origins of human nature. As each new phase of synthesis emerges from biological inquiry, the humanities will expand their reach and capability. In symmetric fashion, with each redirection of the humanities, science will add dimensions to human biology.

ART OBJECTS

Jeanette Winterson

I was in Amsterdam one snowy Christmas when the weather had turned the canals into oblongs of ice. I was wandering happy, alone, playing the *flâneur*, when I passed a little gallery and in the moment of passing saw a painting that had more power to stop me than I had power to walk on.

The quality of the draughtsmanship, the brush strokes in thin oils, had a Renaissance beauty, but the fearful and compelling thing about the picture was its modernity. Here was a figure without a context, in its own context, a haunted woman in blue robes pulling a huge moon face through a subterranean waterway.

What was I to do, standing hesitant, my heart flooded away?

I fled across the road and into a bookshop. There I would be safe, surrounded by things I understood, unchallenged, except by my own discipline. Books I know, endlessly, intimately. Their power over me is profound, but I do know them. I confess that until that day I had not much interest in the visual arts, although I realise now, that my lack of interest was the result of the kind of ignorance I despair of in others. I knew nothing about painting and so I got very little from it. I had never given a picture my full attention even for one hour.

What was I to do?

I had intended to leave Amsterdam the next day. I changed my plans, and sleeping fitfully, rising early, queued to get into the Rijksmuseum, into the Van Gogh Museum, spending every afternoon at any private galleries I could find, and every evening, reading, reading, reading. My turmoil of mind was such that I could only find a kind of peace by attempting to determine the size of the problem. My problem. The paintings were perfectly at ease. I had fallen in love and I had no language. I was dog-dumb. The usual response of 'This painting has nothing to say to me' had become 'I have nothing to say to this painting'. And I desperately wanted to speak.

Long looking at paintings is equivalent to being dropped into a foreign city, where gradually, out of desire and despair, a few key words, then a little syntax make a clearing in the silence. Art, all art, not just painting, is a foreign city, and we deceive ourselves when we think it familiar. No-one is surprised to find that a foreign city follows its own customs and speaks its own language. Only a boor would ignore both and blame his defaulting on the place. Every day this happens to the artist and the art.

We have to recognise that the language of art, all art, is not our mother-tongue.

I read Ruskin's *Modern Painters.* I read Pater's *Studies of the History of the Renaissance.* Joshua Reynolds' *Discourses,* Bernard Berenson, Kenneth Clark, Sickert's *A Free House!,* Whistler's *Ten O'Clock Lecture,* Vasari, Michael Levey, William Morris. I knew my Dante, and I was looking for a guide, for someone astute and erudite with whom I had something in common, a way of thinking. A person dead or alive with whom I could talk things over. I needed someone I could trust, who would negotiate with me the sublimities and cesspits of regions hitherto closed. Someone fluent in this strange language and its dialects, who had spent many years in that foreign city and who might introduce me to the locals and their rather odd habits. Art is odd, and the common method of trying to fit it into the scheme of things, either by taming it or baiting it, cannot succeed. Who at the zoo has any sense of the lion?

At last, back home, and ransacking the shelves of second-hand bookshops, I found Roger Fry.

It may seem hopelessly old-fashioned to have returned to Bloomsbury, but I do not care about fashion, only about permanencies, and if books, music and pictures are happy enough to be indifferent to time, then so am I.

Fry was the one I wanted. For me, at least, a perfect guide, close enough in spirit to Walter Pater, but necessarily firmer. I had better come clean now and say that I do not believe that art (all art) and beauty are ever separate, nor do I believe that either art or beauty are optional in a sane society. That puts me on the side of what Harold Bloom calls 'the ecstasy of the privileged moment'. Art, all art, as insight, as rapture, as transformation, as joy. Unlike Harold Bloom, I really believe that human beings can be taught to love what they do not love already and that the privileged moment exists for all of us, if we let it. Letting art is the paradox of active surrender. I have to work for art if I want art to work on me.

I knew about Roger Fry because I had read Virginia Woolf's biography of him, and because it is impossible to be interested in Modernism without finding reference to him. It was he who gave us the term 'Post-Impressionist', without realising that the late twentieth century would soon be entirely fenced in with posts.

A Quaker, trained as a scientist, passionate about painting, Roger Fry did more than anyone else in Britain to promote and protect new work during the first thirty years of the century. The key quality in Fry's writing is enthusiasm. Nothing to him is dull. Such a life-delighting, art-delighting approach, unashamed of emotion, unashamed of beauty, was what I needed.

I decided that my self-imposed studentship would perform a figure of eight. I would concentrate my reading on priests and prophets of the past, while focusing my looking on modern painters. This saved me from the Old Master syndrome and it allowed me to approach a painting without unfelt reverence or unfit complacency. At the same time it allowed me to test out the theories and assumptions of the art writers whose company I kept. For me, this lemniscate of back and forth has proved the right method. I still know far far less about pictures than I do about books and this will not change. What has changed is my way of seeing. I am learning how to look at pictures. What has changed is my capacity of feeling. Art opens the heart.

Art takes time. To spend an hour looking at a painting is difficult. The public gallery experience is one that encourages art at a trot. There are the paintings, the marvellous speaking works, definite, independent, each with a Self it would be impossible to ignore, if . . . if . . ., it were possible to see it. I do not only mean the crowds and the guards and the low lights and the ropes, which make me think of freak shows, I mean the thick curtain of irrelevancies that screens the painting from the viewer. Increasingly, galleries have a habit of saying when they acquired a painting and how much it cost . . .

Millions! The viewer does not see the colours on the canvas, he sees the colour of the money.

Is the painting famous? Yes! Think of all the people who have carefully spared one minute of their lives to stand in front of it.

Is the painting Authority? Does the guide-book tell us that it is part of The Canon? If Yes, then half of the viewers will admire it on principle, while the other half will dismiss it on principle.

Who painted it? What do we know about his/her sexual practices and have we seen anything about them on the television? If not, the museum will likely have a video full of schoolboy facts and tabloid gossip.

Where is the tea-room/toilet/gift shop?
Where is the painting in any of this?

Experiencing paintings as moving pictures, out of context, disconnected, jostled, over-literary, with their endless accompanying explanations, over-crowded, one against the other, room on room, does not make it easy to fall in love. Love takes time. It may be that if you have as much difficulty with museums as I do, that the only way into the strange life of pictures is to expose yourself to as much contemporary art as you can until you find something, anything, that you will go back and back to see again, and even make great sacrifices to buy. Inevitably, if you start to love pictures, you will start to buy pictures. The time, like the money, can be found, and those who call the whole business élitist, might be fair enough to reckon up the time they spend in front of the television, at the DIY store, and how much the latest satellite equipment and new PC has cost.

For myself, now that paintings matter, public galleries are much less dispiriting. I have learned to ignore everything about them, except for the one or two pieces with whom I have come to spend the afternoon.

Supposing we made a pact with a painting and agreed to sit down and look at it, on our own, with no distractions, for one hour. The painting should be an original, not a reproduction, and we should start with the advantage of liking it, even if only a little. What would we find?

Increasing discomfort. When was the last time you looked at anything, solely, and concentratedly, and for its own sake? Ordinary life passes in a near blur. If we go to the theatre or the cinema, the images before us change constantly, and there is the distraction of language. Our loved ones are so well known to us that there is no need to look at them, and one of the gentle jokes of married life is that we do not. Nevertheless, here is a painting and we have agreed to look at it for one hour. We find we are not very good at looking.

Increasing distraction. Is my mind wandering to the day's work, to the football match, to what's for dinner, to sex, to whatever it is that will give me something to do other than to look at the painting?

Increasing invention. After some time spent daydreaming, the guilty or the dutiful might wrench back their attention to the picture.

What is it about? Is it a landscape? Is it figurative? More promisingly, is it a nude? If the picture seems to offer an escape route then this is the moment to take it. I can make up stories about the characters on the canvas much as art-historians like to identify the people in Rembrandt's *The Night Watch*. Now I am beginning to feel much more confident because I am truly engaging with the picture. A picture is its subject matter isn't it? Oh dear, mine's an abstract. Never mind, would that pink suit me?

Increasing irritation. Why doesn't the picture *do* something? Why is it hanging there staring at me? What is this picture for? Pictures should give pleasure but this picture is making me very cross. Why should I admire it? Quite clearly it doesn't admire me . . .

Admire me is the sub-text of so much of our looking; the demand put on art that it should reflect the reality of the viewer. The true painting, in its stubborn independence, cannot do this, except coincidentally. Its reality is imaginative not mundane.

When the thick curtain of protection is taken away; protection of prejudice, protection of authority, protection of trivia, even the most familiar of paintings can begin to work its power. There are very few people who could manage an hour alone with the *Mona Lisa*.

But our poor art-lover in his aesthetic laboratory has not succeeded in freeing himself from the protection of assumption. What he has found is that the painting objects to his lack of concentration; his failure to meet intensity with intensity. He still has not discovered anything about the painting but the painting has discovered a lot about him. He is inadequate and the painting has told him so.

It is not as hopeless as it seems. If I can be persuaded to make the experiment again (and again and again), something very different might occur after the first shock of finding out that I do not know how to look at pictures, let alone how to like them.

A favourite writer of mine, an American, an animal trainer, a Yale philosopher, Vicki Hearne, has written of the acute awkwardness and embarrassment of those who work with magnificent animals, and find themselves at a moment of reckoning, summed up in those deep and difficult eyes. Art has deep and difficult eyes and for many the gaze is too insistent. Better to pretend that art is dumb, or at least has nothing to say

that makes sense to us. If art, all art, is concerned with truth, then a society in denial will not find much use for it.

In the West, we avoid painful encounters with art by trivialising it, or by familiarising it. Our present obsession with the past has the double advantage of making new work seem raw and rough compared to the cosy patina of tradition, whilst refusing tradition its vital connection to what is happening now. By making islands of separation out of the unbreakable chain of human creativity, we are able to set up false comparisons, false expectations, all the while lamenting that the music, poetry, painting, prose, performance art of Now, fails to live up to the art of Then, which is why, we say, it does not affect us. In fact, we are no more moved by a past we are busy inventing, than by a present we are busy denying. If you love a Cézanne, you can love a Hockney, can love a Boyd, can love a Rao. *If* you love a Cézanne rather than lip-service it.

We are an odd people: We make it as difficult as possible for our artists to work honestly while they are alive; either we refuse them money or we ruin them with money; either we flatter them with unhelpful praise or wound them with unhelpful blame, and when they are too old, or too dead, or too beyond dispute to hinder any more, we canonise them, so that what was wild is tamed, what was objecting, becomes Authority. Canonising pictures is one way of killing them. When the sense of familiarity becomes too great, history, popularity, association, all crowd in between the viewer and the picture and block it out. Not only pictures suffer like this, all the arts suffer like this.

That is one reason why the calling of the artist, in any medium, is to make it new. I do not mean that in new work the past is repudiated; quite the opposite, the past is reclaimed. It is not lost to authority, it is not absorbed at a level of familiarity. It is re-stated and re-instated in its original vigour.

Leonardo is present in Cézanne, Michelangelo flows through Picasso and on into Hockney. This is not ancestor worship, it is the lineage of art. It is not so much influence as it is connection.

I do not want to argue here about great artists, I want to concentrate on true artists, major or minor, who are connected to the past and who themselves make a connection to the future. The true artist is connected. The true artist studies the past, not as a copyist or a pasticheur will study the past, those people are interested only in the final product, the art object, signed sealed and delivered to a public drugged on reproduction. The true artist is interested in the art object as an art process, the thing in being, the being of the thing, the struggle, the excitement, the energy, that have found expression in a particular way. The true artist is after the problem. The false artist wants it solved (by somebody else).

If the true artist is connected, then he or she has much to give us because it is connection that we seek. Connection to the past, to one another, to the physical world, still compelling, in spite of the ravages of technology. A picture, a book, a piece of music, can remind me of feelings, thinkings, I did not even know I had forgot. Whether art tunnels deep under consciousness or whether it causes out of its own invention, reciprocal inventions that we then call memory, I do not know. I do know that the process of art is a series of jolts, or perhaps I mean volts, for art is an extraordinarily faithful transmitter. Our job is to keep our receiving equipment in good working order.

How?

It is impossible to legislate taste, and if it were possible, it would be repugnant. There are no Commandments in art and no easy axioms for art appreciation. 'Do I like this?' is the question anyone should ask themselves at the moment of confrontation with the picture. But if 'yes', why 'yes'? and if 'no', why 'no'? The obvious direct emotional response is never simple, and ninety-nine times out of a hundred, the 'yes' or 'no' has nothing at all to do with the picture in its own right.

'I don't understand this poem'
'I never listen to classical music'
'I don't like this picture'

are common enough statements but not ones that tell us anything about books, painting, or music. They are statements that tell us something about the speaker. That should be obvious, but in fact, such statements are offered as criticisms of art, as evidence against, not least because the ignorant, the lazy, or the plain confused are not likely to want to admit themselves as such. We hear a lot about the arrogance of the artist but nothing about the arrogance of the audience. The audience, who have not done the work, who have not taken any risks, whose life and livelihood are not bound up at every moment with what they are making, who have given no thought to the medium or the method, will glance up, flick through, chatter over the opening chords, then snap their fingers and walk away like some monstrous Roman tyrant. This is not arrogance; of course they can absorb in a few moments, and without any effort, the sum of the artist and the art.

If the obvious direct emotional response is to have any meaning, the question 'Do I like this?' will have to be the opening question and not the final judgement. An examination of our own feelings will have to give way to an examination of the piece of work. This is fair to the work and it will help to clarify the nature of our own feelings; to reveal prejudice, opinion, anxiety, even the mood of the day. It is right to trust our feelings but right to test them too. If they are what we say they are, they will stand the test, if not, we will at least be less insincere. But here we come back to the first hurdle of art, and it is a high one; it shows us up.

When you say 'This work has nothing to do with me'. When you say 'This work is boring/pointless/silly/obscure/élitist etc.', you might be right, because you are looking at a fad, or you might be wrong because the work falls so outside of the safety of your own experience that in order to keep your own world intact, you must deny the other world of the painting. This denial of imaginative experience happens at a deeper level than our affirmation of our daily world. Every day, in countless ways, you and I convince ourselves about ourselves. True art, when it happens to us, challenges the 'I' that we are.

A love-parallel would be just; falling in love challenges the reality to which we lay claim, part of the pleasure of love and part of its terror, is the world turned upside down. We want and we don't want, the cutting edge, the upset, the new views. Mostly we work hard at taming our emotional environment just as we work hard at taming our aesthetic environment. We already have tamed our physical environment. And are we happy with all this tameness? Are you?

Art cannot be tamed, although our responses to it can be, and in relation to The Canon, our responses are conditioned from the moment we start school. The freshness which the everyday regular man or woman pride themselves upon; the untaught 'I know what I like' approach, now encouraged by the media, is neither fresh nor untaught. It is the half-baked sterility of the classroom washed down with liberal doses of popular culture.

The media ransacks the arts, in its images, in its adverts, in its copy, in its jingles, in its little tunes and journalist's jargon, it continually offers up faint shadows of the form and invention of real music, real paintings, real words. All of us are subject to this bombardment, which both deadens our sensibilities and makes us fear what is not instant, approachable, consumable. The solid presence of art demands from us significant effort, an effort anathema to popular culture. Effort of time, effort of money, effort of study, effort of humility, effort of imagination have each been packed by the artist into the art. Is it so unreasonable to expect a percentage of that from us in return? I worry that to ask for effort is to imply élitism, and the charge against art, that it is élitist, is too often the accuser's defence against his or her own bafflement. It is quite close to the remark 'Why can't they all speak English?', which may be why élitist is the favourite insult of the British and the Americans.

But, you may say, how can I know what is good and what is not good? I may wince at the cheap seascape over the mantelpiece but does that necessarily mean I should go to the Tate Gallery and worship a floor full of dyed rice?

Years ago, when I was living very briefly with a stockbroker who had a good cellar, I asked him how I could learn about wine.

'Drink it' he said.

It is true. The only way to develop a palate is to develop a palate. That is why, when I wanted to know about paintings, I set out to look at as many as I could, using always, tested standards, but continuing to test them. You can like a thing out of ignorance, and it is perhaps a blessing that such naiveté stays with us until we die. Even now, we are not as closed and muffled as art-pessimists think we are, we do still fall in love at first sight. All well and good, but the fashion for dismissing a thing out of ignorance is vicious. In fact, it is not essential to like a thing in order to recognise its worth, but to reach that point of self-awareness and sophistication takes years of perseverance.

For most of us the question 'Do I like this?' will always be the formative question. Vital then, that we widen the 'I' that we are as much as we can. Vital then, we recognise that the question 'Do I like this?' involves an independent object, as well as our own subjectivity.

I am sure that if as a society we took art seriously, not as mere decoration or entertainment, but as a living spirit, we should very soon learn what is art and what is not art. The American poet Muriel Rukeyser has said:

There is art and there is non-art; they are two universes (in the algebraic sense) which are exclusive . . . It seems to me that to call an achieved work 'good art' and an unachieved work 'bad art', is like calling one colour 'good red' and another 'bad red' when the second one is green.

If we accept this, it does not follow that we should found an Academy of Good Taste or throw out all our pet water-colours, student posters or family portraits. Let them be but know what they are, and perhaps more importantly, what they are not. If we sharpened our sensibilities, it is not that we would all agree on everything, or that we would suddenly feel the same things in front of the same pictures (or when reading the same book), but rather that our debates and deliberations would come out of genuine aesthetic considerations and not politics, prejudice and fashion . . . And our hearts? Art is aerobic.

It is shocking too. The most conservative and least interested person will probably tell you that he or she likes Constable. But would our stalwart have liked Constable in 1824 when he exhibited at the Paris Salon and caused a riot? We forget that every true shock in art, whether books, paintings or music, eventually becomes a commonplace, even a standard, to later generations. It is not that those works are tired out and have nothing more to offer, it is that their discoveries are gradually diluted by lesser artists who can only copy but do know how to make a thing accessible and desirable. At last, what was new becomes so well known that we cannot separate it from its cultural associations and time-honoured values. To the average eye, now, Constable is a pretty landscape painter, not a revolutionary who daubed bright colour against bright colour ungraded by chiaroscuro. We have had a hundred and fifty years to get used to the man who turned his back on the studio picture, took his easel outdoors and painted in a rapture of light. It is easy to copy Constable. It was not easy to be Constable.

I cannot afford a Constable, or a Picasso, or a Leonardo, but to profess a love of painting and not to have anything original is as peculiar as a booklover with nothing on her shelves. I do not know why the crowds and crowds of visitors to public galleries do not go out and support new work. Are we talking love-affair or peep-show?

I move gingerly around the paintings I own because I know they are looking at me as closely as I am looking at them. There is a constant exchange of emotion between us, between the three of us; the artist I need never meet, the painting in its own right, and me, the one who loves it and can no longer live independent of it. The triangle of exchange alters, is fluid, is subtle, is profound and is one of those unverifiable facts that anyone who cares for painting soon discovers. The picture on my wall, art object and art process, is a living line of movement, a wave of colour that repercusses in my body, colouring it, colouring the new present, the future, and even the past, which cannot now be considered outside of the light of the painting. I think of something I did, the picture catches me, adds to the thought, changes the meaning of thought and past. The totality of the picture comments on the totality of what I am. The greater the picture the more complete this process is.

Process, the energy in being, the refusal of finality, which is not the same thing as the refusal of completeness, sets art, all art, apart from the end-stop world that is always calling 'Time Please!'.

We know that the universe is infinite, expanding and strangely complete, that it lacks nothing we need, but in spite of that knowledge, the tragic paradigm of human life is lack, loss, finality, a primitive doom-saying that has not been repealed by technology or medical science. The arts stand in the way of this doomsaying. Art objects. The nouns become an active force not a collector's item. Art objects.

The cave wall paintings at Lascaux, the Sistine Chapel ceiling, the huge truth of a Picasso, the quieter truth of Vanessa Bell, are part of the art that objects to the lie against life, against the spirit, that it is pointless and mean. The message coloured through time is not lack, but abundance. Not silence but many voices. Art, all art, is the communication cord that cannot be snapped by indifference or disaster. Against the daily death it does not die.

All painting is cave painting; painting on the low dark walls of you and me, intimations of grandeur. The painted church is the tattooed body of Christ, not bound into religion, but unbound out of love. Love, the eloquent shorthand that volumes out those necessary invisibles of faith and optimism, humour and generosity, sublimity of mankind made visible through art.

Naked I came into the world, but brush strokes cover me, language raises me, music rhythms me. Art is my rod and staff, my resting place and shield, and not mine only, for art leaves nobody out. Even those from whom art has been stolen away by tyranny, by poverty, begin to make it again. If the arts did not exist, at every moment, someone would begin to create them, in song, out of dust and mud, and although the artifacts might be destroyed, the energy that creates them is not destroyed. If, in the comfortable West, we have chosen to treat such energies with scepticism and contempt, then so much the worse for us. Art is not a little bit of evolution that late-twentieth-century city dwellers can safely do without. Strictly, art does not belong to our evolutionary pattern at all. It has no biological necessity. Time taken up with it was time lost to hunting, gathering, mating, exploring, building, surviving, thriving. Odd then, that when routine physical threats to ourselves and our kind are no longer a reality, we say we have no time for art.

If we say that art, all art is no longer relevant to our lives, then we might at least risk the question 'What has happened to our lives?' The usual question, 'What has happened to art?' is too easy an escape route.

I did not escape. At an Amsterdam gallery I sat down and wept.

When I sold a book I bought a Massimo Rao. Since that day I have been filling my walls with new light.

78

THE DEATH OF THE MOTH

Virginia Woolf

*M*oths that fly by day are not properly to be called moths; they do not excite that pleasant sense of dark autumn nights and ivy-blossom which in the commonest yellow-underwing asleep in the shadow of the curtain never fails to rouse in us. They are hybrid creatures, neither gay like butterflies nor somber like their own species. Nevertheless the present specimen, with his narrow hay-colored wings, fringed with a tassel of the same color, seemed to be content with life. It was a pleasant morning, mid-September, mild, benignant, yet with a keener breath than that of the summer months. The plough was already scoring the field opposite of the window, and where the share had been, the earth was pressed flat and gleamed with moisture. Such vigor came rolling in from the fields and the down beyond that it was difficult to keep the eyes strictly turned upon the book. The rooks too were keeping one of their annual festivities; soaring round the tree tops until it looked as if a vast net with thousands of black knots in it had been cast up into the air; which, after a few moments sank slowly down upon the trees until every twig seemed to have a knot at the end of it. Then, suddenly, the net would be thrown into the air again in a wider circle this time, with the utmost clamor and vociferation, as though to be thrown into the air and settle slowly down upon the tree tops were a tremendously exciting experience.

The same energy which inspired the rooks, the ploughmen, the horse, and even, it seemed the lean bare-backed downs, sent the moth fluttering from side to side of his square of the windowpane. One could not help watching him. One was, indeed, conscious of a queer feeling of pity for him. The possibilities of pleasure seemed that morning so enormous and so various that to have only a moth's part in life, and a day moth's at that, appeared a hard fate, and his zest in enjoying his meager opportunities to the full, pathetic. He flew vigorously to one corner of his compartment, and after waiting there a second, flew across to the other. What remained for him but to fly to a third corner and then to a fourth? That was all he could do, in spite of the size of the downs, the width of the sky, the far-off smoke of houses, and the romantic voice, now and then, of a steamer out at sea. What he would do he did. Watching him, it seemed as if a fiber, very thin but pure, of the enormous energy of the world had been thrust into his frail and diminutive body. As often as he crossed the pane, I could fancy that a thread of vital light became visible. He was little or nothing but life.

Yet, because he was so small, and so simple a form of the energy that rolling in at the open window and driving its way through so many narrow and intricate corridors in my own brain and in those of other human beings, there was something marvelous as well as pathetic about him. It was as if someone had taken a tiny bead of pure life and decking it as lightly as possible with down and feathers, had set it dancing and zigzagging to show us the true nature of life. Thus displayed one could not get over the strangeness of it. One is apt to forget all about life, seeing it humped and bossed and garnished and cumbered so that it has to move with the greatest circumspection and dignity. Again, the thought of all that life might have been had he been born in any other shape caused one to view his simple activities with a kind of pity.

After a time, tired by his dancing apparently, he settled on the window ledge in the sun, and, the queer spectacle being at an end, I forgot about him. Then, looking up, my eye was caught by him. He was trying to resume his dancing, but seemed either so stiff or so awkward that he could only flutter to the bottom of the windowpane; and when he tried to fly across it he failed. Being intent on other matters I watched these futile attempts for a time without thinking, unconsciously waiting for him to resume his flight, as one waits for a machine, that has stopped momentarily, to start again without considering the reason of its failure. After perhaps a seventh attempt he slipped from the wooden ledge and fell, fluttering his wings, on to his back on the windowsill. The helplessness of his attitude roused me. It flashed upon me that he was in difficulties; he could no longer raise himself; his legs struggled vainly. But, as I stretched out a pencil, meaning to help him to right himself, it came over me that the failure and awkwardness were the approach of death. I laid the pencil down again.

The legs agitated themselves once more. I looked as if for the enemy against which he struggled. I looked out of doors. What had happened there? Presumably it was midday, and work in the fields had stopped. Stillness and quiet had replaced the previous animation. The birds had taken themselves off to feed in the brooks. The horse stood still. Yet the power was there all the same, massed outside, indifferent, impersonal, not attending to anything in particular. Somehow it was opposed to the little hay-colored moth. It was useless to try and do anything. One could only watch the extraordinary efforts made by those tiny legs against an oncoming doom which would, had it chosen, have submerged an entire city, not merely a city, but masses of human beings; nothing, I knew, had any chance against death. Nevertheless after a pause of exhaustion the legs fluttered again. It was superb that this last protest, and so frantic that he succeeded at last in righting himself. One's sympathies, of course, were all on the side of life. Also, when there was nobody to care or to know, this gigantic effort on the part of an insignificant little moth, against a power of such magnitude, to retain what no one else valued or desired to keep, moved one strangely. Again, somehow, one saw life, a pure bead. I lifted the pencil again, useless though I knew it to be. But even as I did so, the unmistakable tokens of death showed themselves. The body relaxed, and instantly grew stiff. The struggle was over. The insignificant little creature now knew death. As I looked over at the dead moth, this minute wayside triumph of so great a force over so mean an antagonist filled me with wonder. Just as life had been strange a few minutes before, so death was now as strange. The moth having righted himself now lay most decently and uncomplainingly composed. O yes, he seemed to say, death is stronger than I am.

THE WHITE BIRD

John Berger

From time to time I have been invited by institutions—mostly American—to speak about aesthetics. On one occasion I considered accepting and I thought of taking with me a bird made of white wood. But I didn't go. The problem is that you can't talk about aesthetics without talking about the principle of hope and the existence of evil. During the long winters the peasants in certain parts of the Haute Savoie used to make wooden birds to hang in their kitchens and perhaps also in their chapels. Friends who are travellers have told me that they have seen similar birds, made according to the same principle, in certain regions of Czechoslovakia, Russia and the Baltic countries. The tradition may be more widespread.

The principle of the construction of these birds is simple enough, although to make a fine bird demands considerable skill. You take two bars of pine wood, about six inches in length, a little less than one inch in height and the same in width. You soak them in water so that the wood has the maximum pliability, then you carve them. One piece will be the head and body with a fan tail, the second piece will represent the wings. The art principally concerns the making of the wing and tail feathers. The whole block of each wing is carved according to the silhouette of a single feather. Then the block is sliced into thirteen thin layers and these are gently opened out, one by one, to make a fan shape. Likewise for the second wing and for the tail feathers. The two pieces of wood are joined together to form a cross and the bird is complete. No glue is used and there is only one nail where the two pieces of wood cross. Very light, weighing only two or three ounces, the birds are usually hung on a thread from an overhanging mantelpiece or beam so that they move with the air currents.

It would be absurd to compare one of these birds to a van Gogh self-portrait or a Rembrandt crucifixion. They are simple, homemade objects, worked according to a traditional pattern. Yet, by their very simplicity, they allow one to categorize the qualities which make them pleasing and mysterious to everyone who sees them.

First there is a figurative representation—one is looking at a bird, more precisely a dove, apparently hanging in mid-air. Thus, there is a reference to the surrounding world of nature. Secondly, the choice of subject (a flying bird) and the context in which it is placed (indoors where live birds are unlikely) render the object symbolic. This primary symbolism then joins a more general, cultural one. Birds, and doves in particular, have been credited with symbolic meanings in a very wide variety of cultures.

Thirdly, there is a respect for the material used. The wood has been fashioned according to its own qualities of lightness, pliability and texture. Looking at it, one is surprised by how well wood becomes bird. Fourthly, there is a formal unity and economy. Despite the object's apparent complexity, the grammar of its making is simple, even austere. Its richness is the result of repetitions which are also variations. Fifthly, this man-made object provokes a kind of astonishment: how on earth was it made? I have given rough indications above, but anyone unfamiliar with the technique wants to take the dove in his hands and examine it closely to discover the secret which lies behind its making.

These five qualities, when undifferentiated and perceived as a whole, provoke at least a momentary sense of being before a mystery. One is looking at a piece of wood that has become a bird. One is looking at a bird that is somehow more than a bird. One is looking at something that has been worked with a mysterious skill and a kind of love.

Thus far I have tried to isolate the qualities of the white bird which provoke an aesthetic emotion. (The word "emotion", although designating a motion of the heart and the imagination, is somewhat confusing for we are considering an emotion that has little to do with the others we experience, notably because the self here is in a far greater degree of abeyance.) Yet my definitions beg the essential question. They reduce aesthetics to art. They say nothing about the relation between art and nature, art and the world.

Before a mountain, a desert just after the sun has gone down, or a fruit tree, one can also experience aesthetic emotion. Consequently we are forced to begin again—not this time with a man-made object but with the nature into which we are born.

Urban living has always tended to produce a sentimental view of nature. Nature is thought of as a garden, or a view framed by a window, or as an arena of freedom. Peasants, sailors, nomads have known better. Nature is energy and struggle. It is what exists without any promise. If it can be thought of by man as an arena, a setting, it has to be thought of as one which lends itself as much to evil as to good. Its energy is fearsomely indifferent. The first necessity of life is shelter. Shelter against nature. The first prayer is for protection. The first sign of life is pain. If the Creation was purposeful, its purpose is a hidden one which can only be discovered intangibly within signs, never by the evidence of what happens.

It is within this bleak natural context that beauty is encountered, and the encounter is by its nature sudden and unpredictable. The gale blows itself out, the sea changes from the colour of grey shit to aquamarine. Under the fallen boulder of an avalanche a flower grows. Over the shanty town the moon rises. I offer dramatic examples so as to insist upon the bleakness of the context. Reflect upon more everyday examples. However it is encountered, beauty is always an exception, always *in despite of*. This is why it moves us.

It can be argued that the origin of the way we are moved by natural beauty was functional. Flowers are a promise of fertility, a sunset is a reminder of fire and warmth, moonlight makes the night less dark, the bright colours of a bird's plumage are (atavistically even for us) a sexual stimulus. Yet such an argument is too reductionist, I believe. Snow is useless. A butterfly offers us very little.

Of course the range of what a given community finds beautiful in nature will depend upon its means of survival, its economy, its geography. What Eskimos find beautiful is unlikely to be the same as what the Ashanti found beautiful. Within modern class societies there are complex ideological determinations: we know, for instance, that the British ruling class in the eighteenth century disliked the sight of the sea. Equally, the social use to which an aesthetic emotion may be put changes according to the historical moment: the silhouette of a mountain can represent the home of the dead or a challenge to the initiative of the living. Anthropology, comparative studies of religion, political economy and Marxism have made all this clear.

Yet there seem to be certain constants which all cultures have found 'beautiful': among them—certain flowers, trees, forms of rock, birds, animals, the moon, running water . . .

One is obliged to acknowledge a coincidence or perhaps a congruence. The evolution of natural forms and the evolution of human perception have coincided to produce the phenomenon of a potential recognition: what is and what we can see (and by seeing also feel) sometimes meet at a point of affirmation. This point, this coincidence, is two-faced: what has been seen is recognized and affirmed and, at the same time, the seer is affirmed by what he sees. For a brief moment one finds oneself—without the pretensions of a creator—in the position of God in the first chapter of Geneses . . . And he saw that it was good. The aesthetic emotion before nature derives, I believe, from the double affirmation.

Yet we do not live in the first chapter of Genesis. We live—if one follows the biblical sequence of events—after the Fall. In any case, we live in a world of suffering in which evil is rampant, a world whose events do not confirm our Being, a world that has to be resisted. It is in this situation that the aesthetic moment offers hope. That we find a crystal or a poppy beautiful means that we are less alone, that we are more deeply inserted into existence than the course of a single life would lead us to believe. I try to describe as accurately as possible the experience in question; my starting point is phenomenological, not deductive; its form, perceived as such, becomes a message that one receives but cannot translate because, in it, all is instantaneous. For an instant, the energy of one's perception becomes inseparable from the energy of the creation.

The aesthetic emotion we feel before a man-made object—such as the white bird with which I started—is a derivative of the emotion we feel before nature. The white bird is an attempt to translate a message received from a real bird. All the languages of art have been developed as an attempt to transform the instantaneous into the permanent. Art supposes that beauty is not an exception—is not *in despite of*—but is the basis for an order.

Several years ago, when considering the historical face of art, I wrote that I judged a work according to whether or not it helped men in the modern world claim their social rights. I hold to that. Art's other, transcendental face raises the question of man's ontological right.

The notion that art is the mirror of nature is the one that only appeals in periods of skepticism. Art does not imitate nature, it imitates a creation, sometimes to propose an alternative world, sometimes simply to amplify, to confirm, to make social the brief hope offered by nature. Art is an organized response to what nature allows us to glimpse occasionally. Art sets out to transform the potential recognition into an unceasing one. It proclaims man in the hope of receiving a surer reply . . . the transcendental face of art is always a form of prayer.

The white wooden bird is wafted by the warm air rising from the stove in the kitchen where the neighbours are drinking. Outside, in minus 25°C, the real birds are freezing to death!

HIROSHIMA

John Berger

The whole incredible problem begins with the need to reinsert those events of August 1945 back into the living consciousness.

I was shown a book last year at the Frankfurt Book Fair. The editor asked me some question about what I thought of its format. I glanced at it quickly and gave some reply. Three months ago I was sent a finished copy of the book. It lay on my desk unopened. Occasionally its title and cover picture caught my eye, but I did not respond. I didn't consider the book urgent, for I believed that I already knew what I would find within it.

Did I not clearly remember the day—I was in the army in Belfast—when we first heard the news of the bomb dropped on Hiroshima? At how many meetings during the first nuclear disarmament movement had I and others not recalled the meaning of that bomb?

And then, one morning last week, I received a letter from America, accompanying an article written by a friend. This friend is a doctor of philosophy and a Marxist. Furthermore, she is a very generous and warm-hearted woman. The article was about the possibilities of a third world war. Vis-à-vis the Soviet Union she took, I was surprised to read, a position very close to Reagan's. She concluded by evoking the likely scale of destruction which would be caused by nuclear weapons, and then welcomed the possibilities that this would offer the social-ist revolution in the United States.

It was on that morning that I opened and read the book on my desk. It is called *Unforgettable Fire*.[i]

The book consists of drawings and paint-ings made by people who were in Hiroshima on the day that the bomb was dropped, thirty-six years ago today. Often the pictures are accompanied by a verbal record of what the image represents. None of them is by a professional artist. In 1974, an old man went to the television centre in Hiroshima to show to whoever was interested a picture he had painted, entitled 'At about 4pm. 6th August 1945, near Yurozuyo bridge'.

This prompted an idea of launching a tel-evision appeal to other survivors of that day to paint or draw their memories of it. Nearly a thousand pictures were sent in, and these were made into an exhibition. The appeal

[i]Edited by Japan Broadcasting Corporation, London, Wildwood House, 1981; New York, Pantheon, 1981.

was worded: 'Let us leave for posterity pictures about the atomic bomb, drawn by citizens.'

Clearly, my interest in these pictures cannot be an art-critical one. One does not musically analyze screams. But after repeatedly looking at them, what began as an impression became a certainty. These were images of hell.

I am not using the word as hyperbole. Between these paintings by women and men who have never painted anything else since leaving school, and who have surely, for the most part, never travelled outside Japan, between these traced memories which had to be exorcised, and the numerous representations of hell in European medieval art, there is a very close affinity.

This affinity is both stylistic and fundamental. And fundamentally it is to do with the situations depicted. The affinity lies in the degree of the multiplication of pain, in the lack of appeal or aid, in the pitilessness, in the equality of wretchedness, and in the disappearance of time.

I am 78 years old. I was living a Midori-machi on the day of the A-bomb blast. Around 9am that morning, when I looked out of my window, I saw several women coming along the street one after another towards the Hiroshima prefectural hospital. I realized for the first time, as it is sometimes said, that when people are very much frightened hair really does stand on end. The women's hair was, in fact, standing straight up and the skin of their arms was peeled off. I suppose they were around 30 years old.

Time and again, the sober eyewitness accounts recall the surprise and horror of Dante's verses about the Inferno. The temperature at the center of the Hiroshima fireball was 300,000 degrees centigrade. The survivors are called in Japanese *hibakuska*— 'those who have seen hell'.

Suddenly, one man who was stark naked came up to me and said in a quavering voice, 'Please help me!' He was burned and swollen all over from the effects of the A-bomb. Since I did not recognize him as my neighbour, I asked who he was. He answered that he was Mr. Sasaki, the son of Mr. Ennosuke Sasaki, who had a lumber shop in Funairi town. That morning he had been doing volunteer labour service, evacuating the houses near the prefectural office in Kato town. He had been burned black all over and had started back to his home in Funairi. He looked miserable—burned and sore, and naked with only pieces of his gaiters trailing behind as he walked. Only the part of his hair covered by his soldier's hat was left, as if he was wearing a bowl. When I touched him, his burned skin slipped off, I did not know what to do, so I asked a passing driver to take him to Eba hospital.

Does not this evocation of hell make it easier to forget that these scenes belonged to life? Is there not something conveniently unreal about hell? The whole history of the twentieth century proves otherwise.

Very systematically in Europe the conditions of hells have been constructed. It is not even necessary to list the sites. It is not necessary to repeat the calculations of the organizers. We know this, and we choose to forget it.

We find it ridiculous and shocking that most of the pages concerning, for example, Trotsky were torn out of official Soviet history. What has been torn out of our history are the pages concerning the experience of the two atom bombs dropped on Japan.

Of course, the facts are there in the textbooks. It may even be that school children learn the dates. But what these facts mean—and originally their meaning was so clear, so monstrously vivid, that every commentator in the world was shocked, and every politician was obliged to say (whilst planning differently), 'Never again'—what these facts mean has now been torn out. It has been a systematic, slow and thorough process of suppression and elimination. This process has been hidden within the reality of politics.

Do not misunderstand me. I am not here using the word 'reality' ironically, I am not politically naïve. I have the greatest respect for political reality, and I believe that the innocence of political idealists is often very dangerous. What we are considering is how in this case in the West—not in Japan for obvious reasons and not in the Soviet Union for different reasons—political and military realities have eliminated another reality.

The eliminated reality is both physical—

Yokogawa bridge above Tenma river,
*   6th August 1945, 8.30am.*
People crying and moaning were run-
*   ning towards the city. I did not*
know why. Steam engines were burn-
*   ing at Yokogawa station.*
Skin of cow Tied to wire.
Skin of girl's hip was hanging down.
'My baby is dead, isn't' she?'

and moral.

The political and military arguments have concerned such issues as deterrence, defense systems, relative strike parity, tactical nuclear weapons and—pathetically—so-called civil defense. Any movement for nuclear disarmament today has to contend with those considerations and dispute their false interpretation. To lose sight of them is to become as apocalyptic as the Bomb and all utopias. (The construction of hells on earth was accompanied in Europe by plans for heavens on earth.)

What has to be redeemed, reinserted, disclosed and never be allowed to be forgotten, is the other reality. Most of the mass means of communication are close to what has been suppressed.

These paintings were shown on Japanese television. Is it conceivable that the BBC would show these pictures on channel one at a peak hour? Without any reference to 'political' and 'military' realities, under the straight title, *This is How It Was, 6TH August 1945?* I challenge them to do so.

What happened on that day was, of course, neither the beginning nor the end of the act. It began months, years before, with the planning of the action, and the eventual final decision to drop two bombs on Japan. However much the world was shocked and surprised by the bomb dropped on Hiroshima, it has to be emphasized that it was not miscalculation, an error, or the result (as can happen in war) of a situation deteriorating so rapidly that it gets out of hand. What happened was consciously and precisely planned. Small scenes like this were part of the plan:

I was walking along the Hihiyama
bridge about 3 pm on 7th August. A
woman, who looked like an expectant
mother, was dead. At her side, a girl of
about three years of age brought some
water in an empty can she had found.
She was trying to let her mother drink
from it.

As soon as I saw this miserable scene
with the pitiful child, I embraced the
girl close to me and cried with her,
telling her that her mother was dead.

There was a preparation. And there was an aftermath. The latter included long, lingering deaths, radiation sickness, many fatal illnesses which developed later as a result of exposure to the bomb, and tragic genetical effects on generations yet to be born.

I refrain from giving the statistics: how many hundreds of thousands of dead, how many injured, how many deformed children. Just as I refrain from pointing out how comparatively 'small' were the atomic bombs dropped on Japan. Such statistics tend to distract. We calculate instead of judging. We relativize instead of refusing.

It is possible today to arouse popular indignation or anger by speaking of the threat and immorality of terrorism. Indeed, this appears to be the central plank of the rhetoric of the new American foreign policy ('Moscow is the world-base of all terrorism') and of British policy towards Ireland. What is able to shock people about terrorist acts is that often their targets are unselected and innocent—a crowd in a railway station, people waiting for a bus to go home after work. The victims are chosen indiscriminately in the hope of producing a shock effect on political decision-making by their government.

The two bombs dropped on Japan were terrorist actions. The calculation was terrorist. The indiscriminacy was terrorist. The small group of terrorists operating today are, by comparison, humane killers.

Another comparison needs to be made. Today terrorist groups mostly represent small nations or groupings, who are disputing large powers in a position of strength. Whereas Hiroshima was perpetrated by the most powerful alliance in the world against an enemy who was already prepared to negotiate, and was admitting defeat.

To apply the epithet 'terrorist' to the acts of bombing Hiroshima and Nagasaki is logically justifiable, and I do so because it may help to re-insert that act into living consciousness today. Yet the word changes nothing in itself.

The first-hand evidence of the victims, the reading of the pages which have been torn out, provokes a sense of outrage. This outrage has two natural faces. One is a sense of horror and pity at what happened; the other face is self-defensive and declares: *this*

should not happen again (here). For some the *here* is in brackets, for others it is not.

The face of horror, the reaction which has now been mostly suppressed, forces us to comprehend the reality of what happened. The second reaction, unfortunately, distances us from that reality. Although it begins as a straight declaration, it quickly leads into the labyrinth of defence policies, military arguments and global strategies. Finally it leads to the sordid commercial absurdity of private fall-out shelters.

This split of the sense of outrage into, on one hand, horror and, on the other hand, expediency occurs because the concept of evil has been abandoned. Every culture, except our own in recent times, has had such a concept.

That its religious or philosophical bases vary is unimportant. The concept of evil implies a force or forces which have to be continually struggled against so that they do not triumph over life and destroy it. One of the very first written texts from Mesopotamia, 1500 years before Homer, speaks of this struggle, which was the first condition of human life. In public thinking nowadays, the concept of evil has been reduced to a little adjective to support an opinion or hypothesis (abortions, terrorism, ayatollahs).

Nobody can confront the reality of 6th August 1945 without being forced to acknowledge that what happened was evil. It is not a question of opinion or interpretation, but of events.

The memory of these events should be continually before our eyes. This is why the thousand citizens of Hiroshima started to draw on their little scraps of paper. We need to show their drawings everywhere. These terrible images can now release an energy for opposing evil and for the life-long struggle of that opposition.

And from this a very old lesson may be drawn. My friend in the United States is, in a sense, innocent. She looks beyond the nuclear holocaust without considering its reality. This reality includes not only its victims but also its planners and those who support them. Evil from time immemorial has often worn a mask of innocence. One of evil's principal modes of being is looking beyond (with indifference) that which is before the eyes.

August 9th: On the west embankment of a military training field was a young boy four or five years old. He was burned black, lying on his back, with his arms pointing towards heaven.

Only by looking beyond or away can one come to believe that such evil is relative, and therefore under certain conditions justifiable. In reality—the reality to which the survivors and dead bear witness—it can never be justified.

HAMMER

Harvey Blume

*M*ark Burnett is a hands-on kind of guy, sort of a real life Mad Max. The ex-British paratrooper, a veteran of combat operations in the Falklands and police actions in Northern Ireland, personally tries out the tests of skill and endurance he designs for *Survivor*, one of the reality shows he produces for American television. In my mind's eye, I see him putting finishing touches on the faux primitive set *Survivor* uses for the tribal councils where contestants gather to vote one of their number off the isle. Burnett is hammering away at a nail, as I see it, but when he pulls his hand back, it no longer belongs to him. It has migrated to the body of Mel Gibson. And we are no longer on the steamy beach of Palau Tiga, off the coast of Borneo, where the first *Survivor* was taped, but on the set of *The Passion of the Christ*, where Gibson filmed himself hammering a faux nail through Christ's crucified flesh.

Burnett and Gibson like to leave traces of themselves on their work, not an uncommon impulse, in one form or another, in the arts. Hitchcock, for example, was famous for his cameos. More to the point, Andre Serrano signified his personal struggle with Catholic tradition by mixing up bodily fluids and cru-

cifixes in his photographs. It could be noted that when Gibson wields his hammer he is more like Serrano, making his controversial testimony, than he would ever care to acknowledge. But bringing religion into it at this point only clouds the issue. It's when you put aside the religious content of *The Passion of the Christ* for a moment that it's apparent that Burnett and Gibson have a lot in common. That hammer I see them using doesn't come from religious fundamentalism, but from an allied if not underlying sensibility, one that might be called aesthetic or narrative fundamentalism. And at the start of a new century it would seem to be aesthetic fundamentalism that lays down the cultural beat, in time with political events.

The Pope's purported review of *The Passion of the Christ*—namely, "it is as it was"—gets to the core of this sensibility, its "it is as it was" approach to storytelling. Burnett and Gibson aim to cut through complications, irony, self-reflection—all that baroque, distracting, postmodern stuff—to give the sensation of raw truth, undoctored experience. They are storytelling revivalists, demanding narrative return to its roots. And they place enormous emphasis on the power of ordeal to seal their pact with reality. By showing protagonists under fire they give viewers the sense of truths that go beyond mere fiction.

In Gibson's case, those truths are Gospel. The Holy Spirit helped him bring them to screen. When he required more detail, a close-up, perhaps, on some underdocumented scene in Christ's life, he turned to *The Dolorous Passion Of Our Lord Jesus Christ*, by the German nun Anne Catherine Emmerich (1774–1824). In Gibson's view, contrary to the settled opinion of historians, the apostles were present at the events they describe. Sister Emmerich believed that she was there, too. Her testimony typically consists of long passages flowing from an "I saw" or an "I beheld." For example, apropos Christ's meeting with Pilate and the High Priest, she writes: "I see numerous devils among the crowd, exciting and encouraging the Jews, whispering in their ears, entering their mouths, inciting them still more against Jesus. . . ." This becomes the sole source for a scene in the Gibson movie, as does the following, which similarly has no basis in scripture: "I saw Pilate going to his wife . . . a tall, fine-looking woman, although extremely pale. Her hair was plaited and slightly ornamented, but partly covered by a long veil. . . . She conversed with Pilate for a long time, and entreated him by all that he held sacred not to injure Jesus, that Prophet, that saint of saints."

The Catholic Church has had enough reservations about Sister Emmerich's trances to deny her sainthood. For one thing, a poet named Clemens Brentano served as her secretary, transcribing her visions, and possibly interpolating material and a slant of his own. But it is precisely such fraught questions of authorship and authenticity that Gibson set out to override in his movie. Its theme, as much as anything, is that certainty *is* available and doubt can be once and for all expunged—or, to put it another way, that a story, *this* story, anyway, is absolutely, incontestably true, true not only in its own particulars but on behalf of all other stories. It's a story that redeems imperfect narratives much as Christ does sinners. Doubts and complexities may gather around Sister Emmerich's tales, but Gibson will not so much as acknowledge them. Her twenty-twenty hindsight puts her there with the apostles. What she saw is as it was.

As compared to Gibson's anxious absolute, the truths spun out by reality television are mundane and provisional. But they share one thing, at least, with *The Passion of the Christ*—its pessimism. For Gibson, we are all sinners—and he wielded that hammer to show that he is, too—all, with few exceptions, responsible for the death of the messiah. The conclusions reality TV comes to about humankind are not much cheerier. They are a sort of secular version, updated with regard to language and setting. The difference has to do with how we take the news: while we may be just as bad as Gibson says, we won't feel as guilty about it. We'll be entertained.

Reality TV's take on human nature is tangled up with the kinds of research performed by Stanley Milgram and Philip Zimbardo, psychologists whose work became notorious for exposing embarrassing aspects of human behavior, especially our obsequiousness toward authority. In his most famous experiment, at Yale in the 1960s, Milgram wanted to know if people would obey white-coated lab technicians even if it meant seeming to do physical injury to others. As we all know by now, it turned out most people would.

Ten years later, Philip Zimbardo pursued a similar line of inquiry in the Stanford Prison Experiment. Curious to learn what would prove stronger under stress, individual morality or peer pressure to conform, Zimbardo randomly divided 24 Stanford student volunteers into cohorts of prisoners and guards. The simulation was scheduled to last two weeks, but Zimbardo intervened to call it off after six days. By then, the distinction between reality and role-playing had collapsed, and guards were imposing genuine punishments on prisoners, depriving them of food, sleep, and clothing, making them wear hoods, and, as Zimbardo recently put it, treating them as sexual "playthings."

As I write, the full scope of prisoner abuse at Iraq's Abu Ghraib is still coming to light, but more than enough is known to make the Stanford experiment seem predictive, down to the "playthings." Often asked by the media to comment on the similarities, Zimbardo repeats that whether at Stanford or in Abu Ghraib, peer pressure will as a rule beat down individual morality. Many of the students who volunteered for the Stanford experiment had been protesters against the war in Vietnam—"peaceniks," as he called them. Six days in the prison simulation: "They became like Nazis." Zimbardo has proposed that psychologists give a sort of conscience award to the guards at Abu Ghraib who managed not to become abusers.

Because it followed no script, and exposed how unstable, how prone to collapse, the walls are between role-playing and reality, the Stanford experiment is a ready-made template for reality TV. Zimbardo attributes renewed interest in the experiment (archived at www.prisonexp.org) to the rise of genre, with which he has had an ambivalent relationship for years. He criticizes reality tube for concocting mini-Stanfords or Abu Ghraibs, while at the same time hoping that in responsible hands the genre could evolve into a psych lab in the rough.

He's not the only psychologist who has been drawn, misgivings and all, to the genre. In 2001, The American Psychological Association (which Zimbardo chaired at the time) sponsored a symposium entitled, "Reality TV: Psychology in Prime Time." As reported by Sam Brenton and Reuben Cohen ("Shooting People: Adventures in Reality TV," 2003), one of the speakers confessed he had a "gut bad feeling" about reality TV, but just didn't have it in him to turn down a job as an advisor for *Survivor*. Should psychologists ever

become eligible, this one would not be in the running for a conscience award.

Milgram- and Zimbardo-type experiments are no longer permitted in the field, due to the possibility of their inflicting harm on participants. Reality TV is in some ways a continuation of their work, with prize money and telegenic contestants to boot, not many of whom could be accused of being peaceniks to start with. The shows reiterate Milgram's, Zimbardo's—and Mel Gibson's—dour view of behavior, while allowing for outbreaks of principle and loyalty. One speaker at the APA symposium expressed the view that reality TV may be to our time what the birth of tragedy was to ancient Greece, an entirely new way of framing and conceiving of human experience. "Reality shows are in their infancy," he argued. "Entertainment since Sophocles has recounted and acted out dramas." Reality TV is "the first time we have been able to create a new form of drama by creating contexts for compelling behaviors." The tragedians have only interpreted the world. Reality TV gives you the world itself, in concentrated, volatile form.

Mark Burnett couldn't agree more about the revolutionary impact of the genre. In the book he wrote to accompany the first year of *Survivor*, he boasted that the show signified "a return to a core element of adventure: staying alive." Whether the adventure takes place in a flea-bitten tropical isle or a backstabbing corporate boardroom, Burnett can be trusted to design the site-specific ordeal. The techniques he uses are disconcertingly similar to the ones employed at Abu Ghraib, but Burnett's not out to punish contestants or extract information from them. He's not even aiming to embarrass or humiliate them, necessarily. All he wants is to squeeze as much "raw emotional drama" out of contestants as he can.

To do that, he keeps them "off-balance" and "out of their comfort zone." Sleep deprivation helps, especially when augmenting the effects of hunger. And then, for *Survivor*, there is the disorienting impact of an alien locale. Burnett writes with almost proprietary glee about the stinging jellyfish that share the waters around Palau Tiga with "the world's highest concentration of deadly sea snakes." The island's interior is no picnic either, populated as it is by fat pythons that drop from trees onto passing animals, not excluding human beings.

This environment can't but trigger that moment dear to Burnett when it dawns on his naïve "castaways" that they're in for an "actual, real-world adventure instead of something pretend." The shock of recognition comes early, he reports, occasioned by questions such as "where to sit without being swarmed by sand fleas and where to sleep without rats crawling over them." Will contestants toughen up or fall apart when they find that in both cases the answer is "nowhere"? The cameras are rolling.

If Burnett cared for a high-cultural gloss on his own procedures he could get one from no less a connoisseur of ordeals than Michel Foucault. Foucault thought of the ordeal as a mode of inquiry that had once rivaled epistemologies based on reason. Unlike science, which aims at reproducible results, ordeals favor outcomes that are "ambiguous [and] reversible." Such mercurial outcomes don't yield themselves to the straightforward approach; they must be "provoked by rituals [and] attained by tricks."

Foucault's thoughts on ordeal arose from his encounter with sadomasochism in San Francisco's gay underworld but seem perfectly applicable to reality TV. The ritual aspect that he refers to structures the experience, moors it, lends it a certain gravity, perhaps as much for the sake of viewers as for participants. Ritual announces that something primal is afoot, something basic is being called forth. And so *Survivor* has its tribal councils and tribal names, and rites like the "Confessional," where contestants can leave the game for a moment and speak openly to the camera. Then, when the last vote comes around, there is a sort of ritual of return for banished contestants who assemble to bear witness, murmur, judge, and curse like unappeased spirits.

Counter to the rituals, there are the tricks. Producers reserve the element of surprise to themselves, and the right to bend or suspend the rules as they see fit. Treating rules as variables is only another way in which reality TV displays an intuitively postmodern touch. In fact, now that the word "postmodern" is worn out, reality shows indicate how many of the themes associated with it have bled into the popular culture (where more than a few of them may have begun in the first place). Postmodern art sought out its rules, frame, definition, limits. In the genre of reality tube, rules have an analogous tendency to mutate.

The obvious question, at this point, is how all this makes a case for talking about reality TV and a film like *The Passion of the Christ* in the same breath? Is the comparison forced in the end? Don't religious fundamentalism and aesthetic or narrative fundamentalism, assuming there is such a thing, go separate ways soon enough, one heading toward church, the other toward ratings, one toward prayer, the other toward celebrity? They do diverge, though possibly only to join up again later, trailing great clouds of zeitgeist behind them. But it's worth holding them together long enough for a thought experiment: conceive, for a moment, of Christ's life in terms of reality television. It doesn't necessarily exalt the television shows or disparage the Gibson movie to do so. Or at least that's not the whole intention.

Think of Christ—Gibson's Christ, to be precise—as the ultimate survivor. He endures torture and vanquishes death itself (though briefly, in the Gibson version) to establish his claim to something infinitely more precious than prize money. (Nor is it at Donald Trump's right hand that he proposes to wind up.) True, Jesus' disciples disown and betray him. In that, they're just like contestants. But wait a minute, maybe they *were* contestants. Add just a touch of Gnosticism and you can get a very different spin from the story of Christ and his disciples. Maybe they weren't disciples at all—until tradition got done with them. Maybe they were competitors, each of them going full tilt after the same prize, none of them conceding, to start with, that the Nazarene had any better right to it.

Of course, if there is any truth to this version, it's been scrubbed out of the official account. The only trace left is the weakness and betrayal among Christ's all too human apostolic inferiors. And Christ doesn't seem to be surprised by any of it, not even by Judas. (Which didn't stop one *Survivor* contestant from exclaiming, when he got voted off the show by supposed allies: "Just like Jesus said, 'Et tu, Brute?'")

Is this to suggest that Christianity is a prototype, a pilot for what after two thousand years becomes reality TV? Can a world religion be boiled down to a game show called, maybe, "Messiah"? If you are Mel Gibson, the answer would seem to be yes. Christ's complex teachings, and the mystery, even if metaphorical, of resurrection, get short shrift from him. What's left is the blunt instrument of the Ordeal and the Survivor who lives through it.

This is where reality TV does peel away. It provides the tales—maybe even, if Burnett and some psychologists can be believed, the tales of and for our time. But that's just for starters. When it's over, there are the stories behind the story, and they are milked for everything they're worth. Check out what Richard Hatch looks like in a suit and tie. Doesn't Amber look terrific when she's not picking nits out of her hair? And let Omarosa have her say—until Donald Trump cuts her off.

Actually, let's stay with Omarosa for a while, the lean, cool ex-beauty queen from the ghetto who turned the first season of "The Apprentice" into a racial minefield. Was she lying when she accused a white competitor of calling her the N-word? The post-mortem indicated that she was. No microphone or producer picked up a trace of the insult. Could be, then, she really was a bitch, reality tube's first of the kind, and a black one to boot. In short, she was delicious, tantalizing, and altogether invaluable to the show. "The Apprentice" lost steam when she was finally dumped, which is why she was called back for encores, all the while glorying in the attention she got from tabloids and talk shows.

Everyone knows reality tube is edited, filtered, constructed, composed. And everyone is invited to join in a guessing game about truth and fiction, or, as a *People Magazine* cover story put it: "Reality TV: What's Real? What's Fake?" It's here that reality television fully distinguishes itself from Gibson's "Passion." Not at the level of story, nor at the level of ordeal, but by slyly folding into itself all that postmodern stuff about subjectivity, point of view, all the suspicion about media slant, the whole Rashomon effect. That's the real genius of reality television, its ability to mix up intimations of primal truths with the open recognition that everyone is media savvy, we all know a show is a show.

It's like a magic show where afterward the magician lets you see how he does it. Except, in this case, he doesn't quite. The disclosure itself is just another level of diversion, keeping your eyes off yet another sleight of hand. For example, the story of Omarosa might have been a story about migraines instead of race. She said she suffered from headaches, and it's perfectly believable. It explains why she couldn't tolerate her teammates' squeals of joy during a victory ride in The Donald's limo. (Well, it doesn't explain why she couldn't just ask them to tone it down, instead of challenging them do so in that provocative way of hers). It explains why she refused to do a lick of work after a teeny particle of plaster fell on her head in one episode. (But it doesn't quite account for why she went outside to play catch with a neighborhood kid not long after.)

The point is, the producers were not about to focus on migraines when they had something juicier to work with. They were not going to tell an edifying tale about neurology when they could shape one around a more explosive N-word. Reality TV has an uncanny way of going right to the hot spots—race and sex. Are the makers just shaking up contestants and letting the cultural pieces fall where they may, or are the dice loaded every time? I don't know how it came about, but I will say that one of my favorite moments in all of television occurred at the end of the first *Survivor* series, when Richard, the spear-fishing gay guy, won the $1,000,000.00 with a vote from Rudy, the leathery, homophobic ex-Navy SEAL, who should have been his nemesis. That wasn't just reality tube; it was a transaction worthy of reality opera.

So they diverge, Burnett and Gibson, and hammer out different rhythms after a while. But with part of their brains they're still marching to the same drummer, or drum machine. For example, Burnett has bought up rights to "The Da Vinci Legacy" and "Daughter of God," two religious potboilers (that, according to Lewis Perdue, their author, were plagiarized by Dan Brown for his own potboiler *The Da Vinci Code*, also, of course, to be a major motion picture). In the *Variety* report on the subject—"Mark Burnett Has Found God"—Burnett explains that he's always been "very passionate" about the origins of religion and looks forward to breaking into Hollywood with "a theological thriller." It won't be an unscripted, reality-type thriller, he says. But someone else may be thinking along those lines. The APA psychologist was correct to point out that reality shows are in their infancy. We may never get a reality Sophocles out of them, but they're nowhere near exhausting their inspiration or influence.

Another example, more disturbing: to date, the best-known photo from the Abu Ghraib trove is of the hooded man, recently identified as Abdou Hussain Saad Faleh, standing on a box, wires fastened to his outstretched arms and genitals, terrified that if he falls off he'll be electrocuted. It's a stunning image in its own right—Susan Sontag calls it "canonical"—with its intimations of Dark Age sacrifice or ritual. What marks it as contemporary is a partial view of a man on the right, adjusting his cellphone or camera.

The pose Abdou Hussain Saad Faleh was forced to assume—standing, arms outstretched—was familiar to the Gestapo and the Soviet secret police, and later to Brazilian interrogators who added the threat of electrocution. Make of it what you will, but the cognoscenti of torture refer to it as crucifixion.

CRITICISM

Matthew Goulish

2.1 THE EXAMPLE OF GLASS

Each time we experience a work of performance, we start over almost from nothing. Despite recognizable trends, we face infinite differences – individual or cultural details, opposing traditions, idiosyncratic forms and settings, all kinds of aesthetic extremes.

Where do we begin, how do we begin, to engage a critical mind?

This question does not limit itself to performance. It relates to all art forms. In fact, it applies to all human endeavors and perceptions, from the humanities to the sciences to the practice of everyday life. Irreducible complexity seems to characterize the late twentieth century itself.

As a result, each field structures itself by propagating its own specialized vocabulary so that its practitioners might share some basic concepts. Yet each field necessarily interfaces and intersects any number of other fields, sometimes even spawning hybrid fields. Even the purist, in order to reach any depth of understanding on any given subject, must confront conflicting discourses. A serious student of performance thus might encounter the terminology of theatre, literature, music, psychology, architecture, anthropology, and biology, among other disciplines.

One might say that we face a landscape of vistas opening only onto more vistas. On the threshold of this landscape we might pause to recall the writer Isaac Babel who described his grandmother's sobering admonition when, as a child, he told her he wanted to grow up to be a writer, and she replied, "To be a writer, you must know everything."

Faced with the impossibility of the task of knowing everything, we sometimes feel the desire to reject intellectuality altogether in favor of passionate expression. Such expression may take the form of the urgently political, the assertion of a solidified identity, or the following of individual inspiration wherever it may lead. And yet even these roads, if sincerely followed lead back to the discourse of complexity.

We have no choice but to accept this terrain, with the hope of discovering its exhilarating creative possibilities. Such acceptance requires a softening of the dividing lines between traditional differences: artist and critic, passion and intellect, accessible and hermetic, success and failure.

The softening of dividing lines does not however imply the disintegration of difference.

Take for example the problem of glass. What is glass? Until recently, glass was considered a mostly transparent solid. It behaved like a solid; if struck, it shattered. But then, in the ancient cathedrals of Europe, it was observed that the tops of windows let in more light than the bottoms. A simple measurement proved that a window of once uniform thickness had grown thicker at the bottom and thinner at the top. Only one explanation exists for this phenomenon. Glass flows in the direction of the pull of gravity, exhibiting the behavior of a liquid. Thus one cannot conclusively define glass without the inclusion of time. At any given moment, glass is a solid, but over a period of one thousand years, it is a liquid. The problem of glass forces us to accept the inaccuracy of the traditional distinctions of solid or liquid. While the qualities of solidity and liquidity retain their difference, glass in fact is both, depending on the duration of observation, thus proving that these two states inextricably coexist.

We must ask not only how to engage the critical mind, but also why. Any act of critical thought finds its value through fulfilling one or both of two interrelated purposes:

    1) to cause a change;
    2) to understand how to understand.

As creative and critical thinkers, we may find it rewarding to attempt works of criticism, which, over time, reveal themselves as works of art, thus following the example of glass.

2.2 THE EXAMPLE OF WINDOWS

Most critics would not contest the idea that criticism exists to cause a change. But to cause a change in what?

Rarely has a work of critical thought successfully caused a change in the artwork it addresses. If a critic sees a film one day, and writes a review the next excoriating the weakness of the lead actor's performance, that same critic could return to the theater on the third day, and, despite the conviction of his argument, encounter the actor's performance unchanged. The same holds true for countless examples: condemned paintings, ridiculed concertos, buildings of reviled design, all survive, oblivious. Yet critics continue to offer their views. What are they trying to change?

Perhaps they attempt to change the future by effecting audience perceptions. If they can convince enough people, they believe they will achieve critical mass, causing an elimination of the despised, and an encouragement of the admired. But is this an accurate assessment of events? A critique may influence the thoughts of many audience members, but in the end they will make up their own minds. And those few powerful individuals who function in a producing capacity have the option of following the will of the majority, the minority, whatever sells the most tickets, or the advice of the critic. In this equation, the critic's power seems slight. If a critic believes in his or her own power to cause a change in audience thinking, that critic lives in delusion. Any changes of this kind are peripheral effects of a more central event.

Criticism only consistently changes the critic – whether further narrowing the views of the art policeman, or incrementally expanding the horizons of the open-minded thinker. If we accept this severe limitation – that in fact the first function of criticism is to cause a change in the critic – then we may begin to act accordingly.

We may agree on the premise that each work of art is at least in part perfect, while each critic is at least in part imperfect. We may then look to each work of art not for its faults and shortcomings, but for its moments of exhilaration, in an effort to bring our own imperfections into sympathetic vibration with these moments, and thus effect a creative change in ourselves. These moments will of course be somewhat subjective, and if we don't see one immediately, we will out of respect look again, because each work contains at least one, even if it occurs by accident. We may look at the totality of the work in the light of this moment – whether it be a moment of humor or sadness, an overarching structural element, a mood, a personal association, a distraction, an honest error, anything at all that speaks to us. In this way we will treat the work of art, in the words of South African composer Kevin Volans, not as an object in this world but as a window into another world. If we can articulate one window's particular exhilaration, we may open a way to inspire a change in ourselves, so that we may value and work from these recognitions.

What I advocate is not so unusual, because if we have been trained at all, we have probably been trained to spot the negatives, and to try to improve the work by eliminating them. Given, as we have established, that criticism always changes the critic, this approach means trouble. Whatever we fix our attention on seems to multiply before our eyes. If we look for problems, we will find them everywhere. Out of concern for ourselves and our psychic well-being, let us look instead for the aspects of wonder.

If others choose to change their own thinking as an inspired result of our critical articulations, or if they decide to dismiss us as idealists, that is their business, and we will leave it to them.

But can we recognize windows to other worlds without some formal, historical, or theoretical understanding of what we are looking at? If we deepen our understanding, might we increase our chances of locating these moments? How do we deepen our understanding?

We may think of critical thought itself as a process through which we deepen our understanding. This brings us to the second proposed function of criticism, to understand how to understand.

2.3 THE EXAMPLE OF RAIN

How do we understand something? We understand something by approaching it. How do we approach something? We approach it from any direction. We approach it using our eyes, our ears, our noses, our intellects, our imaginations. We approach it with silence. We approach it with childhood. We use pain or embarrassment. We use history. We take a safe route or a dangerous one. We discover our approach and we follow it.

In his 1968 essay 'Rain and the Rhinoceros', the American Trappist monk Thomas Merton attempted to understand Eugene Ionesco's play *Rhinoceros* by comparing it to the rain. Trappist monks take vows of silence. They almost never speak. In keeping with their silent life, they live in a silent place. The sound of the rain on the tin roof of his isolated monastic cabin in the Kentucky woods must have given Merton the only inspiration he needed to approach Ionesco's rhinoceros. And when the rain stopped, he heard the sound of the military airplane overhead, leaving the nearby base, on its way to Vietnam. When the airplane passed, he heard the hiss of his lantern burning. The rain provided the window to the rhinoceros, and the rhinoceros the window to the rain. The essay's analysis balances the work of art, with the work of nature, with the work of war. Merton understood critical thought as an act of contemplation, not an act of production. At the same time, he understood it to be, like all human activity, absurd. And thus he liberated his critical mind to follow whatever might cross its path. As the zen saying goes, no matter where we go, we are never far from enlightenment.

How then can we understand the rain? We can understand it as a scientist might, by studying climatic conditions and learning the Latin names for clouds. Or we may understand the rain by looking at it and how it falls – straight down, or at an angle, or lashed by the wind. Is it a light drizzly rain, or is it only a mist and hardly rain at all? Is it the kind that falls when the sun is shining just down the street? We could understand rain by examining its effects – on plants, on people, on cities. Or we may catalogue the sounds it makes on glass, on water, on stone, on metal. We could even study the moods it evokes before it has started and after it has stopped. We could not look at it directly, but rather at what it reminds us of – childhood, violence, love, tears. Who could tell us that any of these approaches to rain is not valid? And yet we would be the first to admit their absurdity.

The modernists believed that each work of art somehow outstretches interpretation, that each criticism reduces the infinite possibilities of the work, that no critique is exhaustive. I agree to the extent that the opposite is also true – each artwork reduces its critique. Only when criticism can step a little away from the artwork that fostered it will it achieve a life of its own as a way of understanding. The way a critique discovers and explores becomes as personal, intellectual, and creative as any artwork; not to offer a comprehensive analysis of the rain, but instead one singular approach to it. Thus it might return us to our first purpose, that of causing a change. If our critique of rain allows us a different rain experience, then it has caused a change, if not in the rain, at least in the critic. And as our approaches to the rain increase, so too increases our understanding of the fleeting and fragile qualities of human life. And as our ways of understanding the rain multiply, so too will we begin to see the presence of rain in even the driest of subjects. We will realize at last that our objective all along was to understand that it is always raining.

An Aesthetic of Blackness

Strange and Oppositional

bell hooks

This is the story of a house. It has been lived in by many people. Our grandmother, Baba, made this house living space. She was certain that the way we lived was shaped by objects, the way we looked at them, the way they were placed around us. She was certain that we were shaped by space. From her I learn about aesthetics, the yearning for beauty that she tells me is the predicament of heart that makes our passion real. A quiltmaker, she teaches me about color. Her house is a place where I am learning to look at things, where I am learning how to belong in space. In rooms full of objects, crowded with things, I am learning to recognize myself. She hands me a mirror, showing me how to look. The color of wine she has made in my cup, the beauty of the everyday. Surrounded by fields of tobacco, the leaves braided like hair, dried and hung, circles and circles of smoke fill the air. We string red peppers fiery hot, with thread that will not be seen. They will hang in front of a lace curtain to catch the sun. Look, she tells me, what the light does to color! Do you believe that space can give life, or take it

away, that space has power? These are the questions she asks which frighten me. Baba dies an old woman, out of place. Her funeral is also a place to see things, to recognize myself. How can I be sad in the face of death, surrounded by so much beauty? Death, hidden in a field of tulips, wearing my face and calling my name. Baba can make them grow. Red, yellow, they surround her body like lovers in a swoon, tulips everywhere. Here a soul on fire with beauty burns and passes, a soul touched by flame. We see her leave. She has taught me how to look at the world and see beauty. She has taught me "we must learn to see."

Years ago, at an art gallery in San Francisco near the Tassajara restaurant, I saw rooms arranged by Buddhist monk Chögyam Trungpa. At a moment in my life when I had forgotten how to see, he reminds me to look. He arranges spaces. Moved by an aesthetic shaped by old beliefs. Objects are not without spirit. As living things they touch us in unimagined ways. On this path one learns that an entire room is a space to be created, a space that can reflect beauty, peace, and a harmony of being, a spiritual aesthetic. Each space is a sanctuary. I remember. Baba has taught me "we must learn to see."

Aesthetics then is more than a philosophy or theory of art and beauty; it is a way of inhabiting space, a particular location, a way of looking and becoming. It is not organic. I grew up in an ugly house. No one there considered the function of beauty or pondered the use of space. Surrounded by dead things, whose spirits had long ago vanished since they were no longer needed, that house contained a great engulfing emptiness. In that house things were not to be looked at, they were to be possessed—space was not to be created but owned—a violent anti-aesthetic. I grew up thinking about art and beauty as it existed in our lives, the lives of poor black people. Without knowing the appropriate language, I understood that advanced capitalism was affecting our capacity to see, that consumerism began to take the place of that predicament of heart that called us to yearn for beauty. Now many of us are only yearning for things.

In one house I learned the place of aesthetics in the lives of agrarian poor black folks. There the lesson was that one had to understand beauty as a force to be made and imagined. Old folks shared their sense that we had come out of slavery into this free space and we had to create a world that would renew the spirit, that would make it life-giving. In that house there was a sense of history. In the other house, the one I lived in, aesthetics had no place. There the lessons were never about art or beauty, but always only to possess things. My thinking about aesthetics has been informed by the recognition of these houses: one which cultivated and celebrated an aesthetic of existence, rooted in the idea that no degree of material lack could keep one from learning how to look at the world with a critical eye, how to recognize beauty, or how to use it as a force

to enhance inner well-being; the other which denied the power of abstract aestheticism. Living in that other house where we were so acutely aware of lack, so conscious of materiality, I could see in our daily life the way consumer capitalism ravaged the black poor, nurtured in us a longing for things that often subsumed our ability to recognize aesthetic worth or value.

Despite these conditions, there was in the traditional southern racially segregated black community a concern with racial uplift that continually promoted recognition of the need for artistic expressiveness and cultural production. Art was seen as intrinsically serving a political function. Whatever African-Americans created in music, dance, poetry, painting, etc., it was regarded as testimony, bearing witness, challenging racist thinking which suggested that black folks were not fully human, were uncivilized, and that the measure of this was our collective failure to create "great" art. White supremacist ideology insisted that black people, being more animal than human, lacked the capacity to feel and therefore could not engage the finer sensibilities that were the breeding ground for art. Responding to this propaganda, nineteenth-century black folks emphasized the importance of art and cultural production, seeing it as the most effective challenge to such assertions. Since many displaced African slaves brought to this country an aesthetic based on the belief that beauty, especially that created in a collective context, should be an integrated aspect of everyday life, enhancing the survival and development of community, these ideas formed the basis of African-American aesthetics. Cultural production and artistic expressiveness were also ways for displaced African people to maintain connections with the past. Artistic African cultural retentions survived long after other expressions had been lost or forgotten. Though not remembered or cherished for political reasons, they would ultimately be evoked to counter assertions by white supremacists and colonized black minds that there remained no vital living bond between the culture of African-Americans and the cultures of Africa. This historical aesthetic legacy has proved so powerful that consumer capitalism has not been able to completely destroy artistic production in underclass black communities.

Even though the house where I lived was ugly, it was a place where I could and did create art. I painted, I wrote poetry. Though it was an environment more concerned with practical reality than art, these aspirations were encouraged. In an interview in *Callaloo* painter Lois Mailou Jones describes the tremendous support she received from black folks: "Well I began with art at a very early stage in my life. As a child, I was always drawing. I loved color. My mother and father, realizing that I had talent, gave me an excellent supply of crayons and pencils and paper—and encouraged me." Poor black parents saw artistic cultural production as crucial to the struggle against racism, but they were also cognizant of the link between creating art and pleasure. Art was necessary to bring delight, pleasure, and beauty into lives that were hard, that were materially deprived. It mediated the harsh conditions of poverty and servitude. Art was also a way to escape one's plight. Protestant black churches emphasized the parable of the talents, and commitment to spirituality also meant appreciating one's talents and using them. In our church if someone could sing or play the piano and they did not offer these talents to the community, they were admonished.

Performance arts—dance, music, and theater—were the most accessible ways to express creativity. Making and listening to black music, both secular and sacred, was one of the ways black folks developed an aesthetic. It was not an aesthetic documented in writing, but it did inform cultural production.

Analyzing the role of the "talent show" in segregated black communities, which was truly the community-based way to support and promote cultural production, would reveal much about the place of aesthetics in traditional black life. It was both a place for collective display of artistry and a place for the development of aesthetic criteria. I cite this information to place African-American concern with aesthetics in a historical framework that shows a continuity of concern. It is often assumed that black folks first began to articulate an interest in aesthetics during the sixties. Privileged black folks in the nineteenth and early twentieth centuries were often, like their white counterparts, obsessed with notions of "high art." Significantly, one of the important dimensions of the artistic movement among black people, most often talked about as the Harlem Renaissance, was the call for an appreciation of popular forms. Like other periods of intense focus on the arts in African-American culture, it called attention to forms of artistic expression that were simply passing away because they were not valued in the context of a conventional aesthetic focusing on "high art." Often African-American intellectual elites appropriated these forms, reshaping them in ways suited to different locations. Certainly the spiritual as it was sung by Paul Robeson at concerts in Europe was an aspect of African-American folk culture evoked in a context far removed from small, hot, Southern church services, where poor black folks gathered in religious ecstasy. Celebration of popular forms ensured their survival, kept them as a legacy to be passed on, even as they were altered and transformed by the interplay of varied cultural forces.

Conscious articulation of a "black aesthetic" as it was constructed by African-American artists and critics in the sixties and early seventies was an effort to forge an unbreakable link between artistic production and revolutionary politics. Writing

103

about the interconnectedness of art and politics in the essay "Frida Kahlo and Tina Modottit," Laura Mulvey describes the way an artistic avant-garde

> . . . was able to use popular form not as a means of communication but as a means of constructing a mythic past whose effectiveness could be felt in the present. Thereby it brought itself into line with revolutionary impetus towards constructing the mythic past of the nation.

A similar trend emerged in African-American art as painters, writers, musicians worked to imaginatively evoke black nationhood, a homeland, re-creating bonds with an African past while simultaneously evoking a mythic nation to be born in exile. During this time Larry Neal declared the Black Arts Movement to be "the cultural arm of the black revolution." Art was to serve black people in the struggle for liberation. It was to call for and inspire resistance. One of the major voices of the black aesthetic movement, Maulana Karenga, in his *Thesis on Black Cultural Nationalism,* taught that art should be functional, collective, and committed.

The black aesthetic movement was fundamentally essentialist. Characterized by an inversion of the "us" and "them" dichotomy, it inverted conventional ways of thinking about otherness in ways that suggested that everything black was good and everything white bad. In his introduction to the anthology *Black Fire,* Larry Neal set the terms of the movement, dismissing work by black artists which did not emerge from black power movement:

> A revolutionary art is being expressed today. The anguish and aimlessness that attended our great artists of the forties and fifties and which drove most of them to early graves, to dissipation and dissolution, is over. Misguided by white cultural references (the models the culture sets for its individuals), and the incongruity of these models with black reality, men like Bird were driven to willful self-destruction. There was no program. And the reality-model was incongruous. It was a white reality-model. If Bird had had a black reality-model, it might have been different . . . In Bird's case, there was a dichotomy between his genius and the society. But that he couldn't find the adequate model of being was the tragic part of the whole thing.

Links between black cultural nationalism and revolutionary politics led ultimately to the subordination of art to politics. Rather than serving as a catalyst promoting diverse artistic expression, the Black Arts Movement began to dismiss all forms of cultural production by African-Americans that did not conform to movement criteria. Often this led to aesthetic judgments that did not allow for recognition of multiple black experience or the complexity of black life, as in the case of Neal's critical interpretation of jazz musician Charlie Parker's fate. Clearly, the problems facing Parker were not simply aesthetic concerns, and they could not have been resolved by art or critical theories about the nature of black artistic production. Ironically, in many of its aesthetic practices the Black Arts Movement was based on the notion that a people's art, cultural production for the masses, could not be either complex, abstract, or diverse in style, form, content, etc.

Despite its limitations, the Black Arts Movement provided useful critique based on radical questioning of the place and meaning of aesthetics for black artistic production.

The movement's insistence that all art is political, that an ethical dimension should inform cultural production, as well as the encouragement of an aesthetic which did not separate habits of being from artistic production, were important to black thinkers concerned with strategies of decolonization. Unfortunately, these positive aspects of the black aesthetic movement should have led to the formation of critical space where there could have been more open discussion of the relevance of cultural production to black liberation struggle. Ironically, even though the Black Arts Movement insisted that it represented a break from white western traditions, much of its philosophical underpinning re-inscribed prevailing notions about the relationship between art and mass culture. The assumption that naturalism or realism was more accessible to a mass audience than abstraction was certainly not a revolutionary position. Indeed the paradigms for artistic creation offered by the Black Arts Movement were most often restrictive and disempowering. They stripped many artists of creative agency by dismissing and devaluing their work because it was either too abstract or did not overtly address a radical politic. Writing about socialist attitudes towards art and politics in *Art and Revolution,* John Berger suggests that the relationship between art and political propaganda is often confused in the radical or revolutionary context. This was often the case in the Black Arts Movement. While Berger willingly accepts the truism "that all works of art exercise an ideological influence—even works by artists who profess to have no interest outside art," he critiques the idea that simplicity of form or content necessarily promotes critical political consciousness or leads to the development of a meaningful revolutionary art. His words of caution should be heeded by those who would revive a prescriptive black aesthetic that limits freedom and restricts artistic development. Speaking against a prescriptive aesthetic, Berger writes:

> *When the experience is "offered up," it is not expected to be in any way transformed. Its apotheosis should be instant, and as it were invisible. The artistic process is taken for granted: it always remains exterior to the spectator's experience. It is no more than the supplied vehicle in which experience is placed so that it may arrive safely at a kind of cultural terminus. Just as academicism reduces the process of art to an apparatus for artists, it reduces it to a vehicle for the spectator. There is absolutely no dialectic between experience and expression, between experience and its formulations.*

The black aesthetic movement was a self-conscious articulation by many of a deep fear that the power of art resides in its potential to transgress boundaries.

Many African-American artists retreated from black cultural nationalism into a retrogressive posture where they suggested there were no links between art and politics, evoking outmoded notions of art as transcendent and pure to defend their position. This was another step backwards. There was no meaningful attempt to counter the black aesthetic with conceptual criteria for creating and evaluating art which would simultaneously acknowledge its ideological content even as it allowed for expansive notions of artistic freedom. Overall the impact of these two movements, black aesthetics and its opponents, was a stifling of artistic production by African-Americans in practically every medium with the exception of music. Significantly, avant-garde jazz musicians, grappling with artistic expressivity that demanded experimentation, resisted restrictive mandates about their work, whether they were imposed by a white public saying their work was not really music or a black public which wanted to see more overt links between that work and political struggle.

To re-open the creative space that much of the black aesthetic movement closed down, it seems vital for those involved in contemporary black arts to engage in a revitalized discussion of aesthetics. Critical theories about cultural production, about aesthetics, continue to confine and restrict black artists, and passive withdrawal from a discussion of aesthetics is a useless response. To suggest, as Clyde Taylor does in his essay "We Don't Need Another Hero: Anti-Theses On Aesthetics," that the failure of black aesthetics or the development of white western theorizing on the subject should negate all African-American concern with the issue is to once again repeat an essentialist project that does not enable or promote artistic growth. An African-American discourse on aesthetics need not begin with white western traditions and it need not be prescriptive. Cultural decolonization does not happen solely by repudiating all that appears to maintain connection with the colonizing culture. It is really important to dispel the notion that white western culture is "the" location where a discussion of aesthetics emerged, as Taylor suggests; it is only one location.

Progressive African-Americans concerned with the future of our cultural production seek to critically conceptualize a radical aesthetic that does not negate the powerful place of theory as both that force which sets up criteria for aesthetic judgment and as vital grounding that helps make certain work possible, particularly expressive work that is transgressive and oppositional. Hal Foster's comments on the importance of an anti-aesthetic in the essay "Postmodernism: A Preface" present a useful paradigm

African-Americans can employ to interrogate modernist notions of aesthetics without negating the discourse on Aesthetics. Foster proposes this paradigm to critically question "the idea that aesthetic experience exists apart, without 'purpose,' all but beyond history, or that art can now affect a world at once (inter) subjective, concrete, and universal—a symbolic totality." Taking the position that an anti-aesthetic "signals a practice, cross-disciplinary in nature, that is sensitive to cultural forms engaged in a politic (e.g., feminist art) or rooted in a vernacular—that is, to forms that deny the idea of a privileged aesthetic realm," Foster opens up the possibility that work by marginalized groups can have a greater audience and impact. Working from a base where difference and otherness are acknowledged as forces that intervene in western theorizing about aesthetics to reformulate and transform the discussion, African-Americans are empowered to break with old ways of seeing reality that suggest there is only one audience for our work and only one aesthetic measure of its value. Moving away from narrow cultural nationalism, one leaves behind as well racist assumptions that cultural productions by black people can only have "authentic" significance and meaning for a black audience.

Black artists concerned with producing work that embodies and reflects a liberatory politic know that an important part of any decolonization process is critical intervention and interrogation of existing repressive and dominating structures. African-American critics and/or artists who speak about our need to engage in ongoing dialogue with dominant discourses always risk being dismissed as assimilationist. There is a grave difference between that engagement with white culture which seeks to deconstruct, demystify, challenge, and transform and gestures of collaboration and complicity. We cannot participate in dialogue that is the mark of freedom and critical agency if we dismiss all work emerging from white western traditions. The assumption that the crisis of African-Americans should or can only be addressed by us must also be interrogated. Much of what threatens our collective well-being is the product of dominating structures. Racism is a white issue as much as it is a black one.

Contemporary intellectual engagement with issues of "otherness and difference" manifest in literary critique, cultural studies, feminist theory, and black studies indicates that there is a growing body of work that can provide and promote critical dialogue and debate across boundaries of class, race, and gender. These circumstances, coupled with a focus on pluralism at the level of social and public policy, are creating a cultural climate where it is possible to interrogate the idea that difference is synonymous with lack and deprivation, and simultaneously call for critical re-thinking of aesthetics. Retrospective examination of the repressive impact a prescriptive black aesthetic had on black cultural production should serve as a cautionary model for African-Americans. There can never be one critical paradigm for the evaluation of artistic work. In part, a radical aesthetic acknowledges that we are constantly changing positions, locations, that our needs and concerns vary, that these diverse directions must correspond with shifts in critical thinking. Narrow limiting aesthetics within black communities tend to place innovative black artistry on the margins. Often this work receives little or no attention. Whenever black artists work in ways that are transgressive, we are seen as suspect, by our group and by the dominant culture. Rethinking aesthetic principles could lead to the development of a critical standpoint that promotes and encourages various modes of artistic and cultural production.

As artist and critic, I find compelling a radical aesthetic that seeks to uncover and restore links between art and revolutionary politics, particularly black liberation struggle, while offering an expansive critical foundation for aesthetic evaluation. Concern for the contemporary plight of black people necessitates that I interrogate my work to see if it functions as a force that promotes the development of critical consciousness and resistance movement. I remain passionately committed to an aesthetic that focuses on the purpose and function of beauty, of artistry in everyday life, especially the lives of poor people, one that seeks to explore and celebrate the connection between our capacity to engage in critical resistance and our ability to experience pleasure and beauty. I want to create work that shares with an audience, particularly oppressed and marginalized groups, the sense of agency artistry offers, the empowerment. I want to share the aesthetic inheritance handed down to me by my grandmother and generations of black ancestors, whose ways of thinking about the issue have been globally shaped in the African diaspora and informed by the experience of exile and domination. I want to reiterate the message that "we must learn to see." Seeing here is meant metaphysically as heightened awareness and understanding, the intensification of one's capacity to experience reality through the realm of the senses.

Remembering the houses of my childhood, I see how deeply my concern with aesthetics was shaped by black women who were fashioning an aesthetic of being, struggling to create an oppositional world view for their children, working with space to make it livable. Baba, my grandmother, could not read or write. She did not inherit her contemplative preoccupation with aesthetics from a white western literary tradition. She was poor all her life. Her memory stands as a challenge to intellectuals, especially those on the left, who assume that the capacity to think critically, in abstract concepts, to be theoretical, is a function of class and educational privilege. Contemporary intellectuals committed to progressive politics must be reminded again and again that the capacity to name something (particularly in writing terms like aesthetics, postmodernism, deconstruction, etc.) is not synonymous with the creation or ownership of the condition or circumstance to which such terms may refer.

Many underclass black people who do not know conventional academic theoretical language are thinking critically about aesthetics. The richness of their thoughts is rarely documented in books. Innovative African-American artists have rarely documented their process, their critical thinking on the subject of aesthetics. Accounts of the theories that inform their work are necessary and essential; hence my concern with opposing any standpoint that devalues this critical project. Certainly many of the revolutionary, visionary critical perspectives on music that were inherent to John Coltrane's oppositional aesthetics and his cultural production will never be shared because they were not fully documented. Such tragic loss retards the development of reflective work by African-Americans on aesthetics that is linked to enabling politics. We must not deny the way aesthetics serves as the foundation for emerging visions. It is, for some of us, critical space that inspires and encourages artistic endeavor. The ways we interpret that space and inhabit it differ.

As a grown black woman, a guest in my mother's house, I explain that my interior landscape is informed by minimalism, that I cannot live in a space filled with too many things. My grandmother's house is only inhabited by ghosts and can no longer shelter or rescue me. Boldly I declare that I am a minimalist. My sisters repeat this word with the kind of glee that makes us laugh, as we celebrate together that particular way language, and the "meaning" of words is transformed when they fall from the hierarchical space they inhabit in certain locations (the predominantly white university setting) into the mouths of vernacular culture and speech, into underclass blackness, segregated communities where there is much illiteracy. Who can say what will happen to this word "minimalist." Who knows how it will be changed, re-fashioned by the thick patois that is our Southern black tongue. This experience cannot be written. Even if I attempt description it will never convey process.

One of my five sisters wants to know how it is I come to think about these things, about houses, and space. She does not remember long conversations with Baba. She remembers her house as an ugly place, crowded with objects. My memories fascinate her. She listens with astonishment as I describe the shadows in Baba's house and what they meant to me, the way the moon entered an upstairs window and created new ways for me to see dark and light. After reading Tanizaki's essay on aesthetics "In Praise of Shadows," I tell this sister in a late night conversation that I am learning to think about blackness in a new way. Tanizaki speaks of seeing beauty in darkness and shares this moment of insight: "The quality that we call beauty, however, must always grow from the realities of life, and our ancestors, forced to live in dark rooms, presently came to discover beauty in shadows, ultimately to guide shadows towards beauty's end." My sister has skin darker than mine. We think about our skin as a dark room, a place of shadows. We talk often about color politics and the ways racism has created an aesthetic that wounds us, a way of thinking about beauty that hurts. In the shadows of late night, we talk about the need to see darkness differently, to talk about it in a new way. In that space of shadows we long for an aesthetic of blackness—strange and oppositional.

IN HISTORY
FROM CALLALOO

Jamaica Kincaid

[handwritten marginalia:] opens up with questions—giving us a sense of what will be talked about and the writer's curiousity

What to call the thing that happened to me and all who look like me?

Should I call it history?

If so, what should history mean to someone like me?

Should it be an idea, should it be an open wound and each breath I take in and expel healing and opening the wound again and again, over and over, or is it a moment that began in 1492 and has come to no end yet? Is it a collection of facts, all true and precise details, and, if so, when I come across these true and precise details, what should I do, how should I feel, where should I place myself?

Why should I be obsessed with all these questions?

My history began like this: in 1492, Christopher Columbus discovered the New World. Since this is only a beginning and I am not yet in the picture, I have not yet made an appearance, the word "discover" does not set off an alarm, and I am not yet confused by this interpretation. I accept it. I am only taken by the personality of this quarrelsome, restless man. His origins are sometimes obscure; sometimes no one knows just where he really comes from, who he really was. His origins are sometimes quite vivid: his father was a tailor, he came from Genoa, he as a boy wandered up and down the Genoese wharf, fascinated by sailors and their tales of lands far away; these lands would be filled with treasures, as all things far away are treasures. I am far away, but I am not yet a treasure: I am not a part of this man's consciousness, he does not know of me, I do not yet have a name. And so the word "discover," as it is applied to this New World, remains uninteresting to me.

He, Christopher Columbus, discovers this New World. That it is new only to him, that it had a substantial existence, physical and spiritual, before he became aware of it, does not occur to him. To cast blame on him now for this childlike immaturity has all the moral substance of a certificate given to a schoolgirl for good behavior. To be a well-behaved schoolgirl is not hard. When he sees this New World, it is really new to him: he has never seen anything like it before, it was not what he had expected, he had images of China and Japan, and, though he thought he was in China and Japan, it was not the China or Japan that he had fixed in his mind. He couldn't find enough words to describe what he saw before him: the people were new, the flora and fauna were new, the way the water met the sky was new, this world itself was new, it was the New World.

"If one does not know the names, one's knowledge of things is useless." This is attributed to Isidorus, and I do not know if this is the Greek Isidorus or the other Isidorus, the bishop of Seville; but now put it another way: to have knowledge of things, one must first give them a name. This, in any case, seems me to have been Christopher Columbus's principle, for he named and he named: he named places, he named people, he named things. This world he saw before him had a blankness to it, the blankness of the newly made, the newly born. It had no before—I could say that it had no history, but I would have to begin again, I would have to ask those questions again: What is history? This blankness, the one Columbus met, was more like the blankness of paradise; paradise emerges from chaos, and this chaos is not history; it is not a legitimate order of things. Paradise, then, is the arrangement of the ordinary and the extraordinary. But in such a way as to make it, paradise, seem as if it had fallen out of the clear air. Nothing about it suggests the messy life of the builder, the carpenter, the quarrels with the contractor, the people who are late with the delivery of materials, their defense which, when it is not accepted, is met with their back chat. This is an unpleasant arrangement; this is not paradise. Paradise is the thing just met when all the troublesome details have been vanquished, overcome.

Christopher Columbus met paradise. It would not have been paradise for the people living there; they would have had the ordinary dreariness of living anywhere day after day, the ordinary dreariness of just being alive. But someone else's ordinary dreariness is another person's epiphany.

The way in which he wanted to know these things was not in the way of satisfying curiosity, or in the way of correcting an ignorance; he wanted to know them, to possess them, and he wanted to possess them in a way that must have been a surprise to him. His ideas kept not so much changing as evolving: he wanted to prove the world was round, and even that, to know with certainty that the world was round, that it did not come to an abrupt end at a sharp cliff from which one could fall into nothing; to know that is to establish a claim also. And then after the world was round, this round world should belong to his patrons, the king and queen of Spain; and then finding himself at the other side of the circumference and far away from his patrons, human and other kind, he loses himself, for it becomes clear: the person who really can name the thing gives it a life, a reality, that it did not have before. His patrons are in Spain, looking at the balance sheet: if they invest so much, will his journey yield a return to make the investment worthwhile? But he—I am still speaking of Columbus—is in the presence of something else.

His task is easier than he thought it would be; his task is harder than he could have imagined. If he had only really reached Japan or China, places like that already had an established narrative. It was not a narrative that these places had established themselves; it was a narrative that someone like him had invented, Marco Polo, for instance; but this world, China or Japan, in the same area of the world to him (even as this familiarity with each other—between China and Japan—would surprise and even offend the inhabitants of these places), had an order, and the order offered a comfort (the recognizable is always so comforting). But this new place, what was it? Sometimes it was just like Seville; sometimes it was like Seville but only more so; sometimes it was more beautiful than Seville. Mostly it was "mar-

110

velous," and this word "marvelous" is the word he uses again and again, and when he uses it, what the reader (and this is what I have been, a reader of this account of the journey, and the account is by Columbus himself) can feel, can hear, can see, is a great person whose small soul has been sundered by something unexpected. And yet the unexpected turned out to be the most ordinary things: people, the sky, the sun, the land, the water surrounding the land, the things growing on the land.

What were the things growing on the land? I pause for this. What were the things growing on that land, and why do I pause for this?

I come from a place called Antigua. I shall speak of it as if no one has ever heard of it before; I shall speak of it as if it is just new. In the writings, in anything representing a record of the imagination of Christopher Columbus, I cannot find any expectation for a place like this. It is a small lump of insignificance, green, green, green, and green again. Let me describe this landscape again: it is green, and unmistakably so; another person, who would have a more specific interest, a painter, might say it is a green that often verges on blue, a green that often is modified by reds and yellows and even other more intense or other shades of green. To me, it is green and green and green again. I have no interest other than this immediate and urgent one: the landscape is green. For it is on this green landscape that, suddenly, I and the people who look like me made an appearance.

I, me. The person standing in front of you started to think of all this while really focused on something and someone else altogether. I was standing in my garden; my garden is in a place called Vermont; it is in a village situated in a place called Vermont. From the point of view of growing things, that is the gardener's, Vermont is not in the same atmosphere as that other place I am from, Antigua. But while standing in that place, Vermont, I think about the place I am from, Antigua. Christopher Columbus never saw Vermont at all; it never entered his imagination. He saw Antigua, I believe on a weekday, but if not, then it would have been a Sunday, for in this life there would have been only weekdays or Sundays, but he never set foot on it, he only came across it while passing by. My world then—the only world I might have known if circumstances had not changed, intervened, would have entered the human imagination, the human imagination that I am familiar with, the only one that dominates the world in which I live—came into being as a footnote to someone just passing by. By the time Christopher Columbus got to the place where I am from, the place that forms the foundation of the person you see before you, he was exhausted, he was sick of the whole thing, he longed for his old home, or he longed just to sit still and enjoy the first few things that he had come upon. The first few things that he came on were named after things that were prominent in his thinking, his sponsors especially; when he came to the place I am from, he (it) had been reduced to a place of worship; the place I am from is named after a church. This church might have been an important church to Christopher Columbus, but churches are not important, originally, to people who look like me. And if people who look like me have an inheritance, among this inheritance will be this confusion of intent; nowhere in his intent when he set out from his point of embarkation (for him, too, there is not origin: he originates from Italy, he sails from Spain, and this is the beginning of another new traditional American narrative, point of origin and point of embarkation): "here is something I have never seen before, I especially like it because it has no precedent, but it is frightening because it has no precedent, and so to make it less frightening I will frame it in the thing I know; I know a church, I know the name of the church, even if I do not like or know the people connected to this church, it is more familiar to me, this church, than the very ground I am standing on; the ground has changed, the church, which is in my mind, remains the same."

I, the person standing before you, close the quotation marks. Up to this point, I and they that look like me am not yet a part of this narrative. I can look at all these events: a man setting sail with three ships, and after many, many days on the ocean, finding new lands whose existence he had never even heard of before, and then finding in these new lands people and their things and these people and their things, he had never heard of them before, and he empties the land of these people, and then he empties the people, he just empties the people. It is when this land is completely empty that I and the people who look like me begin to make an appearance, the food I eat begins to make an appearance, the trees I will see each day come from far away and begin to make an appearance, the sky is as it always was, the sun is as it always was, the water surrounding the land on which I am just making an appearance is as it always was; but these are the only things left from before that man, sailing with his three ships, reached the land on which I eventually make an appearance.

When did I begin to ask all this? When did I begin to think of all this and in just this way? What is history? Is it a theory? I no longer live in the place where I and those who look like me first made an appearance. I live in another place. It has another narrative. Its narrative, too, can start with that man sailing on his ships for days and days, for that man sailing on his ships for days and days is the source of many narratives, for he was like a deity in the simplicity of his beliefs, in the simplicity of his actions; just listen to the straightforward way many volumes featuring this man sailing on his ships begin: "In fourteen hun-dred and ninety-two . . ." But it was while standing in this other place, which has a narrative mostly different from the place in which I make an appearance, that I began to think of this.

One day, while looking at the things that lay before me at my feet, I was having an argument with myself over the names I should use when referring to the things that lay before me at my feet. These things were plants. The plants, all of them and they were hundreds, had two names: they had a common name—that is, the name assigned to them by people for whom these plants have value—and then they have a proper name, or a Latin name, and that is a name assigned to them by an agreed-on group of botanists. For a long time I resisted using the proper names of the things that lay before me. I believed that it was an affectation to say "eupatorium" when you could say "joe-pye weed." I then would only say "joe-pye weed." The botanists are from the same part of the world as the man who sailed on the three ships, that same man who started the narrative from which I trace my beginning. And in a way, too, the botanists are like that man who sailed on the ships: they emptied the worlds of things animal, mineral, and vegetable of their names, and replaced these names with names pleasing to them; the recognized names are now reasonable, as reason is a pleasure to them.

Carl Linnaeus was born on May 23, 1707, somewhere in Sweden. (I know where, but I like the highhandedness of not saying so.) His father's name was Nils Ingemarsson; the Ingemarssons were farmers. Apparently, in Sweden then, surnames were uncommon among ordinary people, and so the farmer would add "son" to his name or he was called after the farm on which he lived. Nils Ingemarsson became a Lutheran minister, and on doing so he wanted to have a proper surname, not just a name with "son" attached to it. On his family's farm grew a linden tree. It had grown there for generations and had come to be regarded with reverence among neighboring farmers; people believed that misfortune would fall on you if you harmed this tree in any way. This linden tree was so well regarded that people passing by used to pick up twigs that had dropped from it and carefully place them at the base of the tree. Nils Ingemarsson took his surname from this tree: Linnaeus is the Latinized form of the Swedish word *lind*, which means linden. Other branches of this family who also needed a surname drew inspiration from this tree; some took the name Tiliander—the Latin word for linden is *tilia*—and some others who also needed a surname took the name Lindelius, from the same Swedish word *lind*.

Carl Linnaeus's father had a garden. I do not know what his mother had. His father loved growing things in this garden and would point them out to the young Carl, but when the young Carl could not remember the names of the plants, his father gave him a scolding and told him he would not tell him the names of any more plants. (Is this story true? But how could it not be?) He grew up not far from a forest filled with beech, a forest with pine, a grove filled with oaks, meadows. His father had a collection of rare plants in his garden (but what would be rare to him and in that place, I do not know). At the time Linnaeus was born, Sweden—this small country that I now think of as filled with well-meaning and benign people interested mainly in the well-being of children, the well-being of the unfortunate no matter their age—was the ruler of an empire, but the remains of it are visible only in the architecture of the main square of the capital of places like Estonia. And so what to make of all this, this small detail that is the linden tree, this large volume of the Swedish empire, and a small boy whose father was a Lutheran pastor? At the beginning of this narrative, the narrative that is Linnaeus, I

have not made an appearance yet; the Swedes are not overly implicated in the Atlantic slave trade, not because they did not want to have a part in it, only because they weren't allowed to do so; other people were better at it than they.

He was called "the little botanist" because he would neglect his studies and go out looking for flowers; if even then he had already showed an interest in or the ability to name and classify plants, this fact is not in any account of his life that I have come across. He went to university at Uppsala; he studied there with Olof Rudbeck. I can pause at this name, Rudbeck, and say rudbeckia, and say, I do not like rudbeckia. I never have it in my garden, but then I remember a particularly stately, beautiful yellow flower in a corner of my field garden, *Rudbeckia nitida*, growing there. He met Anders Celsius (the Celsius scale of temperature measurement), who was so taken with Linnaeus's familiarity and knowledge of botany that he gave Linnaeus free lodging in his house. Linnaeus became one of the youngest lecturers at the university. He went to Lapland and collected plants and insects native to that region of the world; he wrote and published an account of it called *Flora Lapponica*. In Lapland, he acquired a set of clothing that people native to that region of the world wore on festive occasions; I have seen a picture of him dressed in these clothes, and the caption under the picture says that he is wearing his Lapland costume. Suddenly I am made a little uneasy, for just when is it that other people's clothes become your costume? But I am not too uneasy, I haven't really entered this narrative yet, I shall soon. In any case, I do not know the Laplanders, they live far away, I don't believe they look like me.

I enter the picture only when Linnaeus takes a boat to Holland. He becomes a doctor to an obviously neurotic man (obvious only to me, I arbitrarily deem him so; no account of him I have ever come across has described him so) named George Clifford. George Clifford is often described as a rich merchant banker; just like that, a rich merchant banker, and this description often seems to say that to be a rich merchant banker is just a type of person one could be, an ordinary type of person, anyone could be that. And now how to go on, for on hearing that George Clifford was a rich merchant in the eighteenth century, I now am sure I have become a part of the binomial-system-of-plant-nomenclature narrative.

George Clifford had glass houses full of vegetable material from all over the world. This is what Linnaeus writes of it:

I was greatly amazed when I entered the greenhouses, full as they were of so many plants that a son of the North must feel bewitched, and wonder to what strange quarter of the globe he had been transported. In the first house were cultivated an abundance of flowers from southern Europe, plants from Spain, the South of France, Italy, Sicily and the isles of Greece. In the second were treasures from Asia, such as Poincianas, coconut and other palms, etc.; in the third, Africa's strangely shaped, not to say mis-shapen plants, such as the numerous forms of Aloe and Mesembryanthe-mum families, carnivorous flowers, Euphorbias, Crassula and Proteas species, and so on. And finally in the fourth greenhouse were grown the charming inhabitants of America and the rest of the New World; large masses of Cactus varieties, orchids, cruciferea, yams, magnolias, tulip-trees, calabash trees, arrow, cassias, acacias, tamarinds, pepper-plants, Anona, manicinilla, cucurbitaceous trees and many others, and sur-rounded by these, plantains, the most

stately of all the world's plants, the most beauteous Hernandia, silver-gleaming species of Protea and cam-phor trees. When I then entered the positively royal residence and the extremely instructive museum, whose collections no less spoke in their owner's praise, I, a stranger, felt com-pletely enraptured, as I had never before seen its like. My heartfelt wish was that I might lend a helping hand with its management.

In almost every account of an event that has taken place sometime in the last five hundred years, there is always a moment when I feel like placing an asterisk some-where in its text, and at the end of this offi-cial story place my own addition. This chap-ter in the history of botany is such a moment. But where shall I begin? George Clifford is interesting—shall I look at him? He has long ago entered my narrative; I now feel I must enter his. What could it possibly mean to be a merchant banker in the eigh-teenth century? He is sometimes described as making his fortune in spices. Only once have I come across an account of him that says he was a director of the Dutch East India Company. The Dutch East India Com-pany would not have been involved in the Atlantic trade in human cargo from Africa, but human cargo from Africa was a part of world trade. To read a brief account of the Dutch East India trading company in my very old encyclopedia is not unlike reading the label on an old can of paint. The entry mentions dates, the names of Dutch gover-nors or people acting in Dutch interest; it mentions trade routes, places, commodities, incidents of war between the Dutch and other European people; it never mentions the people who lived in the area of the Dutch trading factories. Places like Ceylon, Java, the Cape of Good Hope, are emptied of their people as the landscape itself was emptied of the things they were familiar with, the things that Linnaeus found in George Clifford's greenhouse.

"If one does not know the names, one's knowledge of things is useless." It was in George Clifford's greenhouse that Linnaeus gave some things names. The Adam-like quality of this effort was lost on him. "We revere the Creator's omnipotence," he says, meaning, I think, that he understood he had not made the things he was describing, he was only going to give them names. And even as a relationship exists between George Clifford's activity in the world, the world as it starts out on ships leaving the seaports of the Netherlands, traversing the earth's seas, touching on the world's peoples and the places they are in, the things that have meant something to them being renamed and a whole new set of narratives imposed on them, narratives that place them at a disadvantage in relationship to George Clifford and his fellow Dutch, even as I can say all this in one breath or in one large volume, so too then does an invisible thread, a thread that no deep breath or large volume can contain, hang between Carolus Linnaeus, his father's desire to give himself a distinguished name, the name then coming from a tree, the linden tree, a tree whose existence was regarded as not ordinary, and his invention of a system of naming that even I am forced to use?

The invention of this system has been a good thing. Its narrative would begin this way: in the beginning, the vegetable kingdom was chaos; people everywhere called the same things by a name that made sense to them, not by a name that they arrived at by an objective standard. But who has an interest in an objective standard? Who would need one? It makes me ask again what to call the thing that happened to me and all who look like me? Should I call it history? And if so, what should history mean to someone who looks like me? Should it be an idea, should it be an open wound and each breath I take in and expel healing and opening the wound again and again, over and over, or is it a long moment that begins anew each day since 1492?

Some Questions About Tolerance

Presented at the "Tolerance as an Art Form" conference,
New York City, February 9, 1993.

Tony Kushner

*T*wanted to participate in this conference because bigotry of every kind seems these days to be getting an upper hand. I don't know whether or not we are witnessing a massive regression in the face of economic and social disorganization, or the turbulence that invariably accompanies a transformation—the last ugly efforts of reactionary forces worldwide to prevent an imminent and unstoppable outbreak of sanity and peace. Not all signs are negative these days, but there's much cause for alarm.

Only once I'd agreed to participate I became completely confused and conflicted about what I wanted to say. I've finally located my conflict and rendered it in the form of a kind of dissenting opinion. I worry that I haven't fulfilled my assignment. I'm sure I can count on being tolerated.

The title of this conference uses two words I don't trust: "Tolerance" and "Art."

If Equality is the chief civic virtue of liberal democracy, and Fraternity and Sorority the chief virtues of socialist democracy, then Tolerance, to borrow from Robert Wolff, is the chief virtue of a pluralist democracy, which is the best description of and possibly the best prescription for the kind of society the United States is and ought to be. In a large, industrialized pluralist democracy, groups of people, arranged along lines of race, ethnicity, religion, gender and sexual orientation, must develop strategies for living together in spite of what may prove to be incommensurable differences. The art of doing this is called Tolerance. Or so the theory goes.

Tolerance has its uses, but not all of them are good. It seems to me that frequently when people are asked to tolerate one another, something is wrong that Tolerance will not fix. Tolerance as a virtue derives from the humanist notion that we are all, as the old saying goes, brothers under the skin; and in this bland, unobjectionable assertion is much that can be objected to. We are divided not simply by "intolerance" but by brutal discrepancies in wealth and power; the qualities that distinguish us from each other are not simply surface irrelevancies but our histories and cultures; and we aren't all "brothers."

When we hear the word "intolerance" in the context of contemporary events we think of Crown Heights; the Los Angeles uprisings; the rape of Moslem women in Bosnia; gay-bashing; born-again anti-Semitism in Germany and here at home. These are events too various to be grouped under one rubric, and any word broad enough to seem to encompass so much should immediately arouse our suspicions.

Intolerance implies a passive, xenophobic bridling at foreignness, while the various phenomena that have impelled us to assemble here today are far more active, passionate and exuberantly malevolent than that. In other countries, where it is polite to use the word, the agents of what we are calling intolerance are called fascists. And Tolerance is not an adequate response to fascism.

Tolerance can be used to normalize an insupportable situation, or it can serve to warn those groups which lack real power that they exist on sufferance, that they are tolerated. If you are oppressed, if those characteristics which make you identifiable to yourself make you loathsome to a powerful majority which does not share those characteristics, then you are at great risk if your existence is predicated on being tolerated. Toleration is necessary when power is unequal; if you have power, you will not need to be tolerated. People who are oppressed need to strive for power, which in a pluralistic democracy means they have to strive for civil rights, for legal protection, for enfranchisement. Ineffable benevolences like Tolerance are easily and tracelessly withdrawn. Civic peace is most secure when the law guarantees it. In other words, people seeking to rid their society of racism, homophobia, anti-Semitism and misogyny must engage in political struggles.

The dismaying lack of solidarity for the oppressed by the oppressed is historically at its worst when the Right is most successful. This, too, is a political issue.

There is a false notion that Culture unites people and Politics divides them. I believe this to be untrue. Every people, every group has a culture, but each culture is different; the artistic expressions of each culture embody those differences in form and content, and indeed one might say that the art a culture produces is the clearest statement that culture can make of difference. While we may say, hopefully, that no difference is insuperable, the recognition and embracing of difference, rather than its effacement, is what real integration and real multiculturalism mandate. We do not want to be overhasty in seeking out unity in culture. We understand very little about the processes by which different cultures may engage constructively with one another, for our history is a history of cultural murder, genocide, holocaust, ethnic cleansing—our history is the history of the violent eradication of Otherness. Where we have succeeded in striking balances which allow for the possibility of mutual coexistence, we have relied on politics as the instrument of peace.

How much sense does it make to separate Culture and Politics as distinct categories? If culture can be thought of as both the exalted and the quotidian expressions of a people's life, then all culture is ideological, political, rooted in history and informed by present circumstance. And art has to reflect this, as well as reflect the artist's desires for society and social change which will, whether revolutionary or reactionary, find expression in the work he or she creates.

If art (and here I lapse into the sin of being generic, though it is really the art of the theater I know and am speaking about) has any political impact, and I believe it does, it seems to me that it's most likely to have it by being effective as art—in other words, that political agendas can't successfully be imposed on the act of making art, of creation, for all that those agendas will invariably surface from within once the art is made.

The artist embraces or expresses difference, spends her or his time imagining it with as powerful and graceful empathic leaps as the limitations of human consciousness permit. This embrace of difference can be instructive: The artist is involved in a process of synthesis when imagining the Other—synthesis, and not compromise. As in any process of true synthesis, the two principles, the Self and the Other, create something new without losing those features which make each principle distinctly itself. This process is difficult and doomed to at least partial failure—if the Other is to stay truly Other then failure is axiomatic. But when an audience watches an artist in this process it is exhilarated, because a miracle of sorts is taking place, in which the Self's isolation is being discarded but not at the cost of its integrity. It is in moments like these, when art is most successful, that it may perhaps teach useful gestures to society, to political action.

I do not believe that a lack of exposure to other cultures in and of itself breeds the virulent forms of hatred that lead to violence. Nor does exposure guarantee Tolerance. In the communities of what was formerly Yugoslavia, different cultures living in the greatest intimacy possible, including inter-marriage, integrated schools and housing, have split into stark factions, and the Serbs are now massacring Bosnian Moslems who were formerly next-door neighbors.

Neither cultural intimacy nor art can ensure coexistence, not when politics makes faction profitable, or seem so. I would like it to be the case, for instance, that New York City schoolboard homophobe Mary Cummins or John J. O'Connor watch one of my plays and subsequently abandon their energetic persecution of gay men and women. I think it unlikely that they will buy tickets, much less be moved to decency by art, when the manifest suffering of people around them has not moved them at all. Perhaps there is more hope for less grimly committed ideologues: but the homophobic rage on display during the battle over the Children of the Rainbow curriculum does not seem to me to be of the sort that will yield to theater. The failure of that initiative is a useful example of the ways in which mistakes in the political arena led to a firestorm of hysterical intolerance, and much worse. The remedy, I believe, lies not in cultural exchange, an unmediated example of which could be seen at those nightmare Board of Education meetings, where the Legions of Decency screeched their opposition into silence, but in politics.

New York City drew me from my native Louisiana seventeen years ago because I imagined it a place in which people of fantastically varied backgrounds could live, intimately, intricately mixed. When I first arrived, every subway car seemed to me a peaceable kingdom in miniature, in which Difference charged the air with curiosity, mystery, possibility and sex. As a gay man, I desperately wanted to believe that such a city existed, and even if New York never really was such a place, in the early seventies it still appeared to be headed towards a reasonable approximation. Twelve years of the anti-urban initiatives of the Reagan and Bush administrations, of polarizing and hate-mongering leaders like Ed Koch, of increased homelessness and joblessness and decreased funding for health care, education, and social services have changed this city. The hope offered by the identity-politics movements has collided catastrophically with the counterrevolution, and the temporary deferral of that hope has given birth to frustration and desperation: which in turn has given birth to a politics based on nationalism. Nationalism, however useful it might prove to be in weathering a hostile social environment, brings with it moral blindness and heavily defended, bristling boundaries. Our best hope, I believe, for reclaiming lost ground and for pushing ahead lies not so much in cultural exchange but in securing civil rights. Before we can lay claim to our common humanity, we must learn to recognize and respect Difference and what it tells us about the infinite complexities of human behavior—recognize and respect Difference, not just tolerate it. The foregrounding of such respect is social justice.

Is Gender Necessary? Redux

Ursula K. Le Guin

IS GENDER NECESSARY?
1976

In the mid-1960s the women's movement was just beginning to move again, after a fifty-year halt. There was a groundswell gathering. I felt it, but I didn't know it was a groundswell; I just thought it was something wrong with me. I considered myself a feminist; I didn't see how you could be a thinking woman and not be a feminist; but I had never taken a step beyond the ground gained for us by Emmeline Pankhurst and Virginia Woolf.[1]

Along about 1967, I began to feel a certain unease, a need to step on a little farther, perhaps, on my own. I began to want to define and understand the meaning of sexuality and the meaning of gender, in my life and in our society. Much had gathered in the unconscious—both personal and collective—which must either be brought up into consciousness, or else turn destructive. It was that same need, I think, that had led Beauvoir to write *The Second Sex*, and Friedan to write *The Feminine Mystique*, and that was, at the same time, leading Kate Millett and others to write their books, and to create the new feminism. But I was not a theoretician, a political thinker or activist, or a sociologist. I was and am a fiction writer. The way I did my thinking was to write a novel. That novel, *The Left Hand of Darkness*, is the record of my consciousness, the process of my thinking.

---

[1] Feminism has enlarged its ground and strengthened its theory and practice immensely, and enduringly, in these past twenty years; but has anyone actually taken a step "beyond" Virginia Woolf? The image, implying on ideal of "progress," is not one I would use now.

Perhaps, now that we have all[2] moved on to a plane of heightened consciousness about these matters, it might be of some interest to look back on the book, to see what it did, what it tried to do, and what it might have done, insofar as it is a "feminist"[3] book. (Let me repeat that last qualification, once. The fact is that the real subject of the book is not feminism or sex or gender or anything of the sort; as far as I can see, it is a book about betrayal and fidelity. That is why one of its two dominant sets of symbols is an extended metaphor of winter, of ice, snow, cold: the winter of journey. The rest of this discussion will concern only half, the lesser half, of the book.)[4]

It takes place on a planet called Gethen, whose human inhabitants differ from us in their sexual physiology. Instead of our continuous sexuality, the Gethenians have an oestrus period, called *kemmer*. When they are not in kemmer, they are sexually inactive and impotent; they are also androgynous. An observer in the book describes the cycle:

> *In the first phase of kemmer [the individual] remains completely androgynous. Gender, and potency, are not attained in isolation. . . . Yet the sexual impulse is tremendously strong in this phase, controlling the entire personality. . . . When the individual finds a partner in kemmer, hormonal secretion is further stimulated (most importantly by touch—secretion? scent?) until in one partner either a male or female hormonal dominance is established. The genitals engorge or shrink accordingly, foreplay intensifies, and the part-ner, triggered by the change, takes on the other sexual role (apparently without exception). . . . Normal individuals have no predisposition to either sexual role in kemmer; they do not know whether they will be the male or the female, and have no choice in the matter. . . . The culminant phase of kemmer . . . lasts from two to five days, during which sexual drive and capacity are at maximum. It ends fairly abruptly, and if conception has not taken place, the individual returns to the latent phase and the cycle begins anew. If the individual was in the female role and was impregnated, hormonal activity of course continues, and for the gestation and lactation periods this individual remains female. . . . With the cessation of lactation the female becomes once more a perfect androgyne. No physiological habit is established, and the mother of several children may be the father of several more.*

Why did I invent these peculiar people? Not just so that the book could contain, halfway through it, the sentence, "The king was pregnant"—though I admit that I am fond of that sentence. Not, certainly not, to propose Gethen as a model for humanity. I am not in favor of genetic alteration of the human organism—not at our present level of understanding. I was not recommending the Gethenian sexual setup: I was using it. It was a heuristic device, a thought-experiment. Physicists often do thought-experiments. Einstein shoots a light ray through a moving elevator; Schrödinger puts a cat in a box. There

---

[2] Well, quite a lot of us, anyhow.

[3] Strike the quotation marks from the word *feminist*, please.

[4] This parenthesis is overstated; I was feeling defensive, and resentful that critics of the book insisted upon talking only about its "gender problems," as if it were an essay not a novel. "*The fact is* that the *real* subject of the book is. . . ." This is bluster. I had opened a can of worms and was trying hard to shut it. "The fact is," however, that there are other aspects to the book, which are involved with its sex/gender aspects quite inextricably.

is no elevator, no cat, no box. The experiment is performed, the question is asked, in the mind. Einstein's elevator, Schrödinger's cat, my Gethenians, are simply a way of thinking. They are questions, not answers; process, not stasis. One of the essential functions of science fiction, I think, is precisely this kind of question-asking: reversals of an habitual way of thinking, metaphors for what our language has no words for as yet, experiments in imagination.

The subject of my experiment, then, was something like this: Because of our life-long social conditioning, it is hard for us to see clearly what, besides purely physiological form and function, truly differentiates men and women. Are there real differences in temperament, capacity, talent, psychic processes, etc.? If so, what are they? Only comparative ethnology offers, so far, any solid evidence on the matter, and the evidence is incomplete and often contradictory. The only going social experiments that are truly relevant are the kibbutzim and the Chinese communes, and they too are inconclusive—and hard to get unbiased information about. How to find out? Well, one can always put a cat in a box. One can send an imaginary, but conventional, indeed rather stuffy, young man from Earth into an imaginary culture which is totally free of sex roles because there is no, absolutely no, physiological sex distinction. I eliminated gender, to find out what was left. Whatever was left would be, presumably, simply human. It would define the area that is shared by men and women alike.

I still think that this was a rather neat idea. But as an experiment, it was messy. All results were uncertain; a repetition of the experiment by someone else, or by myself seven years later, would probably[5] give quite different results. Scientifically, this is most disreputable. That's all right; I am not a sci-

entist. I play the game where the rules keep changing.

Among these dubious and uncertain results, achieved as I thought, and wrote, and wrote, and thought, about my imaginary people, three appear rather interesting to me.

First: The absence of war. In the 13,000 years of recorded history on Gethen, there has not been a war. The people seem to be as quarrelsome, competitive, and aggressive as we are; they have fights, murders, assassinations, feuds, forays, and so on. But there have been no great invasions by peoples on the move, like the Mongols in Asia or the Whites in the New World: partly because Gethenian populations seem to remain stable in size, they do not move in large masses, or rapidly. Their migrations have been slow, no one generation going very far. They have no nomadic peoples, and no societies which live by expansion and aggression against other societies. Nor have they formed large, hierarchically governed nation-states, the mobilizable entity that is the essential factor in modern war. The basic social unit all over the planet is a group of from 200 to 800 people, called a "hearth," a structure founded less on economic convenience than on sexual necessity (there must be others in kemmer at the same time), and therefore more tribal than urban in nature, though overlaid and interwoven with a later urban pattern. The hearth tends to be communal, independent, and somewhat introverted. Rivalries between hearths, as between individuals, are channeled into a socially approved form of aggression called *shifgrethor*, a conflict without physical violence, involving one-upsmanship, the saving and losing of face—conflict ritualized, stylized, controlled. When *shifgrethor* breaks down there may be physical violence, but it does not become mass violence, remaining

---

[5] Strike the word *probably* and replace it with *certainly.*

limited, personal. The active group remains small. The dispersive trend is as strong as the cohesive. Historically, when hearths gathered into a nation for economic reasons, the cellular pattern still dominated the centralized one. There might be a king and a parliament, but authority was not enforced so much by might as by the use of *shifgrethor* and intrigue, and was accepted as custom, without appeal to patriarchal ideals of divine right, patriotic duty, etc. Ritual and parade were far more effective agents of order than armies or police. Class structure was flexible and open; the value of the social hierarchy was less economic than aesthetic, and there was no great gap between rich and poor. There was no slavery or servitude. Nobody owned anybody. There were no chattels. Economic organization was rather communistic or syndicalistic than capitalistic, and was seldom highly centralized.

During the time span of the novel, however, all this is changing. One of the two large nations of the planet is becoming a genuine nation-state, complete with patriotism and bureaucracy. It has achieved state capitalism and the centralization of power, authoritarian government, and a secret police; and it is on the verge of achieving the world's first war.

Why did I present the first picture, and show it in the process of changing to a different one? I am not sure. I think it is because I was trying to show a balance—and the delicacy of a balance. To me the "female principle" is, or at least historically has been, basically anarchic. It values order without constraint, rule by custom not by force. It has been the male who enforces order, who constructs power-structures, who makes, enforces, and breaks laws. On Gethen, these two principles are in balance: the decentralizing against the centralizing, the flexible against the rigid, the circular against the linear. But balance is a precarious state, and at the moment of the novel the balance, which had leaned toward the "feminine," is tipping the other way[6].

Second: The absence of exploitation. The Gethenians do not rape their world. They have developed a high technology, heavy industry, automobiles, radios, explosives, etc., but they have done so very slowly, absorbing their technology rather than letting it overwhelm them. They have no myth of Progress at all. Their calendar calls the current year always the Year One, and they count backward and forward from that.

In this, it seems that what I was after again was a balance: the driving linearity of the "male," the pushing forward to the limit, the logicality that admits no boundary—and the circularity of the "female," the valuing of patience, ripeness, practicality, livableness. A model for this balance, of course, exists on Earth: Chinese civilization over the past six millennia. (I did not know when I wrote the book that the parallel extends even to the

---

[6] At the very inception of the whole book, I was interested in writing a novel about people in a society that had never had a war. That came first. The androgyny come second. (Cause and effect? Effect and cause?) I would now rewrite this paragraph this way: The "female principle" has historically been anarchic; that is, anarchy has been historically identified as female. The domain allotted to women—"the family," for example—is the area of order without coercion, rule by custom not by force. Men have reserved the structures of social power to themselves (and those few women whom they admit to it on male terms, such as queens, prime ministers); men make the wars and peaces, men make, enforce, and break the laws. On Gethen, the two polarities we perceive through our cultural conditioning as male and female are neither, and are in balance: consensus with authority, decentralizing with centralizing, flexible with rigid, circular with linear, hierarchy with network. But it is not a motionless balance, there being no such thing in life, and at the moment of the novel, it is wobbling perilously.

calendar; the Chinese historically never had a linear dating system, such as ours that dates from the birth of Christ.)[7]

Third: The absence of sexuality as a continuous social factor. For four-fifths of the month, a Gethenian's sexuality plays no part at all in his social life (unless he's pregnant); for the other one-fifth, it dominates him absolutely. In kemmer, one must have a partner, it is imperative. (Have you ever lived in a small apartment with a tabby-cat in heat?) Gethenian society fully accepts this imperative. When a Gethenian has to make love, he does make love, and everybody expects him to, and approves of it.[8]

But still, human beings are human beings, not cats. Despite our continuous sexuality and our intense self-domestication (domesticated animals tend to be promiscuous, wild animals pairbonding, familial, or tribal in their mating), we are very seldom truly promiscuous. We do have rape, to be sure—no other animal has equaled us there. We have mass rape, when an army (male, of course) invades; we have prostitution, promiscuity controlled by economics; and sometimes ritual abreactive promiscuity controlled by religion; but in general we seem to avoid genuine license. At most we award it as a price to the Alpha Male, in certain situations; it is scarcely ever permitted to the female without social penalty. It would seem, perhaps, that the mature human being, male or female, is not satisfied by sex-ual gratification without psychic involvement, and in fact may be afraid of it, to judge by the tremendous variety of social, legal, and religious controls and sanctions exerted over it in all human societies. Sex is a great mana, and therefore the immature society, or psyche, sets great taboos about it. The maturer culture, or psyche, can integrate these taboos or laws into an internal ethical code, which, while allowing great freedom, does not permit the treatment of another person as an object. But, however irrational or rational, there is always a code.

Because the Gethenians cannot have sexual intercourse unless both partners are willing, because they cannot rape or be raped, I figured that they would have less fear and guilt about sex than we tend to have; but still it is a problem for them, in some ways more than for us, because of the extreme, explosive, imperative quality of the oestrous phase. Their society would have to control it, though it might move more easily than we from the taboo stage to the ethical stage. So the basic arrangement, I found, is that of the kemmerhouse, in every Gethenian community, which is open to anyone in kemmer, native or stranger, so that he can find a partner.[9] Then there are various customary (not legal) institutions, such as the kemmering group, a group who choose to come together during kemmer as a regular thing; this is like the primate tribe, or group marriage. Or there is the possibility of vowing

[7] A better model might be some of the pre-Conquest cultures of the Americas, though not those hierarchical and imperialistic ones approvingly termed, by our hierarchical and imperialistic standards, "high." The trouble with the Chinese model is that their civilisation instituted and practiced male domination as thoroughly as the other "high" civilisations. I was thinking of a Taoist ideal, not of such practices as bride-selling and foot-binding, which we are trained to consider unimportant, nor of the deep misogyny of Chinese culture, which we are trained to consider normal.

[8] I would now write this paragraph this way: . . . For four-fifths of the month, sexuality plays no part at all in a Gethenian's social behavior; for the other one-fifth, it controls behavior absolutely. In kemmer, one must have a partner, it is imperative. (Have you ever lived in a small apartment with a tabby-cat in heat?) Gethenian society fully accepts this imperative. When Gethenians have to make love, they do make love, and everybody else expects it and approves of it.

kemmering, which is marriage, pairbonding for life, a personal commitment without legal sanction. Such commitments have intense moral and psychic significance, but they are not controlled by Church or State. Finally, there are two forbidden acts, which might be taboo or illegal or simply considered contemptible, depending on which of the regions of Gethen you are in: first, you don't pair off with a relative of a different generation (one who might be your own parent or child); second, you may mate, but not vow kemmering, with your own sibling. These are the old incest prohibitions. They are so general among us—and with good cause, I think, not so much genetic as psychological—that they seemed likely to be equally valid on Gethen.

These three "results," then, of my experiment, I feel were fairly clearly and successfully worked out, though there is nothing definitive about them.

In other areas where I might have pressed for at least such plausible results, I see now a failure to think things through, or to express them clearly. For example, I think I took the easy way in using such familiar governmental structures as a feudal monar-chy and a modern-style bureaucracy for the two Gethenian countries that are the scene of the novel. I doubt that Gethenian governments, rising out of the cellular "hearth," would resemble any of our own so closely. They might be better, they might be worse, but they would certainly be different.

I regret even more certain timidities or ineptnesses I showed in following up the psychic implications of Gethenian physiology.[10] Just for example, I wish I had known Jung's work, when I wrote the book: so that I could have decided whether a Gethenian had *no* animus or anima, or *both*, or an animum. . . . But the central failure in this area comes up in the frequent criticism I receive, that the Gethenians seem like *men*, instead of menwomen.

This rises in part from the choice of pronoun. I call Gethenians "he," because I utterly refuse to mangle English by inventing a pronoun for "he/she."[11] "He" is the generic pronoun, damn it, in English. (I envy the Japanese, who, I am told, do have a he/she pronoun.) But I do not consider this really very important.[12] The pronouns wouldn't matter at all if I had been cleverer at *showing* the "female" component of the Gethenian

[9] Read: so that they can find sexual partners.

[10] For another example (and Jung wouldn't have helped with this, more likely hindered) I quite unnecessarily locked the Gethenians into heterosexuality. It is a naively pragmatic view of sex that insists that sexual partners must be of opposite sex! In any kemmerhouse homosexual practice would, of course, be possible and acceptable and welcomed—but I never thought to explore this option; and the omission, alas, implies that sexuality is heterosexuality. I regret this very much.

[11] This "utter refusal" of 1968 restated in 1976 collapsed, utterly, within a couple of years more. I still dislike invented pronouns, but I now dislike them less than the so-called generic pronoun he/ him/his, which does in fact exclude women from discourse; and which was on invention of male grammarians, for until the sixteenth century the English generic singular pronoun was they/them/ their, as it still is in English and American colloquial speech. It should be restored to the written language, and let the pedants and pundits squeak and gibber in the streets.

In a screenplay of *The Left Hand of Darkness* written in 1985, I referred to Gethenians not pregnant or in kemmer by the invented pronouns a/un/a's, modelled on a British dialect. These would drive the reader mad in print, I suppose; but I have read parts of the book aloud using them, and the audience was perfectly happy, except that they pointed out that the subject pronoun, "a" pronounced "uh" [ə]sounds too much like "I" said with a Southern accent.

[12] I now consider it very important.

characters in *action*.[13] Unfortunately, the plot and structure that arose as I worked the book out cast the Gethenian protagonist, Estraven, almost exclusively into roles which we are culturally conditioned to perceive as "male"—a prime minister (it takes more than even Golda Meit and Indira Gandhi to break a stereotype), a political schemer, a fugitive, a prison-breaker, a sledge-hauler. . . . I think I did this because I was privately delighted at watching, not a man, but a manwoman, do all these things, and do them with considerable skill and flair. But, for the reader, I left out too much. One does not see Estraven as a mother, with his children, in any role which we automatically perceive as "female": and therefore, we tend to see him as a man. This is a real flaw in the book, and I can only be very grateful to those readers, men and women, whose willingness to participate in the experiment led them to fill in that omission with the work of their own imagination, and to see Estraven as I saw him, as man and woman, familiar and different, alien and utterly human.[14]

It seems to be men, more often than women, who thus complete my work for me: I think because men are often more willing to identify as they read with poor, confused, defensive Genly, the Earthman, and therefore to participate in his painful and gradual discovery of love.

Finally, the question arises, is the book a Utopia? It seems to me that it is quite clearly not; it poses no *practicable* alternative to contemporary society, since it is based on an imaginary, radical change in human anatomy. All it tries to do is open up an alternative viewpoint, to widen the imagination, without making any definite suggestions as to what might be seen from the new viewpoint. The most it says is, I think, something like this: If we were socially ambisexual, if men and women were completely and genuinely equal in their social roles, equal legally and economically, equal in freedom, in responsibility, and in self-esteem, then society would be a very different thing. What our problems might be, God knows; I only know we would have them. But it seems likely that our central problem would not be the one it is now: the problem of exploitation—exploitation of the woman, of the weak, of the earth. Our curse is alienation, the separation of yang from yin.[15] Instead of a search for balance and integration, there is a struggle for dominance. Divisions are insisted upon, interdependence is denied. The dualism of value that destroys us, the dualism of superior/inferior, ruler/ruled, owner/owned, user/used, might give way to what seems to me, from here, a much healthier, sounder, more promising modality of integration and integrity.

[13] If I had realised how the pronouns I used shaped, directed, controlled my own thinking, I might have been "cleverer."

[14] I now see it thus: Men were inclined to be satisfied with the book, which allowed them a safe trip into androgyny and back, from a conventionally male viewpoint. But many women wanted it to go further, to dare more, to explore androgyny from a woman's point of view as well as a man's. In fact, it does so, in that it was written by a woman. But this is admitted directly only in the chapter "The Question of Sex," the only voice of a woman in the book. I think women were justified in asking more courage of me and a more rigorous thinking through of implications.

[15] —and the moralisation of yang as good—of yin as bad.

THE DOCUMENTARY DEBATE: AESTHETIC OR ANAESTHETIC?

Or, What's So Funny about Peace, Love, Understanding, and Social Documentary Photography?

David Levi Strauss

So, what does a photograph expose? It exposes, says Derrida, the relation to the law. What he means is that every photo poses itself as this question: Are we allowed to view what is being exposed?

—Avital Ronell, interviewed by Andrea Juno in *Angry Women*

It is excellent that people should be starting to argue about this again.

—Opening line of Ernst Bloch's defense of Expressionism (contra Georg Lukás), 1938

The relation between aesthetics and politics was a matter of great contention at the end of the twentieth century. Although too much of the discussion about it consisted of apodictic pronouncements and invective dismissals, it was good to have people arguing about it again. From where there is heat there may occasionally come some light.

When the "Culture Wars" in the United States spread to censorship battles over the photographs of Robert Mapplethorpe, Andres Serrano, and David Wojnoarowicz, the documentary veracity and political content of aesthetic images were put on public trial. From the beginning of these conflicts, the right recognized what the real stakes were in this "war between cultures and . . . about the meaning of 'culture'" (per Indiana Republican Representative Henry Hyde); they recognized the subversive nature of art and responded accordingly. On the other hand, one of the left's most articulate antecedents to this trial was the "anti-aesthetic" branch of postmodern criticism, which Hal Foster characterized in 1983 as questioning "the very notion of the aesthetic, its network of ideas," including "the notion of the aesthetic as subversive," claiming that "its criticality is now largely illusory."[1]

---

[1] Hal Foster, "Postmodernism: A Preface," in *The Anti-Aesthetic: Essays on Postmodern Culture*, ed. by Foster (Port Townsend, WA: Bay Press, 1983), p. xv.

During this same time, the theory and criticism of photography was being transformed by the emergence of a new, strong materialist analysis of photography by writers such as Martha Rosler, Allan Sekula, Abigail Solomon-Godeau, and John Tagg, among others. One of the most trenchant and persistent critiques arising from this tendency was that of "social documentary" photography, focusing especially on the aestheticization of the documentary image. One measure of the success of this critique is the extent to which its assumptions and conclusions were accepted and absorbed into mainstream writing about photography.

The September 9, 1991 issue of the *New Yorker* carried an article by Ingrid Sischy, titled "Good Intentions," on the work of Brazilian photographer Sebastião Salagado. Sischy upbraids Salagado for being too popular and too successful, and also for being too "uncompromisingly serious" and "weighty"; for being opportunistic and self-aggrandizing, and also too idealistic; for being too spiritual, and also for being "kitschy" and "schmaltzy." But Sischy's real complaint about Salagado's photographs is that they threaten the boundary between aesthetics and politics. The complaint is couched in the familiar terms of a borrowed political critique: *Salagado is too busy with the compositional aspects of his pictures—and with finding the "grace" and "beauty" in the twisted forms of his anguished subjects. And this beautification of tragedy results in pictures that ultimately reinforce our passivity toward the experience they reveal. To aestheticize tragedy is the fastest way to anaesthetize the feelings of those who are witnessing it. Beauty is a call to admiration, not to action.*[2] The

substantive critique upon which this by now conventional criticism is based can be found in the classic debate within German Marxism that occurred from the 1930s to the 1950s, involving Ernst Bloch, Georg Lukás, Bertolt Brecht, Walter Benjamin, and Theodor Adorno.[3]

The principal source for the "aestheticization of tragedy" argument is Walter Benjamin's essay "The Author As Producer," in which he speaks of "the way certain modish photographers proceed in order to make human misery an object of consumption."[4] What is often forgotten by those who appropriate this critique is its historical context within this debate. Benjamin's criticisms here specifically refer to certain products of the Neue Sachlichkeit (New Objectivity) movement in literature and art, which was itself a reaction against Expressionism, professing a return to objectivity of vision. When Benjamin charges that "it has succeeded in turning abject poverty itself, by handling it in a modish, technically perfect way, into an object of enjoyment," he is referring to the well-known picture book by Albert Renger-Patzsch titled *Die Welt ist schön* (The world is beautiful). And he is expressly referring to the New Objectivity as a literary movement when he says that "it transforms political struggle so that it ceases to be a compelling motive for decision and becomes an object of comfortable contemplation." There are contemporary photographers who are heirs to the New Objectivity, but Salgado is not one of them, and to apply these criticisms to his work is a politically pointed inversion.

The distinction is made eloquently, and in a way that Benjamin would surely have

---

[2] Ingrid Sischy, "Good Intentions," *The New Yorker*, September 9, 1991, p. 92 When I read this passage to the poet Susan Thackrey, she said, "And what is she going to do with King Lear?"

[3] *Aesthetics and Politics*, Afterword by Fredric Jameson, translation ed. by Ronald Taylor (London and New York: Verso, 1980).

[4] Walter Benjamin, "The Author As Producer," in *Thinking Photography,* ed. by Victor Burgin (London: Macmillan,1982), p.24.

appreciated, by Uruguayan writer Eduardo Galeano in his essay "Salgado, 17 Times," which appeared in the San Francisco Museum of Modern Art's catalog to the 1990 Salgado show: *Salgado photographs people. Casual photographers photograph phantoms. As an article of consumption poverty is a source of morbid pleasure and much money. Poverty is a commodity that fetches a high price on the luxury market. Consumer-society photographers approach but do not enter. In hurried visits to scenes of despair or violence, they climb out of the plane or helicopter, press the shutter release, explode the flash: they shoot and run. They have looked without seeing and their images say nothing. Their cowardly photographs soiled with horror or blood may extract a few crocodile tears, a few coins, a pious word or two from the privileged of the earth, none of which changes the order of their universe. At the sight of the dark-skinned wretched, forsaken by God and pissed on by dogs, anybody who is nobody confidentially congratulates himself: life hasn't done too badly by me, in comparison. Hell serves to confirm the virtues of paradise. Charity, vertical, humiliates. Solidarity, horizontal, helps. Salgado photographs from inside, in solidarity.* [5] Are Galeano and Sischy looking at the same images? What is the political difference in the way they are looking? In another part of his essay, Galeano (who was forced into exile from his native Uruguay for having "ideological ideas," as one of the dictator's functionaries put it) locates Salgado's transgression: "From their mighty silence, these images, these portraits, question the hypocritical frontiers that safeguard the bourgeois order and protect its right to power and inheritance." [6]

This is the disturbing quality of Salgado's work that so divides viewers. Like all politically effective images, the best of Salgado's photographs work in the fissures, the wounds, of the social. They cause those who see them to ask themselves: *Are we allowed to view what is being exposed?* In an essay on "Active Boundaries," the poet Michael Palmer relates Salgado's work to that of Paul Celan, and notes: *The subject of Salgado's photojournalism, we must continually remind ourselves, is* not there, *is not in fact the visible but the invisible: what has been repressed and will not be spoken. It appears always at the edge of the frame or in the uneasy negotiation among the space of origin, the framed space of the work, and the social space to which it has been removed, which is also a cultural space, of the aesthetic.* [7] The anti-aesthetic tendency can easily become an anaesthetic one, an artificially induced unconsciousness to protect oneself from pain, and to protect the "hypocritical frontiers" of propriety and privilege. It is unseemly to look right into the face of hunger, and then to represent it in a way that compels others to look right into it as well. It is an abomination, and obscenity, an ideological crime.

When one, anyone, tries to represent someone else, to "take their picture" or "tell their story," they run headlong into a minefield of real political problems. The first question is: what right have *I* to represent *you*? Every photograph of this kind must be a negotiation, a complex act of communication. As with all such acts, the likelihood of success is extremely remote, but does that mean it shouldn't be attempted? In his magnificent defense of Modern art against Lukás,

[5] Eduardo Galeano, "Salgado, 17 Times," trans. by Asa Zatz, in *Sebastião Salgado: An Uncertain Grace* (New York: Aperture, in association with the San Francisco Museum of Modern Art, 1990), p.11.

[6] Ibid., p.12.

[7] Michael Palmer, "Active Boundaries: Poetry at the Periphery," unpublished manuscript, 1992. Later published in *Onward: Contemporary Poetry and Poetics,* ed. by Peter Baker (New York: Peter Lang Publishing, 1996), p.265.

Brecht wrote: *In art there is the fact of failure, and the fact of partial success. Our metaphysicians must understand this. Works of art can fail so easily; it is so difficult for them to succeed. One man will fall silent because of lack of feeling; another, because his emotion chokes him. A third frees himself, not from the burden that weighs on him, but only from a feeling of unfreedom. A fourth breaks his tools because they have too long been used to exploit him. The world is not obliged to be sentimental. Defeats should be acknowledged; but one should never conclude from them that there should be no more struggles.*[8] A documentary practice that tries to avoid the difficulties of such communication is not worthy of the name. After the aestheticization argument made social documentary photography of any kind theoretically indefensible, a number of articles appeared calling for its recuperation as "new documentary." In his essay "Toward a New Social Documentary," Grant Kester wrote: *If social documentary can be recuperated as a new documentary, it is precisely because it was never entirely aestheticized in the first place. There must be a core of authentic practice in documentary. It seems clear that this authenticity rests in its ability to act not only as art, but also in the kind of concrete social struggles that gave it its original character.*[9] The assumptions here are clear: the "aestheticized" (art) is not "authentic," but always already supplementary—perhaps even antithetical—to "concrete social struggles." Isn't this just the flip side of the right's view of art: that art is inauthentic and supplementary and politically suspect? The doctrinaire right contends that politics has no place in art, while the doctrinaire left contends that art has no place in politics. Both takes are culturally restrictive and historically inaccurate.

The idea that the more transformed or "aestheticized" an image is, the less "authentic" or politically valuable it becomes, is one that needs to be seriously questioned. Why *can't* beauty be a call to action? The unsupported and careless use of "aestheticization" to condemn artists who deal with politically charged subjects recalls Brecht's statement that "the 'right thinking' people among us, whom Stalin in another context distinguishes from creative people, have a habit of spell-binding our minds with certain words used in an extremely arbitrary sense."[10]

To represent is to aestheticize; that is, to transform. It presents a vast field of choices but it does not include the choice *not* to transform, not to change or alter whatever is being represented. It can not be a pure process, in practice. This goes for photography as much as for any other means of representation. But this is no reason to back away from the process, in practice. The aesthetic is not objective and is not reducible to quantitative scientific terms. Quantity can only measure physical phenomena, and is misapplied in aesthetics, which often deals with what is *not* there, imagining things into existence. To become legible to others, these imaginings must be socially and culturally encoded. That is aestheticization.

When Benjamin wrote that "the tendency of a work of literature can be politically correct only if it is also correct in the literary sense," he meant that the way something is made (its poetics) is political. Carried over into photography, that might mean that being politically correct doesn't signify much unless the work is also visually and conceptually compelling, or rather that these two things are not mutually exclusive, nor even separate. To be compelling, there must be tension in the work; if everything

[8] *Aesthetics and Politics,* p.74.

[9] Grant Kester, "Toward a New Social Documentary," *Afterimage* vol. 14, no. 8 (March 1987), p.14.

[10] *Aesthetics and Politics,* p.76.

has been decided beforehand, there will be no tension and no compulsion to the work. In the latter kind of imagery, the viewer's choice is reduced to acceptance or rejection of the "message," without becoming involved in a more complex response. Such images may work as propaganda (the effectiveness of which is quantitatively measurable), but they will not work at other points on the spectrum of communication.

Aestheticization is one of the ways that disparate peoples recognize themselves in one another. Photographs by themselves certainly cannot tell "the whole truth"—they are always only instants. What they do most persistently is to register the relation of photographer to subject—the distance from one to another—and this understanding is a profoundly important political process, as Marx himself suggested: "Let us suppose that we had carried out production as human beings. . . . Our products would be so many mirrors in which we saw reflected our essential nature."[11]

---

[11] Karl Marx, "Comments on James Mill" (1844) in the *Collected Works*. Quoted by W.J.T. Mitchell in *Iconology: Image, Test, Ideology* (Chicago and London: University of Chicago Press, 1986), p.186.

PUBLIC INTELLECTUALS

Cynthia Ozick

The term "public intellectual" has been in fashion for some time now, but its embodiment has always been with us. Socrates was what we would call a public intellectual; and Isaiah; and Maimonides; and Voltaire; and Emerson. But observe: presumably not Aristotle, not Montaigne, not George Eliot, not Santayana. George Eliot presided over a salon, of which she was the undisputed center and engine; and still we would not cite her as a public intellectual. Hannah Arendt and Mary McCarthy were certainly public intellectuals; Lionel Trilling was not.

If there are public intellectuals, it must follow that there are also private intellectuals. What is the difference between them? It cannot be a difference of substance or subject matter. William James, despite countless public lectures, was not really a public intellectual; Emerson, who confronted many of the same themes, was. Nor could it have been simply reticence of temperament that separated Lionel Trilling from, say, Irving Howe, an almost prototypical public intellectual. And if we could clearly define the difference, is it important, would it matter?

There recently came into my hands a thin little chapbook, bound in the pallor of an aging blue and entitled "The New Disorder," containing remarks set down in 1941 by E. M. Forster. Now you may instantly object: why bring up Forster, a novelist, an artist, in the context of the public intellectual? The reason is this. Before we had the dispassionate phrase "public intellectual," there was a simpler name in common use that appeared to cover everyone who attends to, and rallies around, and pokes at and palpates ideas. That name was "thinker." No one can deny that Forster, though distinguished for fiction, was also a thinker. He surely addressed literary issues, but now and then he touched on political issues, the hallmark of the public intellectual. *A Passage to India* is inevitably read as a protest against British colonialism in India; that it is a masterwork able to escape the fate of a tract is a measure of Forster's both delicate and robust art. And the indelible epigraph of *Howards End,* "Only connect," is a slogan as political in its intention as it is private.

Beyond the novels there are the essays—pre-eminently "On Liberty in England," a talk delivered at an international writers' conference in Paris in 1935. Here Forster defends freedom of expression and attacks censorship, particularly of homosexual writing. And here also he situates himself as any number of writers and intellectuals situated themselves in the nineteen-thirties: "As for my politics," he tells his audience, "you will have guessed that I am not a Fascist—Fascism does evil that evil may come. And you may have guessed that I am not a Communist, though perhaps I might be one if I was a younger and braver man, for in Communism I can see hope. It does many things which I think evil, but I know that it intends good." Lately, it goes without saying, these latter words are achingly hollow; and there were some for whom they were terribly hollow even two-thirds of a century ago.

But let us return to my little blue pamphlet. It is now 1941; England has been fighting Hitler for two years; in December Pearl Harbor will catapult America into the war. Fascism's evil, recognized as such by Forster six years earlier—the force that "does evil that evil may come"—is furiously at work. In Germany and elsewhere the Jews have been stripped of citizenship and are now official prey, ready candidates for a destiny which, while perhaps not yet overtly revealed as murderous, has already plunged whole populations into unspeakable suffering and degradation. Once again the occasion is a writers' conference, this one the seventeenth International PEN Congress. "We had with us," Forster wrote afterward, "representatives from about thirty nations, many of whom had suffered; all of whom had cause for fear. Politics had not ignored them, so how could they ignore politics? . . . They valued literature only if it helped their particular cause or what they regarded as the good of humanity." He granted that his speech was politely dismissed; the Congress "reverted to what it considered important and did not discuss the issue raised."

And the issue Forster raised, in 1941, was this: "Art for Art's sake? I should just think so, and more so than ever at the present time. It is the one orderly product which our muddling race has produced." He offers history as proof: "Ancient Athens made a mess," he says, "but the 'Antigone' stands up. Renaissance Rome made a mess—but the ceiling of the Sistine got painted," and so on. He ends by citing Shelley—the usual quote about poets as the unacknowledged legislators of mankind.

As an adolescent English major in college, I know I would have warmed to this, and taken it as my own life's credo. I did, in fact, do exactly that. But now, when I look at this date—1941!—I can only wonder how, with all of torn-up Europe dangling from German jaws, Forster could dare to take the view from Mount Olympus. Did Forster in 1941 not remember the political impulse out of which he conceived his Indian novel, published in 1924? Yet no one can tell him he is in error: the Sistine Chapel *did* get painted, the "Antigone" *does* stand up (though Forster seems to have forgotten what it stands *for*.) But suppose Sophocles had been run through by a tyrant's sword, or suppose Michelangelo had been taken off and shot? Then there would be no play and no painted ceiling. Art may well be the most worthy of all human enterprises; that is why it needs to be defended; and in crisis, in a barbarous time, even the artists must be visible among the defending spear-carriers. Art at its crux—certainly the "Antigone"!—doesn't fastidiously separate itself from the human roil; neither should artists. I like to imagine a conversation between Forster and Isaac Babel—let us say in 1939, the year Babel was arrested and tortured, or early in 1940, when he was sentenced to death at a mock trial. History isn't only what we inherit, safe and sound and after the fact; it is also what we are ourselves obliged to endure.

And just here, you may conclude, is the distinction between the public intellectual and the other kind. Public intellectuals know that history is where we swim, that we are *in* it, that we can't see over or around it, that it is our ineluctable task to grapple with it; and that we may not murmur, with Forster, Look: the past came through, and so will we. Thinkers, after all, do not simply respond to existing conditions; in the buzz, confusion, and chaos of the Zeitgeist they strive to sort out—to formulate—the cognitive and historic patterns that give rise to public issues. That, we may presume, is what Forster thought he was doing when he picked out art-for-art's-sake as the salient issue of 1941. Why this choice was a disappointing one hardly demands analysis. "I realized," he had admitted that same year, living in Cambridge, protected by the British Army, "that as soon as I myself had been hurt or frightened I should forget about books too." Still, he continued, "even when the cause of humanity is lost, the possibility of the aesthetic order will remain and it seems well to assert it at this moment . . . I hope it is not callous to do this, and certainly no callousness is intended."

Intended or not, the callousness was there. Not because Forster was in any way a callous man; the absolute opposite is true. Yet even in 1949, when Forster appended a postscript to that talk—at an hour when the ovens were scarcely cooled and the D.P. camps were filled with wandering ghosts— he did not acknowledge that his 1941 formulation had been inadequate to its own context. Out of the turbulence of a Europe in extremis he had formulated an issue, as thinkers are wont to do, and he had formulated it badly. He put an ideal above immediate reality: the reality that kills. You might protest that Primo Levi did the same when he recited Dante in Auschwitz; but that was because he had the privilege of being a slave laborer rather than a gassed corpse. If you are still barely alive in Auschwitz, it is barely possible that poetry will salve your soul; but if you are comfortably alive well beyond the inferno, the exaltation of art as exclusive of the suffering of your own time does take on the lineaments of callousness.

How do we know when a thinker formulates an issue badly? In just this way: when an ideal, however comely, fails to accord with deep necessity. In 1941, "blood, sweat, and tears" is apropos; in an era of evil joy— Mark Twain's chilling phrase—a dream of the "possibility of aesthetic order" is not. Only a fantasist will not credit the reality of the contagion of evil joy; the world engenders it; it exists. There are those—human beings both like and unlike ourselves—who relish evil joy, and pursue it, and make it their cause; who despise compromise, reason, negotiation; who, in Forster's words, do evil that evil may come—and then the possibility of aesthetic order fails to answer. It stands only as a beautiful thought, and it is not sufficient to have beautiful thoughts while the barbarians rage on. The best ideal then becomes the worst ideal, and the worst ideal, however comely, is that there *are* no barbarians; or that the barbarians will be so impressed by your beautiful thoughts that they too will begin thinking beautiful thoughts; or that in actuality the barbarians are no different from you and me, with our beautiful thoughts; and that therefore loyalty belongs to the barbarians' cause as much as it belongs to our own.

Some will say, how is it you have the gall to use so unforgivably denigrating a term as "barbarians"? Must you despise your opponents as other, as not of your own flesh? What of the humanity of the other? Are we not all equally flawed, equally capable of mercy? Are we ourselves not in some respects worse? Shall we not be decent to the other?

But—in a jurisprudential democracy especially—a moment may come when it is needful to be decent to our own side, concerning whom we are not to witness falsely or even carelessly in order to prove how worse we are. Without such loyalty—not always a popular notion among the global sentimentalists—you may find you are too weak in self-respect to tell the truth or to commit yourself to the facts. The responsibility of intellectuals ought to include this recognition, or it is no responsibility at all.

The responsibility of intellectuals includes also the recognition that we cannot live above or apart from our own time and what it imposes on us; that willy-nilly we breathe inside the cage of our generation, and must perform within it. Thinkers—whether they count as public intellectuals or the more reticent and less visible sort—are obliged above all to make distinctions, particularly in an age of mindlessly spreading moral equivalence. "I have seen the enemy and he is us" is not always and everywhere true; and self-blame can be the highest form of self-congratulation. People who are privileged to be thinkers are obliged to respect exigency and to admit to crisis. They are obliged to expose and war against those rampant Orwellian coinages that mean their opposite and lead to purposeful deception. And political intellectuals who have the capacity, and the inclination, to reflect on fresh public issues from new perspectives are obliged to reflect on them in so careful a way that their propositions will not seem callous or morally embarrassing or downright despicable decades on.

At the end of the day, a verge can perhaps be measured out: those who favor the guarded life should not risk contemplation in public. Contemplation in public is what political intellectuals commonly do, and what the quieter private thinkers on occasion slip into doing, not always inadvertently. The private thinkers have the advantage of being written off as bunglers when they do speak out, or as cowards when they don't. But for the public thinkers, who are always audible in the forum, the risk is far more perilous, far more destructive to the honor of a generation: they risk being judged mistaken.

LOOKING AT WAR

BY SUSAN SONTAG

In June, 1938, Virginia Woolf published *Three Guineas*, her brave, unwelcomed reflections on the roots of war. Written during the preceding two years, while she and most of her intimates and fellow-writers were rapt by the advancing Fascist insurrection in Spain, the book was couched as a tardy reply to a letter from an eminent lawyer in London who had asked, "How in your opinion are we to prevent war?" Woolf begins by observing tartly that a truthful dialogue between them may not be possible. For though they belong to the same class, "the educated class," a vast gulf separates them: the lawyer is a man and she is a woman. Men make war. Men (most men) like war, or at least they find "some glory, some necessity, some satisfaction in fighting" that women (most women) do not seek or find. What does an educated—that is, privileged, well-off—woman like her know of war? Can her reactions to its horrors be like his?

Woolf proposes they test this "difficulty of communication" by looking at some images of war that the beleaguered Spanish government has been sending out twice a week to sympathizers abroad. Let's see "whether when we look at the same photographs we feel the same things," she writes. "This morning's collection contains the photograph of what might be a man's body, or a woman's; it is so mutilated that it might, on the other hand, be the body of a pig. But those certainly are dead children, and that undoubtedly is the section of a house. A bomb has torn open the side; there is still a bird-cage hanging in what was presumably the sitting room." One can't always make out the subject, so thorough is the ruin of flesh and stone that the photographs depict. "However different the education, the traditions behind us," Woolf says to the lawyer, "we"— and here women are the "we"—and he might well have the same response: "War, you say, is an abomination; a barbarity; war must be stopped at whatever cost. And we echo your words. War is an abomination; a barbarity; war must be stopped."

Who believes today that war can be abolished? No one, not even pacifists. We hope only (so far in vain) to stop genocide and bring to justice those who commit gross violations of the laws of war (for there are laws of war, to which combatants should be held), and to stop specific wars by imposing negotiated alternatives to armed conflict. But protesting against war may not have seemed so futile or naïve in the nineteen-thirties. In 1924, on the tenth anniversary of the national mobilization in Germany for the First World

War, the conscientious objector Ernst Friedrich published *War Against War! (Krieg dem Kriege!)*, an album of more than a hundred and eighty photographs that were drawn mainly from German military and medical archives, and almost all of which were deemed unpublishable by government censors while the war was on. The book starts with pictures of toy soldiers, toy cannons, and other delights of male children everywhere, and concludes with pictures taken in military cemeteries. This is photography as shock therapy. Between the toys and the graves, the reader has an excruciating photo tour of four years of ruin, slaughter, and degradation: wrecked and plundered churches and castles, obliterated villages, ravaged forests, torpedoed passenger steamers, shattered vehicles, hanged conscientious objectors, naked personnel of military brothels, soldiers in death agonies after a poison-gas attack, skeletal Armenian children.

Friedrich did not assume that heart-rending, stomach-turning pictures would speak for themselves. Each photograph has an impassioned caption in four languages (German, French, Dutch, and English), and the wickedness of militarist ideology is excoriated and mocked on every page. Immediately denounced by the German government and by veterans' and other patriotic organizations— in some cities the police raided bookstores, and lawsuits were brought against public display of the photographs— Friedrich's declaration of war against war was acclaimed by left-wing writers, artists, and intellectuals, as well as by the constituencies of the numerous antiwar leagues, who predicted that the book would have a decisive influence on public opinion. By 1930, *War Against War!* had gone through ten editions in Germany and been translated into many languages.

In 1928, in the Kellogg-Briand Pact, fifteen nations, including the United States, France, Great Britain, Germany, Italy, and Japan, solemnly renounced war as an instrument of national policy. Freud and Einstein were drawn into the debate four years later, in an exchange of letters published under the title "Why War?" *Three Guineas*, which appeared toward the close of nearly two decades of plangent denunciations of war and war's horrors, was at least original in its focus on what was regarded as too obvious to be mentioned, much less brooded over: that war is a man's game—that the killing machine has a gender, and it is male. Nevertheless, the temerity of Woolf's version of "Why War?" does not make her revulsion against war any less conventional in its rhetoric, and in its summations, rich in repeated phrases. Photographs of the victims of war are themselves a species of rhetoric. They reiterate. They simplify. They agitate. They create the illusion of consensus.

Woolf professes to believe that the shock of such pictures cannot fail to unite people of good will. Although she and the lawyer are separated by the age-old affinities of feeling and practice of their respective sexes, he is hardly a standard-issue bellicose male. After all, his question was not, What are your thoughts about preventing war? It was, How in your opinion are we to prevent war? Woolf challenges this "we" at the start of her book, but after some pages devoted to the feminist point she abandons it.

"Here then on the table before us are photographs," she writes of the thought experiment she is proposing to the reader as well as to the spectral lawyer, who is eminent enough to have K.C., King's Counsel, after his name— and may or may not be a real person. Imagine a spread of loose photographs extracted from an envelope that arrived in the morning mail. They show the mangled bodies of adults and children. They show how war evacuates, shatters, breaks apart, levels the built world. A bomb has torn open the side of a house. To be sure, a cityscape is not made of flesh. Still, sheared-off buildings are almost as eloquent as body parts (Kabul; Sarajevo; East Mostar; Grozny; sixteen acres of Lower Manhattan after September 11, 2001; the refugee camp in

Jenin). Look, the photographs say, *this* is what it's like. This is what war *does*. And *that*, that is what it does, too. War tears, rends. War rips open, eviscerates. War scorches. War dismembers. War *ruins*. Woolf believes that not to be pained by these pictures, not to recoil from them, not to strive to abolish what causes this havoc, this carnage, is a failure of imagination, of empathy.

But surely the photographs could just as well foster greater militancy on behalf of the Republic. Isn't this what they were meant to do? The agreement between Woolf and the lawyer seems entirely presumptive, with the grisly photographs confirming an opinion already held in common. Had his question been, How can we best contribute to the defense of the Spanish Republic against the forces of militarist and clerical fascism?, the photographs might have reinforced a belief in the justness of that struggle.

The pictures Woolf has conjured up do not in fact show what war—war in general—does. They show a particular way of waging war, a way at that time routinely described as "barbaric," in which civilians are the target. General Franco was using the tactics of bombardment, massacre, torture, and the killing and mutilation of prisoners that he had perfected as a commanding officer in Morocco in the nineteen-twenties. Then, more acceptably to ruling powers, his victims had been Spain's colonial subjects, darker-hued and infidels to boot; now his victims were compatriots. To read in the pictures, as Woolf does, only what confirms a general abhorrence of war is to stand back from an engagement with Spain as a country with a history. It is to dismiss politics.

For Woolf, as for many antiwar polemicists, war is generic, and the images she describes are of anonymous, generic victims. The pictures sent out by the government in Madrid seem, improbably, not to have been labelled. (Or perhaps Woolf is simply assuming that a photograph should speak for itself.) But to those who are sure that right is on one side, oppression and injustice on the other, and that the fighting must go on, what matters is precisely who is killed and by whom. To an Israeli Jew, a photograph of a child torn apart in the attack on the Sbarro pizzeria in downtown Jerusalem is first of all a photograph of a Jewish child killed by a Palestinian suicide bomber. To a Palestinian, a photograph of a child torn apart by a tank round in Gaza is first of all a photograph graph of a Palestinian child killed by Israeli ordnance. To the militant, identity is everything. And all photographs wait to be explained or falsified by their captions. During the fighting between Serbs and Croats at the beginning of the recent Balkan wars, the same photographs of children killed in the shelling of a village were passed around at both Serb and Croat propaganda briefings. Alter the caption: alter the use of these deaths.

Photographs of mutilated bodies certainly can be used the way Woolf does, to vivify the condemnation of war, and may bring home, for a spell, a portion of its reality to those who have no experience of war at all. But someone who accepts that in the world as currently divided war can become inevitable, and even just, might reply that the photographs supply no evidence, none at all, for renouncing war— except to those for whom the notions of valor and of sacrifice have been emptied of meaning and credibility. The destructiveness of war— short of total destruction, which is not war but suicide—is not in itself an argument against waging war, unless one thinks (as few people actually do) that violence is always unjustifiable, that force is always and in all circumstances wrong: wrong because, as Simone Weil affirms in her sublime essay on war, "The Iliad, or, The Poem of Force," violence turns anybody subjected to it into a thing. But to those who in a given situation see no alternative to armed struggle, violence can exalt someone subjected to it into a martyr or a hero.

In fact, there are many uses of the innumerable opportunities that a modern life supplies for regarding—at a distance, through the medium of photography— other people's pain.

Photographs of an atrocity may give rise to opposing responses: a call for peace; a cry for revenge; or simply the bemused awareness, continually restocked by photographic information, that terrible things happen. Who can forget the three color pictures by Tyler Hicks that the *New York Times* ran on November 13, 2001, across the upper half of the first page of its daily section devoted to America's new war? The triptych depicted the fate of a wounded Taliban soldier who had been found in a ditch by some Northern Alliance soldiers advancing toward Kabul. First panel: the soldier is being dragged on his back by two of his captors—one has grabbed an arm, the other a leg—along a rocky road. Second panel: he is surrounded, gazing up in terror as he is pulled to his feet. Third panel: he is supine with arms outstretched and knees bent, naked from the waist down, a bloodied heap left on the road by the dispersing military mob that has just finished butchering him. A good deal of stoicism is needed to get through the newspaper each morning, given the likelihood of seeing pictures that could make you cry. And the disgust and pity that pictures like Hicks's inspire should not distract from asking what pictures, whose cruelties, whose deaths you are *not* being shown.

II

Awareness of the suffering that accumulates in wars happening elsewhere is something constructed. Principally in the form that is registered by cameras, it flares up, is shared by many people, and fades from view. In contrast to a written account, which, depending on its complexity of thought, references, and vocabulary, is pitched at a larger or smaller readership, a photograph has only one language and is destined potentially for all.

In the first important wars of which there are accounts by photographers, the Crimean War and the American Civil War, and in every other war until the First World War, combat itself was beyond the camera's ken. As for the war photographs published between 1914 and 1918, nearly all anonymous, they were—insofar as they did convey something of the terrors and devastation endured —generally in the epic mode, and were usually depictions of an aftermath: corpse-strewn or lunar landscapes left by trench warfare; gutted French villages the war had passed through. The photographic monitoring of war as we know it had to wait for a radical upgrade of professional equipment: lightweight cameras, such as the Leica, using 35-mm. film that could be exposed thirty-six times before the camera needed to be reloaded. The Spanish Civil War was the first war to be witnessed ("covered") in the modern sense: by a corps of professional photographers at the lines of military engagement and in the towns under bombardment, whose work was immediately seen in newspapers and magazines in Spain and abroad. Pictures could be taken in the thick of battle, military censorship permitting, and civilian victims and exhausted, begrimed soldiers studied up close. The war America waged in Vietnam, the first to be witnessed day after day by television cameras, introduced the home front to a new intimacy with death and destruction. Ever since, battles and massacres filmed as they unfold have been a routine ingredient of the ceaseless flow of domestic, small-screen entertainment. Creating a perch for a particular conflict in the consciousness of viewers exposed to dramas from everywhere requires the daily diffusion and rediffusion of snippets of footage about the conflict. The understanding of war among people who have not experienced war is now chiefly a product of the impact of these images.

Non-stop imagery (television, streaming video, movies) surrounds us, but, when it comes to remembering, the photograph has the deeper bite. Memory freeze-frames; its basic unit is the single image. In an era of information overload, the photograph provides a quick way of apprehending something and a compact form for memorizing it. The photograph is like a quotation, or a maxim or proverb. Each of us mentally stocks hundreds of photographs, subject to instant recall. Cite the most famous photograph taken during the

Spanish Civil War, the Republican soldier "shot" by Robert Capa's camera at the same moment he is hit by an enemy bullet, and virtually everyone who has heard of that war can summon to mind the grainy black-and-white image of a man in a white shirt with rolled-up sleeves collapsing backward on a hillock, his right arm flung behind him as his rifle leaves his grip—about to fall, dead, onto his own shadow.

It is a shocking image, and that is the point. Conscripted as part of journalism, images were expected to arrest attention, startle, surprise. As the old advertising slogan of *Paris Match*, founded in 1949, had it: "The weight of words, the shock of photos." The hunt for more dramatic—as they're often described—images drives the photographic enterprise, and is part of the normality of a culture in which shock has become a leading stimulus of consumption and source of value. "Beauty will be convulsive, or it will not be," André Breton proclaimed. He called this aesthetic ideal "surrealist," but, in a culture radically revamped by the ascendancy of mercantile values, to ask that images be jarring, clamorous, eye-opening seems like elementary realism or good business sense. How else to get attention for one's product or one's art? How else to make a dent when there is incessant exposure to images, and overexposure to a handful of images seen again and again? The image as shock and the image as cliché are two aspects of the same presence. Sixty-five years ago, all photographs were novelties to some degree. (It would have been inconceivable to Virginia Woolf—who did appear on the cover of *Time* in 1937—that one day her face would become a much reproduced image on T-shirts, book bags, refrigerator magnets, coffee mugs, mouse pads.) Atrocity photographs were scarce in the winter of 1936–37: the depiction of war's horrors in the photographs Woolf discusses in *Three Guineas* seemed almost like clandestine knowledge. Our situation is altogether different. The ultra-familiar, ultra-celebrated image— of an agony, of ruin—is an unavoidable feature of our camera-mediated knowledge of war.

Photography has kept company with death ever since cameras were invented, in 1839. Because an image produced with a camera is, literally, a trace of something brought before the lens, photographs had an advantage over any painting as a memento of the vanished past and the dear departed. To seize death in the making was another matter: the camera's reach remained limited as long as it had to be lugged about, set down, steadied. But, once the camera was emancipated from the tripod, truly portable, and equipped with a range finder and a variety of lenses that permitted unprecedented feats of close observation from a distant vantage point, picture-taking acquired an immediacy and authority greater than any verbal account in conveying the horror of mass-produced death. If there was one year when the power of photographs to define, not merely record, the most abominable realities trumped all the complex narratives, surely it was 1945, with the pictures taken in April and early May in Bergen-Belsen, Buchenwald, and Dachau, in the first days after the camps were liberated, and those taken by Japanese witnesses such as Yosuke Yamahata in the days following the incineration of the populations of Hiroshima and Nagasaki, in early August.

Photographs had the advantage of uniting two contradictory features. Their credentials of objectivity were inbuilt, yet they always had, necessarily, a point of view. They were a record of the real— incontrovertible, as no verbal account, however impartial, could be (assuming that they showed what they purported to show)—since a machine was doing the recording. And they bore witness to the real, since a person had been there to take them.

The photographs Woolf received are treated as windows on the war: transparent views of what they show. It was of no interest to her that each had an "author"—that photographs represent the view of someone—although it was precisely in the late nineteen-thirties that the profession of bearing individual witness to war and war's atrocities with a camera was forged. Before, war photography had mostly appeared in daily and weekly newspapers. (Newspapers had been printing photographs since 1880.) By 1938, in addition to the older popular magazines that used photographs as illustrations—such as *National Geographic* and *Berliner Illustrierte Zeitung*, both founded in the late nineteenth century —there were large-circulation weekly magazines, notably the French *Vu*, the American *Life*, and the British *Picture Post*, devoted entirely to pictures (accompanied by brief texts keyed to the photos) and "picture stories" (four or five pictures by the same photographer attached to a story that further dramatized the images); in a newspaper, it was the photograph —and there was only one—that accompanied the story.

In a system based on the maximal reproduction and diffusion of images, witnessing requires star witnesses, renowned for their bravery and zeal. War photographers inherited what glamour going to war still had among the anti-bellicose, especially when the war was felt to be one of those rare conflicts in which someone of conscience would be impelled to take sides. In contrast to the 1914–18 war, which, it was clear to many of the victors, had been a colossal mistake, the second "world war" was unanimously felt by the winning side to have been a necessary war, a war that had to be fought. Photojournalism came into its own in the early nineteen-forties — wartime. This least controversial of modern wars, whose necessity was sealed by the full revelation of Nazi infamy in Europe, offered photojournalists a new legitimacy. There was little place for the left-wing dissidence that had informed much of the serious use of photographs in the interwar period, including Friedrich's *War Against War!* and the early work of Robert Capa, the most celebrated figure in a generation of politically engaged photographers whose work centered on war and victimhood.

In 1947, Capa and a few friends formed a coöperative, the Magnum Photo Agency. Magnum's charter, moralistic in the way of the founding charters of other international organizations and guilds created in the immediate postwar period, spelled out an enlarged, ethically weighted mission for photojournalists: to chronicle their own time as fair-minded witnesses free of chauvinistic prejudices. In Magnum's voice, photography declared itself a global enterprise. The photographer's beat was "the world." He or she was a rover, with wars of unusual interest (for there were many wars) a favorite destination.

The memory of war, however, like all memory, is mostly local. Armenians, the majority in diaspora, keep alive the memory of the Armenian genocide of 1915; Greeks don't forget the sanguinary civil war in Greece that raged through most of the second half of the nineteen-forties. But for a war to break out of its immediate constituency and become a subject of international attention it must be regarded as something of an exception, as wars go, and represent more than the clashing interests of the belligerents themselves. Apart from the major world conflicts, most wars do not acquire the requisite fuller meaning. An example: the Chaco War (1932–35), a butchery engaged in by Bolivia (population one million) and Paraguay (three and a half million) that took the lives of a hundred thousand soldiers, and which was covered by a German photojournalist, Willi Ruge, whose superb closeup battle pictures are as forgotten as that war. But the Spanish Civil War, in the second half of the nineteen-thirties, the Serb and Croat wars against Bosnia in the mid-nineties, the drastic worsening of the Israeli-Palestinian conflict that began in 2000—these relatively small wars were guaranteed the attention of many cameras because they were invested with the meaning of larger struggles: the Spanish Civil War because it was a stand against the Fascist menace, and was understood to be a dress rehearsal for the coming European, or "world," war; the Bosnian war because it was the stand of a small, fledgling European country wishing to remain multicultural as well as independent against the dominant power in the region and its neo-Fascist program of ethnic cleansing; and the conflict in the Middle East because the United States supports the State of Israel. Indeed, it is felt by many who champion the Palestinian side that what is ultimately at stake, by proxy, in the struggle to end the Israeli domination of the territories captured in 1967 is the strength of the forces opposing the juggernaut of American-sponsored globalization, economic and cultural.

The memorable sites of suffering documented by admired photographers in the nineteen-fifties, sixties, and early seventies were mostly in Asia and Africa— Werner Bischof's photographs of famine victims in India, Don McCullin's pictures of war and famine in Biafra, W. Eugene Smith's photographs of the victims of the lethal pollution of a Japanese fishing village. The Indian and African famines were not just "natural" disasters: they were preventable; they were crimes of the greatest magnitude. And what happened in Minamata was obviously a crime; the Chisso Corporation knew that it was dumping mercuryladen waste into the bay. (Smith was severely and permanently injured by Chisso goons who were ordered to put an end to his camera inquiry.) But war is the largest crime, and, starting in the mid-sixties, most of the best-known photographers covering wars set out to show war's "real" face. The color photographs of tormented Vietnamese villagers and wounded American conscripts that Larry Burrows took and *Life* published, starting in 1962, certainly fortified the outcry against the American presence in Vietnam. Burrows was the first important photographer to do a whole war in color—another gain in verisimilitude and shock.

In the current political mood, the friendliest to the military in decades, the pictures of wretched hollow-eyed G.I.s that once seemed subversive of militarism and imperialism may seem inspirational. Their revised subject: ordinary American young men doing their unpleasant, ennobling duty.

III

The iconography of suffering has a long pedigree. The suffering most often deemed worthy of representation is that which is understood to be the product of wrath, divine or human. (Suffering brought on by natural causes, such as illness or childbirth, is scantily represented in the history of art; that brought on by accident virtually not at all—as if there were no such thing as suffering by inadvertence or misadventure.) The statue group of the writhing Laocoön and his sons, the innumerable versions in painting and sculpture of the Passion of Christ, and the immense visual catalogue of the fiendish executions of the Christian martyrs— these are surely intended to move and excite, to instruct and exemplify. The viewer may commiserate with the sufferer's pain—and, in the case of the Christian saints, feel admonished or inspired by model faith and fortitude— but these are destinies beyond deploring or contesting.

It seems that the appetite for pictures showing bodies in pain is almost as keen as the desire for ones that show bodies naked. For a long time, in Christian art, depictions of Hell offered both of these elemental satisfactions. On occasion, the pretext might be a Biblical decapitation story (Holofernes, John the Baptist) or massacre yarn (the newborn Hebrew boys, the eleven thousand virgins) or some such, with the status of a real historical event and of an implacable fate. There was also the repertoire of hard-to-look-at cruelties from classical antiquity —the pagan myths, even more than the Christian stories, offer something for every taste. No moral charge attaches to the representation of these cruelties. Just the provocation: Can you look at this? There is the satisfaction at being able to look at the image without flinching. There is the pleasure of flinching.

To shudder at Goltzius's rendering, in his etching "The Dragon Devouring the Companions of Cadmus" (1588), of a man's face being chewed off his head is very different from shuddering at a photograph of a First

World War veteran whose face has been shot away. One horror has its place in a complex subject— figures in a landscape—that displays the artist's skill of eye and hand. The other is a camera's record, from very near, of a real person's unspeakably awful mutilation; that and nothing else. An invented horror can be quite overwhelming. (I, for one, find it difficult to look at Titian's great painting of the flaying of Marsyas, or, indeed, at any picture of this subject.) But there is shame as well as shock in looking at the closeup of a real horror. Perhaps the only people with the right to look at images of suffering of this extreme order are those who could do something to alleviate it—say, the surgeons at the military hospital where the photograph was taken—or those who could learn from it. The rest of us are voyeurs, whether we like it or not.

In each instance, the gruesome invites us to be either spectators or cowards, unable to look. Those with the stomach to look are playing a role authorized by many glorious depictions of suffering. Torment, a canonical subject in art, is often represented in painting as a spectacle, something being watched (or ignored) by other people. The implication is: No, it cannot be stopped—and the mingling of inattentive with attentive onlookers underscores this.

The practice of representing atrocious suffering as something to be deplored, and, if possible, stopped, enters the history of images with a specific subject: the sufferings endured by a civilian population at the hands of a victorious army on the rampage. It is a quintessentially secular subject, which emerges in the seventeenth century, when contemporary realignments of power become material for artists. In 1633, Jacques Callot published a suite of eighteen etchings titled *The Miseries and Misfortunes of War*, which depicted the atrocities committed against civilians by French troops during the invasion and occupation of his native Lorraine in the early sixteen-thirties. (Six small etchings on the same subject that Callot had executed prior to the large series appeared in 1635, the year of his death.) The view is wide and deep; these are scenes with many figures, scenes from a history, and each caption is a sententious comment in verse on the various energies and dooms portrayed in the images. Callot begins with a plate showing the recruitment of soldiers; brings into view ferocious combat, massacre, pillage, and rape, the engines of torture and execution (strappado, gallows tree, firing squad, stake, wheel), and the revenge of the peasants on the soldiers; and ends with a distribution of rewards. The insistence in plate after plate on the savagery of a conquering army is startling and without precedent, but the French soldiers are only the leading malefactors in the orgy of violence, and there is room in Callot's Christian humanist sensibility not just to mourn the end of the independent Duchy of Lorraine but to record the postwar plight of destitute soldiers who squat on the side of the road, begging for alms.

Callot had his successors, such as Hans Ulrich Franck, a minor German artist who, in 1643, toward the end of the Thirty Years' War, began making what would be (by 1656) a suite of twenty-five etchings depicting soldiers killing peasants. But the preëminent concentration on the horrors of war and the vileness of soldiers run amok is Goya's, in the early nineteenth century. *The Disasters of War*, a numbered sequence of eighty-three etchings made between 1810 and 1820 (and first published, except for three plates, in 1863, thirty-five years after his death), depicts the atrocities perpetrated by Napoleon's soldiers, who invaded Spain in 1808 to quell the insurrection against French rule. Goya's images move the viewer close to the horror. All the trappings of the spectacular have been eliminated: the landscape is an atmosphere, a darkness, barely sketched in. War is not a spectacle. And Goya's print series is not a narrative: each image, captioned with a brief phrase lamenting the wickedness of the invaders and the monstrousness of the suffering they inflicted, stands independent of the others. The cumulative effect is devastating.

"Some freshly mined salt?"

The ghoulish cruelties in *The Disasters of War* are meant to awaken, shock, wound the viewer. Goya's art, like Dostoyevsky's, seems a turning point in the history of moral feelings and of sorrow —as deep, as original, as demanding. With Goya, a new standard for responsiveness to suffering enters art. (And new subjects for fellow-feeling: for example, the painting of an injured laborer being carried away from a construction site.) The account of war's cruelties is constructed as an assault on the sensibility of the viewer. The expressive phrases in script below each image comment on the provocation. While the image, like all images, is an invitation to look, the caption, more often than not, insists on the difficulty of doing just that. A voice, presumably the artist's, badgers the viewer: Can you bear this? One caption declares, "*No se puede mirar*" ("One can't look"). Another says, "*Esto es malo*" ("This is bad"). "*Esto es peor*" ("This is worse"), another retorts.

The caption of a photograph is traditionally neutral, informative: a date, a place, names. A reconnaissance photograph from the First World War (the first war in which cameras were used extensively for military intelligence) was unlikely to be captioned "Can't wait to overrun this!" or the X-ray of a multiple fracture to be annotated "Patient will probably have a limp!" It seems no less inappropriate to speak for the photograph in the photographer's voice, offering assurances of the image's veracity, as Goya does in *The Disasters of War*, writing beneath one image, "*Yo lo vi*" ("I saw this"). And beneath another, "*Esto es lo verdadero*" ("This is the truth"). Of course the photographer saw it. And, unless there's been some tampering or misrepresenting, it is the truth.

Ordinary language fixes the difference between handmade images like Goya's and photographs through the convention that artists "make" drawings and paintings while photographers "take" photographs. But the photographic image, even to the extent that it is a trace (not a construction made out of disparate photographic traces), cannot be simply a transparency of something that happened. It is always the image that someone chose; to photograph is to frame, and to frame is to exclude. Moreover, fiddling with the picture long antedates the era of digital photography and Photoshop manipulations: it has always been possible for a photograph to misrepresent. A painting or drawing is judged a fake when it turns out not to be by the artist to whom it had been attributed. A photograph— or a filmed document available on television or the Internet —is judged a fake when it turns out to be deceiving the viewer about the scene it purports to depict.

That the atrocities perpetrated by Napoleon's soldiers in Spain didn't happen exactly as Goya drew them hardly disqualifies *The Disasters of War*. Goya's images are a synthesis. Things *like* this happened. In contrast, a single photograph or filmstrip claims to represent exactly what was before the camera's lens. A photograph is supposed not to evoke but to show. That is why photographs, unlike handmade images, can count as evidence. But evidence of what? The suspicion that Capa's "Death of a Republican Soldier"—recently retitled "The Falling Soldier," in the authoritative compilation of Capa's work—may not show what it has always been said to show continues to haunt discussions of war photography. Everyone is a literalist when it comes to photographs.

Images of the sufferings endured in war are so widely disseminated now that it is easy to forget that, historically, photographers have offered mostly positive images of the warrior's trade, and of the satisfactions of starting a war or continuing to fight one. If governments had their way, war photography, like much war poetry, would drum up support for soldiers' sacrifices. Indeed, war photography begins with such a mission, such a disgrace. The war was the Crimean War, and the photographer, Roger Fenton, invariably called the first war photographer, was no less than that war's "official" photographer, having been sent to the Crimea in early 1855 by the British government, at the instigation of Prince Albert. Acknowledging the need to counteract the alarming printed accounts of the dangers and privations endured by the British soldiers dispatched there the previous year, the government invited a well-known professional photographer to give another, more positive impression of the increasingly unpopular war.

Edmund Gosse, in *Father and Son*, his memoir of a mid-nineteenth-century English childhood, relates how the Crimean War penetrated even his stringently pious, unworldly family, which belonged to an evangelical sect called the Plymouth Brethren: "The declaration of war with Russia brought the first breath of outside life into our Calvinist cloister. My parents took in a daily newspaper, which they had never done before, and events in picturesque places, which my Father and I looked out on the map, were eagerly discussed." War was, and still is, the most irresistible—and picturesque— news, along with that invaluable substitute for war, international sports. But this war was more than news. It was bad news. The authoritative, pictureless London newspaper to which Gosse's parents had succumbed, the *Times*, attacked the military leadership whose incompetence was responsible for the war's dragging on, with so much loss of British life. The toll on the soldiers from causes other than combat was horrendous— twenty-two thousand died of illnesses; many thousands lost limbs to frostbite during the long Russian winter of the protracted siege of Sebastopol—and several of the military engagements were disasters. It was still winter when Fenton arrived in the Crimea for a four-month stay, having contracted to publish his photographs (in the form of engravings) in a less venerable and less critical weekly paper,

the *Illustrated London News*, exhibit them in a gallery, and market them as a book upon his return home.

Under instructions from the War Office not to photograph the dead, the maimed, or the ill, and precluded from photographing most other subjects by the cumbersome technology of picture-taking, Fenton went about rendering the war as a dignified all-male group outing. With each image requiring a separate chemical preparation in the darkroom and a long exposure time, he could photograph British officers in open-air staff meetings or common soldiers tending the cannons only after asking them to stand or sit together, follow his directions, and hold still. His pictures are tableaux of military life behind the front lines; the war—movement, disorder, drama—stays off-camera. The one photograph Fenton took in the Crimea that reaches beyond benign documentation is "The Valley of the Shadow of Death," whose title evokes the consolation offered by the Biblical Psalmist as well as the disaster in which six hundred British soldiers were ambushed on the plain above Balaklava—Tennyson called the site "the valley of Death" in his memorial poem, "The Charge of the Light Brigade." Fenton's memorial photograph is a portrait of absence, of death without the dead. It is the only photograph that would not have needed to be staged, for all it shows is a wide rutted road, studded with rocks and cannonballs, that curves onward across a barren rolling plain to the distant void.

A bolder portfolio of after-the-battle images of death and ruin, pointing not to losses suffered but to a fearsome British triumph over the enemy, was made by another photographer who had visited the Crimean War. Felice Beato, a naturalized Englishman (he was born in Venice), was the first photographer to attend a number of wars: besides being in the Crimea in 1855, he was at the Sepoy Rebellion (what the British call the Indian Mutiny) in 1857–58, the Second Opium War in China, in 1860, and the Sudanese colonial wars in 1885. Three years after Fenton made his anodyne images of a war that did not go well for England, Beato was celebrating the fierce victory of the British Army over a mutiny of native soldiers under its command, the first important challenge to British rule in India. Beato's "Ruins of Sikandarbagh Palace," an arresting photograph of a palace in Lucknow that has been gutted by bombardment, shows the courtyard strewn with the rebels' bones.

The first full-scale attempt to document a war was carried out a few years later, during the American Civil War, by a firm of Northern photographers headed by Mathew Brady, who had made several official portraits of President Lincoln. The Brady war pictures— most were shot by Alexander Gardner and Timothy O'Sullivan, although their employer was invariably credited with them—showed conventional subjects, such as encampments populated by officers and foot soldiers, towns in war's way, ordnance, ships, and also, most famously, dead Union and Confederate soldiers lying on the blasted ground of Gettysburg and Antietam. Though access to the battlefield came as a privilege extended to Brady and his team by Lincoln himself, the photographers were not commissioned, as Fenton had been. Their status evolved in rather typical American fashion, with nominal government sponsorship giving way to the force of entrepreneurial and freelance motives.

The first justification for the brutally legible pictures of a field of dead soldiers was the simple duty to record. "The camera is the eye of history," Brady is supposed to have said. And history, invoked as truth beyond appeal, was allied with the rising prestige of a certain notion of subjects needing more attention, known as realism, which was soon to have a host of defenders among novelists as well as photographers. In the name of realism, one was permitted—required— to show unpleasant, hard facts. Such pictures also convey "a useful moral" by showing "the blank horror and reality of war, in opposition to

its pageantry," as Gardner wrote in a text accompanying O'Sullivan's picture of fallen Confederate soldiers, their agonized faces clearly visible. "Here are the dreadful details! Let them aid in preventing another such calamity falling upon the nation." But the frankness of the most memorable pictures in an album of photographs by Gardner and other Brady photographers, which Gardner published after the war, did not mean that he and his colleagues had necessarily photographed their subjects as they found them. To photograph was to compose (with living subjects, to pose); the desire to arrange elements in the picture did not vanish because the subject was immobilized, or immobile.

Not surprisingly, many of the canonical images of early war photography turn out to have been staged, or to have had their subjects tampered with. Roger Fenton, after reaching the much shelled valley near Sebastopol in his horse-drawn darkroom, made two exposures from the same tripod position: in the first version of the celebrated photograph he was to call "The Valley of the Shadow of Death" (despite the title, it was not across this landscape that the Light Brigade made its doomed charge), the cannonballs are thick on the ground to the left of the road; before taking the second picture—the one that is always reproduced—he oversaw the scattering of cannonballs on the road itself. A picture of a desolate site where a great deal of dying had indeed recently taken place, Beato's "Ruins of Sikandarbagh Palace," involved a more thorough theatricalization of its subject, and was one of the first attempts to suggest with a camera the horrific in war. The attack occurred in November, 1857, after which the victorious British troops and loyal Indian units searched the palace room by room, bayoneting the eighteen hundred surviving Sepoy defenders who were now their prisoners and throwing their bodies into the courtyard; vultures and dogs did the rest. For the photograph he took in March or April, 1858, Beato constructed the courtyard as a deathscape, stationing some natives by two pillars in the rear and distributing human bones about the foreground.

At least they were old bones. It's now known that the Brady team rearranged and displaced some of the recently dead at Gettysburg; the picture titled "The Home of a Rebel Sharpshooter, Gettysburg" in fact shows a dead Confederate soldier who was moved from where he had fallen on the field to a more photogenic site, a cove formed by several boulders flanking a barricade of rocks, and includes a prop rifle that Gardner leaned against the barricade beside the corpse. (It seems not to have been the special rifle a sharpshooter would have used, but a common infantryman's rifle; Gardner didn't know this or didn't care.)

Only starting with the Vietnam War can we be virtually certain that none of the best-known photographs were setups. And this is essential to the moral authority of these images. The signature Vietnam War horror photograph, from 1972, taken by Huynh Cong Ut, of children from a village that has just been doused with American napalm running down the highway, shrieking with pain, belongs to the universe of photographs that cannot possibly be posed. The same is true of the well-known pictures from the most widely photographed wars since.

That there have been so few staged war photographs since the Vietnam War probably should not be attributed to higher standards of journalistic probity. One part of the explanation is that it was in Vietnam that television became the defining medium for showing images of war, and the intrepid lone photographer, Nikon or Leica in hand, operating out of sight much of the time, now had to compete with, and endure the proximity of, TV crews. There are always witnesses to a filming. Technically, the possibilities for doctoring or electronically manipulating pictures are greater than ever—almost unlimited. But the practice of inventing dramatic news pictures, staging them for the camera, seems on its way to becoming a lost art.

IV

Central to modern expectations, and modern ethical feeling, is the conviction that war is an aberration, if an unstoppable one. That peace is the norm, if an unattainable one. This, of course, is not the way war has been regarded throughout history. War has been the norm and peace the exception.

Descriptions of the exact fashion in which bodies are injured and killed in combat is a recurring climax in the stories told in the *Iliad*. War is seen as something men do, inveterately, undeterred by the accumulation of suffering it inflicts; to represent war in words or in pictures requires a keen, unflinching detachment. When Leonardo da Vinci gives instructions for a battle painting, his worry is that artists will lack the courage or the imagination to show war in all its ghastliness: "Make the conquered and beaten pale, with brows raised and knit, and the skin above their brows furrowed with pain. . .and the teeth apart as with crying out in lamentation.. . . Make the dead partly or entirely covered with dust. . .and let the blood be seen by its color flowing in a sinuous stream from the corpse to the dust. Others in the death agony grinding their teeth, rolling their eyes, with their fists clenched against their bodies, and the legs distorted." The concern is that the images won't be sufficiently upsetting: not concrete, not detailed enough.

Pity can entail a moral judgment if, as Aristotle suggests, pity is considered to be the emotion that we owe only to those enduring undeserved misfortune. But pity, far from being the natural twin of fear in the dramas of catastrophic misfortune, seems diluted—distracted—by fear, while fear (dread, terror) usually manages to swamp pity. Leonardo is suggesting that the artist's gaze be, literally, pitiless. The image should appall, and in that *terribilità* lies a challenging kind of beauty.

That a gory battlescape could be beautiful—in the sublime or awesome or tragic register of the beautiful—is a commonplace about images of war made by artists. The idea does not sit well when applied to images taken by cameras: to find beauty in war photographs seems heartless. But the landscape of devastation is still a landscape. There is beauty in ruins. To acknowledge the beauty of photographs of the World Trade Center ruins in the months following the attack seemed frivolous, sacrilegious. The most people dared say was that the photographs were "surreal," a hectic euphemism behind which the disgraced notion of beauty cowered. But they *were* beautiful, many of them—by veteran photographers such as Gilles Peress, Susan Meiselas, and Joel Meyerowitz and by many little-known and nonprofessional photographers. The site itself, the mass graveyard that had received the name Ground Zero, was, of course, anything but beautiful. Photographs tend to transform, whatever their subject; and as an image something may be beautiful—or terrifying, or unbearable, or quite bearable—as it is not in real life.

Transforming is what art does, but photography that bears witness to the calamitous and the reprehensible is much criticized if it seems "aesthetic"; that is, too much like art. The dual powers of photography—to generate documents and to create works of visual art—have produced some remarkable exaggerations about what photographers ought or ought not to do. These days, most exaggerations is of the puritanical kind. Photographs that depict suffering shouldn't be beautiful, as captions shouldn't moralize. In this view, a beautiful photograph drains attention from the sobering subject and turns it toward the medium itself, inviting the viewer to look "aesthetically," and thereby compromising the picture's status as a document. The photograph gives mixed signals. Stop this, it urges. But it also exclaims, What a spectacle!

Take one of the most poignant images from the First World War: a column of English soldiers blinded by poison gas—each rests his hand on the shoulder of the man ahead of him— stumbling toward a dressing station. It could be an image from one of the searing movies made about the war—King Vidor's *The Big Parade*, of 1925, or G. W. Pabst's *Westfront 1918*, Lewis Milestone's *All Quiet on the Western Front*, and Howard Hawks's *Dawn Patrol*, all from 1930. The way in which still photography finds its perfection in the reconstruction of battle scenes in the great war movies has begun to backfire on the photography of war. What assured the authenticity of Steven Spielberg's much admired re-creation of the Omaha Beach landing on D Day in *Saving Private Ryan* (1998) was that it was based on, among other sources, the photographs taken with immense bravery by Robert Capa during the landing. But a war photograph seems inauthentic, even though there is nothing staged about it, when it looks like a still from a movie. Sebasti???ao Salgado, a photographer who specializes in world misery (including but not restricted to the effects of war), has been the principal target of the new campaign against the inauthenticity of the beautiful. Particularly with the seven-year project he calls "Migrations: Humanity in Transition," Salgado has come under steady attack for producing spectacular, beautifully composed big pictures that are said to be "cinematic."

The sanctimonious Family of Manstyle rhetoric that accompanies Salgado's exhibitions and books has worked to the detriment of the pictures, however unfair this may be. The pictures have also been sourly treated in response to the highly commercialized situations in which, typically, Salgado's portraits of misery are seen. But the problem is in the pictures themselves, not the way they are exhibited: in their focus on the powerless, reduced to their powerlessness. It is significant that the powerless are not named in the captions. A portrait that declines to name its subject becomes complicit, if inadvertently, in the cult of celebrity that has fuelled an insatiable appetite for the opposite sort of photograph: to grant only the famous their names demotes the rest to representative instances of their occupations, their ethnicities, their plights. Taken in thirty-five countries, Salgado's migration pictures group together, under this single heading, a host of different causes and kinds of distress. Making suffering loom larger, by globalizing it, may spur people to feel they ought to "care" more. It also invites them to feel that the sufferings and misfortunes are too vast, too irrevocable, too epic to be much changed by any local, political intervention. With a subject conceived on this scale, compassion can only flounder—and make abstract. But all politics, like all history, is concrete.

It used to be thought, when candid images were not common, that showing something that needed to be seen, bringing a painful reality closer, was bound to goad viewers to feel—feel more. In a world in which photography is brilliantly at the service of consumerist manipulations, this naïve relation to poignant scenes of suffering is much less plausible. Morally alert photographers and ideologues of photography are concerned with the issues of exploitation of sentiment (pity, compassion, indignation) in war photography, and how to avoid rote ways of arousing feeling.

Photographer-witnesses may try to make the spectacular *not* spectacular. But their efforts can never cancel the tradition in which suffering has been understood throughout most of Western history. To feel the pulse of Christian iconography in certain wartime or disaster-time photographs is not a sentimental projection. It would be hard not to discern the lineaments of the Pietà in W. Eugene Smith's picture of a woman in Minamata cradling her deformed, blind, and deaf daughter, or the template of the Descent from the Cross in several of Don McCullin's pictures of dying American soldiers in Vietnam.

The problem is not that people remember through photographs but that they remember only the photographs. This remembering through photographs eclipses other forms of understanding —and remembering. The concentration camps—that is, the photographs taken when the camps were liberated, in 1945—are most of what people associate with

Nazism and the miseries of the Second World War. Hideous deaths (by genocide, starvation, and epidemic) are most of what people retain of the clutch of iniquities and failures that have taken place in postcolonial Africa.

To remember is, more and more, not to recall a story but to be able to call up a picture. Even a writer as steeped in nineteenth-century and early-modern literary solemnities as W. G. Sebald was moved to seed his lamentation-narratives of lost lives, lost nature, lost cityscapes with photographs. Sebald was not just an elegist; he was a militant elegist. Remembering, he wanted the reader to remember, too.

Harrowing photographs do not inevitably lose their power to shock. But they don't help us much to understand. Narratives can make us understand. Photographs do something else: they haunt us. Consider one of the most unforgettable images of the war in Bosnia, a photograph of which the *New York Times* foreign correspondent John Kifner wrote, "The image is stark, one of the most enduring of the Balkan wars: a Serb militiaman casually kicking a dying Muslim woman in the head. It tells you everything you need to know." But of course it doesn't tell us everything we need to know.

From the identification supplied by the photographer, Ron Haviv, we learn that the photograph was taken in the town of Bijeljina in April, 1992, the first month of the Serb rampage through Bosnia. From behind, we see a uniformed Serb soldier, a youthful figure with sunglasses perched on the top of his head, a cigarette between the second and third fingers of his raised left hand, rifle dangling in his right hand, right leg poised to kick a woman lying face down on the sidewalk between two other bodies. The photograph doesn't tell us that she is Muslim, but she is not likely to have been labelled in any other way, or why would she and the two others be lying there, as if dead (why "dying"?), under the gaze of some Serb soldiers? In fact, the photograph tells us very little—except that war is hell, and that graceful young men with guns are capable of kicking in the head overweight older women lying helpless, or already killed.

The pictures of Bosnian atrocities were seen soon after they took place. Like pictures from the Vietnam War, such as Ron Haberle's documents of the massacre by a company of American soldiers of some five hundred unarmed civilians in the village of My Lai in March, 1968, they became important in bolstering indignation at this war which had been far from inevitable, far from intractable; and could have been stopped much sooner. Therefore one could feel an obligation to look at these pictures, gruesome as they were, because there was something to be done, right now, about what they depicted. Other issues are raised when the public is invited to respond to a dossier of hitherto unknown pictures of horrors long past.

An example: a trove of photographs of black victims of lynching in small towns in the United States between the eighteen-nineties and the nineteen-thirties, which provided a shattering, revelatory experience for the thousands who saw them in a gallery in New York in 2000. The lynching pictures tell us about human wickedness. About inhumanity. They force us to think about the extent of the evil unleashed specifically by racism. Intrinsic to the perpetration of this evil is the shamelessness of photographing it. The pictures were taken as souvenirs and made, some of them, into postcards; more than a few show grinning spectators, good churchgoing citizens, as most of them had to be, posing for a camera with the backdrop of a naked, charred, mutilated body hanging from a tree. The display of the pictures makes us spectators, too.

What is the point of exhibiting these pictures? To awaken indignation? To make us feel "bad"; that is, to appall and sadden? To help us mourn? Is looking at such pictures really necessary, given that these horrors lie in a past remote enough to be beyond punishment? Are we the better for seeing these images? Do they actually teach us anything?

Don't they rather just confirm what we already know (or want to know)?

All these questions were raised at the time of the exhibition and afterward when a book of the photographs, *Without Sanctuary*, was published. Some people, it was said, might dispute the need for this grisly photographic display, lest it cater to voyeuristic appetites and perpetuate images of black victimization— or simply numb the mind. Nevertheless, it was argued, there is an obligation to "examine"—the more clinical "examine" is substituted for "look at"—the pictures. It was further argued that submitting to the ordeal should help us understand such atrocities not as the acts of "barbarians" but as the reflection of a belief system, racism, that by defining one people as less human than another legitimizes torture and murder. But maybe they *were* barbarians. Maybe *this* is what barbarians look like. (They look like everybody else.)

That being said, whom do we wish to blame? More precisely, whom do we believe we have the right to blame? The children of Hiroshima and Nagasaki were no less innocent than the young African-American men (and a few women) who were butchered and hanged from trees in small-town America. More than a hundred thousand German civilians, three-fourths of them women, were incinerated in the R.A.F. fire bombing of Dresden on the night of February 13, 1945; seventy-two thousand civilians were killed by the American bomb dropped on Hiroshima. The roll call could be much longer. Again, whom do we wish to blame? What atrocities from the incurable past do we think we are obliged to see?

Probably, if we are Americans, we think that it would be "morbid" to go out of our way to look at pictures of burned victims of atomic bombing or the napalmed flesh of the civilian victims of the American war on Vietnam but that we have some kind of duty to look at the lynching pictures—if we belong to the party of the right-thinking, which on this issue is now large. A stepped-up recognition of the monstrousness of the slave system that once existed, unquestioned by most, in the United States is a national project of recent decades that many Euro-Americans feel some tug of obligation to join. This ongoing project is a great achievement, a benchmark of civic virtue. But acknowledgment of American use of disproportionate firepower in war (in violation of one of the cardinal laws of war) is very much not a national project. A museum devoted to the history of America's wars that included the vicious war the United States fought against guerrillas in the Philippines from 1899 to 1902 (expertly excoriated by Mark Twain), and that fairly presented the arguments for and against using the atomic bomb in 1945 on the Japanese cities, with photographic evidence that showed what those weapons did, would be regarded—now more than ever—as an unpatriotic endeavor.

V

Consider two widespread ideas— now fast approaching the stature of platitudes—on the impact of photography. Since I find these ideas formulated in my own essays on photography, the earliest of which was written thirty years ago, I feel an irresistible temptation to quarrel with them.

The first idea is that public attention is steered by the attentions of the media—which means images. When there are photographs, a war becomes "real." Thus, the protest against the Vietnam War was mobilized by images. The feeling that something had to be done about the war in Bosnia was built from the attentions of journalists: "the CNN effect," it was sometimes called, which brought images of Sarajevo under siege into hundreds of millions of living rooms night after night for more than three years. These examples illustrate the determining influence of photographs in shaping what catastrophes and crises we pay attention to, what we care about, and ultimately what evaluations are placed on these conflicts.

The second idea—it might seem the converse of what has just been described —is that in a world saturated, even hypersaturated, with images, those which should matter to us have a diminishing effect: we become callous. In the end, such images make us a little less able to feel, to have our conscience pricked.

In the first of the six essays in *On Photography*, which was published in 1977, I argued that while an event known through photographs certainly becomes more real than it would have been if one had never seen the photographs, after repeated exposure it also becomes less real. As much as they create sympathy, I wrote, photographs shrivel sympathy. Is this true? I thought it was when I wrote it. I'm not so sure now. What is the evidence that photographs have a diminishing impact, that our culture of spectacle neutralizes the moral force of photographs of atrocities?

The question turns on a view of the principal medium of the news, television. An image is drained of its force by the way it is used, where and how often it is seen. Images shown on television are, by definition, images of which, sooner or later, one tires. What looks like callousness has its origin in the instability of attention that television is organized to arouse and to satiate, by its surfeit of images. Image-glut keeps attention light, mobile, relatively indifferent to content. Image-flow precludes a privileged image. The whole point of television is that one can switch channels, that it is normal to switch channels: to become restless, bored. Consumers droop. They need to be restimulated, jump-started, again and again. Content is no more than one of these stimulants. A more reflective engagement with content would require a certain intensity of awareness—just what is weakened by the expectations brought to images disseminated by the media. The leaching out of content is what contributes most to the deadening of feeling.

The argument that modern life consists of a menu of horrors by which we are corrupted

154

and to which we gradually become habituated is a founding idea of the critique of modernity— a tradition almost as old as modernity itself. In 1800, Wordsworth, in the Preface to *Lyrical Ballads*, denounced the corruption of sensibility produced by "the great national events which are daily taking place, and the increasing accumulation of men in cities, where the uniformity of their occupations produces a craving for extraordinary incident, which the rapid communication of intelligence hourly gratifies." This process of overstimulation acts "to blunt the discriminating powers of the mind" and "reduce it to a state of almost savage torpor."

Wordsworth singled out the blunting of mind produced by "daily" events and "hourly" news of "extraordinary incident." (In 1800!) Exactly what kind of events and incidents was discreetly left to the reader's imagination. Some sixty years later, another great poet and cultural diagnostician—French, and therefore as licensed to be hyperbolic as the English are prone to understate—offered a more heated version of the same charge. Here is Baudelaire writing in his journal in the early eighteen-sixties: "It is impossible to glance through any newspaper, no matter what the day, the month or the year, without finding on every line the most frightful traces of human perversity.. . .Every newspaper, from the first line to the last, is nothing but a tissue of horrors. Wars, crimes, thefts, lecheries, tortures, the evil deeds of princes, of nations, of private individuals; an orgy of universal atrocity. And it is with this loathsome appetizer that civilized man daily washes down his morning repast."

Newspapers did not yet carry photographs when Baudelaire wrote. But this doesn't make his accusatory description of the bourgeois sitting down with his morning newspaper to breakfast with an array of the world's horrors any different from the contemporary critique of how much desensitizing horror we take in every day, via television as well as the morning paper. Newer technology provides a non-stop feed: as many images of disaster and atrocity as we can make time to look at.

Since *On Photography* was published, many critics have suggested that the agonies of war—thanks to television— have devolved into a nightly banality. Flooded with images of the sort that once used to shock and arouse indignation, we are losing our capacity to react. Compassion, stretched to its limits, is going numb. So runs the familiar diagnosis. But what is really being asked for here? That images of carnage be cut back to, say, once a week? More generally, that we work toward an "ecology of images," as I suggested in *On Photography*? But there *isn't* going to be an ecology of images. No Committee of Guardians is going to ration horror, to keep fresh its ability to shock. And the horrors themselves are not going to abate.

The view proposed in *On Photography* — that our capacity to respond to our experiences with emotional freshness and ethical pertinence is being sapped by the relentless diffusion of vulgar and appalling images— might be called the conservative critique of the diffusion of such images. I call this argument "conservative" because it is the sense of reality that is eroded. There is still a reality that exists independent of the attempts to weaken its authority. The argument is in fact a defense of reality and the imperilled standards for responding to it more fully. In the more radical—cynical—spin on this critique, there is nothing to defend, for, paradoxical as it may sound, there is no reality anymore. The vast maw of modernity has chewed up reality and spat the whole mess out as images. According to a highly influential analysis, we live in a "society of spectacle." Each thing has to be turned into a spectacle to be real— that is, interesting—to us. People themselves become images: celebrities. Reality has abdicated. There are only representations: media.

Fancy rhetoric, this. And very persuasive to many, because one of the characteristics of modernity is that people like to feel they can anticipate their own experience. (This view is associated in particular with the writings of the late Guy Debord, who thought he was describing an illusion, a hoax, and of Jean Baudrillard, who claims to believe that images, simulated realities, are all that exists now; it seems to be something of a French specialty.) It is common to say that war, like everything else that seems to be real, is *médiatique*. This was the diagnosis of several distinguished French day-trippers to Sarajevo during the siege, among them André Glucksmann: that the war would be won or lost not by anything that happened in Sarajevo, or Bosnia generally, but by what happened in the media. It is often asserted that "the West" has increasingly come to see war itself as a spectacle. Reports of the death of reality—like the death of reason, the death of the intellectual, the death of serious literature—seem to have been accepted without much reflection by many who are attempting to understand what feels wrong, or empty, or idiotically triumphant in contemporary politics and culture.

To speak of reality becoming a spectacle is a breathtaking provincialism. It universalizes the viewing habits of a small, educated population living in the rich part of the world, where news has been converted into entertainment—a mature style of viewing that is a prime acquisition of the "modern," and a prerequisite for dismantling traditional forms of party-based politics that offer real disagreement and debate. It assumes that everyone is a spectator. It suggests, perversely, unseriously, that there is no real suffering in the world. But it is absurd to identify "the world" with those zones in the rich countries where people have the dubious privilege of being spectators, or of declining to be spectators, of other people's pain, just as it is absurd to generalize about the ability to respond to the sufferings of others on the basis of the mind-set of those consumers of news who know nothing at first hand about war and terror. There are hundreds of millions of television watchers who are far from inured to what they see on television. They do not have the luxury of patronizing reality.

VI

Is there an antidote to the perennial seductiveness of war? And is this a question a woman is more likely to pose than a man? (Probably yes.)

Could one be mobilized actively to oppose war by an image (or a group of images), as one might be enrolled among the opponents of capital punishment by reading, say, Dreiser's *An American Tragedy* or Turgenev's "The Execution of Troppmann," an account of a night spent with a notorious criminal who is about to be guillotined? A narrative seems likely to be more effective than an image. Partly it is a question of the length of time one is obliged to look, and to feel. No photograph, or portfolio of photographs, can unfold, go further, and further still, as does *The Ascent* (1977), by the Ukrainian director Larisa Shepitko, the most affecting film about the horror of war I know.

Among single antiwar images, the huge photograph that Jeff Wall made in 1992 entitled "Dead Troops Talk (A vision after an ambush of a Red Army Patrol, near Moqor, Afghanistan, winter 1986)" seems to me exemplary in its thoughtfulness, coherence, and passion. The antithesis of a document, the picture, a Cibachrome transparency seven and a half feet high and more than thirteen feet wide and mounted on a light box, shows figures posed in a landscape, a blasted hillside, that was constructed in the artist's studio. Wall, who is Canadian, was never in Afghanistan. The ambush is a made-up event in a conflict he had read about. His imagination of war (he cites Goya as an inspiration) is in the tradition of nineteenth-century history painting and other forms of history-as-spectacle that emerged in the late eighteenth and early nineteenth centuries—just before the invention of the camera—such as tableaux vivants, wax displays, dioramas, and panoramas, which made the past, especially the immediate past, seem astonishingly, disturbingly real.

The figures in Wall's visionary photowork are "realistic," but, of course, the image is not. Dead soldiers don't talk. Here they do.

Thirteen Russian soldiers in bulky winter uniforms and high boots are scattered about a pocked, blood-splashed pit lined with loose rocks and the litter of war: shell casings, crumpled metal, a boot that holds the lower part of a leg. The soldiers, slaughtered in the Soviet Union's own late folly of a colonial war, were never buried. A few still have their helmets on. The head of one kneeling figure, talking animatedly, foams with his red brain matter. The atmosphere is warm, convivial, fraternal. Some slouch, leaning on an elbow, or sit, chatting, their opened skulls and destroyed hands on view. One man bends over another, who lies on his side in a posture of heavy sleep, perhaps encouraging him to sit up. Three men are horsing around: one with a huge wound in his belly straddles another, who is lying prone, while the third, kneeling, dangles what might be a watch before the laughing man on his stomach. One soldier, helmeted, legless, has turned to a comrade some distance away, an alert smile on his face. Below him are two who don't seem quite up to the resurrection and lie supine, their bloodied heads hanging down the stony incline.

Engulfed by the image, which is so accusatory, one could fantasize that the soldiers might turn and talk to us. But no, no one is looking out of the picture at the viewer. There's no threat of protest. They're not about to yell at us to bring a halt to that abomination which is war. They are not represented as terrifying to others, for among them (far left) sits a white-garbed Afghan scavenger, entirely absorbed in going through somebody's kit bag, of whom they take no note, and entering the picture above them (top right), on the path winding down the slope, are two Afghans, perhaps soldiers themselves, who, it would seem from the Kalashnikovs collected near their feet, have already stripped the dead soldiers of their weapons. These dead are supremely uninterested in the living: in those who took their lives; in witnesses—or in us. Why should they seek our gaze? What would they have to say to us? "We"— this "we" is everyone who has never experienced anything like what they went through—don't understand. We don't get it. We truly can't imagine how dreadful, how terrifying war is— and how normal it becomes. Can't understand, can't imagine. That's what every soldier, and every journalist and aid worker and independent observer who has put in time under fire and had the luck to elude the death that struck down others nearby, stubbornly feels. And they are right. ♦

LAUGHING WITH KAFKA

David Foster Wallace

One reason for my willingness to speak publicly on a subject for which I am sort of under qualified is that it affords me a chance to declaim for you a short story of Kafka's that I have given up teaching in literature classes and miss getting to read aloud. Its English title is "A Little Fable":

"Alas," said the mouse, "the world is growing smaller every day. At the beginning it was so big that I was afraid, I kept running and running, and I was glad when at last I saw walls far away to the right and left, but these long walls have narrowed so quickly that I am in the last chamber already, and there in the corner stands the trap that I must run into." "You only need to change your direction," said the cat, and ate it up.

For me, a signal frustration in trying to read Kafka with college students is that it is next to impossible to get them to see that Kafka is funny . . . Nor to appreciate the way funniness is bound up with the extraordinary power of his stories. Because, of course, great short stories and great jokes have a lot in common. Both depend on what communication-theorists sometimes call "exformation," which is a certain quantity of vital information *removed from* but *evoked by* a communication in such a way as to cause a kind of explosion of associative con-

nections within the recipient. This is probably why the effect of both short stories and jokes often feels sudden and percussive, like the venting of a long-stuck valve. It's not for nothing that Kafka spoke of literature as "a hatchet with which we chop at the frozen seas inside us." Nor is it an accident that the technical achievement of great short stories is often called "compression"—for both the pressure and the release are already inside the reader. What Kafka seems able to do better than just about anyone else is to orchestrate the pressure's increase in such a way that it becomes intolerable at the precise instant it is released.

The psychology of jokes helps account for part of the problem in teaching Kafka. We all know that there is no quicker way to empty a joke of its peculiar magic than to try to explain it—to point out, for example, that Lou Costello is mistaking the proper name "Who" for the interrogative pronoun "who," etc. We all know the weird antipathy such explanations arouse in us, a feeling not so much of boredom as offence, like something has been blasphemed. This is a lot like the teacher's feeling at running a Kafka story through the gears of your standard undergrad-course literary analysis—plot to chart, symbols to decode, etc. Kafka, of

159

course, would be in a unique position to appreciate the irony of submitting his short stories to this kind of high-efficiency critical machine, the literary equivalent of tearing the petals off and grinding them up and running the goo through a spectrometer to explain why a rose smells so pretty.[1] Franz Kafka, after all, is the writer whose story "Poseidon" imagines a sea-god so overwhelmed with administrative paperwork that he never gets to sail or swim, and whose "In the Penal Colony" conceives description as punishment and torture as edification and the ultimate critic as a needled harrow whose *coup de grâce* is a spike through the forehead.

Another handicap, even for gifted students, is that—unlike, say, Joyce's or Pound's—the exformative associations Kafka's work creates are not intertextual or even historical. Kafka's evocations are, rather, unconscious and almost *sub*-archetypal, the little-kid stuff from which myths derive; this is why we tend to call even his weirdest stories *nightmarish* rather than *surreal*. Not to mention that the particular sort of funniness Kafka deploys is deeply alien to kids whose neural resonances are American. The fact is that Kafka's humor has almost none of the particular forms and codes of contemporary U.S. amusement. There's no recursive wordplay or verbal stunt-pilotry, little in the way of wisecracks or mordant lampoon. There is no body-function humor in Kafka, nor sexual entendre, nor stylized attempts to rebel by offending convention. No Pynchonian slapstick with banana peels or rapacious adenoids. No Rothish satyriasis or Barthish metaparody or arch Woody-Allenish kvetching. There are none of the ba-bing ba-bang reversals of modern sitcoms; nor are there precocious children or profane grandparents or cynically insurgent co-workers. Perhaps most alien of all, Kafka's authority figures are never just hollow buffoons to be ridiculed, but are always absurd and scary and sad all at once, like "In the Penal Colony"'s Lieutenant.

My point is not that his wit is too subtle for U.S. students. In fact, the only halfway effective strategy I've come up with for exploring Kafka's funniness in class involves suggesting to students that much of his humor is actually sort of unsubtle, or rather *anti*-subtle. The claim is that Kafka's funniness depends on some kind of radical literalization of truths we tend to treat as metaphorical. I opine to them that some of our deepest and most profound collective intuitions seem to be expressible only as figures of speech, that that's why we call these figures of speech "expressions." With respect to *The Metamorphosis*, then, I might invite students to consider what is really being expressed when we refer to someone as "creepy" or "gross" or say that somebody was forced to "eat shit" in his job. Or to reread "In the Penal Colony" in light of expressions like "tonguelashing" or "She sure tore me a new asshole" or the gnomic "By a certain age, everybody has the face he deserves." Or to approach "A Hunger Artist" in terms of tropes like "starved for attention" or "love-starved" or the double entendre in the term "self-denial," or even as innocent a factoid as that the etymological root of "anorexia" happens to be the Greek word for longing.

The students usually end up engaged here, which is great, but the teacher still sort of writhes with guilt, because the comedy-as-literalization-of-metaphor tactic doesn't begin to countenance the deeper

---

[1] A more grad-schoolish literary-theory-type machine, on the other hand, is designed to yield the conclusion that one has been deluded into imagining there was any scent in the first place.

alchemy by which Kafka's comedy is always also a tragedy, and this tragedy always also an immense and reverent joy. This usually leads to an excruciating hour during which I backpedal and hedge and warn students that, for all their wit and exformative voltage, Kafka's stories are not fundamentally jokes, and that the rather simple and lugubrious gallows humor which marks so many of Kafka's personally statements—stuff like his "There is hope, but not for us"—is *not* what is stories have got going on.

What Kafka's stories have, rather, is a grotesque and gorgeous and thoroughly modern complexity, Kafka's humor—not only not neurotic but ant-neurotic, heroically sane—is, finally a religious humor, but religious in the manner of Kierkegaard and the Rilke and the Psalms, a harrowing spirituality against which even Ms. O'Connor's bloody grace seems a little bit easy, the souls at stake pre-made.

And it is this, I think, that makes Kafka's wit inaccessible to children whom our culture has trained to see jokes as entertainment and entertainment as reassurance.[2] It's not that students don't "get" Kafka's humor but that we've taught them to see humor as something you get—the same way we've taught them that a self is something you just have. No wonder they cannot appreciate the really central Kafka joke—that the horrific struggle to establish a human self results in a self whose humanity is inseparable from that horrific struggle. That home is in fact our home. It's hard to put into words up at the blackboard, believe me. You can tell them that maybe it's good they don't "get" Kafka. You can ask them to imagine his art as a kind of door. To envision us readers coming up and pounding on this door, pounding and pounding, not just wanting admission but needing it, we don't know what it is but we can feel it, this total desperation to enter, pounding and pushing and kicking, etc. That, finally, the door opens...and it opens outward: we've been inside what we wanted all along. *Das ist komisch.*

---

[2]There are probably whole Johns Hopkins U. Press books to be written on the particular lallating function humor serves at this point in the U.S. psyche. Nonetheless, a crude but concise way to put the whole thing is that our present culture is, both developmentally and historically, "adolescent." Since adolescence is pretty much acknowledged to be the single most stressful and frightening period of human development—the stage when the adulthood we claim to crave begins to present itself as a real and narrowing system of responsibilities and limitations[2a]—it's not difficult to see why we as a culture are so susceptible to art and entertainment whose primary function is to "escape." Jokes are a kind of art, and since most of us Americans come to art essentially to forget ourselves—to pretend for a while that we're not mice and all walls are parallel and the cat can be outrun—it's no accident that we're going to see "A Little Fable" as not all that funny, in fact as maybe being the exact sort of downer-type death-and-taxes thing for which "real" humor serves as a respite.

[2a]You think it's a coincidence that it's in college that most Americans do their most serious falling-down drinking and drugging and reckless driving and rampant fucking and mindless general Dionysian-type reveling? It's not. They're adolescents, and they're terrified, and they're dealing with their terror in a distinctively American way. Those naked boys hanging upside down out of their frat-house's windows on Friday night are simply trying to get a few hours' escape from the stuff that any decent college has forced them to think about all week.

VERMEER IN BOSNIA

Lawrence Weschler

*T*happened to be in The Hague several weeks ago, sitting in on the preliminary hearings of the Yugoslav War Crimes Tribunal—specifically, those related to the case of Dusko Tadic, the only one of more than forty accused war criminals whom the Tribunal has actually been able to get its hands on up to this point. While there, I had occasion to talk with some of the principal figures involved in this unprecedented judicial undertaking.

At one point, for instance, I was having lunch with Antonio Cassese, a distinguished Italian jurist who has been serving for the past two years as the president of the court (the head of its international panel of eleven judges). He'd been rehearsing for me some of the more gruesome stories that have crossed his desk—maybe not the most gruesome but just the sort of thing he has to contend with every day and which perhaps accounts for the sense of urgency he brings to his mission. The story, for instance, of a soccer player. As Cassese recounted, "Famous guy, a Muslim. When he was captured, they said, 'Aren't you So-and-So?' He admitted he was. So they broke both his legs, handcuffed him to a radiator, and forced him to watch as they repeat-

edly raped his wife and two daughters and then slit their throats. After that, he begged to be killed himself, but his tormentors must have realized that the cruelest thing they could possibly do to him now would simply be to set him free, which they did. Somehow, this man was able to make his way to some U.N. investigators, and told them about his ordeal—a few days after which, he committed suicide." Or, for instance, as Cassese went on, "some of the tales about Tadic himself, how, in addition to the various rapes and murders he's accused of, he is alleged to have supervised the torture and torments of a particular group of Muslim prisoners, at one point forcing one of his charges to emasculate another—*with his teeth*. The one fellow died, and the guy who bit him went mad."

Stories like that: one judge's daily fare. And, at one point, I asked Judge Cassese how, regularly obliged to gaze into such an appalling abyss, he had kept from going mad himself. His face brightened. "Ah," he said with a smile. "You see, as often as possible I make my way over to the Mauritshuis museum, in the center of town, so as to spend a little time with the Vermeers."

* * *

163

Sitting there over lunch with Cassese, I'd been struck by the perfect aptness of his impulse. I, too, had been spending time with the Vermeers at the Mauritshuis, and at the Rijksmuseum, in Amsterdam, as well. For Vermeer's paintings, almost uniquely in the history of art, radiate "a centeredness, a peacefulness, a serenity" (as Cassese put it), a sufficiency, a sense of perfectly equipoised grace. In his exquisite *Study of Vermeer,* Edward Snow has deployed as an epigraph a line from Andrew Forge's essay "Painting and the Struggle for the Whole Self," which reads, "In ways that I do not pretend to understand fully, painting deals with the only issues that seem to me to count in our benighted time—freedom, autonomy, fairness, love." And I've often found myself agreeing with Snow's implication that somehow these issues may be more richly and fully addressed in Vermeer than anywhere else.

But that afternoon with Cassese I had a sudden further intuition as to the true extent of Vermeer's achievement—something I hadn't fully understood before. For, of course, when Vermeer was painting those images, which for us have become the very emblem of peacefulness and serenity, *all Europe was Bosnia* (or had only just recently ceased to be): awash in incredibly vicious wars of religious persecution and proto-nationalist formation, wars of an at-that-time unprecedented violence and cruelty, replete with sieges and famines and massacres and mass rapes, unspeakable tortures and wholesale devastation. To be sure, the sense of Holland during Vermeer's lifetime which we are usually given—that of the country's so-called Golden Age—is one of becalmed, burgherlike efficiency; but that Holland, to the extent that it ever existed, was of relatively recent provenance, and even then under the continual threat of being overwhelmed once again.

Jan Vermeer was born in 1632, sixteen years before the end of the Thirty Years' War, which virtually shredded neighboring Germany and repeatedly tore into the Netherlands as well. Between 1652 and 1674, England and the United Provinces of the Netherlands went to war three times, and though most of the fighting was confined to sea battles, the wars were not without their consequences for the Dutch mainland: Vermeer's Delft, in particular, suffered terrible devastation in 1654, when some eighty thousand pounds of gunpowder in the town's arsenal accidentally exploded, killing hundreds, including Vermeer's great contemporary, the painter Carel Fabritius. (By the conclusion of those wars, the Dutch had ended up ceding New Amsterdam to the British, who quickly changed its name to New York.) These were years of terrible religious conflict throughout Europe—the climaxes of both the Reformation and the Counter-Reformation and their various splintering progeny. And though the Dutch achieved an enviable atmosphere of tolerance during this period, Holland was regularly over-run with refugees from religious conflicts elsewhere. (Vermeer himself, incidentally, was a convert to Catholicism, which was a distinctly minority creed in the Dutch context.) Finally, in 1672, the Dutch fell under the murderous assault of France's Louis XIV and were subjected to a series of campaigns that lasted until 1678. In fact, the ensuing devastation of the Dutch economy and Vermeer's own resulting bankruptcy may have constituted a proximate cause of the painter's early death, by stroke, in 1675: he was only forty-two.

Another preliminary session of the Tribunal was scheduled for late in the afternoon of the day I had lunch with Judge Cassese, and, following our conversation, I decided to spend the intervening hours at the Mauritshuis. On the taxi ride out, as I looked through a Vermeer catalogue, I began to realize that, in fact, the pressure of all that violence (remembered, imagined, foreseen) is what those paintings are all about. Of course, not directly—in fact, quite the opposite: the literary critic Harry Berger, in his essays on Vermeer, frequently invokes the notion of the "conspicuous exclusion" of themes that are saturatingly present but only as *felt absence*—themes that are being held at bay, but conspicuously so. It's almost as if Vermeer can be seen, amid the horrors of his age, to have been asserting or *inventing* the very idea of peace. But Hobbes's state of nature, or state of war (Hobbes: 1588–1679; Vermeer: 1632–75), is everywhere adumbrated around the edges of Vermeer's achievement. That's what the roaring lions carved into the chair posts are all about—those and also the maps on the wall. The maps generally portray the Netherlands, but the whole point is that during Vermeer's lifetime the political and geographic dispensation of the Netherlands, the distribution of its Protestants and Catholics, the grim legacy of its only just recently departed Spanish overlords, and the still current threats posed by its English and French neighbors—all these matters were still actively, and sometimes bloodily, being contested. When soldiers visit young girls in Vermeer's paintings, where does one think they have been off soldiering—and why, one wonders, does the country need all those civic guards? When pregnant young women are standing still, bathed in the window light, intently reading those letters, where is one invited to imagine the letters are coming from?

Or consider the magisterial *View of Delft*—as I now did, having arrived at the Mauritshuis and taken a seat before the magnificent canvas up on the second floor. It is an image of unalloyed civic peace and quiet. But it is also the image of a town only just emerging from a downpour, the earth in the foreground still saturated with moisture, the walls of the town bejewelled with wet, the dark clouds breaking up at last, and the sunlight breaking through, though not just anywhere: a shaft of fresh, clean light gets lavished on one spire in particular, that of the

radiantly blond Nieuwe Kerk, in whose interior, as any contemporary of Vermeer's would doubtless have known, stands the mausoleum of William the Silent, one of the heroes of the wars of Dutch independence, assassinated in Delft at the end of the previous century by a French Catholic fanatic.

I found myself being reminded of a moment in my own life, over twenty-five years ago. I was in college and Nixon had just invaded Cambodia and we were, of course, all up in arms; the college had convened as a committee of the whole in the dining commons—the students, the professors, the administrators—what were we going to do? How were we going to respond? Our distinguished American history professor got up and declared this moment *the* crisis of American history. Not to be outdone, our eminent new-age classicist got up and declared it the crisis of *universal* history. And we all nodded our fervent concurrence. But then our visiting religious historian from England, a tall, lanky lay-Catholic theologian, as it happened, with something of the physical bearing of Abraham Lincoln, got up and suggested mildly, "We really ought to have a little modesty in our crises. I suspect," he went on, "that the people during the Black Plague must have thought they were in for a bit of a scrape."

Having momentarily lanced our fervor, he went on to allegorize, deploying the story of Jesus on the Waters (from Matthew 8:23–27). "Jesus," he reminded us, "needed to get across the Sea of Galilee with his disciples, so they all boarded a small boat, whereupon Jesus quickly fell into a nap. Presently a storm kicked up, and the disciples, increasingly edgy, finally woke Jesus up. He told them not to worry, everything would be all right, whereupon he fell back into his nap. The storm meanwhile grew more and more intense, winds slashing the ever-higher waves. The increasingly anxious disciples woke Jesus once again, who once again told them not to worry and again fell back asleep. And still the storm worsened, now tossing the little boat violently all to and fro. The disciples, beside themselves with terror, awoke Jesus one more time, who now said, 'Oh ye of little faith'—that's where that phrase comes from—and then proceeded to pronounce, 'Peace!' Whereupon the storm instantaneously subsided and calm returned to the water." Our historian waited a few moments as we endeavored to worry out the glancing relevance of this story. "It seems to me," he finally concluded, "that what that story is trying to tell us is simply that in times of storm, we mustn't allow the storm to enter ourselves; rather we have to find peace inside ourselves and then breathe it out."

And it now seemed to me, sitting among the Vermeers that afternoon at the Mauritshuis, that that was precisely what the Master of Delft had been about in his life's work: at a tremendously turbulent juncture in the history of his continent, he had been finding—and, yes, inventing—a zone filled with peace, a small room, an intimate vision . . . and then breathing it out.

It's one of the great things about great works of art that they can bear—and, indeed, that they invite—a superplenitude of possible readings, some of them contradictory. One of the most idiosyncratic responses to Vermeer I have ever encountered was that of the Afrikaner poet and painter Breyten Breytenbach during a walk we took one morning through the galleries of New York's Metropolitan Museum. Breytenbach, who was a clandestine antiapartheid activist, had only recently emerged from seven years of incarceration in the monochrome dungeons of the apartheid regime, and most of his comments that morning had to do with the lusciousness of all the colors in the paintings we were passing. For the most part, though, we were silent, moving at a fairly even pace from room to room—that is, until we came to Vermeer's painting of the young girl in the deep-blue skirt standing by a window, her hand poised on a silver pitcher, the window light spreading evenly across a map on the wall behind her. Here Breytenbach stopped cold for many moments, utterly absorbed. "Huh," he said finally, pointing to the gallery's caption giving the date of the painting: circa 1664–65. "It's hard to believe how from all that serenity emerge the *Boere*. Look." He jabbed a finger at the little boats delicately daubed on the painted map's painted coastline. *"That's them leaving right now!"* (And, indeed, Cape Town had been founded by the Dutch East India Company only a decade earlier, and would soon start filling up with some of the Huguenots who had flooded into Holland following a fresh upsurge of repression back in France.)

Edward Snow, for his part, makes quite a convincing case that Vermeer's art is above all about sexuality and as such provides one of the most profound explorations of the wellsprings of the erotic in the entire Western tradition. It is about female reserve and autonomy and self-sufficiency in the face of the male gaze, Snow suggests, or even in the seeming absence of such a gaze.

In this context, the pièce de résistance in his argument is a brilliantly sustained twenty-page close reading of Vermeer's magnificent (though uncannily diminutive) *Head of a Young Girl*—sometimes referred to, alternatively, as *The Girl in a Turban* or *The Girl with a Pearl* (at the Mauritshuis, it happens to face *The View of Delft,* just across the room). Snow's approach to this overexposed and by now almost depleted image is to ask, Has the girl just turned toward us or is she just about to turn away? Looked at with this question in mind, it does seem that such immanence, one way or the other, is of its essence. As Snow points out, if we momentarily blot out the face itself, everything else conspires to make us expect a simple profile of a head—so that afterward, as we allow ourselves to look again on the face unobstructed, the girl does seem to have only just now turned to face us. But if we look for a moment at the pendant of cloth cascading down from the knot at the top of her turban, it seems at first as if that pendant ought to fall behind her far shoulder; in fact it falls far forward, provoking a visual torsion precisely opposite to that of the one we'd surmised earlier: no, on second thought, she seems to be pulling away. The answer is that she's actually doing both. This is a woman who has just turned toward us and is already about to look away: and the melancholy of the moment with its impending sense of loss, is transferred from her eyes to the tearlike pearl dangling from her ear. *It's an entire movie in a single frozen image.* (One is in turn reminded of the obverse instance of Chris Marker's ravishing short film from 1962, *La Jetée*, a Vermeer-saturated romance made up entirely of still shots unfurling evenly, hypnotically, one after the next, with the sole exception of a single moving-picture sequence: the woman asleep in bed, her eyes closed, her eyes opening to gaze up at us, and then closing once again. A sequence that passes so quickly—in the blink, we say, of an eye—that it's only moments later that we even register its having been a moving-picture sequence at all.)

The girl's lips are parted in a sudden intake of breath—much, we suddenly notice, as are our own as we gaze back upon her. And in fact an astonishing transmutation has occurred. In the moment of painting, it was Vermeer who'd been looking at the girl and registering the imminent turning-away of her attention (the speculation among some critics that Vermeer's model for this image may have been his daughter renders the conceit all the more poignant); subsequently, it was, of course, the painte-image that would stay frozen in time, eternally attentive, while it was he as artist who'd eventually be the one turning away; and, still later, it would be Vermeer

himself who, through the girl's gaze, would remain faithful, whereas it would be we viewers, casually wandering through the museum and tarrying before the image for a few, breath-inheld moments, who would be the ones eventually turning away. *The Head of a Young Girl* thus becomes a picture about presence and eternity, or, at any rate, posterity.

But this is only because it is first and foremost a painting about inter-subjectivity: about the autonomy, the independent agency, dignity, and self-sufficiency of the Other, in whose eyes we in turn are likewise autonomous, self-sufficient, suffuse with individual dignity and potential agency. And here is where we come full circle: because if Vermeer's work can be said to be one extended invention—or assertion—of a certain concept of peace-filledness, this is precisely how he's doing it, by imagining or asserting the possibility of such an autonomous, inhabited sense of self-hood.

The scale of Vermeer's achievement becomes even clearer if, like me, you have a chance to walk among some of the genre pieces by Vermeer's Dutch contemporaries, also scattered about the Mauritshuis (it was getting late now and I wanted to make it back for the final session of the preliminary Tadic hearing, but I did tarry for a few minutes longer in some of the museum's adjoining rooms).

For many years, Vermeer's works were themselves seen primarily as instances of these sorts of moralizing genre images. The Metropolitan's *Girl Asleep* was thus cast as yet another castigating allegory of feminine sloth and drunkenness, while Berlin's *Woman Putting on Pearls* was folded into the tradition of vanity motifs. The Frick's *Officer and Laughing Girl* was assigned to the tradition of vaguely unsavory prostitution images (as, naturally, was Dresden's *Procuress,* from earlier in Vermeer's career); conversely, the Louvre's *Lacemaker* was seen in the context of more positively tinged illustrations of industriousness, and the Rijksmuseum's *Milkmaid* was cast as yet another prototypically Dutch celebration of the domestic virtues. All of which misses the essential point, because in each of these instances and in virtually every other one of his paintings, Vermeer deploys the conventional iconography precisely so as to upend it. No, his paintings all but cry out, this person is not to be seen as merely a type, a trope, an allegory. If she is standing in for anything, she is standing in for the condition of being a unique individual human being, worthy of our own unique individual response. (Which is more than can be said, generally, for the men in Vermeer's paintings, who do seem, hovering there beside the women, to stand in for the condition of being somewhat oafishly de trop.)

Or so, anyway, I found myself thinking in the taxi as I returned to the Tribunal—of that and of the way in which the entire Yugoslavian debacle has been taking place in a context wherein the Other, even one's own neighbor, is suddenly being experienced no longer as a subject like oneself but as an instance, a type, a vile expletive: a Serb, a Croat, a Turk, and, as such, pre-ordained for an ages-old, inevitable fate. (Note that such a construction has to be as assiduously "invented" as its obverse: people who've been living in relative peace for decades have to be goaded into seeing one another, once again, in this manner.) No wonder that Cassese flees to Vermeer for surcease.

A Dutch journalist named Alfred van Cleef recently published a remarkable book, *De Verloren Wereld van de Familie Berberovic (The Lost World of the Berberovic Family),* in which he traces the downward spiral of the last five years in Yugoslavia through the shattered prism of one Bosnian family's experience. Early in his narrative, he recounts how the war came to the Berberovic family's village, how for many months its members had been picking up

the increasingly strident harangues welling out from the Belgrade and Zagreb television stations but hadn't worried because theirs was a peaceful village, where Serbs and Croats and Muslims lived equably together, with a high degree of intermarriage, and so forth. Then the war was just two valleys over, but still they didn't worry, and then it was in the very next valley, but, even so, no one could imagine its actually intruding into their quiet lives. But one day a car suddenly careered into the village's central square, four young men in militia uniforms leaping out, purposefully crossing the square, seeming to single out a particular house and cornering its occupant, whereupon the leader of the militiamen calmly leveled a gun at the young man and blew him away. The militiamen hustled back to their car and sped off. As van Cleef subsequently recounted the incident for me, "They left behind them a village almost evenly divided. Those under fifty years of age had been horrified by the seeming randomness of the act, while those over fifty realized, with perhaps even greater horror, that the young man who'd just been killed was the son of a man who, back during the partisan struggles of the Second World War, happened to have killed the uncle of the kid who'd just done the killing. And the older villagers immediately realized, with absolute clarity, that if this was now possible everything was going to be possible."

David Rieff tells a story about visiting a recent battlefield at one point during the war in the company of a small band of fellow journalists: Muslim corpses strewn across the muddy meadow, a Serb soldier grimly standing guard. " 'So,' we asked the soldier, this young kid," Rieff recalls, " 'What happened here?' At which point the soldier took a drag on his cigarette and began, 'Well, in 1385 . . .' "

Yugoslavia today has been turned back into one of those places where people not only seem incapable of forgetting the past but barely seem capable of thinking about anything else: the Serbs and Croats and Muslims now appear to be so deeply mired in a poisonous legacy of grievances, extending back fifty years, years—indeed, all the way back to the fourteenth century—that it's almost as if the living had been transformed into pale, wraithlike shades haunting the ghosts of the long-dead rather than the other way around.

Which is to say that we're back in the moral universe of epic poetry: the Iliad, Beowulf, the Chanson de Roland, the Mahabharata, and, of course, *Finnegans Wake*—a modernist recasting of the entire epic tradition, composed during the thirties by James Joyce, who once characterized history as "two bloody Irishmen in a bloody fight over bloody nothing." Not so much over bloody nothing, perhaps, as vengeance for vengeance for vengeance for who-any-longer-knows-what? That's the heart of the epic tradition: those twinned themes of the relentless maw of vengeance and the ludicrous incommensurability of its first causes recur time and again, from one culture to the next. It's worth remembering how, also during the thirties, when the great Harvard classicist Milman Parry was trying to crack the Homeric code—to determine just how the ancient Greek bards were able to improvise such incredibly long poems, and what mnemonic devices they had devised to assist them—he scoured the world for places where such oral epic traditions were still alive, and the place he finally settled on as perfect for his purposes was Yugoslavia (see his disciple Albert Lord's seminal account in *The Singer of Tales*).

Vermeer was not a painter in the epic tradition: on the contrary, his life's work can be seen, within its historical moment, as a heroic, extended attempt to steer his (and his viewers') way clear of such a depersonalizing approach to experiencing one's fellow human beings. It was a project, I now realized, as I took my seat in the visitors' gallery facing the Tribunal's glassed-in hearing room, not all that dissimilar from that of the Tribunal itself.

The day before, I'd spoken with Richard Goldstone, the eminent South African jurist who has been serving as the Yugoslav Tribunal's lead prosecutor. (He is serving the same role on the Tribunal that has been established to prosecute the war criminals in Rwanda.) I'd asked him how he envisioned the mission of the Tribunal, and he'd described it as nothing less than a breaking of the historic cycle of vengeance-inspired ethnic mayhem. He does not believe in the inevitability of such violence. "For the great majority of their histories, the Croats and Serbs and Muslims, and the Tutsis and Hutus, have lived in relative peace with one another—and they were all doing that relatively nicely once again until just recently," he told me. "Such interethnic violence usually gets stoked by specific individuals intent on immediate political or material advantage, who then call forth the legacies of earlier and previously unaddressed grievances. But the guilt for the violence that results does not adhere to the entire group. Specific individuals bear the major share of the responsibility, and it is they, not the group as a whole, who need to be held to account, through a fair and meticulously detailed presentation and evaluation of evidence, precisely so that the next time around no one will be able to claim that all Serbs did this, or all Croats or all Hutus—so that people are able to see how it is specific individuals in their communities who are continually endeavoring to manipulate them in that fashion. I really believe that this is the only way the cycle can be broken."

The preliminary hearings now resumed. Tadic was seated in a sort of aquarium of bulletproof glass, a panoply of high-tech gadgetry arrayed all around him and around the various lawyers and judges: instantaneous-translation devices, video cameras and monitors, computerized evidence screens, and so forth.

Inventing peace: I found myself thinking of Vermeer with his camera obscura—an empty box fronted by a lens through which the chaos of the world might be drawn in and tamed back to a kind of sublime order. And I found myself thinking of these people here with their legal chamber, the improbably calm site for a similar effort at transmutation.

I looked up at the TV monitor: the automated camera was evidently scanning the room. It caught the prosecutors in their flowing robes shuffling papers, the judges, the defense table, and now Tadic himself. The camera lingered on him—a handsome young man, improbably dapper in a navy-blue jacket and a gleaming white T-shirt—and then zeroed in for a closer shot of his face.

There he was, not some symbol or trope or a stand-in for anybody other than himself: a quite specific individual, in all his sublime self-sufficiency; a man of whom, as it happened, terrible, terrible allegations had been made, and who was now going to have to face those allegations, stripped of any rationales except his own autonomous free agency.

For a startling split second, he looked up at the camera. And then he looked away.

(1995)

Postscript

The Tadic trial dragged on for many more months, evidence for the depravity of the defendant's alleged crimes vying against equally compelling evidence of the relative insignificance of his role in the wider conflict: he had, after all, merely been a guard at the camp in question, and some felt that he was being singled out at that early stage of the Tribunal's proceedings primarily because he'd had the bad luck to get caught while much more significant malefactors had so far eluded arrest, and the Tribunal had to be seen to be doing *something*. In the end, he was found guilty on eleven counts, not guilty on nine others (for which there was found to be insufficient evidence of his specific involvement) and sentenced to twenty years in prison (a sentence which, after both sides appealed the verdict, was presently lengthened to twenty-five years).

With the passing years, the Tribunal did begin netting more—and more significant—suspects. By the end of 2003, ninety-two individuals had been brought before it, with forty-two already tried, their cases disposed. Several of these were "big fish" indeed—Biljana Plavsic, one of the highest civilian authorities among the Bosnian Serbs, for example, pled guilty in advance of her trial—though two of the most significant, the Bosnian Serb civilian and military commanders Radovan Karadzic and Ratko Mladic had thus far still managed to elude arrest.

THE SEMIOTICS OF SEX

Jeanette Winterson

I was in a bookshop recently when a young woman approached me.

She told me she was writing an essay on my work and that of Radclyffe Hall. Could I help?

"Yes," I said. "Our work has nothing in common."

"I thought you were a lesbian," she said.

I have become aware that the chosen sexual difference of one writer is, in itself, thought sufficient to bind her in semiotic sisterhood with any other writer, also lesbian, dead or alive.

I am, after all, a pervert, so I will not mind sharing a bed with a dead body. This bed in the shape of a book, this book in the shape of a bed, must accommodate us every one, because, whatever our style, philosophy, class, age, preoccupations and talent, we are lesbians and isn't that the golden key to the single door of our work?

In any discussion of art and the artist, heterosexuality is backgrounded, whilst homosexuality is foregrounded. What you fuck is much more important than how you write. This may be because reading takes more effort than sex. It may be because the word "sex" is more exciting than the word "book." Or is it? Surely that depends on what kind of sex and what kind of book? I can only assume that straight sex is so dull that even a book makes better reportage. No one asks Iris Murdoch about her sex life. Every interviewer I meet asks me about mine and what they do not ask they invent. I am a writer who happens to love women. I am not a lesbian who happens to write.

What is it about? Prurience? Stupidity? And as Descartes didn't say, "I fuck therefore I am."? The straight world is wilful in its pursuit of queers and it seems to me that to continually ask someone about their homosexuality, when the reason to talk is a book, a picture, a play, is harassment by the back door.

The Queer world has colluded in the misreading of art as sexuality. Art is difference, but not necessarily sexual difference, and while to be outside of the mainstream of imposed choice is likely to make someone more conscious, it does not automatically make that someone an artist. A great deal of gay writing, especially gay writing around the AIDS crisis, is therapy, is release, is not art. It is its subject matter and no more and I hope by now that I have convinced my readers in these essays, that all art, including literature, is much more than its subject matter. It is true that a number of gay and lesbian writers have attracted an audience and some attention simply because they are queer. Lesbians and gays do need their own culture, as any sub-group does, including the sub-group of heterosexuality, but the problems start when we assume that the fact of our queerness bestows on us special powers. It might make for certain advantages (it is helpful for a woman artist not to have a husband) but it cannot, of itself, guarantee art. Lesbians and gay men, who have to examine so much of what the straight world takes for granted, must keep on examining their own standards in all things, and especially the standards we set for our own work.

I think this is particularly urgent where fiction and poetry are concerned and where it is most tempting to assume that the autobiography of Difference will be enough.

Let me put it another way: if I am in love with Peggy and I am a composer I can express that love in an ensemble or a symphony. If I am in love with Peggy and I am a painter, I need not paint her portrait, I am free to express my passion in splendid harmonies of colour and line. If I am a writer, I will have to be careful, I must not fall into the trap of believing that my passion, of itself, is art. As a composer or a painter I know that it is not. I know that I shall have to find a translation of form to make myself clear. I know that the language of my passion and the language of my art are not the same thing.

Of course there is a paradox here; the most powerful written work often masquerades as autobiography. It offers itself as raw when in fact it is sophisticated. It presents itself as a kind of diary when really it is an oration. The best work speaks intimately to you even though it has been consciously made to speak intimately to thousands of others. The bad writer believes that sincerity of feeling will be enough, and pins her faith on the power of experience. The true writer knows that feeling must give way to form. It is through the form, not in spite of, or accidental to it, that the most powerful emotions are let loose over the greatest number of people.

Art must resist autobiography if it hopes to cross boundaries of class, culture . . . and . . . sexuality. Literature is not a lecture delivered to a special interest group, it is a force that unites its audience. The subgroups are broken down.

How each artist learns to translate autobiography into art is a problem that each artist solves for themselves. When solved, unpicking is impossible, we cannot work backwards from the finished text into its raw material. The commonest mistake of critics and biographers is to assume that what holds significance for them necessarily held significance for the writer. Forcing the work back into autobiography is a way of trying to contain it, of making what has become unlike anything else into what is just like everything else. It may be that in the modern world, afraid of feeling, it is more comfortable to turn the critical gaze away from a fully realised piece of work. It is always easier to focus on sex. The sexuality of the writer is a wonderful diversion.

If Queer culture is now working against assumptions of identity as sexuality, art goes there first, by implicitly or explicitly creating emotion around the forbidden. Some of the early feminist arguments surrounding the wrongfulness of men painting provocative female nudes seem to me to have overlooked the possibility or the fact of another female as the viewer. Why should she identify with the nude? What deep taboos make her unable to desire the nude?

Opera, before and after the nineteenth century, but not during, enjoyed serious games of sexual ambiguity, and opera fans will know the delicious and disturbing pleasure of watching a woman disguised as a man and hearing her woo another woman with a voice unmistakably female. Our opera ancestors knew the now forbidden pleasure of listening to a man sing as a woman; in his diary, Casanova writes of the fascination and desire felt for these compromising creatures by otherwise heterosexual men. Music is androgynously sexy and with the same sensuous determination penetrates male and female alike. Unless of course one resists it, and how much sex-resistance goes on under the lie of "I don't like opera"?

Similarly, I am sure that a lot of the coyness and silliness that accompanies productions of Shakespeare that include cross-dressing roles, is an attempt to steer them clear of Queer. As long as we all know that a pretence is happening; the pretence of Principal Boy or music-hall camp, we are safe in our het-suits. Too many directors overlook the obvious fact that in Shakespeare, the disguises are meant to convince. They are not a comedian's joke. We too must fall in love. We too must know what it is to find that we have desired another woman, desired another man. And should we really take at face value those fifth acts where everyone simply swops their partner to the proper sex and goes home to live happily ever after?

I am not suggesting that we should all part with our husbands and live Queer.

I am not suggesting that a lesbian who recognises desire for a man sleep with him. We need not be so crude. What we do need is to accept in ourselves, with pleasure, the subtle and various emotions that are the infinity of a human being. More, not less, is the capacity of the heart. More not less is the capacity of art.

Art coaxes out of us emotions we normally do not feel. It is not that art sets out to shock (that is rare), it is rather that art occu-pies ground unconquered by social niceties. Seeking neither to please nor to displease, art works to enlarge emotional possibility. In a dead society that inevitably puts it on the side of the rebels. Do not mistake me, I am not of the voting party of bohemians and bad boys, and the rebelliousness of art does not make every rebel an artist. The rebellion of art is a daily rebellion against the state of living death routinely called real life.

Where every public decision has to be justified in the scale of corporate profit, poetry unsettles these apparently self-evident propositions, not through ideology, but by its very presence and ways of being, its embodiment of states of longing and desire.

ADRIENNE RICH, WHAT IS FOUND THERE: NOTEBOOKS ON POETRY AND POLITICS (1993)

And not only public decisions but also private compromises. Calculations of the heart that should never be made. It is through the acceptance of breakdown; breakdown of fellowship, of trust, of community, of communication, of language, of love, that we begin to break down ourselves, a fragmented society afraid of feeling.

Against this fear, art is fresh healing and fresh pain. The rebel writer who brings healing and pain, need not be a Marxist or a Socialist; need not be political in the journalistic sense and may fail the shifting tests of Correctness, while standing as a rebuke to the hollowed out days and as a refuge for our stray hearts. Communist and People's Man, Stephen Spender, had the right credentials, but Catholic and cultural reactionary T. S. Eliot made the poetry. It is not always so paradoxical but it can be, and the above example should be reason enough not to judge the work by the writer. Judge the writer by the work.

When I read Adrienne Rich or Oscar Wilde, rebels of very different types, the fact of their homosexuality should not be uppermost. I am not reading their work to get at their private lives. I am reading their work because I need the depth-charge it carries.

Their formal significance, the strength of their images, their fidelity to language makes it possible for them to reach me across distance and time. If each were not an exceptional writer, neither would be able to reach beyond the interests of their own sub-group. The truth is that both have an audience who do not share the sexuality of the subversiveness of playwright and poet but who cannot fail to be affected by those elements when they read Rich and Wilde. Art succeeds where polemic fails.

Nevertheless, there are plenty of heterosexual readers who won't touch books by Queers and plenty of Queer readers who are only out to scan a bent kiss. We all know of men who won't read books by women and in spite of the backlash that dresses this up in high sounding notions of creativity, it is ordinary terror of difference. Men do not feel comfortable looking at the world through eyes that are not male. It has nothing to do with sentences or syntax, it is sexism by any other name. It would be a pity if lesbians and gay men retreated into the same kind of cultural separatism. We learn early how to live in two words; our own and that of the dominant model, why not learn how to live in multiple worlds? The strange prismatic worlds that art offers? I do not want to read only books by women, only books by Queers, I want all that there is, so long as it is genuine and it seems to me that to choose our reading matter according to the sex and/or sexuality of the writer is a dismal way to read. For lesbians and gay men it has been vital to create our own counter-culture but that does not mean that there is nothing in straight culture that we can use. We are more sophisticated than that and it is worth remembering that the conventional mind is its own prison.

The man who won't read Virginia Woolf, the lesbian who won't touch T. S. Eliot, are both putting subjective concerns in between themselves and the work. Literature, whether made by heterosexuals or homosexuals, whether to do with lives gay or straight, packs in it supplies of energy and emotion that all of us need. Obviously if a thing is not art, we will not get any artistic pleasure out of it and we will find it void of the kind of energy and emotion we can draw on indefinitely. It is difficult, when we are surrounded by trivia makers and trivia merchants, all claiming for themselves the power of art, not to fall for the lie that there is no such thing or that it is anything. The smallness of it all is depressing and it is inevitable that we will have to whip out the magnifying glass of our own interests to bring the thing up to size. "Is it about me?" "Is it amusing?" "Is it dirty?" "What about the sex?" are not aesthetic questions but they are the questions asked by most reviewers and by most readers most of the time. Unless we setup criteria of judgement that are relevant to literature, and not to sociology, entertainment, topicality etc., we are going to find it harder and harder to know what it is that separates art from everything else.

Learning to read is more than learning to group the letters on a page. Learning to read is a skill that marshals the entire resources of body and mind. I do not mean the endless dross-skimming that passes for literacy, I mean the ability to engage with a text as you would another human being. To recognise it in its own right, separate, particular, to let it speak in its own voice, not in a ventriloquism of yours. To find its relationship to you that is not its relationship to anyone else. To recognise, at the same time, that you are neither the means nor the method of its existence and that the love between you is not a mutual suicide. The love between you offers an alternative paradigm; a complete and fully realised vision in a chaotic unrealised world. Art is not amnesia, and the popular idea of books as escapism or diversion, misses altogether what art is. There is plenty of escapism and diversion to be had, but it cannot be had from real books, real pictures, real music, real theatre. Art is the realisation of complex emotion.

We value sensitive machines. We spend billions of pounds to make them more sensitive yet, so that they detect minerals deep in the earth's crust, radioactivity thousands of miles away. We don't value sensitive human beings and we spend no money on their priority. As machines become more delicate and human beings coarser, will antennae and fibreoptic claim for themselves what was uniquely human? Not rationality, not logic, but that strange network of fragile perception, that means I can imagine, that teaches me to love, a lodging of recognition and tenderness where I sometimes know the essential beat that rhythms life.

The artist as radar can help me. The artist who combines an exceptional sensibility with an exceptional control over her material. This equipment, unfunded, unregarded, gift and discipline kept tuned to untapped frequencies, will bring home signals otherwise lost to me. Will make for my ears and eyes what was the proper of the hawk. This sharpness and stretch of wings has not in it the comfort of escape. It has in it warnings and chances and painful beauty. It is not what I know and it is not what I am. The mirror turns out to be a through looking-glass, and beyond are places I have never reached. Once reached there is no need to leave them again. Art is not tourism it is an ever-expanding territory. Art is not Capitalism, what I find in it, I may keep. The title takes my name.

The realisation of complex emotion.

Complex emotion is pivoted around the forbidden. When I feel the complexities of a situation I am feeling the many-sidedness of it, not the obvious smooth shape, grasped at once and easily forgotten. Complexity leads to perplexity. I do not know my place. There is a clash between what I feel and what I had expected to feel. My logical self fails me, and no matter how I try to pace it out, there is still something left over that will not be accounted for. All of us have felt like this, all of us have tried to make the rough places smooth; to reason our way out of a gathering storm. Usually dishonesty is our best guide. We call inner turbulence "blowing things up out of all proportion." We call it "seven-year itch." We call it "over-tiredness." Like Adam we name our beasts, but not well, and we find they do not come when called.

Complex emotion often follows some major event in our lives; sex, falling in love, birth, death, are the commonest and in each of these potencies are strong taboos. The striking loneliness of the individual when confronted with these large happenings that we all share, is a loneliness of displacement. The person is thrown out of the normal groove of their life and whilst they stumble, they also have to carry a new weight of feeling, feeling that threatens to overwhelm them. Consequences of misery and breakdown are typical and in a repressive society that pretends to be liberal, misery and breakdown can be used as subtle punishments for what we no longer dare legislate against. Inability to cope is defined as a serious weakness in a macho culture like ours, but what is inability to cope, except a spasmodic, faint and fainter protest against a closed-in drugged-up life where suburban values are touted as the greatest good? A newborn child, the moment of falling in love, can cause in us seismic shocks that will, if we let them, help to re-evaluate what things matter, what things we take for granted. This is frightening, and as we get older it is harder to face such risks to the deadness that we are. Art offers the challenge we desire but also the shape we need when our own world seems most shapeless. The formal beauty of art is threat and relief to the formless neutrality of unrealised life.

"Ah" you will say, "She means Art as Consolation. The lonely romantic who reads Jane Eyre. The computer misfit wandering with Wordsworth."

I do not think of art as Consolation. I think of it as Creation. I think of it as an energetic space that begets energetic space. Works of art do not reproduce themselves, they re-create themselves and have at the same time sufficient permanent power to create rooms for us, the dispossessed. In other words, art makes it possible to live in energetic space.

When I talk about creating emotion around the forbidden, I do not mean disgust around the well known. Forget the lowlife, tourist, squeaky clean middle-class bad boys who call their sex-depravity in blunt prose, fine writing. Forget the copycat girls who wouldn't know the end of a dildo from a vacuum rod. They are only chintz dipped in mud and we are after real material. What is forbidden is scarier, sexier, unnightmared by the white-collar cataloguers of crap. "Don't do that" makes for easy revolt. What is forbidden is hidden. To worm into the heart and mind until what one truly desires has been encased in dark walls of what one ought to desire, is the success of the serpent. Serpents of state, serpents of religion, serpents in the service of education, monied serpents, mythic serpents, weaving their lies backwards into history. Two myths out of many: the first, Hebrew: Eve in the garden persuaded to eat that which she has never desired to eat ("The serpent bade me eat"). The second, Greek: Medusa, the Gorgon, whose serpent hair turns all who look on her to stone.

There are many ways of reading these myths, that is the way with myths, but for the purposes of this argument, I want us to be wary of bodies insinuated to desire what they do not desire and of hearts turned to stone.

How can I know what I feel? When a writer asks herself that question she will have to find the words to answer it, even if the answer is another question. The writer will have to make her words into a true equivalent of her heart. If she cannot, if she can only hazard at the heart, arbitrarily temporarily, she may be a psychologist but she will not be a poet.

It is the poet who goes further than any human scientist. The poet who with her dredging net must haul up difficult things and return them to the present. As she does this, the reader will begin to recognise parts of herself so neatly buried that they seem to have been buried from birth. She will be able to hear clearly the voices that have whispered at her for so many years. Some of those voices will prove false, she will perhaps learn to fear her own fears. The attendant personalities that are clinically labelled as schizophrenia, can be brought into a harmonious balance. It is not necessary to be shut up in one self, to grind through life like an ox at a mill, always treading the same ground. Human beings are capable of powered flight; we can travel across ourselves and find that self multiple and vast. The artist knows this; at the same time that art is prising away old dead structures that have rusted almost unnoticed into our flesh, art is pushing at the boundaries we thought were fixed. The convenient lies fall; the only boundaries are the boundaries of our imagination.

How much can we imagine? The artist is an imaginer. The artist imagines the forbidden because to her it is not forbidden. If she is freer than other people it is the freedom of her single allegiance to her work. Most of us have divided loyalties, most of us have sold ourselves. The artist is not divided and she is not for sale. Her clarity of purpose protects her although it is her clarity of purpose that is most likely to irritate most people. We are not happy with obsessives, visionaries, which means, in effect, that we are not happy with artists. Why do we flee from feeling? Why do we celebrate those who lower us in the mire of their own making while we hound those who come to us with hands full of difficult beauty?

If we could imagine ourselves out of despair?

If we could imagine ourselves out of helplessness?

What would happen if we could imagine in ourselves authentic desire?

What would happen if one woman told the truth about herself? The world would split open.

MURIEL RUKEYSER

In search of this truth, beyond the fear of the consequences of this truth, are the flight-maps of art. When truth is at stake, and in a society that desperately needs truth, we have to be wary of those side-tracks to nowhere that mislead us from the journey we need to make. There are plenty of Last Days signposts to persuade us that nothing is worth doing and that each one of us lives in a private nightmare occasionally relieved by temporary pleasure.

Art is not a private nightmare, not even a private dream, it is a shared human connection that traces the possibilities of past and future in the whorl of now. It is a construct, like science, like religion, like the world itself. It is as artificial as you and me and as natural too. We have never been able to live without it, we have never been able to live with it. We claim it makes no difference whilst nervously barring it out of our lives. Part of this barring is to gender it, to sex it, to find ways of containing and reducing this fascinating fear. But to what are our efforts directed? What is it that we seek to mock and discourage? It is the human spirit free.

I was in a bookshop recently and a young man came up to me and said "Is *Sexing the Cherry* a reading of *Four Quartets?*"

"Yes," I said, and he kissed me.

FROM CAMERA LUCIDA
REFLECTIONS ON PHOTOGRAPHY

Roland Barthes

1

*O*ne day, quite some time ago, I happened on a photograph of Napoleon's youngest brother, Jerome, taken in 1852. And I realized then, with an amazement I have not been able to lessen since: "I am looking at eyes that looked at the Emperor." Sometimes I would mention this amazement, but since no one seemed to share it, nor even to understand it (life consists of these little touches of solitude), I forgot about it. My interest in Photography took a more cultural turn. I decided I liked Photography *in opposition* to the Cinema, from which I nonetheless failed to separate it. This question grew insistent. I was overcome by an "ontological" desire: I wanted to learn at all costs what Photography was "in itself," by what essential feature it was to be distinguished from the community of images. Such a desire really meant that beyond the evidence provided by technology and usage, and despite its tremendous contemporary expansion, I wasn't sure that Photography existed, that it had a "genius" of its own.

2

Who could help me?

From the first step, that of classification (we must surely classify, verify by samples, if we want to constitute a corpus), Photography evades us. The various distributions we impose upon it are in fact either empirical (Professionals/Amateurs), or rhetorical (Landscapes/Objects/Portraits/Nudes), or else aesthetic (Realism/Pictorialism), in any case external to the object, without relation to its essence, which can only be (if it exists at all) the New of which it has been the advent; for these classifications might very well be applied to other, older forms of representation. We might say that Photography is unclassifiable. Then I wondered what the source of this disorder might be.

The first thing I found was this. What the Photograph reproduces to infinity has occurred only once: the Photograph mechanically repeats what could never be repeated existentially. In the Photograph, the event is never transcended for the sake of something else: the Photograph always leads the corpus I need back to the body I see; it is the absolute Particular, the sovereign Contingency, matte and somehow stupid, the *This* (this photograph, and not Photography), in short, what Lacan calls the *Tuché,* the Occasion, the Encounter, the Real, in its indefatigable expression. In order to designate reality, Buddhism says *sunya,* the void; but better still: *tathata,* as Alan Watts has it, the fact of being this, of being thus, of being so; *tat* means *that* in Sanskrit and suggests the gesture of the child pointing his finger at something and saying: *that, there it is, lo!* but says nothing else; a photograph cannot be transformed (spoken) philosophically, it is wholly ballasted by the contingency of which it is the weightless, transparent envelope. Show your photographs to someone—he will immediately show you his: "Look, this is my brother; this is me as a child," etc.; the Photograph is never anything but an antiphon of "Look," "See," "Here it is"; it points a finger at certain *vis-à-vis,* and cannot escape this pure deictic language. This is why, insofar as it is licit to speak of *a* photograph, it seemed to me just as improbable to speak of *the* Photograph.

A specific photograph, in effect, is never distinguished from its referent (from what it represents), or at least it is not *immediately* or *generally* distinguished from its referent (as is the case for every other image, encumbered—from the start, and because of its status—by the way in which the object is simulated): it is not impossible to perceive the photographic signifier (certain professionals do so), but it requires a secondary action of knowledge or of reflection. By nature, the Photograph (for convenience's sake, let us accept this universal, which for the moment refers only to the tireless repetition of contingency) has something tautological about it: a pipe, here, is always and intractably a pipe. It is as if the Photograph always carries its referent with itself, both affected by the same amorous or funereal immobility, at the very heart of the moving world: they are glued together, limb by limb, like the condemned man and the corpse in certain tortures; or even like those

pairs of fish (sharks, I think, according to Michelet) which navigate in convoy, as though united by an eternal coitus. The Photograph belongs to that class of laminated objects whose two leaves cannot be separated without destroying them both: the windowpane and the landscape, and why not: Good and Evil, desire and its object: dualities we can conceive but not perceive (I didn't yet know that this stubbornness of the Referent in always being there would produce the essence I was looking for).

This fatality (no photograph without *something* or *someone*) involves Photography in the vast disorder of objects—of all the objects in the world: why choose (why photograph) this object, this moment, rather than some other? Photography is unclassifiable because there is no reason to *mark* this or that of its occurrences; it aspires, perhaps, to become as crude, as certain, as noble as a sign, which would afford it access to the dignity of a language: but for there to be a sign there must be a mark; deprived of a principle of marking, photographs are signs which don't *take,* which *turn,* as milk does. Whatever it grants to vision and whatever its manner, a photograph is always invisible: it is not it that we see.

In short, the referent adheres. And this singular adherence makes it very difficult to focus on Photography. The books which deal with it, much less numerous moreover than for any other art, are victims of this difficulty. Some are technical; in order to "see" the photographic signifier, they are obliged to focus at very close range. Others are historical or sociological; in order to observe the total phenomenon of the Photograph, these are obliged to focus at a great distance. I realized with irritation that none discussed precisely the photographs which interest me, which give me pleasure or emotion. What did I care about the rules of composition of the photographic landscape, or, at the other end, about the Photograph as family rite? Each time I would read something about Photography, I would think of some photograph I loved, and this made me furious. Myself, I saw only the referent, the desired object, the beloved body; but an importunate voice (the voice of knowledge, of *scientia*) then adjured me, in a severe tone: "Get back to Photography. What you are seeing here and what makes you suffer belongs to the category 'Amateur Photographs,' dealt with by a team of sociologists; nothing but the trace of a social protocol of integration, intended to reassert the Family, etc." Yet I persisted; another, louder voice urged me to dismiss such sociological commentary; looking at certain photographs, I wanted to be a primitive, without culture. So I went on, not daring to reduce the world's countless photographs, any more than to extend several of mine to Photography: in short, I found myself at an impasse and, so to speak, "scientifically" alone and disarmed.

3

Then I decided that this disorder and this dilemma, revealed by my desire to write on Photography, corresponded to a discomfort I had always suffered from: the uneasiness of being a subject torn between two languages, one expressive, the other critical; and at the heart of this critical language, between several discourses, those of sociology, of semiology, and of psychoanalysis—but that, by ultimate dissatisfaction with all of them, I was bearing witness to the only sure thing that was in me (however naïve it might be): a desperate resistance to any reductive system. For each time, having resorted to any such language to whatever degree, each time I felt it hardening and thereby tending to reduction and reprimand, I would gently leave it and seek elsewhere: I began to speak differently. It was better, once and for all, to make my protestation of singularity into a virtue—to try making what Nietzsche called

the "ego's ancient sovereignty" into an heuristic principle. So I resolved to start my inquiry with no more than a few photographs, the ones I was sure existed *for me*. Nothing to do with a corpus: only some bodies. In this (after all) conventional debate between science and subjectivity, I had arrived at this curious notion: why mightn't there be, somehow, a new science for each object? A *mathesis singularis* (and no longer *universalis*)? So I decided to take myself as mediator for all Photography. Starting from a few personal impulses, I would try to formulate the fundamental feature, the universal without which there would be no Photography.

4

So I make myself the measure of photographic "knowledge." What does my body know of Photography? I observed that a photograph can be the object of three practices (or of three emotions, or of three intentions): to do, to undergo, to look. The *Operator* is the Photographer. The *Spectator* is ourselves, all of us who glance through collections of photographs—in magazines and newspapers, in books, albums, archives . . . And the person or thing photographed is the target, the referent, a kind of little simulacrum, any *eidolon* emitted by the object, which I should like to call the *Spectrum* of the Photograph, because this word retains, through its root, a relation to "spectacle" and adds to it that rather terrible thing which is there in every photograph: the return of the dead.

One of these practices was barred to me and I was not to investigate it: I am not a photographer, not even an amateur photographer: too impatient for that: I must see right away what I have produced (Polaroid? Fun, but disappointing, except when a great photographer is involved). I might suppose that the *Operator's* emotion (and consequently the essence of Photography-according-to-the-Photographer) had some relation to the "little hole" *(stenope)* through which he looks, limits, frames, and perspectivizes when he wants to "take" (to surprise). Technically, Photography is at the intersection of two quite distinct procedures; one of a chemical order: the action of light on certain substances; the other of a physical order: the formation of the image through an optical device. It seemed to me that the *Spectator's* Photograph descended essentially, so to speak, from the chemical revelation of the object (from which I receive, by deferred action, the rays), and that the *Operator's* Photograph, on the contrary, was linked to the vision framed by the key-hole of the *camera obscura*. But of that emotion (or of that essence) I could not speak, never having experienced it; I could not join the troupe of those (the majority) who deal with Photography-according-to-the-Photographer. I possessed only two experiences: that of the observed subject and that of the subject observing . . .

5

It can happen that I am observed without knowing it, and again I cannot speak of this experience, since I have determined to be guided by the consciousness of my feelings. But very often (too often, to my taste) I have been photographed and knew it. Now, once I feel myself observed by the lens, everything changes: I constitute myself in the process of "posing," I instantaneously make another body for myself, I transform myself in advance into an image. This transformation is an active one: I feel that the Photograph creates my body or mortifies it, according to its caprice (apology of this mortiferous power: certain Communards paid with their lives for their willingness or even their eagerness to pose on the barricades: defeated, they were recognized by Thiers's police and shot, almost every one).

Posing in front of the lens (I mean: knowing I am posing, even fleetingly), I do not risk so much as that (at least, not for the moment). No doubt it is metaphorically that I derive my existence from the photographer. But though this dependence is an imaginary one (and from the purest image-repertoire), I experience it with the anguish of an uncertain filiation: an image—my image—will be generated: will I be born from an antipathetic individual or from a "good sort"? If only I could "come out" on paper as on a classical canvas, endowed with a noble expression—thoughtful, intelligent, etc.! In short, if I could be "painted" (by Titian) or drawn (by Clouet)! But since what I want to have captured is a delicate moral texture and not a mimicry, and since Photography is anything but subtle except in the hands of the very greatest portraitists, I don't know how to work upon my skin from within. I decide to "let drift" over my lips and in my eyes a faint smile which I mean to be "indefinable," in which I might suggest, along with the qualities of my nature, my amused consciousness of the whole photographic ritual: I lend myself to the social game, I pose, I know I am posing, I want you to know that I am posing, but (to square the circle) this additional message must in no way alter the precious essence of my individuality: what I am, apart from any effigy. What I want, in short, is that my (mobile) image, buffeted among a thousand shifting photographs, altering with situation and age, should always coincide with my (profound) "self"; but it is the contrary that must be said: "myself" never coincides with my image; for it is the image which is heavy, motionless, stubborn (which is why society sustains it), and "myself" which is light, divided, dispersed; like a bottle-imp, "myself" doesn't hold still, giggling in my jar: if only Photography could give me a neutral, anatomic body, a body which signifies nothing! Alas, I am doomed by (well-meaning) Photography always to have an expression: my body never finds its zero degree, no one can give it to me (perhaps only my mother? For it is not indifference which erases the weight of the image—the Photomat always turns you into a criminal type, wanted by the police—but love, extreme love).

To see oneself (differently from in a mirror): on the scale of History, this action is recent, the painted, drawn, or miniaturized portrait having been, until the spread of Photography, a limited possession, intended moreover to advertise a social and financial status—and in any case, a painted portrait, however close the resemblance (this is what I am trying to prove) is not a photograph. Odd that no one has thought of the *disturbance* (to civilization) which this new action causes. I want a History of Looking. For the Photograph is the advent of myself as other: a cunning dissociation of consciousness from identity. Even odder: it was *before* Photography that men had the most to say about the vision of the double. Heautoscopy was compared with an hallucinosis; for centuries this was a great mythic theme. But today it is as if we repressed the profound madness of Photography: it reminds us of its mythic heritage only by that faint uneasiness which seizes me when I look at "myself" on a piece of paper.

This disturbance is ultimately one of ownership. Law has expressed it in its way: to whom does the photograph belong? Is landscape itself only a kind of loan made by the owner of the terrain? Countless cases, apparently, have expressed this uncertainty in a society for which being was based on having. Photography transformed subject into object, and even, one might say, into a museum object: in order to take the first portraits (around 1840) the subject had to assume long poses under a glass roof in bright sunlight; to become an object made one suffer as much as a surgical operation; then a device was invented, a kind of prosthesis invisible to the lens, which supported and maintained the body in its passage to immobility: this head-rest was the pedestal of the statue I would become, the corset of my imaginary essence.

The portrait-photograph is a closed field of forces. Four image-repertoires intersect here, oppose and distort each other. In front of the lens, I am at the same time: the one I think I am, the one I want others to think I am, the one the photographer thinks I am, and the one he makes use of to exhibit his art. In other words, a strange action: I do not stop imitating myself, and because of this, each time I am (or let myself be) photographed, I invariably suffer from a sensation of inauthenticity, sometimes of imposture (comparable to certain nightmares). In terms of image-repertoire, the Photograph (the one I *intend*) represents that very subtle moment when, to tell the truth, I am neither subject nor object but a subject who feels he is becoming an object: I then experience a micro-version of death (of parenthesis): I am truly becoming a specter. The Photographer knows this very well, and himself fears (if only for commercial reasons) this death in which his gesture will embalm me. Nothing would be funnier (if one were not its passive victim, its *plastron*, as Sade would say) than the photographers' contortions to produce effects that are "lifelike": wretched notions: they make me pose in front of my paint-brushes, they take me outdoors (more "alive" than indoors), put me in front of a staircase because a group of children is playing behind me, they notice a bench and immediately (what a windfall!) make me sit down on it. As if the (terrified) Photographer must exert himself to the utmost to keep the Photograph from becoming Death. But I—already an object, I do not struggle. I foresee that I shall have to wake from this bad dream even more uncomfortably; for what society makes of my photograph, what it reads there, I do not know (in any case, there are so many readings of the same face); but when I discover myself in the product of this operation, what I see is that I have become Total-Image, which is to say, Death in person; others—the Other—do not dispossess me of myself, they turn me, ferociously, into an object, they put me at their mercy, at their disposal, classified in a file, ready for the subtlest deceptions: one day an excellent photographer took my picture; I believed I could read in his image the distress of a recent bereavement: for once Photography had restored me to myself, but soon afterward I was to find this same photograph on the cover of a pamphlet; by the artifice of printing, I no longer had anything but a horrible disinternalized countenance, as sinister and repellent as the image the authors wanted to give of my language. (The "private life" is nothing but that zone of space, of time, where I am not an image, an object. It is my *political* right to be a subject which I must protect.)

Ultimately, what I am seeking in the photograph taken of me (the "intention" according to which I look at it) is Death: Death is the *eidos* of that Photograph. Hence, strangely, the only thing that I tolerate, that I like, that is familiar to me, when I am photographed, is the sound of the camera. For me, the Photographer's organ is not his eye (which terrifies me) but his finger: what is linked to the trigger of the lens, to the metallic shifting of the plates (when the camera still has such things). I love these mechanical sounds in an almost voluptuous way, as if, in the Photograph, they were the very thing—and the only thing—to which my desire clings, their abrupt click breaking through the mortiferous layer of the Pose. For me the noise of Time is not sad: I love bells, clocks, watches—and I recall that at first photographic implements were related to techniques of cabinetmaking and the machinery of precision: cameras, in short, were clocks for seeing, and perhaps in me someone very old still hears in the photographic mechanism the living sound of the wood.

6

The disorder which from the very first I had observed in Photography—all practices and all subjects mixed up together—I was to rediscover in the photographs of the *Spectator* whom I was and whom I now wanted to investigate.

I see photographs everywhere, like everyone else, nowadays; they come from the world to me, without my asking; they are only "images," their mode of appearance is heterogeneous. Yet, among those which had been selected, evaluated, approved, collected in albums or magazines and which had thereby passed through the filter of culture, I realized that some provoked tiny jubilations, as if they referred to a stilled center, an erotic or lacerating value buried in myself (however harmless the subject may have appeared); and that others, on the contrary, were so indifferent to me that by dint of seeing them multiply, like some weed, I felt a kind of aversion toward them, even of irritation: there are moments when I detest Photographs: what have I to do with Atget's old tree trunks, with Pierre Boucher's nudes, with Germaine Krull's double exposures (to cite only the old names)? Further: I realized that I have never liked *all* the pictures by any one photographer: the only thing by Stieglitz that delights me (but to ecstasy) is his most famous image ("The Horse-Car Terminal," New York, 1893); a certain picture by Mapplethorpe led me to think I had found "my" photographer; but I hadn't—I don't like all of Mapplethorpe. Hence I could not accede to that notion which is so convenient when we want to talk history, culture, aesthetics—that notion known as an artist's style. I felt, by the strength of my "investments," their disorder, their caprice, their enigma, that Photography is an *uncertain* art, as would be (were one to attempt to establish such a thing) a science of desirable or detestable bodies.

I saw clearly that I was concerned here with the impulses of an overready subjectivity, inadequate as soon as articulated: *I like/ I don't like:* we all have our secret chart of tastes, distastes, indifferences, don't we? But just so: I have always wanted to remonstrate with my moods; not to justify them; still less to fill the scene of the text with my individuality; but on the contrary, to offer, to extend this individuality to a science of the subject, a science whose name is of little importance to me, provided it attains (as has not yet occurred) to a generality which neither reduces nor crushes me. Hence it was necessary to take a look for myself.

7

I decided then to take as a guide for my new analysis the attraction I felt for certain photographs. For of this attraction, at least, I was certain. What to call it? Fascination? No, this photograph which I pick out and which I love has nothing in common with the shiny point which sways before your eyes and makes your head swim; what it produces in me is the very opposite of hebetude; something more like an internal agitation, an excitement, a certain labor too, the pressure of the unspeakable which wants to be spoken. Well, then? Interest? Of brief duration; I have no need to question my feelings in order to list the various reasons to be interested in a photograph; one can either desire the object, the landscape, the body it represents; or love or have loved the being it permits us to recognize; or be astonished by what one sees; or else admire or dispute the photographer's performance, etc.; but these interests are slight, heterogeneous; a certain photograph can satisfy one of them and interest me slightly; and if another photograph interests me powerfully, I should like to know what there is in it that sets me off. So it seemed that the best word to designate (temporarily) the attraction certain photographs exerted upon me was *advenience* or even *adventure.* This picture *advenes,* that one doesn't.

The principle of adventure allows me to make Photography exist. Conversely, without adventure, no photograph. I quote Sartre: "Newspaper photographs can very well 'say nothing to me.' In other words, I look at them without assuming a posture of existence. Though the persons whose photograph I see are certainly present in the photograph, they are so without existential posture, like the Knight and Death present in Dürer's engraving, but without my positing them. Moreover, cases occur where the photograph leaves me so indifferent that I do not even bother to see it 'as an image.' The photograph is vaguely constituted as an object, and the persons who figure there are certainly constituted as persons, but only because of their resemblance to human beings, without any special intentionality. They drift between the shores of perception, between sign and image, without ever approaching either."

In this glum desert, suddenly a specific photograph reaches me; it animates me, and I animate it. So that is how I must name the attraction which makes it exist: an *animation.* The photograph itself is in no way animated (I do not believe in "lifelike" photographs), but it animates me: this is what creates every adventure.

8

In this investigation of Photography, I borrowed something from phenomenology's project and something from its language. But it was a vague, casual, even cynical phenomenology, so readily did it agree to distort or to evade its principles according to the whim of my analysis. First of all, I did not escape, or try to escape, from a paradox: on the one hand the desire to give a name to Photography's essence and then to sketch an eidetic science of the Photograph; and on the other the intractable feeling that Photography is essentially (a contradiction in terms) only contingency, singularity, risk: my photographs would always participate, as Lyotard says, in "something or other": is it not the very weakness of Photography, this difficulty in existing which we call banality? Next, my phenomenology agreed to compromise with a power, *affect;* affect was what I didn't want to reduce; being irreducible, it was thereby what I wanted, what I ought to reduce the Photograph *to;* but could I retain an affective intentionality, a view of the object which was immediately steeped in desire, repulsion, nostalgia, euphoria? Classical phenomenology, the kind I had known in my adolescence (and there has not been any other since), had never, so far as I could remember, spoken of desire or of mourning. Of course I could make out in Photography, in a very orthodox manner, a whole network of essences: material essences (necessitating the physical, chemical, optical study of the Photography), and regional essences (deriving, for instance, from aesthetics, from History, from sociology); but at the moment of reaching the essence of Photography in general, I branched off; instead of following the path of a formal ontology (of a Logic), I stopped, keeping with me, like a treasure, my desire or my grief; the anticipated essence of the Photograph could not, in my mind, be separated from the "pathos" of which, from the first glance, it consists. I was like that friend who had turned to Photography only because it allowed him to photograph his son. As *Spectator* I was interested in Photography only for "sentimental" reasons; I wanted to explore it not as a question (a theme) but as a wound: I see, I feel, hence I notice, I observe, and I think.

9

I was glancing through an illustrated magazine. A photograph made me pause. Nothing very extraordinary: the (photographic) banality of a rebellion in Nicaragua: a ruined street, two helmeted soldiers on patrol; behind them, two nuns. Did this photograph please me? Interest me? Intrigue me? Not even. Simply, it existed (for me). I understood at once that its existence (its "adventure") derived from the co-presence of two discontinuous elements, heterogeneous in that they did not belong to the same world (no need to proceed to the point of contrast): the soldiers and the nuns. I foresaw a structural rule (conforming to my own observation), and I immediately tried to verify it by inspecting other photographs by the same reporter (the Dutchman Koen Wessing): many of them attracted me because they included this kind of duality which I had just become aware of. Here a mother and daughter sob over the father's arrest (Baudelaire: "the emphatic truth of gesture in the great circumstances of life"), and this happens *out in the countryside* (where could they have learned the news? for whom are these gestures?). Here, on a torn-up pavement, a child's corpse under a white sheet; parents and friends stand around it, desolate: a banal enough scene, unfortunately, but I noted certain interferences: the corpse's one bare foot, the sheet carried by the weeping mother (why this sheet?), a woman in the background, probably a friend, holding a handkerchief to her nose. Here again, in a bombed-out apartment, the huge eyes of two little boys, one's shirt raised over his little belly (the excess of those eyes disturb the scene). And here, finally, leaning against the wall of a house, three Sandinists, the lower part of their faces covered by a rag (stench? secrecy? I have no idea, knowing nothing of the realities of guerrilla warfare); one of them holds a gun that rests on his thigh (I can see his nails); but his other hand is stretched out, open, as if he were explaining and demonstrating something. My rule applied all the more closely in that other pictures from the same reportage were less interesting to me; they were fine shots, they expressed the dignity and horror of rebellion, but in my eyes they bore no mark or sign: their homogeneity remained cultural: they

186

were "scenes," rather *à la* Greuze, had it not been for the harshness of the subject.

10

My rule was plausible enough for me to try to name (as I would need to do) these two elements whose co-presence established, it seemed, the particular interest I took in these photographs.

The first, obviously, is an extent, it has the extension of a field, which I perceive quite familiarly as a consequence of my knowledge, my culture; this field can be more or less stylized, more or less successful, depending on the photographer's skill or luck, but it always refers to a classical body of information: rebellion, Nicaragua, and all the signs of both: wretched un-uniformed soldiers, ruined streets, corpses, grief, the sun, and the heavy-lidded Indian eyes. Thousands of photographs consist of this field, and in these photographs I can, of course, take a kind of general interest, one that is even stirred sometimes, but in regard to them my emotion requires the rational intermediary of an ethical and political culture. What I feel about these photographs derives from an *average* affect, almost from a certain training. I did not know a French word which might account for this kind of human interest, but I believe this word exists in Latin: it is *studium,* which doesn't mean, at least not immediately, "study," but application to a thing, taste for someone, a kind of general, enthusiastic commitment, of course, but without special acuity. It is by *studium* that I am interested in so many photographs, whether I receive them as political testimony or enjoy them as good historical scenes: for it is culturally (this connotation is present in *studium*) that I participate in the figures, the faces, the gestures, the settings, the actions.

The second element will break (or punctuate) the *studium.* This time it is not I who seek it out (as I invest the field of the *studium* with my sovereign consciousness),

it is this element which rises from the scene, shoots out of it like an arrow, and pierces me. A Latin word exists to designate this wound, this prick, this mark made by a pointed instrument: the word suits me all the better in that it also refers to the notion of punctuation, and because the photographs I am speaking of are in effect punctuated, sometimes even speckled with these sensitive points; precisely, these marks, these wounds are so many *points.* This second element which will disturb the *studium* I shall therefore call *punctum;* for *punctum* is also: sting, speck, cut, little hole—and also a cast of the dice. A photograph's *punctum* is that accident which pricks me (but also bruises me, is poignant to me).

Having thus distinguished two themes in Photography (for in general the photographs I liked were constructed in the manner of a classical sonata), I could occupy myself with one after the other.

11

Many photographs are, alas, inert under my gaze. But even among those which have some existence in my eyes, most provoke only a general and, so to speak, *polite* interest: they have no *punctum* in them: they please or displease me without pricking me: they are invested with no more than *studium.* The *studium* is that very wide field of unconcerned desire, of various interest, of inconsequential taste: *I like/I don't like.* The *studium* is of the order of *liking,* not of *loving;* it mobilizes a half desire, a demi-volition; it is the same sort of vague, slippery, irresponsible interest one takes in the people, the entertainments, the books, the clothes one finds "all right."

To recognize the *studium* is inevitably to encounter the photographer's intentions, to enter into harmony with them, to approve or disapprove of them, but always to understand them, to argue them within myself, for culture (from which the *studium* derives) is a contract arrived at between creators and consumers. The *studium* is a kind of education (knowledge and civility, "politeness") which allows me to discover the *Operator,* to experience the intentions which establish and animate his practices, but to experience them "in reverse," according to my will as a *Spectator.* It is rather as if I had to read the Photographer's myths in the Photograph, fraternizing with them but not quite believing in them. These myths obviously aim (this is what myth is for) at reconciling the Photograph with society (is this necessary?—Yes, indeed: the Photograph is *dangerous*) by endowing it with *functions,* which are, for the Photographer, so many alibis. These functions are: to inform, to represent, to surprise, to cause to signify, to provoke desire. And I, the *Spectator,* I recognize them with more or less pleasure: I invest them with my *studium* (which is never my delight or my pain).

12

Since the Photograph is pure contingency and can be nothing else (it is always *something* that is represented)—contrary to the text which, by the sudden action of a single word, can shift a sentence from description to reflection—it immediately yields up those "details" which constitute the very raw material of ethnological knowledge. When William Klein photographs "Mayday, 1959" in Moscow, he teaches me how Russians dress (which after all I don't know): I *note* a boy's big cloth cap, another's necktie, an old woman's scarf around her head, a youth's haircut, etc. I can enter still further into such details, observing that many of the men photographed by Nadar have long fingernails: an ethnographical question: how long were nails worn in a certain period? Photography can tell me this much better than painted portraits. It allows me to accede to an infra-knowledge; it supplies me with a collection of partial objects and can flatter a certain fetishism of mine: for this "me" which likes knowledge, which nourishes a kind of amorous preference for it. In the same way, I like certain biographical features which, in a writer's life, delight me as much as certain photographs; I have called these features "biographemes"; Photography has the same relation to History that the biographeme has to biography.

LEAVING THE MOVIE THEATER

Roland Barthes

There is something to confess: your speaker likes to *leave* a movie theater. Back out on the more or less empty, more or less brightly lit sidewalk (it is invariably at night, and during the week, that he *goes*), and heading uncertainly for some café or other, he walks in silence (he doesn't like discussing the film he's just seen), a little dazed, wrapped up in himself, feeling the cold—he's *sleepy,* that's what he's thinking, his body had become something *sopitive,* soft, limp, and he feels a little disjointed, even (for a moral organization, relief comes only from this quarter) irresponsible. In other words, obviously, he's coming out of hypnosis. And hypnosis (an old psychoanalytic device—one that psychoanalysis nowadays seems to treat quite condescendingly) means only one thing to him: the most venerable of powers: healing. And he thinks of music: isn't there such a thing as hypnotic music? The castrato Farinelli, whose messa *di voce* was "as incredible for its duration as for its emission," relieved the morbid melancholy of Philip V of Spain by singing him the same aria every night for fourteen years.

This is often how he leaves a movie theater. How does he go in? Except for the—increasingly frequent—case of a specific cultural quest (a selected, sought-for, desired film, object of a veritable preliminary alert), he goes to movies as a response to idleness, leisure, free time. It's as if, even before he went into the theater, the classic conditions of hypnosis were in force: vacancy, want of occupation, lethargy; it's not in front of the film and because of the film that he *dreams off*—it's without knowing it, even before he becomes a spectator. There is a "cinema situation," and this situation is pre-hypnotic. According to a true metonymy, the darkness of the theater is prefigured by the "twilight reverie" (a prerequisite for hypnosis, according to Breuer-Freud) which precedes it and leads him from street to street, from poster to poster, finally burying himself in a dim, anonymous, indifferent cube where that festival of affects known as a film will be presented.

What does the "darkness" of the cinema mean? (Whenever I hear the word *cinema,* I can't help thinking *hall,* rather than *film.*) Not only is the dark the very substance of

189

reverie (in the pre-hypnoid meaning of the term); it is also the "color" of a diffused eroticism; by its human condensation, by its absence of worldliness (contrary to the cultural *appearance* that has to be put in at any "legitimate theater"), by the relaxation of postures (how many members of the cinema audience slide down into their seats as if into a bed, coats or feet thrown over the row in front!), the movie house (ordinary model) is a site of availability (even more than cruising), the inoccupation of bodies, which best defines modern eroticism—not that of advertising or strip-tease, but that of the big city. It is in this urban dark that the body's freedom is generated; this invisible work of possible affects emerges from a veritable cinematographic cocoon; the movie spectator could easily appropriate the silkworm's motto: *Inclusum labor illustrat;* it is because I am enclosed that I work and glow with all my desire.

In this darkness of the cinema (anonymous, populated, numerous—oh, the boredom, the frustration of so-called private showings!) lies the very fascination of the film (any film). Think of the contrary experience: on television, where films are also shown, no fascination; here darkness is erased, anonymity repressed; space is familiar, articulated (by furniture, known objects), tamed: the eroticism—no, to put it better, to get across the particular kind of lightness, of unfulfillment we mean: the eroticization of the place is foreclosed: television *doomed* us to the Family, whose household instrument it has become—what the hearth used to be, flanked by its communal kettle.

In that opaque cube, one light: the film, the screen? Yes, of course. But also (especially?), visible and unperceived, that dancing cone which pierces the darkness like a laser beam. This beam is minted, according to the rotation of its particles, into changing figures; we turn our face toward the *currency* of a gleaming vibration whose imperious jet brushes our skull, glancing off someone's hair, someone's face. As in the old hypnotic experiments, we are fascinated—without seeing it head-on—by this shining site, motionless and dancing.

It's exactly as if a long stem of light had outlined a keyhole, and then we all peered, flabbergasted, through that hole. And nothing in this ecstasy is provided by sound, music, words? Usually—in current productions—the audio protocol can produce no *fascinated* listening; conceived to reinforce the *lifelikeness* of the anecdote, sound is merely a supplementary instrument of representation; it is meant to integrate itself unobtrusively into the object shown, it is in no way detached from this object; yet it would take very little in order to separate this sound track: one displaced or magnified sound, the grain of a voice milled in our eardrums, and the fascination begins again; for it never comes except from artifice, or better still: from the *artifact*— like the dancing beam of the projector— which comes from overhead or to the side, blurring the scene shown by the screen *yet without distorting its image* (its *gestalt,* its meaning).

For such is the narrow range—at least for me—in which can function the fascination of film, the cinematographic hypnosis: I must be in the story (there must be verisimilitude), but I must also be elsewhere: a slightly disengaged image-repertoire, that is what I must have—like a scrupulous, conscientious, organized, in a word *difficult* fetishist, that is what I require of the film and of the situation in which I go looking for it.

The film image (including the sound) is what? *A lure.* I am confined with the image as if I were held in that famous dual relation which establishes the image-repertoire. The image is there, in front of me, for me: coalescent (its signified and its signifier melted together), analogical, total, pregnant; it is a perfect lure: I fling myself upon it like an animal upon the scrap of "lifelike" rag held out to him; and, of course, it sustains in me the misreading attached to Ego and to image-repertoire. In the movie theater, however far away I am sitting, I press my nose against the screen's mirror, against that "other" image-repertoire with which I narcissistically identify myself (it is said that the spectators who choose to sit as close to the screen as possible are children and movie buffs); the image captivates me, captures me: I am *glued* to the representation, and it is this glue which established the *naturalness* (the pseudo-nature) of the filmed scene (a glue prepared with all the ingredients of "technique"); the Real knows only distances, the Symbolic knows only masks; the image alone (the image-repertoire) is *close,* only the image is *"true"* (can produce the resonance of truth). Actually, has not the image, statutorily, all the characteristics of the *ideological?* The historical subject, like the cinema spectator I am imagining, is also *glued* to ideological discourse: he experiences its coalescence, its analogical security, its naturalness, its "truth": it is a lure (*our* lure, for who escapes it?); the Ideological would actually be the image-repertoire of a period of history, the Cinema of a society; like the film which lures its clientele, it even has its photograms; is not the stereotype a fixed image, a quotation to which our language is glued? And in the commonplace have we not a dual relation: narcissistic and maternal?

How to come unglued from the mirror? I'll risk a pun to answer: by *taking off* (in the aeronautical and narcotic sense of the term).

Of course, it is still possible to conceive of an art which will break the dual circle, the fascination of film, and loosen the glue, the hypnosis of the lifelike (of the analogical), by some recourse to the spectator's critical vision (or listening); is this not what the Brechtian alienation-effect involves? Many things can help us to "come out of" (imaginary and/or ideological) hypnosis: the very methods of an epic art, the spectator's culture or his ideological vigilance; contrary to classical hysteria, the image-repertoire vanishes once one observes that it exists. But there is another way of going to the movies (besides being armed by the discourse of counter-ideology); by letting oneself be fascinated *twice over,* by the image and by its surroundings—as if I had two bodies at the same time: a narcissistic body which gazes, lost, into the engulfing mirror, and a perverse body, ready to fetishize not the image but precisely what exceeds it: the texture of the sound, the hall, the darkness, the obscure mass of the other bodies, the rays of light, entering the theater, leaving the hall; in short, in order to distance, in order to "take off," I complicate a "relation" by a "situation." What I use to distance myself from the image—that, ultimately, is what fascinates me: I am hypnotized by a distance; and this distance is not critical (intellectual); it is, one might say, an amorous distance: would there be, in the cinema itself (and taking the word at its etymological suggestion) a possible bliss of *discretion?*

—*Translated by Richard Howard*

TRANSGRESSION AND TRANSFORMATION

LEAVING LAS VEGAS

bell hooks

Six years ago I published a book of essays, *Yearning: race, gender, and cultural politics,* which included this dedication: "for you to whom i surrender—to you for whom i wait." When the book was about to go to press, several feminist editors working on the project expressed concern about this dedication. They found the use of the word "surrender" problematic, disempowering to women. It suggested for them a loss of control, powerlessness. While I agreed that the word "surrender" has this connotation, it also means to give up, to submit. I argued that there are moments when submission is a gesture of agency and power, that a distinction has to be made between conscious surrender, an act of choice and the submission of someone who is victimized and without choice. It seemed to me then, as it does now that women would need to know the difference if we were ever to be capable of self-actualization within patriarchal culture.

To love fully one must be able to surrender—to give up control. If we are to know love, then we cannot escape the practice of surrender. In patriarchal culture women who love men take a risk that our willingness to surrender may create a space of vulnerability where we can be wounded, violated. This is why there was such a critique of romantic love in early radical feminist discussions and why it was believed that it was difficult for any woman to fully realize feminist practice in a heterosexual relationship. Hence the saying: "feminism is the theory and lesbianism is the practice." Women active in the feminist movement who continued relating to men sexually had to grapple with the meaning of a politics of surrender in the context of heterosexual love in patriarchal society.

Unfortunately, feminist thinkers have to a grave extent abandoned radical discussions of sexuality and the meaning of love in heterosexual relationships. At times these concerns are dismissed as irrelevant and the issues are addressed by simply calling attention to male sexism as though acknowledgement of that reality precludes any need to understand the construction of female and female sexual agency within this context. These issues are raised by Mike Figgis's film *Leaving Las Vegas*. Many feminist viewers simply dismissed this film as another example of the male pornographic imagination at work. Despite the ways in which sexism informs female sexuality is in this film, *Leaving Las Vegas* is a daring work in so far as it suggests that within patriarchy female masochism need not be disempowering, that it can be the space of abjection and surrender wherein the powerless regain a sense of agency. However utopian, this vision does not condemn women to play forever the role of victim.

Leaving Las Vegas chronicles the story of Sera, a prostitute who falls in love with a washed up movie executive named Ben who is drinking himself to death. Ben chooses to travel to Las Vegas to abandon himself to dying. When the film begins we witness him bottoming out at work and in relationships. The film makes it clear that he is not seeking help (this is not about recovery). Addressing the issue of alcoholism in his popular work *Further Along the Road Less Traveled,* psychologist M. Scott Peck contends: "Alcoholics are not any more broken than people who are not alcoholic. We all have our griefs and our terrors, we may not be conscious of them, but we all have them. We are all broken people, but alcoholics can't hide it anymore, whereas the rest of us can hide behind our masks of composure. We are not able to talk with each other about the things that are most important to us, about the way our hearts are breaking. So the great lesson of alcoholism is the nature of the disease. It puts people into visible crisis." Yet Figgis creates an alcoholic in crisis who is not seeking redemption. He has surrendered to his fate. He is courting death.

In the midst of this flirtation, he seeks community and finds it with Sera. Mistakenly, reviewers of the film talk about it as a romantic love story between two individuals who are both broken. The sign of Sera's brokenness is presumably that she is a sex worker. However, audiences and critics arrive at this assessment of her through the lens of their own morality, their own sense that to work as a prostitute means that one is a loser. In actuality, the film disturbs many feminist viewers precisely because Sera is not presented as a victim. In *Leaving Las Vegas* Sera is depicted as a prostitute who enjoys her work. She likes the power to take charge, to use sexuality as a means of making money. Like the actual prostitute in Sallie Tisdale's *Talk Dirty to Me* who states that she would like to be able to display the material comforts of her life and say to people: "See? I am really good in bed! Look at this apartment! Look at what my pussy got me!" It is this assertion of female agency in relation to her body that Sera's character exhibits in the film that is so unsettling for viewers. Many of them choose to see this characterization as male fantasy rather than accept that there are women in the sex industry who feel this way about their work.

Unlike Ben, the alcoholic male, Sera is not washed up. Her vulnerability lies not in her profession but in her longing to be seen as more than her job. In fact, she is resisting the dehumanization that working as a prostitute in patriarchal culture would have her succumb to. It is this resistance, this refusal to be a victim, or object without choices that attracts her to Ben. He seduces her by recognizing her humanity, by seeing that she is not defined by her work and the stigma attached to it. This recognition enables Sera to share with someone critical awareness of the burden of having other people treat you as a loser when you do not see yourself that way. Sera responds to this recognition, to Ben's willingness to address her in the complexity of her being, by falling in love. Yet later, once she has trusted him, he continually reminds her, "We both know that I am a drunk and you are a hooker." Love matters to Sera more than to Ben.

Wary of her and love, instead of returning that love fully, Ben violates the trust she shows him by swiftly becoming an intimate terrorist. While Sera can express her need for Ben without shame, he resists. It is his resistance that turns the potential love relationship into a torturous sadomasochistic bond. Michael Miller argues in *Intimate Terrorism* that when the psychological fate of the self becomes enmeshed with erotic passion, individuals panic: "When people fear what they need, they become angry both at themselves and at those from whom they seek to get their needs met . . . Often you see a man and a woman in an intimate relationship . . . treat one another with cruelty that they would never consider directing toward anyone who meant less to them." This is precisely what happens with Ben in *Leaving Las Vegas*.

Having made the decision to surrender to death, Ben resists the pull of eros—the call to return to life that sexual longing and connection make on his psyche. His impotence is the sign of that resistance. Hence his insistence that Sera never suggest that he seek help. He demands that she completely surrender any longing for him to be well—to stay alive. It is the unequal demand in the relationship that creates the sadomasochistic dynamic. Sera becomes the slave of love. In the end it is she who confesses in therapy that" "We realized we didn't have much time and I accepted him for what he was."

Throughout the film, Ben remains enthralled by his flirtation with death. In the forward to *The Tears of Eros* Georges Bataille celebrates a love affair like Ben's, declaring: "The essence of man as given in sexuality—which is his origin and beginning—poses a problem for him that has no other outcome than wild turmoil. This turmoil is given in

the 'little death.' How can I fully live the 'little death' if not as a foretaste of the final death? The violence of spasmodic joy lies deep in my heart. This violence, at the same time, and I tremble as I say it, is the heart of death: it opens itself up to me." To a grave extent, Ben the wasted lost male soul, is the personification of the patriarchal betrayal of masculinity. Before he leaves for Las Vegas, everyone he reaches out to for connection is male. His friend Peter tells him "Never contact me again." Once he is broken, the world of homosocial patriarchal bonding that once sustained him shuns him. Lost to himself and others precisely because his lust for death is the extreme living out of the patriarchal masculine ethos, he is naked and exposed.

As Sera's sense of wholeness is restored by the act of loving Ben, he loses his power over her. She begins to long for him to be well. When she expresses that longing he violently rejects her. Later he violates her home by bringing another woman prostitute there and sharing with her the erotic passion he withholds from Sera. Even though she has willingly surrendered to love, Sera refuses violation, especially in the domestic space that is her sanctuary and refuge. Despite her love for Ben, she demands that he leave. It is at this filmic moment that the misogynist pornographic imagination rears its ugly head and we see that Sera's refusal to be a victim in romantic love sets the stage for her to be brutally raped. This is the sequence in the film that appears as pure, unadulterated sexist male fantasy. Up until this point in the movie, Sera has been a savvy, tough woman of the streets who can take care of herself. Suddenly, she is portrayed as dumb, as blinded by the sight of three college males with money seeking sexual servicing. In this sequence Sera is triply betrayed: First by the men who rape her, then by the lover who has violated her in the first place, and ultimately by the filmmaker who succumbs to the usual stereotypes and has the "bad" girl punished. This male punishment of the sexually assertive woman who refuses to be a victim gives the film a conventional, predictable patriarchal pornographic slant.

Indeed, this brutal anal rape sequence undermines the more progressive narrative in the film wherein Sera's sense of self is restored by having a healthy interaction with a male she loves. Interviewed in *The Power to Dream,* writer Maxine Hong Kingston states: "I believe that in order to truly grow up, women must love men. That has to be the next stage of feminism. I can't believe that feminism just breaks off at the point where we get to join the Marines." Significantly, Sera is the quintessentially sexually liberated woman in modern society. Her overactive sexuality serves to mask her desire to be loved. It is in the act of loving that Sera risks vulnerability, not in being sexual with men. In sex she can be indifferent—in control. To love she must let go. It is this letting go that makes it possible for her to be redeemed. Unlike Ben, she begins a love affair with life. Loving him makes her want to live. In *Rituals of Love* Ted Polhemus and Housk Randall suggest that in the sadomasochistic power ritual the submissive believes that by "submitting to humiliating indignity she will discover in herself a 'sublime dignity' and that by the loss of control over her own actions (the will that wills self-abandon) she will discover a greater selfhood." This is Sera's quest.

After she has gained recognition of her selfhood through the reciprocal bond she forms with Ben, she finds it impossible to reinhabit a social space where she is not being truly seen. Although she has asked Ben to leave, she continues to love him. Throughout their affair she has felt powerless because she cannot sexually seduce him. Seduction is the way that she previously controlled men. Describing the power relations embedded in the process of seduction, Jean Baudrillard in *Seduction* states:

"There is something impersonal in every process of seduction, as in every crime, something ritualistic, something suprasubjective and supra-sensual, the lived experience, whether of the seducer or his victim, being only its unconscious reflection." Sera the experienced seducer is seduced. Baudrillard claims that "seduction always seeks to overturn and exorcise a power. If seduction is artificial, it is also sacrificial. One is playing with death, it always being a matter of capturing or immolating the desire of the other." When Ben calls Sera, like the slave of love she is, she obeys. Entering the sleazy hotel room where he lies in the throes of death, she gives him the mingling of tears and eros Georges Bataille extols in his work. For Ben ecstasy is merely a preparation for death. Meditating on death, on the "last instant," Bataille observed: "When there is physical pain, a high degree of what may be termed narcissistic cathexis of the painful place occurs: this cathexis continues to increase and tends, as it were, to 'empty' the ego." It is this state of emptiness that gives Ben his aura of blissful indifference. That bliss would be eradicated at the moment of death, were it not for Sera's presence. As Bataille testifies: "In myself, the satisfaction of a desire is often opposed to my interests. But I give in to it, for in a brutal way it has become for me the ultimate end . . . the end of reason, which exceeds reason, is not opposed to the overcoming of reason! In the violence of the overcoming, in the disorder of my laughter and my sobbing, in the excess of raptures that shatter me, I seize on the similarity between a horror and a voluptuousness that goes beyond me, between an ultimate pain and an unbearable joy!" Ben fails in his quest to meet death alone. The desire for connection triumphs. He is able to go—to truly leave Las Vegas—only when he is connected, only when he has a witness.

Sera gives him the recognition he needs before dying, just as he has given her the recognition that restores her to full humanity, that brings her back to life. Coming back to life for Sera means acknowledging pain and suffering. To cope with the very realties Ben has failed to cope with, she seeks connection and healing. The wounds of passion in her life become the source of that healing.

As a witness to death, Sera is ultimately transformed. She experiences a world that is deeper than the one she knows every day. All experiences are essential for self-actualization, including those of suffering, degradation, and pain. Through her acceptance of Ben and of herself, Sera finds a way to experience unity. In *On the Way to the Wedding,* the Jungian therapist Linda Leonard shares this insight: "As Heidegger has said, our being is to 'be there' where Being opens up and reveals itself, and our task is to open to the revelation and to try to preserve it through expression. For Heidegger, the fundamental opening-up of experience for the human being occurs when one is able to accept and affirm the mystery of death within one's being. For in the acceptance of our 'being-unto-death' we surrender our desire to control reality and thus are able to accept whatever offers itself to us. . . . For death is the ultimate transformation and threshold." Sera crosses the threshold of death and enters life. She is born again through her redemptive love. The tragedy of *Leaving Las Vegas* lies in the way in which Ben's transgression of boundaries does not lead to redemption. This is the danger of being seduced by transgression. At the end of her essay "Is Transgression Transgressive?" Elizabeth Wilson concludes: "We transgress in order to insist that we are, that we exist, and to place a distance between ourselves and the dominant culture. But we have to go further—we have to have an idea of how things could be different, otherwise transgression is mere posturing. In other words, transgression on its own leads eventually to entropy, unless we carry within us some idea of transformation. It is therefore not transgression that should be our watchword, but transformation." If audiences watching *Leaving Las Vegas* are merely enthralled by sexual scenarios of pleasure and danger, by alcoholic hedonistic excess, by the various tropes of transgression, they will feast on the tragedy and ignore the call to love—to be transformed utterly. To love is to endure.

MAD DOGS AND COMPANY MEN

Michael Pressler

*L*ast season everybody turned out for *The Piano,* that damp fable about a silent woman and the two men who desire her, but most people stayed home from *The Music of Chance,* a story about the relationship of two men in which the only woman, a girlish prostitute, appears late in the movie, in a brief scene designed to show how the two guys behave in the presence of the opposite sex. In *A League of Their Own,* a women's baseball team overcame catcalls and went all the way to the Hall of Fame, but the all-male team of diamond robbers in *Reservoir Dogs* struck out. Sally Potter may have cast a woman as a male lead in her film adaptation of Virginia Woolf's *Orlando,* but there were nothing but genuine leading men in the cast of the film version of David Mamet's *Glengarry Glen Ross.* (It takes brass balls to sell real estate, Alec Baldwin tells us in the opening scene.) In the wake of Hollywood's Year of the Woman, despite the high visibility of movies by women directors featuring remarkable women, several male directors have continued to make movies about unremarkable men in whose lives women scarcely figure at all.

Inadequate female representation is common in American films, of course. In traditional Westerns, women are conventionally either schoolmarm madonnas or gold-hearted whores; they stay behind closed shutters when drama breaks out on main street. On Hollywood front lines during World War II, a good woman could be a real liability. Any movie GI who eulogized his mom to a buddy during a pause in battle, or mooned over a snapshot of the girl back home, was doomed in the next round of fighting. Nor have women been peripheral or absent only in such patently "masculine" genres from yesterday. Recently much scholarly attention has been given to gender issues in film, with a number of theorists arguing persuasively that even many "woman's pictures" are really male films in disguise, being based on patriarchal assumptions, Oedipal structures and, embedded in classical filmmaking technique itself, a voyeuristic "look" or "gaze" that perpetuates male values in subtle ways.

I don't mean to talk about such "disguised" male films, though, or about undisguised macho action movies with priapic titles like *Die Hard* or *Lethal Weapon*. I'm talking about films that focus on men at work, locked in their jobs and all but quarantined from women. The rules of this dubious genre, laid down by such classics as *The Treasure of the Sierra Madre, Twelve Angry Men, Dr. Strangelove, The Wild Bunch, Cool Hand Luke*, and *The Last Detail*, make up what I call the Guys Production Code:

I. No woman may appear except in a decidedly minor role, and then only in a service capacity—as, for example, a waitress, maid, checkout girl, nurse, concubine, prostitute, or innocent victim of violence. Treatment of normal heterosexual desire is permitted when drama or proper characterization requires, but only in moderation, and never in such a way as to suggest close friendship or romantic love.

II. The male workplace, broadly defined as any place where men have a certain job to do, shall function as the exclusive sphere of operation. Though brief reference may be made to marriage and the home, scenes of domestic life must never be directly presented, nor allowed to exert any significant positive influence in the exclusionary male world of work.

III. Whether as imminent threat or clear and present danger, verbal and/or physical violence must be presented as an essential fact of life in the workplace. Scenes involving cruelty and brutality, gruesomeness, pointed profanity, or malicious, hostile, or sadistic behavior will make it clear that nothing less than personal survival is at stake for the male characters.

IV. Though some attention may be paid to latent homosexuality, the treatment must be governed by good taste and delicacy. The presentation of male comradeship

and competition must never be compromised by homoeroticism, and audiences should be reassured that unmanly behavior is not accepted nor common and usually has dire consequences.

Reservoir Dogs illustrates these principles vividly. In a short scene, before the opening credits and the diamond robbery that is the line of work in this film, a waitress serves breakfast in the background while in the foreground a group of men at a table discusses the sexual politics of Madonna's "Like a Virgin" and argues about the ethics of tipping. "She don't make enough money, she can quit," says Mr. Pink (Steve Buscemi), refusing to ante up with the rest of the gang who, like him, have assumed false names to preserve anonymity on the heist. "Waitressing is the number one occupation for female non-graduates in this country," the older and more sensitive Mr. White (Harvey Keitel) objects, fixing a steely eye on Pink. "It's the one job basically any woman can get and make a living on—the reason is because of their tips." Quentin Tarantino, who wrote and directed the film and who also appears in this scene as Mr. Brown, was a light tipper when it came to casting: besides the waitress, only two other female characters appear, and they are listed at the bottom of the closing credits merely as "Shocked Woman" and "Shot Woman."

After this scene and the opening credits, we cut to the aftermath of the robbery-gone-sour. The survivors assemble in a vacant warehouse, like players meeting in the locker room after a game they lost. During their post-mortem, what was supposed to happen and what actually did happen is disclosed by flashbacks to the robbery, along with other flashbacks titled "Mr. White," "Mr. Blonde," and "Mr. Orange" showing these key players hiring on and prepping for the job with its boss, Joe Cabot (Lawrence Tierney) and his son and honcho, "Nice Guy" Eddie (Christopher Penn). Gradually we discover what went wrong with the heist: a manager set off the alarm; Mr. Blonde (Michael Madsen), the bona fide psychopath of the group, retaliated by shooting him and several citizens ("real people," Pink calls them, as opposed to cops and robbers); and the police quickly moved in, having been tipped off in advance by Mr. Orange (Tim Roth), who is actually an undercover informer. While we are figuring all this out, there is enough violence to send any Merchant-Ivory fan running for cover. Through all ninety-plus minutes of the film, Mr. Orange lies bleeding to death on a loading ramp. A young cop dies horribly. All the other perpetrators, save Pink, who's nabbed trying to sneak away, are shot dead or mortally wounded before the afternoon is over.

Sure the workplace in *Reservoir Dogs* is bloody, but viewers learned at least as long ago as *The Godfather* to see violent gangsterism as a metaphor for American business-as-usual, and these guys are even wearing plain dark suits and ties, white collars. They don't need prison to keep them in uniform. The idea is buttoned down with a complaint by Mr. Pink, on three occasions, that the others are freaking out when they should be acting "like professionals" (Tarantino has cited Howard Hawks as an important influence), and by Boss Joe Cabot's insistence at the robbery planning meeting that the job is strictly "a matter of business." Accordingly, almost all of the action is confined to two interior sets: the boss's office and the warehouse, or main workplace. Joe Cabot's office is a cozy study in rose and brown. It is decorated with an old territorial map, a gold-framed quattrocento painting of the crucifixion, a world globe, a stuffed elephant's foot and, most commanding of all, a huge pair of ivory tusks rising up from the top of Joe's desk. This office is nothing less than the seat of Imperialist Western Civilization. At the desk sits Joe himself, framed by the elephant tusks and as bald as Brando's Kurtz in *Apocalypse Now*. The warehouse, by distinction, is a sparsely furnished void where the actors are shown in deep, wide-angle shots, set against blank expanses of tile and concrete, their characters keyed in lyrically with pipes, ladders, toilet fixtures, ventilation ducts, unopened cargo, workbenches with paint cans, and so on (Tarantino has cited Jean-Luc Godard as another important influence). In short, these are men at work, and no place like home is in evidence.

Nor homemakers. Early on, in the flashback to White's meeting with Cabot, the door is shut for good on marriage and domesticity when we learn that White once had a female partner named Alabama, but after four jobs together they called it quits. "You push that woman-man thing too long and it gets to you after a while," he tells Cabot, who nods and says he understands. Alabama has since teamed up with another man, but White's not bitter: "Hell of a woman," he adds, closing the subject. "Good little thief." We are told nothing more about White's personal life, and the film presents no evidence of relationships with women in the lives of his boss and co-workers.

White and Orange are the operative figures in the personal drama. We are more sympathetically disposed toward White than toward the others, not just because he's Harvey Keitel and feels for working-class women, but because he's the only one who cares about the dying Orange. White's explanation for this is peculiar: he confesses to Pink that Orange's survival "means a hell of a lot" because "the bullet in his belly is my fault"; as we see in a flashback, White did order Orange to commandeer a car during the getaway, but it was its driver, the Shot Woman, who put the bullet in Orange, earning her name tag when he returned fire. Thus the self-accusation seems flimsy, and we wonder about the real source of White's guilt. Why does he feel so personally responsible for Orange? The answer comes when we learn that White has revealed his first name to Orange, meaning he cannot drop him off at the hospital for fear of being compromised. "The man was dying in my arms," White shouts, trying to justify having gotten so personal on the job: "What was I supposed to do? Tell him I'm sorry, I can't give out that fuckin' information, it's against the *rules*? I don't *trust* you enough?"

White, it turns out, trusts Orange far too much—too much for the facts of the film to bear. Any suggestion of unmanliness in their relationship is diffused, however, if not entirely dispelled, by counterpoint with the equally ambiguous and more sinister relationship between Mr. Blonde and "Nice Guy" Eddie Cabot. In the flashback titled "Mr. Blonde," we learn that he is just out of prison, having taken the fall for Joe and Eddie Cabot on a previous job. Mr. Blonde and Eddie greet one another with backslaps, bearhugs, and some affectionate jabbing, trade some insults, and before long they're wrestling on the rug of Joe's office. The insult ritual touches grim depths: Blonde mocks Eddie for screwing up the job that put him behind bars, but when Eddie counters by smirking that Blonde has been sodomized so much in prison that he's become a "butt cowboy," Blonde flinches. With barbed grins the two chums square off again before Joe orders them to cut the horseplay, but a reason has been insinuated for Blonde's sadism, not to say his lousy attitude toward work. ("I don't have a boss," he snaps at the cop he's about to torture, mutilate, and try to set afire. "Nobody tells me what to do.") At the climax, Eddie's reaction to the death of Blonde is of a fierceness that may lead one to think there is more to it than disappointment at losing a good employee, and that helps to keep us from wondering too much about the stubbornness of White's defense of Orange. After all, Eddie may be wrong to assume Blonde's company loyalty, but he's right that Orange is the rat.

The film closes with a gruesome tableau: when Orange confesses that he's an undercover cop, White, seriously wounded in his shootout with the Cabots, crawls over and, grunting from the effort, hoists Orange up and puts a gun to his head. With Orange in his lap gurgling repeatedly that he's sorry instead of begging for his life, White faces the final choice of saving Orange by surrendering himself and probably dying in the hands of the law, or punishing the traitor and using himself up in the sacrifice, and this is no choice worth having. Tarantino has prepared this last shot as though it were the *Pietà*, with Harvey Keitel as the Madonna and Tim Roth as the bleeding Christ. Slow dolly in to a tight close-up of Keitel, agonizing, as we hear the cops break in and order him to drop the gun. More close-up agonizing. Shots are fired. Keitel slumps, then falls down and out of the frame as Joel McCrea did at the end of *Ride the High Country*. Has the personal male bond or the impersonal group code prevailed? Tarantino isn't saying, though independent investigators weary of the Kennedy assassination may want to make something of that offscreen gunfire.

Substitute words for weapons, make salesmanship the crime, and you have *Glengarry Glen Ross*. Back-stabbing guys working out of back rooms is familiar Mamet territory. This time they are in real estate, peddling investment land to "leads" (i.e., names of "real people") handed down by the top management of Premiere Properties. An opening sales conference talk by supersalesman and company VIP Blake (Alec Baldwin) takes as its theme the play's epigram, the no-nonsense sales maxim "Always Be Closing," and his series of confrontations with the salesmen exposes them as a small inventory of types. In the good old days of Glen Ross property, Shelley Levene earned the nickname "The Machine" for his salesmanship, but now he's got a hospitalized daughter and worries if he's still "man enough" to make the grade. Jack Lemmon plays him with full frontal anxiety. Levene has his begging bowl out, but Dave Moss (Ed Harris) is too proud to beg. Angry and embittered by enslavement in a system he cannot control, Moss pursues his leads with the tenacity of a pit bull, calling them "deadbeats" if they flake out. When he's confronted by Blake, though, it's Bambi Meets Godzilla: Blake demolishes Moss by comparing their cars, brandishing his expensive watch, and generally appealing to the Gatsby Principle that material goods equal status and happiness. George Aaronow (Alan Arkin) is tame and correct, a quietly neurotic Bartleby who feels degraded and abused by his job but blames himself: "Somethin's wrong with me," he confides to Moss. "I can't push through. I can't make any sales." Ricky Roma (Al Pacino), the only salesman not at the presentation, doesn't have to be there because he's the top dog and is busy with a prospect. In this "man's game," Blake makes clear, there are only two outcomes—you're either a "closer" or a "loser."

Blake's talk also tightens the dramatic pressure by setting a draconian performance standard and a deadline. The salesmen can get the premium Glengarry leads only by selling second-rate property to the tapped-out old leads; at the end of the month, the lowest men on "the board," the official register of sales figures, will be fired. The young office manager, John Williamson (Kevin Spacey), thinks this is a neat idea, but as the salesmen see it, it's a no-win situation: they can't succeed on the board without the good leads, but they can't get the good leads without succeeding on the board. Desperate measures are in order.

Mamet's original play, produced on Broadway in 1984, does not include Blake nor this scene and is sparer and more schematic. The salesmen are listed as "men in their fifties" (Levene, Moss, Aaronow) and

"men in their early forties" (Williamson and Roma). Act One consists of three scenes set in a Chinese restaurant: Levene tries to strike a deal with Williamson for some of the new leads; Moss tries to talk Aaronow into stealing all the new leads and selling them to Graff, a competitor; and Roma tries to sell property to a mousy client named Lingk. Three pairs, three pitches—cheating within the system, cheating the system, cheating *as* the system. In Act Two, set entirely at the office, the play seeks out the culprit who burglarized the new leads during intermission, most of the others are somehow incriminated, and all deals fall out.

In his screenplay, Mamet has tried to lend some outdoor excitement to an indoor stage play by setting the first two scenes in moving cars. Director James Foley follows the characters with the camera as they move between the office and the restaurant or parking lot, but a stage-managed air of claustrophobia remains. The city is unspecified, though the office looks to be located somewhere between Baltic and Mediterranean Avenues. There's a noisy elevated train nearby that dogs the tracks of the characters like fate whenever they go outside. Inside the office, the ceilings are low and oppressive, the windows are girded with chain-link fencing, and the cluttered *mise en scène*, rendered in shades of gray, blue, and beige, makes the place look like the inside of a cheap telephone. The cinematographer keeps the key light harsh, but otherwise has done everything to darken the place but drape it in black bunting. This workplace is plainly inhospitable to human behavior, and the salesmen's costumes suggest that, if anything, there is less humanity in them than in the white-collar criminals of *Reservoir Dogs*. Dressed entirely in shades of gray, blue, and beige, they are barely distinguishable from the walls and furniture. This is what life at the office has done to them.

Their bosses certainly are inhuman. Unlike Joe Cabot, who takes a personal interest in his employees, the co-owners of this business, "Mitch and Murray," are frequently invoked but never in touch, never appear. Their policies are relayed through Williamson, the office manager, who shrugs off complaints by disclaiming responsibility. "I don't make the rules," he tells his men. "I'm given the rules." And again: "I'm paid to run the office. I do what I'm told." Small wonder that the salesmen feel demoralized and crippled by a rotten system, or that, like Williamson, they persist in believing that responsibility for their unprincipled behavior lies elsewhere, that "the strategy comes from downtown."

Like the gangsters in *Reservoir Dogs*, these men are stapled to their jobs. For all practical dramatic purposes, they have no homes, no personal lives. No women. In the Chinese restaurant, the only female character in the film, a coat check girl, delivers her one line, "Slow tonight," to Levene while handing him his gray hat and raincoat. "I guess everybody's staying home," he replies, alluding to the weather. Not these guys. Though Blake may accuse them of crying on their wives' shoulders, and Williamson may claim to have spent a rare night at home with his kids, we have no dramatic license to see these aspects of their lives. Onscreen they are all business, constantly on the make, locked in the trademarks of their jobs. They have no time to reflect on their soulless professional lives. Beneath the smiles and the handshakes, the charade of intimacy that characterizes the trade, they're too caught up trying to gain advantages over one another. Like those of their fellow robbers from across the tracks in *Reservoir Dogs*, their interests are not domestic nor philosophical, but territorial.

Aggressive sexist language comes with the territory, finger-pointing standing in for firearms, for in this man's business (as the salesmen often refer to the real-estate world) one wins by intimidation. Moreover, not having the opportunity for normal sex lives, these men have displaced sexuality entirely into their work: virility is measured in terms of sales performance, and closing a deal amounts to a sexual conquest. Describing his victory over the Nyborgs, Levene boasts to Roma about holding his fountain pen poised for five—no, he corrects himself, for twenty or more minutes by the kitchen clock before they gave in and signed on the dotted line. "It was like they wilted, all at once," he marvels. "They both kind of imperceptibly slumped." Blake has called him and the others "faggots" for failing in "the man's game," but now Levene can crow in the office. "I closed the cocksuckers!" he brags, urging Williamson to pour on more leads—"I've got my balls back now!" Roma's pitch to Lingk provides further evidence that the female Other is the salesmen's main prey. We know right off that Lingk is an easy mark because he's a wedlocked pipsqueak whose wife wears the pants, and he may even be cowering in the closet ("You think you're queer?" Roma is saying as we pick up his spiel *in medias res*). Like the Shocked Woman or the Shot Woman, Lingk is a made-to-order victim. "My wife said I have to cancel the deal," he pleads weakly to Roma. "It's not me, it's my wife." With well-oiled glibness, Roma counters Lingk's pleas as though he were swatting flies. Women are constitutionally afraid of taking financial risks, he tells him; you've got to stop being weak-kneed and stand up for yourself as an independent man. When Williamson speaks out of turn and scotches the deal, however, Lingk begs forgiveness for his impotency: "I don't have the power ... to negotiate," he apologizes, backing out the door, hat in hand. Roma turns hotly on Williamson: "Whoever told you you could work with *men*?" Then, in a calmer mood, he laments to Aaronow at the end of the movie, "I swear, it is *not* a world of men." The trouble is, that's all it is—men hot for sales figures.

Like the outworn symbol of the train, Mamet's scorn for the marketplace has some cobwebs on it, and to an even greater degree than *Reservoir Dogs, Glengarry Glen Ross* overstates the malice of ordinary men at work. Documentarian Philip Haas's quiet debut as fiction film director, *The Music of Chance*—adapted from Paul Auster's novel by Haas and his wife Belinda, who also edited—offers the freshest recent look at the all-male workplace. Jim Nashe (Mandy Patinkin) has spent a year crisscrossing the States in his BMW when he encounters Jack Pozzi (James Spader), a fast-talking young cardsharp whom Nashe agrees to back in a poker game with a couple of cream puffs named Flower and Stone. In time we learn that Nashe is on a headlong rush from his past: after his wife ran off, leaving him with their three-year-old daughter, a windfall inheritance prompted him to quit his job as a Boston fireman, buy the BMW, deposit the daughter with a sister in Minnesota, and take to the road. After a year, money is running out, and Pozzi—an energetic, self-confident con man—promises financial renewal. No such luck. Following a series of incautious bets, Nashe and Pozzi find themselves victims to a Mephistophelian bargain: to repay the ten thousand dollars they've lost, they agree to spend fifty days constructing a stone wall in the middle of a meadow on a back corner of Flower and Stone's estate. They will live as virtual prisoners in a mobile home on the site, while Calvin Murks, Flower and Stone's hired man, will oversee their labor and satisfy requests for food and other necessities. Having little choice, Nashe and Pozzi sign the contract Flower has drawn up and become working stiffs.

Like the boss figures in *Reservoir Dogs* and *Glengarry Glen Ross*, Flower and Stone represent the American Powers That Be,

though as their names suggest, the characterization here is more explicitly symbolic. Pozzi has prepared us for the meeting by dubbing them "Laurel and Hardy," and they turn out to be a very odd couple indeed. Bankrolls of fat around his waist, Flower (Charles Durning) gloats and clucks about their good fortune as he relates the story of their success. "It's as if God had singled us out from other men," he exults, puffing on a huge cigar as he explains how he and Stone, formerly an accountant and an optometrist, struck it rich in the state lottery by playing prime numbers, "numbers that refuse to cooperate, that don't change or divide, numbers that remain the same for all eternity"— these provided "the magic combination, the key to the gates of heaven." Meanwhile, Stone (Joel Grey), the quiet one, leans on the arm of his chair toward Flower, adding a word now and then, his eyes twinkling appreciatively at the bluster while the thin, ghoulish grin he used in *Cabaret* spreads from ear to ear. The caricaturing of the pair extends to their costumes and the general decor: both sport foppish paisley ties, breast-pocket handkerchiefs, and off-white, Tennessee-Williams-style suits, and the inside of their mansion looks like a mock-up of a Victorian men's club. Rulers by fluke, Flower and Stone have remained American philistines at heart. Their candlelight dinner consists of hamburgers and Cokes, the latter served in the bottle, with plastic drinking straws.

Before the poker game, Nashe and Pozzi are invited into the east wing of the mansion, where Stone keeps his "City of the World," an impressive small-scale model of civilization as he'd like it to look, replete with miniature figures of himself and Flower at different stages of their lives—as kids in the playground, grown-ups working busily at their trades, playing poker together on the weekend, holding their winning lottery ticket—and with extensive replicas of public

205

buildings, houses, churches, a cemetery, their own mansion, even a prison with tiny smiling inmates: "They're glad they're being punished," Flower explains. "They're learning how to recover the goodness within them through hard work." In Auster's novel the tour of the mansion also includes Flower's half of the east wing, which helps to clarify his and Stone's dual function as arbiters of the American way of life: it includes a cluttered library of first editions and history books, plus a museum filled with glass cabinets displaying what Flower calls "tangible remnants of the past"—a pearl earring worn by Sir Walter Raleigh, a pair of Voltaire's spectacles, a pencil that dropped from Enrico Fermi's pocket in 1942, Woodrow Wilson's desk telephone, William Seward's Bible, Babe Ruth's sweatshirt. In short, Stone presides over the American Dream of the ideal commonwealth, Flower over the shards of European-American culture on which that dream is built (a "graveyard of shadows," Nashe reflects in the postmodern novel, trivial relics wrenched out of their historical context, material objects long "defunct, devoid of purpose"). The wall in the meadow, a "joint project" for Flower and Stone, is to be constructed of stones shipped overseas from a fifteenth-century Irish castle destroyed by Oliver Cromwell. It will be "a monument in the shape of a wall," says Stone; "a memorial to itself," expounds Flower, "a symphony of resurrected stones" that every day "will sing a dirge for the past we carry within us."

Pozzi thinks they're off their rockers—and no wonder—though Nashe is strangely fascinated by Stone's model city. Sneaking upstairs for a second look during the poker game, he witnesses a telling series of close-ups: a faceless crowd of people in dark sunglasses marching down the street; a masked burglar slipping on a banana peel in an alley; and, deep within the walls of the prison, an *un*masked man about to be executed by a fir-

ing squad. If he'd been an English major instead of a firefighter, Nashe might see some foreshadowing here, but instead, acting in obedience to some passion he does not understand, he pops off the figure of Flower and Stone holding the winning lottery ticket and sticks it in his pocket. Big Mistake: when he returns to the poker game, Pozzi, who was way ahead before Nashe left, has lost everything.

As they set about building the wall, like the gangsters in *Reservoir Dogs* and the hucksters in *Glengarry Glen Ross*, Nashe and Pozzi begin defining themselves by their attitudes toward work and their reactions to its pressures. Pozzi feels as though he's in prison, and he doesn't smile like the jailbirds in Stone's model world. He has held only one regular job before, as a shoe salesman in a department store, which he quit after three weeks. "It was the pits, the absolute worst," he tells Nashe, "getting down on your hands and knees like some kind of dog, having to breathe in all those dirty sock smells." No more bootlicking for him. He regards Flower and Stone as a pair of half-witted clowns undeserving of serious attention, but once work begins he convinces himself that he is the victim of an injustice, that the bosses cheated in the poker game and are now abusing his rights by making him work. One night he gets drunk and throws a rock through their window: "You're gonna pay for what you did to me!" he shouts, shaking his fist at the mansion. Calvin Murks (M. Emmet Walsh), the job foreman, becomes the focal point of Pozzi's resentment (once the contract is signed, Stone and Flower retire from sight, and Nashe and Pozzi find themselves serving an absent pair of masters like Mitch and Murray). Murks, like Pink in *Reservoir Dogs* and Williamson in *Glengarry Glen Ross*, is a company man: "I'm just doing my job," he drawls, thumbs hitched in his coverall jeans. "The bosses have always been fair with me. I never had no reason for complaining." Pozzi greets this imperturbable loyalty with a shower of vilification, calling Murks "potato head" and "king of the numbskulls" to his face, and extending himself in conversation with Nashe to some crazy images of virulence: "I spit on that sonuvabitch pumpkin-faced pork-bellied rodent." After twenty days on the job, cracking under the strain, Pozzi throws a punch at the foreman and has to be subdued by Nashe, who has been urging him to cool down and stick to business. It's no use. Convinced that "the world is fuckin' run by assholes," Pozzi is almost as unassimilable to the world of work as Mr. Blonde.

Nashe may agree with Pozzi's opinion of the bosses, but he doesn't see the workplace as a prison; to him, it's more like a rehabilitation farm. He's courteous to Murks despite the latter's refusal to let him make a phone call or send a telegram to his sister ("Nuh, I can't do that. The bosses wouldn't like it."), and when he and Pozzi discover a barbed-wire fence surrounding the property, Nashe supposes that it's to keep people from sneaking in rather than to keep them from leaving, as Pozzi thinks. Building the wall begins to take on a monastic character, providing a means of atonement for Nashe. He becomes a life-size smiling inmate. He persuades Pozzi to stay on the job beyond the fifty-day deadline to earn some ready cash. To celebrate their fulfillment of the fifty-day contract, he decorates a cake with lighted candles and sings William Blake's "Jerusalem" over it while Pozzi seduces the prostitute they've imported for the night (Flower and Stone's silent "colored" maid in uniform is the only other woman to appear). When Murks presents them with an unexpected three-thousand-dollar invoice for food and other expenses (including a charge for repair of the broken mansion window), Nashe helps Pozzi escape from the estate but decides to stay and keep working on the wall by himself in

order to settle the tab. The next morning, when Pozzi's badly beaten body turns up on the front lawn, Nashe physically attacks Murks for refusing to allow him to accompany Pozzi to the hospital, and he weeps in the trailer at night, but the next day he's back on the job, taking out his anger on the wall—working "like a powerhouse," says Murks. Confronted by a brutal world that tries to break his will, Nashe throws himself more deeply into his work. No matter now that the wall is an impractical and ultimately foolish project, a senseless "monument to itself." The business of building it has become a matter of personal survival, a means of keeping his desire for revenge in check. He's not working for Murks and the bosses anymore, but for himself.

The Nashe-Pozzi relationship has psychological overtones that are more distinct in Auster's novel, in which Nashe often ponders the "curious correspondence" between himself and "the kid," as he routinely calls Pozzi. Both were abandoned by their fathers at an early age. ("I think he wound up in Florida selling real estate," Pozzi tells Nashe.) Both received unexpected gifts of money from their fathers—Nashe the inheritance that paid for the car and his travels, Pozzi a stake to begin his gambling career. And since then both have been freewheeling toward destinations unknown, improvising their lives as they go along. ("We belong to the same club," Nashe tells Pozzi: "The International Brotherhood of Lost Dogs.") That Pozzi is Nashe's youthful "double," the symbol of his own flight from responsible adulthood, is implied early in the novel, when Nashe describes him as looking like a young kid "trying to impersonate an older man who dressed to look younger than he was." The idea becomes more evident later on, when Nashe, speaking of the two of them as "king and jester," determines to "play the old man to Pozzi's upstart" in the poker game with Flower and Stone. And finally it gets downright explicit near the end of the novel, with Pozzi gone and Nashe "mourning the kid as though a part of himself had been lost forever."

Critics often point out that in Auster's fiction the main character's ambiguous identity is the central mystery, and this may explain why in the movie Mandy Patinkin seems to keep trying to look like an Easter Island statue. But while the novel is Nashe's psychodrama, the movie has the logic of a parable. Jack Pozzi's disappearance is the price Nashe pays for stealing the figure, for wanting to hit the jackpot like Flower and Stone so he can go on living with no strings attached, forget about his three-year-old daughter in Minnesota. With the disappearance of Pozzi, rebellious independence—defiance of work and bosses—is purged for being adolescent, irresponsible, even dangerous. "Minnesota," Nashe tells the driver (Auster himself) who picks him up at the end of the film and asks if he's going to New York—no, "I'm going to Minnesota." In the book Nashe perishes in a car crash with Murks and his son-in-law Floyd, but in the movie the sacrifice of Pozzi provides the occasion for Nashe's redemption as a mature man, maturity in this case meaning his recognition of how and why the (male) world works.

Such workplaces as these are the stuff of popular drama, of course, not to be confused with the "real world." But when we consider what we do *not* see in these films—the "structuring absences" that comprise the Guys Code—a catalogue of male fears of loss emerges. Loss of woman, and with her the civilizing virtues of love, home, and family that are still gender-specific in most American films. (Without women, it's a jungle out there.) Loss of male friendship, a casualty of the pressure of a defective work ethic on personal relationships between men. Loss of job (both social status and financial security). Loss of manhood and of male identity. Implicit in the reduced circumstances of these fictional workplaces is our real worry that out of habit, fear, and compliance, a man can come to be defined solely by his work, that Shelley Levene could turn out to be right when he insists that "a man *is* his job." In this movie business fueled by self-preservation and run by absent but almighty superiors, it isn't always clear whether the workers or the institution is at fault; it is apparent, though, that life in the workplace, like war as Hector describes it in Jean Giraudoux's *Tiger at the Gates*, can kill men and rob them of the two great gifts of life, "warmth and the sky."

AGAINST INTERPRETATION

Susan Sontag

Content is a glimpse of something, an encounter like a flash. It's very tiny—very tiny, content.

—Willem de Kooning, *in an interview*

It is only shallow people who do not judge by appearances. The mystery of the world is the visible, not the invisible.

—Oscar Wilde, *in a letter*

The earliest experience of art must have been that it was incantatory, magical; art was an instrument of ritual. (*Cf.* the paintings in the caves at Lascaux, Altamira, Niaux, La Pasiega,[1] etc.) The earliest *theory* of art, that of the Greek philosophers, pro-posed that art was mimesis, imitation of reality.[2]

It is at this point that the peculiar question of the value of art arose. For the mimetic theory, by its very terms, challenges art to justify itself.

Plato,[3] who proposed the theory, seems to have done so in order to rule that the value of art is dubious. Since he considered ordinary material things as themselves mimetic objects, imitations of transcendent forms or structures, even the best painting of a bed would be only an "imitation of an imitation." For Plato, art is neither particularly useful (the painting of a bed is no good to sleep on) nor, in the strict sense, true. And Aristotle's arguments in defense of art do not really challenge Plato's view that all art is an elaborate *trompe l'oeil,*[4] and therefore a lie. But he does dispute Plato's idea that art is

---

[1] **Lascaux, Altamira, Niaux, La Pasiega** Limestone caves in France and Spain on the walls of which are magnificent prehistoric paintings dating possibly to 15,000 B.C. The subjects of the paintings are animals, and the paintings are thought to have been part of magic rituals designed to gain control over the animals.

[2] **mimesis, imitation of reality** In his *Poetics,* Aristotle suggests that art, whether painting or drama, imitates life because art imitates an action.

[3] **Plato (c. 428–348 B.C.)** In "The Allegory of the Cave" (see Part Four), he demonstrates that reality is in "heaven" and that what we see on earth is only art imitation of the divine ideal.

[4] **trompe l'oeil** French, "fool the eye": an optical illusion, a style of painting that gives the illusion of actual objects or a photograph.

useless. Lie or no, art has a certain value according to Aristotle because it is a form of therapy. Art is useful, after all, Aristotle counters, medicinally useful in that it arouses and purges dangerous emotions.

In Plato and Aristotle, the mimetic theory of art goes hand in hand with the assumption that art is always figurative. But advocates of the mimetic theory need not close their eyes to decorative and abstract art. The fallacy that art is necessarily a "realism" can be modified or scrapped without ever moving outside the problems delimited by the mimetic theory.

The fact is, all Western consciousness of and reflection upon art have remained within the confines staked out by the Greek theory of art as mimesis or representation. It is through this theory that art as such—above and beyond given works of art—becomes problematic, in need of defense. And it is the defense of art which gives birth to the odd vision by which something we have learned to call "form" is separated off from something we have learned to call "content," and to the well-intentioned move which makes content essential and form accessory.

Even in modern times, when most artists and critics have discarded the theory of art as representation of an outer reality in favor of the theory of art as subjective expression, the main feature of the mimetic theory persists. Whether we conceive of the work of art on the model of a picture (art as a picture of reality) or on the model of a statement (art as the statement of the artist), content still comes first. The content may have changed. It may now be less figurative, less lucidly realistic. But it is still assumed that a work of art is its content. Or, as it's usually put today, that a work of art by definition says something. ("What X is saying is . . ." "What X is trying to say is . . ." "What X said is . . ." etc., etc.)

None of us can ever retrieve that innocence before all theory when art knew no need to justify itself, when one did not ask of a work of art what it said because one knew (or thought one knew) what it did. From now to the end of consciousness, we are stuck with the task of defending art. We can only quarrel with one or another means of defense. Indeed, we have an obligation to overthrow any means of defending and justifying art which becomes particularly obtuse or onerous or insensitive to contemporary needs and practice.

This is the case, today, with the very idea of content itself. Whatever it may have been in the past, the idea of content is today mainly a hindrance, a nuisance, a subtle or not so subtle philistinism.[5]

Though the actual developments in many arts may seem to be leading us away from the idea that a work of art is primarily its content, the idea still exerts an extraordinary hegemony. I want to suggest that this is because the idea is now perpetuated in the guise of a certain way of encountering works of art thoroughly ingrained among most people who take any of the arts seriously. What the overemphasis on the idea of content entails is the perennial, never-consummated project of *interpretation*. And, conversely, it is the habit of approaching works of art in order to *interpret* them that sustains the fancy that there really is such a thing as the content of a work of art.

Of course, I don't mean interpretation in the broadest sense, the sense in which Nietzsche[6] (rightly) says, "There are no

[5]**philistinism** A smugly uncultured or anticultural position.
[6]**Friedrich Nietzsche (1844–1900)** One of the most important nineteenth-century German philosophers. His theory of the superman asserts that certain individuals are above conventional wisdom and should be permitted to live and act as they wish.

facts, only interpretations." By interpretation, I mean here a conscious act of the mind which illustrates a certain code, certain "rules" of interpretation.

Directed to art, interpretation means plucking a set of elements (the X, the Y, the Z, and so forth) from the whole work. The task of interpretation is virtually one of translation. The interpreter says. Look, don't you see that X is really—or, really means—A? That Y is really B? That Z is really C?

What situation could prompt this curious project for transforming a text? History gives us the materials for an answer. Interpretation first appears in the culture of late classical antiquity, when the power and credibility of myth had been broken by the "realistic" view of the world introduced by scientific enlightenment. Once the question that haunts post-mythic consciousness—that of the *seemliness* of religious symbols—had been asked, the ancient texts were, in their pristine form, no longer acceptable. Then interpretation was summoned, to reconcile the ancient texts to "modern" demands. Thus, the Stoics,[7] to accord with their view that the gods had to be moral, allegorized away the rude features of Zeus and his boisterous clan in Homer's epics. What Homer really designated by the adultery of Zeus with Leto, they explained, was the union between power and wisdom. In the same vein, Philo of Alexandria[8] interpreted the literal historical narratives of the Hebrew Bible as spiritual paradigms. The story of the exodus from Egypt, the wandering in the desert for forty years, and the entry into the promised land, said Philo, was really an allegory of the individual soul's emancipation, tribulations, and final deliverance. Interpretation thus presupposes a discrepancy between the clear meaning of the text and the demands of (later) readers. It seeks to resolve that discrepancy. The situation is that for some reason a text has become unacceptable; yet it cannot be discarded. Interpretation is a radical strategy for conserving an old text, which is thought too precious to repudiate, by revamping it. The interpreter, without actually erasing or rewriting the text, is altering it. But he can't admit to doing this. He claims to be only making it intelligible, by disclosing its true meaning. However far the interpreters alter the text (another notorious example is the rabbinic and Christian "spiritual" interpretations of the clearly erotic Song of Songs[9]), they must claim to be reading off a sense that is already there.

Interpretation in our own time, however, is even more complex. For the contemporary zeal for the project of interpretation is often prompted not by piety toward the troublesome text (which may conceal an aggression) but by an open aggressiveness, an overt contempt for appearances. The old style of interpretation was insistent, but

---

[7]**the Stoics . . . Homer's epics** The Stoic philosophers in ancient Greece interpreted the Greek myths in accordance with their views of a morality of self-sacrifice and public welfare. Homer (9th–8th centuries B.C.), who preceded the Stoics, could retell the adulterous myths of Zeus without having to interpret them to fit a "higher" public morality.

[8]**Philo of Alexandria (30 B.C.–A.D. 45)** A Jewish philosopher of importance to our knowledge of Jewish thought in the first century A.D. His theories were closely aligned with Stoicism (see note 7). His most important work is a commentary on Genesis in which he sees all the characters as allegorical representations of states of the soul.

[9]**Song of Songs** This is the Song of Solomon in the Bible, referred to in the headnote. The inclusion of the Song of Solomon in the Bible was marked by much dispute because it is an erotic, though beautiful, piece of literature. The dispute was settled when agreement was reached in its interpretation: it was seen as a metaphor of the love of God for his creation.

respectful; it erected another meaning on top of the literal one. The modern style of interpretation excavates, and as it excavates, destroys; it digs "behind" the text, to find a subtext which is the true one. The most celebrated and influential modern doctrines, those of Marx and Freud,[10] actually amount to elaborate systems of hermeneutics,[11] aggressive and impious theories of interpretation. All observable phenomena are bracketed, in Freud's phrase, as *manifest content*. This manifest content must be probed and pushed aside to find the true meaning—the *latent content*—beneath. For Marx, social events like revolutions and wars; for Freud, the events of individual lives (like neurotic symptoms and slips of the tongue) as well as texts (like a dream or a work of art)—all are treated as occasions for interpretation. According to Marx and Freud, these events only *seem* to be intelligible. Actually, they have no meaning without interpretation. To understand *is* to interpret. And to interpret is to restate the phenomenon, in effect to find an equivalent for it.

Thus, interpretation is not (as most people assume) an absolute value, a gesture of mind situated in some timeless realm of capabilities. Interpretation must itself be evaluated, within a historical view of human consciousness. In some cultural contexts, interpretation is a liberating act. It is a means of revising, of transvaluing[12] of escaping the dead past. In other cultural contexts, it is reactionary, impertinent, cowardly, stifling.

Today is such a time, when the project of interpretation is largely reactionary, stifling.

Like the fumes of the automobile and of heavy industry which befoul the urban atmosphere, the effusion of interpretations of art today poisons our sensibilities. In a culture whose already classical dilemma is the hypertrophy[13] of the intellect at the expense of energy and sensual capability, interpretation is the revenge of the intellect upon art.

Even more. It is the revenge of the intellect upon the world. To interpret is to impoverish, to deplete the world—in order to set up a shadow world of "meanings." It is to turn *the* world into *this* world. ("This world"! As if there were any other.)

The world, our world, is depleted, impoverished enough. Away with all duplicates of it, until we again experience more immediately what we have.

In most modern instances, interpretation amounts to the philistine refusal to leave the work of art alone. Real art has the capacity to make us nervous. By reducing the work of art to its content and then interpreting *that,* one tames the work of art. Interpretation makes art manageable, conformable.

This philistinism of interpretation is more rife in literature than in any other art. For decades now, literary critics have understood it to be their task to translate the elements of the poem or play or novel or story into something else. Sometimes a writer will be so uneasy before the naked power of his art that he will install within the work itself—albeit with a little shyness, a touch of the good taste of irony—the clear and explicit interpretation of it. Thomas Mann[14] is an example of such an overcooperative author. In the case of more

---

[10]**Marx and Freud** See the introductions for each of these authors in Parts Three and Four, respectively.

[11]**hermeneutics** A system of critical analysis that examines texts for their deeper meanings.

[12]**transvaluing** The act of evaluating by a new principle, such as interpreting a sonnet of Shakespeare by means of Freudian principles.

[13]**hypertrophy** Overdevelopment.

[14]**Thomas Mann (1875–1955)** A major modern German novelist. Sontag may be referring to his most important novel, *The Magic Mountain* (1924).

stubborn authors, the critic is only too happy to perform the job.

The work of Kafka,[15] for example, has been subjected to a mass ravishment by no less than three armies of interpreters. Those who read Kafka as a social allegory see case studies of the frustrations and insanity of modern bureaucracy and its ultimate issuance in the totalitarian state. Those who read Kafka as a psychoanalytic allegory see desperate revelations of Kafka's fear of his father, his castration anxieties, his sense of his own impotence, his thralldom to his dreams. Those who read Kafka as a religious allegory explain that K. in *The Castle* is trying to gain access to heaven, that Joseph K. in *The Trial* is being judged by the inexorable and mysterious justice of God. . . . Another body of work that has attracted interpreters like leeches is that of Samuel Beckett,[16] Beckett's delicate dramas of the withdrawn consciousness—pared down to essentials, cut off, often represented as physically immobilized—are read as a statement about modern man's alienation from meaning or from God, or as an allegory of psychopathology.

Proust, Joyce, Faulkner, Rilke, Lawrence, Gide[17] . . . one could go on citing author after author; the list is endless of those around whom thick encrustations of interpretation have taken hold. But it should be noted that interpretation is not simply the compliment that mediocrity pays to genius.

It is, indeed, the modern way of understanding something, and is applied to works of every quality. Thus, in the notes that Elia Kazan[18] published on his production of *A Streetcar Named Desire,* it becomes clear that, in order to direct the play, Kazan had to discover that Stanley Kowalski represented the sensual and vengeful barbarism that was engulfing our culture, while Blanche DuBois was Western civilization, poetry, delicate apparel, dim lighting, refined feelings and all, though a little the worse for wear, to be sure. Tennessee Williams's forceful psychological melodrama now became intelligible: it was about something, about the decline of Western civilization. Apparently, were it to go on being a play about a handsome brute named Stanley Kowalski and a faded mangy belle named Blanche DuBois, it would not be manageable.

It doesn't matter whether artists intend, or don't intend, for their works to be interpreted. Perhaps Tennessee Williams thinks *Streetcar* is about what Kazan thinks it to be about. It may be that Cocteau[19] in *The Blood of a Poet* and in *Orpheus* wanted the elaborate readings which have been given these films, in terms of Freudian symbolism and social critique. But the merit of these works certainly lies elsewhere than in their "meanings." Indeed, it is precisely to the extent that Williams's plays and Cocteau's films do suggest these portentous

[15]**Franz Kafka (1883–1924)** A largely surrealist writer whose dreamworlds are often close to the nightmare. The novels referred to, *The Castle* (1926) and *The Trial* (1925), concentrate on the struggles of the individual against institutions whose nature is baffling and intimidating.

[16]**Samuel Beckett (1906–1989)** Irish writer whose work is enigmatic. He is best known for his play *Waiting for Godot* (1956).

[17]**Marcel Proust (1871–1922), James Joyce (1882–1941), William Faulkner (1897–1962), Rainer Maria Rilke (1875–1926), D. H. Lawrence (1885–1930), André Gide (1869–1951)** Important modern writers whose work has attracted considerable interpretive attention.

[18]**Elia Kazan (b. 1909)** American theatrical director who championed the early productions of Tennessee Williams (1914–1984), particularly *A Streetcar Named Desire* (1947).

[19]**Jean Cocteau (1889–1963)** French writer, painter, filmmaker. His *Orpheus* (1924) reinterpreted the Greek myth for modern times.

meanings[20] that they are defective, false, contrived, lacking in conviction.

From interviews, it appears that Resnais and Robbe-Grillet[21] consciously designed *Last Year at Marienbad* to accommodate a multiplicity of equally plausible interpretations. But the temptation to interpret *Marienbad* should be resisted. What matters in *Marienbad* is the pure, untranslatable, sensuous immediacy of some of its images, and its rigorous if narrow solutions to certain problems of cinematic form.

Again, Ingmar Bergman[22] may have meant the tank rumbling down the empty night street in *The Silence* as a phallic symbol. But if he did, it was a foolish thought. ("Never trust the teller, trust the tale," said Lawrence.) Taken as a brute object, as an immediate sensory equivalent for the mysterious abrupt armored happenings going on inside the hotel, that sequence with the tank is the most striking moment in the film. Those who reach for a Freudian interpretation of the tank are only expressing their lack of response to what is there on the screen.

It is always the case that interpretation of this type indicates a dissatisfaction (conscious or unconscious) with the work, a wish to replace it by something else.

Interpretation, based on the highly dubious theory that a work of art is composed of items of content, violates art. It makes art into an article for use, for arrangement into a mental scheme of categories.

Interpretation does not, of course, always prevail. In fact, a great deal of today's art may be understood as motivated by a flight from interpretation. To avoid interpretation, art may become parody. Or it may become abstract. Or it may become ("merely") decorative. Or it may become non-art.

The flight from interpretation seems particularly a feature of modern painting. Abstract painting is the attempt to have, in the ordinary sense, no content; since there is no content, there can be no interpretation. Pop Art[23] works by the opposite means to the same result; using a content so blatant, so "what it is," it, too, ends by being uninterpretable.

A great deal of modern poetry as well, starting from the great experiments of French poetry (including the movement that is misleadingly called Symbolism)[24] to put silence into poems and to reinstate the *magic* of the word, has escaped from the rough grip of interpretation. The most recent revolution in contemporary taste in poetry—the revolution that has deposed Eliot and elevated Pound[25]—represents a turning away from content in poetry in the old sense, an impatience with what made modern poetry prey to the zeal of interpreters.

---

[20]**portentous meanings** Meanings that imply great significance or seriousness and that may imply ominous developments. Sontag implies that the meanings suggested for the works are overblown and unlikely.

[21]**Alain Resnais (b. 1922) and Alain Robbe-Grillet (b. 1922)** The filmmaker and screenwriter, respectively, for an experimental film, *Last Year at Marienbad* (1961).

[22]**Ingmar Bergman (b. 1918)** Swedish film director, one of the most influential of modern filmmakers.

[23]**Pop Art** A form of art that in the late 1950s and the 1960s reacted against the high seriousness of abstract expressionism and other movements of the 1940s and 1950s. Instead of stressing deep content, it stressed no content; instead of profound meaning, no meaning other than what was observable.

[24]**Symbolism** A movement in poetry begun in France in the late nineteenth century and popularized in England by Arthur Symons. It sought expression through the symbol rather than through discursive language. By silencing the discourse, the symbolists hoped to put magic back into poetry—the magic representing what was inexpressible in words but could be felt in symbol.

[25]**T. S. Eliot (1888–1965) and Ezra Pound (1885–1972)** Two of America's most important modern poets.

I am speaking mainly of the situation in America, of course. Interpretation runs rampant here in those arts with a feeble and negligible avant-garde:[26] fiction and the drama. Most American novelists and playwrights are really either journalists or gentlemen sociologists and psychologists. They are writing the literary equivalent of program music. And so rudimentary, uninspired, and stagnant has been the sense of what might be done with form in fiction and drama that even when the content isn't simply information, news, it is still peculiarly visible, handier, more exposed. To the extent that novels and plays (in America), unlike poetry and painting and music, don't reflect any interesting concern with changes in their form, these arts remain prone to assault by interpretation.

But programmatic avant-gardism—which has meant, mostly, experiments with form at the expense of content—is not the only defense against the infestation of art by interpretations. At least, I hope not. For this would be to commit art to being perpetually on the run. (It also perpetuates the very distinction between form and content which is, ultimately, an illusion.) Ideally, it is possible to elude the interpreters in another way, by making works of art whose surface is so unified and clean, whose momentum is so rapid, whose address is so direct that the work can be . . . just what it is. Is this possible now? It does happen in films, I believe. This is why cinema is the most alive, the most exciting, the most important of all art forms right now. Perhaps the way one tells how alive a particular art form is is by the latitude it gives for making mistakes in it and still being good. For example, a few of the films of Bergman—though crammed with lame messages about the modern spirit, thereby inviting interpretations—still triumph over the pretentious intentions of their director. In *Winter Light* and *The Silence,* the beauty and visual sophistication of the images subvert before our eyes the callow pseudo-intellectuality of the story and some of the dialogue. (The most remarkable instance of this sort of discrepancy is the work of D. W. Griffith.)[27] In good films, there is always a directness that entirely frees us from the itch to interpret. Many old Hollywood films, like those of Cukor, Walsh, Hawks,[28] and countless other directors, have this liberating antisymbolic quality, no less than the best work of the new European directors, like Truffaut's *Shoot the Piano Player* and *Jules and Jim,* Godard's *Breathless* and *Vivre sa Vie,* Antonioni's *L'Avventura,* and Olmi's *The Fiancés.*[29]

The fact that films have not been overrun by interpreters is in part due simply to the newness of cinema as an art. It also owes to the happy accident that films for such a long time were just movies; in other words, that they were understood to be part of mass, as opposed to high, culture, and were left alone by most people with minds. Then, too, there is always something other than content in the cinema to grab hold of, for those who want to analyze. For the cinema, unlike the novel, possesses a vocabulary of forms—the explicit, complex, and discussable technology of camera movements, cutting, and composition of the frame that goes into the making of a film.

---

[26]**avante-garde** Art that is ahead of its time: literally, in the advance guard of a movement forward.
[27]**D. W. Griffith (1875–1948)** The first major American film director.
[28]**George Cukor (1899–1983), Raoul Walsh (1887–1980), Howard Hawks (1896–1977)** American filmmakers who were important before 1950.
[29]**François Truffaut (1932–1984), Jean-Luc Godard (b. 1930), Michelangelo Antonioni (b. 1912), Ermanno Olmi (b. 1931)** Important modern influences in filmmaking.

What kind of criticism, of commentary on the arts, is desirable today? For I am not saying that works of art are ineffable, that they cannot be described or paraphrased. They can be. The question is how. What would criticism look like that would serve the work of art, not usurp its place?

What is needed, first, is more attention to form in art. If excessive stress on *content* provokes the arrogance of interpretation, more extended and more thorough descriptions of *form* would silence. What is needed is a vocabulary—a descriptive, rather than prescriptive, vocabulary[30]—for forms.[31] The best criticism, and it is uncommon, is of this sort that dissolves considerations of content into those of form. On film, drama, and painting respectively, I can think of Erwin Panofsky's essay "Style and Medium in the Motion Pictures," Northrop Frye's essay "A Conspectus of Dramatic Genres," Pierre Francastel's essay "The Destruction of a Plastic Space." Roland Barthes's book *On Racine* and his two essays on Robbe-Grillet are examples of formal analysis applied to the work of a single author. (The best essays in Erich Auerbach's *Mimesis,* like "The Scar of Odysseus," are also of this type.) An example of formal analysis applied simulta-

neously to genre and author is Walter Benjamin's essay "The Storyteller: Reflections on the Works of Nicolai Leskov."[32]

Equally valuable would be acts of criticism which would supply a really accurate, sharp, loving description of the appearance of a work of art. This seems even harder to do than formal analysis. Some of Manny Farber's film criticism, Dorothy Van Ghent's essay "The Dickens World: A View from Todgers'," Randall Jarrell's essay on Walt Whitman are among the rare examples of what I mean.[33] These are essays which reveal the sensuous surface of art without mucking about in it.

Transparence is the highest, most liberating value in an art—and in criticism—today. Transparence means experiencing the luminousness of the thing in itself, of things being what they are. This is the greatness of, for example, the films of Bresson and Ozu and Renoir's[34] *The Rules of the Game.*

Once upon a time (say, for Dante),[35] it must have been a revolutionary and creative move to design works of art so that they might be experienced on several levels. Now it is not. It reinforces the principle of redundancy that is the principal affliction of modern life.

---

[30]**descriptive, rather than prescriptive, vocabulary** A prescriptive vocabulary in criticism aims to establish what a work of art ought to be: a descriptive vocabulary concentrates on what is. Sontag encourages a criticism that tells us what has happened, not one that tells us what ought to happen.

[31]One of the difficulties is that our idea of form is spatial (the Greek metaphors for form are all derived from notions of space). This is why we have a more ready vocabulary of forms for the spatial than for the temporal arts. The exception among the temporal arts, of course, is the drama; perhaps this is because the drama is a narrative (i.e., temporal) form that extends itself visually and pictorially, upon a stage. What we don't have yet is a poetics of the novel, any clear notion of the forms of narration. Perhaps film criticism will be the occasion of a breakthrough here, since films are primarily a visual form yet they are also a subdivision of literature. [Sontag's note].

[32]**On film . . . Leskov** These are all works by modern critics; they are the kind that Sontag feels will help to reinstate formal analysis.

[33]**Some of . . . I mean** These are examples of critics whose purpose is to describe accurately the surfaces of works of art.

[34]**Robert Bresson (b. 1907), Yasujiro Ozu (1903–1963), Alain Renoir (1894–1979)** Directors who are or were significant influences on contemporary filmmakers.

[35]**Dante Alighieri (1265–1321)** Italian poet and scholar. His most important work was *The Divine Comedy.*

Once upon a time (a time when high art was scarce), it must have been a revolutionary and creative move to interpret works of art. Now it is not. What we decidedly do not need now is further to assimilate Art into Thought, or (worse yet) Art into Culture.

Interpretation takes the sensory experience of the work of art for granted, and proceeds from there. This cannot be taken for granted now. Think of the sheer multiplication of works of art available to every one of us, super-added to the conflicting tastes and odors and sights of the urban environment that bombard our senses. Ours is a culture based on excess, on overproduction; the result is a steady loss of sharpness in our sensory experience. All the conditions of modern life—its material plenitude, its sheer crowdedness—conjoin to dull our sensory faculties. And it is in the light of the condition of our senses, our capacities (rather than those of another age), that the task of the critic must be assessed.

What is important now is to recover our senses. We must learn to *see* more, to *hear* more, to *feel* more.

Our task is not to find the maximum amount of content in a work of art, much less to squeeze more content out of the work than is already there. Our task is to cut back content so that we can see the thing at all.

The aim of all commentary on art now should be to make works of art—and, by analogy, our own experience—more, rather than less, real to us. The function of criticism should be to show *how it is what it is, even that it is what it is,* rather than to show *what it means.*

In place of a hermeneutics we need an erotics of art.

THE CINEMA[1]

Virginia Woolf

People say that the savage no longer exists in us, that we are at the fag-end of civilization, that everything has been said already, and that it is too late to be ambitious. But these philosophers have presumably forgotten the movies. They have never seen the savages of the twentieth-century watching the pictures. They have never sat themselves in front of the screen and thought how for all the clothes on their backs and the carpets at their feet, no great distance separates them from those bright-eyed naked men who knocked two bars of iron together and heard in that clangour a foretaste of the music of Mozart.

The bars in this case, of course, are so highly wrought and so covered over with accretions of alien matter that it is extremely difficult to hear anything distinctly. All is hubble-bubble, swarm and chaos. We are peering over the edge of a cauldron in which fragments of all shapes and savours seem to simmer; now and again some vast form heaves itself up and seems about to haul itself out of chaos. Yet at first sight the art of the cinema seems simple, even stupid. There is the king shaking hands with a football team; there is Sir Thomas Lipton's yacht; there is Jack Horner winning the Grand National. The eye licks it all up instantaneously, and the brain, agreeably titillated, settles down to watch things happening without bestirring itself to think. For the ordinary eye, the English unæsthetic eye, is a simple mechanism which takes care that the body does not fall down coal-holes, provides the brain with toys and sweetmeats to keep it quiet, and can be trusted to go on behaving like a competent nursemaid until the brain comes to the conclusion that it is time to wake up. What is its purpose, then, to be roused suddenly in the midst of its agreeable somnolence and asked for help? The eye is in difficulties. The eye wants help. The eye says to the brain, "Something is happening which I do not in the least understand. You are needed." Together they look at the king, the boat, the horse, and the brain sees at once that they have taken on a quality which does not belong to the simple

[1]Written in 1926.

photograph of real life. They have become not more beautiful in the sense in which pictures are beautiful, but shall we call it (our vocabulary is miserably insufficient) more real, or real with a different reality from that which we perceive in daily life? We behold them as they are when we are not there. We see life as it is when we have no part in it. As we gaze we seem to be removed from the pettiness of actual existence. The horse will not knock us down. The king will not grasp our hands. The wave will not wet our feet. From this point of vantage, as we watch the antics of our kind, we have time to feel pity and amusement, to generalize, to endow one man with the attributes of the race. Watching the boat sail and the wave break, we have time to open our minds wide to beauty, and register on top of it the queer sensation— this beauty will continue, and this beauty will flourish whether we behold it or not. Further, all this happened ten years ago, we are told. We are beholding a world which has gone beneath the waves. Brides are emerging from the abbey—they are now mothers; ushers are ardent—they are now silent; mothers are tearful; guests are joyful; this has been won and that has been lost, and it is over and done with. The war sprung its chasm at the feet of all this innocence and ignorance but it was thus that we danced and pirouetted, toiled and desired, thus that the sun shone and the clouds scudded, up to the very end.

But the picture-makers seem dissatisfied with such obvious sources of interest as the passage of time and the suggestiveness of reality. They despise the flight of gulls, ships on the Thames, the Prince of Wales, the Mile End Road, Piccadilly Circus. They want to be improving, altering, making an art of their own—naturally, for so much seems to be within their scope. So many arts seemed to stand by ready to offer their help. For example, there was literature. All the famous novels of the world, with their well-known char-

acters and their famous scenes, only asked, it seemed, to be put on the films. What could be easier and simpler? The cinema fell upon its prey with immense rapacity, and to the moment largely subsists upon the body of its unfortunate victim. But the results are disastrous to both. The alliance is unnatural. Eye and brain are torn asunder ruthlessly as they try vainly to work in couples. The eye says "Here is Anna Karenina." A voluptuous lady in black velvet wearing pearls comes before us. But the brain says, "That is no more Anna Karenina than it is Queen Victoria." For the brain knows Anna almost entirely by the inside of her mind— her charm, her passion, her despair. All the emphasis is laid by the cinema upon her teeth, her pearls, and her velvet. Then "Anna falls in love with Vronsky"—that is to say, the lady in black velvet falls into the arms of a gentleman in uniform and they kiss with enormous succulence, great deliberation, and infinite gesticulation, on a sofa in an extremely well-appointed library, while a gardener incidentally mows the lawn. So we lurch and lumber through the most famous novels of the world. So we spell them out in words of one syllable, written, too, in the scrawl of an illiterate school-boy. A kiss is love. A broken cup is jealousy. A grin is happiness. Death is a hearse. None of these things has the least connexion with the novel that Tolstoy wrote, and it is only when we give up trying to connect the pictures with the book that we guess from some accidental scene—like the gardener mowing the lawn—what the cinema might do if left to its own devices.

But what, then, are its devices? If it ceased to be a parasite, how would it walk erect? At present it is only from hints that one can frame any conjecture. For instance, at a performance of Dr. Caligari the other day a shadow shaped like a tadpole suddenly appeared at one corner of the screen. It swelled to an immense size, quivered, bulged, and sank back again into nonentity. For a moment it seemed to embody some monstrous diseased imagination of the lunatic's brain. For a moment it seemed as if thought could be conveyed by shape more effectively than by words. The monstrous quivering tadpole seemed to be fear itself, and not the statement "I am afraid." In fact, the shadow was accidental and the effect unintentional. But if a shadow at a certain moment can suggest so much more than the actual gestures and words of men and women in a state of fear, it seems plain that the cinema has within its grasp innumerable symbols for emotions that have so far failed to find expression. Terror has besides its ordinary forms the shape of a tadpole; it burgeons, bulges, quivers, disappears. Anger is not merely rant and rhetoric, red faces and clenched fists. It is perhaps a black line wriggling upon a white sheet. Anna and Vronsky need no longer scowl and grimace. They have at their command—but what? Is there, we ask, some secret language which we feel and see, but never speak, and, if so, could this be made visible to the eye? Is there any characteristic which thought possesses that can be rendered visible without the help of words? It has speed and slowness; dartlike directness and vaporous circumlocution. But it has, also, especially in moments of emotion, the picture-making power, the need to lift its burden to another bearer; to let an image run side by side along with it. The likeness of the thought is for some reason more beautiful, more comprehensible, more available, than the thought itself. As everybody knows, in Shakespeare the most complex ideas form chains of images through which we mount, changing and turning, until we reach the light of day. But obviously the images of a poet are not to be cast in bronze or traced by pencil. They are compact of a thousand suggestions of which the visual is only the most obvious or the upper-most. Even the simplest image

"My luve's like a red, red, rose, that's newly-sprung in June" presents us with impressions of moisture and warmth and the glow of crimson and the softness of petals inextricably mixed and strung upon the lift of a rhythm which is itself the voice of the passion and hesitation of the lover. All this, which is accessible to words and to words alone, the cinema must avoid.

Yet if so much of our thinking and feeling is connected with seeing, some residue of visual emotion which is of no use either to painter or to poet may still await the cinema. That such symbols will be quite unlike the real objects which we see before us seems highly probable. Something abstract, something which moves with controlled and conscious art, something which calls for the very slightest help from words or music to make itself intelligible, yet justly uses them subserviently—of such movements and abstractions the films may in time to come be composed. Then indeed when some new symbol for expressing thought is found, the film-maker has enormous riches at his command. The exactitude of reality and its surprising power of suggestion are to be had for the asking. Annas and Vronskys—there they are in the flesh. If into this reality he could breathe emotion, could animate the perfect form with thought, then his booty could be hauled in hand over hand. Then, as smoke pours from Vesuvius, we should be able to see thought in its wildness, in its beauty, in its oddity, pouring from men with their elbows on a table; from women with their little handbags slipping to the floor. We should see these emotions mingling together and affecting each other.

We should see violent changes of emotion produced by their collision. The most fantastic contrasts could be flashed before us with a speed which the writer can only toil after in vain; the dream architecture of arches and battlements, of cascades falling and fountains rising, which sometimes visits us in sleep or shapes itself in half-darkened rooms, could be realized before our waking eyes. No fantasy could be too far-fetched or insubstantial. The past could be unrolled, distances annihilated, and the gulfs which dislocate novels (when, for instance, Tolstoy has to pass from Levin to Anna and in doing so jars his story and wrenches and arrests our sympathies) could by the sameness of the background, by the repetition of some scene, be smoothed away.

How all this is to be attempted, much less achieved, no one at the moment can tell us. We get intimations only in the chaos of the streets, perhaps, when some momentary assembly of colour, sound, movement, suggests that here is a scene waiting a new art to be transfixed. And sometimes at the cinema in the midst of its immense dexterity and enormous technical proficiency, the curtain parts and we behold, far off, some unknown and unexpected beauty. But it is for a moment only. For a strange thing has happened—while all the other arts were born naked, this, the youngest, has been born fully-clothed. It can say everything before it has anything to say. It is as if the savage tribe, instead of finding two bars of iron to play with, had found scattering the seashore fiddles, flutes, saxophones, trumpets, grand pianos by Erard and Bechstein, and had begun with incredible energy, but without knowing a note of music, to hammer and thump upon them all at the same time.

FALSE PAPERS

André Aciman

Farrar · Straus · Giroux

New York

Underground

Whenever the Seventh Avenue train races between Eighty-sixth and Ninety-sixth Streets and offers a fleeting, darkened glimpse of what looks like latter-day catacombs, the question invariably arises: What is it? From the windows of the Broadway Local the ghost of this Stone Age grotto, suddenly illumined by the speeding train, is a place only Dante or Kafka might have imagined. The walls are begrimed with thick 1970s-style graffiti, while something resembling a platform, strewn with debris, stands in the ashen dimness of places most cities would rather forget about.

But we stare all the same, until springing into view like painted letters on the hull of a sunken liner are the telltale faded mosaics spelling a station's name: Ninety-first Street. The name appears again on a higher panel, framed by terra-cotta molding with golden numerals in relief, a combination typical of the cartouche created by Heins & LaFarge, the firm originally commissioned to design subway ceramics.

I became intrigued by the Ninety-first Street Station while riding the Broadway Local during one of its arbitrary halts. The train idled to a halt outside Ninety-first, and during my enforced wait, I became aware of, then curious about, this abandoned stop. On my first extended view of the place, I was most struck by what was absent: no old-fashioned wooden token booth, no benches. The benches, says Joe Cunningham, a transportation and engineering historian, were removed as fire hazards, while turnstiles, originally installed in the early twenties, were salvaged for parts. There were no print ads along the walls. A sealed bathroom door was slightly discernible behind a loud smear of graffiti.

Of course, there couldn't be an outlet to the street, though a shaft of light seemed to beam along the skeletal treads of a stairway. At the tail end of the station, a barely perceptible, differently styled ceramic tile suggested that however short its life span, even this station had gone through a face-lift and bore the traces of its various incarnations.

Similar alterations are hardly unusual in New York's subways or in the city itself, where everything is a patchwork of swatches and layers, of bits and pieces, slapped together until you cannot see the fault lines for the surface, nor the surface for the patchwork.Subway corridors, stairwells, and sidewalk entrances are known to have disappeared, and tiled alcoves, designed to accommodate vintage phone booths, have vanished behind newly erected walls that sprout doors to become makeshift toolsheds. Ancient men's rest rooms, famed for their shady practices, have mended their ways and been converted into candy stands.

Nothing is ever really demolished or dismantled down below, but everything is tentative and amorphous. From the width of platforms to the shape of lamp sockets down to the form of pillars (round, square, steel-beam), everything changes in the space of a few yards and betrays the many ways in which the city has always had to adjust to shifting demographics.

Stations whose token booths are absurdly positioned at the extreme end of the platform—Seventy-ninth, Eighty-sixth, and 110th Streets on Broadway, for example—will have their madness forgiven once you are told that they were designed to accommodate trains far shorter than those of today. It was because the Eighty-sixth and Ninety-sixth Street platforms were extended to twice their size to receive ten-car trains that the Ninety-first Street Station, caught between the two and nearly touching both, saw the writing on the wall. It became obsolete. Its time, like that of the Eighteenth Street Station on the East Side or of the Worth Street and City Hall Stations, had run out. On February 2, 1959, the Ninety-first Street Station was closed permanently.

When asked, middle-aged New Yorkers seldom recall even missing the station. Like a friend who died and whose name mysteriously disappears from the Manhattan telephone book, the Ninety-first Street Station no longer exists on any of the Metropolitan Transportation Authority's maps. It is extinct. Or is it, perhaps, just vestigial?

Indeed, the question I ask when passing the Ninety-first Street Station is not simply *What is it?* or *What happened here?* but something more wistful and unwieldy: *What if?* What if, instead of having the train dawdle awhile between stations, the conductor stopped at Ninety-first Street and on a mad impulse announced the station's name, and then, carried away by the sound of his own words, forgot himself and suddenly opened the doors and began discharging passengers? Some of them would actually walk out, half startled and dazed, heading for imaginary turnstiles, past the old token booth, clambering up the stairway onto a sidewalk awash in the early-evening light as passengers had done for six decades until that fateful day forty years ago.

What if, for a split second, the mid-fifties were suddenly to rush in, the way the thought of them invariably takes hold whenever I think of using not the side entrance to a prewar building on Riverside Drive but the defunct main gate on the drive itself, a gate no one uses any longer, but that, being sealed, beckons like a portal to vanished times?

And what if awaiting me barely a block away is the New Yorker Theater at Eighty-ninth Street, and farther up, the Riviera and the Riverside at Ninety-sixth Street? What if the films they're about to show this year are *Black Orpheus, Room at the Top, North by Northwest, The 400 Blows,* and other late-fifties classics? What if things didn't always have to disappear? What if time took another track, as subways do when there's work ahead? Not backward, just different: a track we can't quite fathom and whose secret conduits linking up the new with the old and the very, very old are known only to the loud yellow repair train that appears from nowhere in the dead of night and then lumbers away like a demoted god.

What if, in spite of its dead silence now, this station were a gateway to an underground that is ultimately less in the city than in ourselves, and that what we see in it is what we dare not see in ourselves? What if, for all its beguiling presence, the Ninety-first Street Station is really not even about time, or about hating to see things go, or about watching places grow more lonely and dysfunctional over time? Instead, what if this underground cavern were my double, a metaphor for the pulsating, dirty, frightened dungeon within all of us which feels as lonely and abandoned, and as out of place and out of sync with the rest of the world, as we all fear we are, though we try to hide it, eager as we are to patch up our uneasiness as fast as we can, hoping that, as fast as it can, too, our train will pass this station by, put it behind us, and take us, like people who have been to see Hades, back to the world of the living?

I finally went to visit the old station one day with a small group of subway aficionados led by Mr. Cunningham on a tour run by the New York Transit Museum at Boerum Place and Schermerhorn Street in downtown Brooklyn. We got on at Ninety-sixth Street and rode in the first car of the Broadway Local. At Ninety-first the train did in fact stop, just as I had fantasized. The conductor opened the front doors only, and to the baffled gaze of the other passengers, we stepped out. Then the doors closed again, and the train left, everyone watching us as though we were spectral travelers headed into a time warp. Wandering through this modern underworld, I tried to think of the great poets and the caves of Lascaux and *Planet of the Apes,* but all I could focus on as I negotiated my way through a thick mantle of soot was dirt, rats, and a faint queasiness.

The platform was filled with trash: broken beams, old cardboard, and a litter of foam cups. This wasn't just the detritus of a subway station but the leftovers of mole people. There was enough of it to confuse future archaeologists, whose job, it suddenly occurred to me, is not only to dig up the past but also to scrape the rubble of squatters from that of the great civilizations whose abandoned homes squatters made their own.

I stood there, staring at what must surely have once been the gleaming tiles of a perfectly proportioned station with its perfectly curved platform. Like all armchair archaeologists, I had come here to prod the raw cells of the city's past and see how everything, down to an unused subway station, can be touched by time and, like the layers underneath the city of Troy, is ultimately sanctified by time.

I wanted to see how inanimate objects refuse to forget or suggest that all cities—like people, like palimpsests, like the remains of a Roman temple hidden beneath an ancient church—do not simply have to watch themselves go but strive to remember, because in the wish to remember lies the wish to restore, to stay alive, to continue to be.

I knew I would never come here again. But I also knew that I had not put this station behind me either. In a few days I would pass by again and, again as if I'd never stopped here at all or had bungled an experiment I now needed to repeat, would ask myself, again and again, the one question I've been asking each time I speed by Ninety-first on the Broadway Local line and am invariably brought to think of the past: What if the train were to stop one day and let me off?

MARSEILLES

Walter Benjamin

The street . . . the only valid field of experience.
—André Breton

*M*arseilles—the yellow-studded maw of a seal with salt water running out between the teeth. When this gullet opens to catch the black and brown proletarian bodies thrown to it by ship's companies according to their timetables, it exhales a stink of oil, urine, and printer's ink. This comes from the tartar baking hard on the massive jaws: newspaper kiosks, lavatories, and oyster stalls. The harbour people are a bacillus culture, the porters and whores products of decomposition with a resemblance to human beings. But the palate itself is pink, which is the colour of shame here, of poverty. Hunchbacks wear it, and beggar-women. And the discoloured women of rue Bouterie are given their only tint by the sole pieces of clothing they wear: pink shifts.

"Les bricks," the red-light district is called, after the barges moored a hundred paces away at the jetty of the old harbour. A vast agglomeration of steps, arches, bridges, turrets, and cellars. It seems to be still awaiting its designated use, but it already has it. For this depot of worn-out alleyways is the prostitutes' quarter. Invisible lines divide the area up into sharp, angular territories like African colonies. The whores are strategically placed, ready at a sign to encircle hesitant visitors, and to bounce the reluctant guest like a ball from one side of the street to the other. If he forfeits nothing else in this game, it is his hat. Has anyone yet probed deeply enough into this refuse heap of houses to reach the innermost place in the gynaeceum, the chamber where the trophies of manhood—boaters, bowlers, hunting hats, trilbies, jockey caps—hang in rows on consoles or in layers on racks? From the interiors of taverns the eye meets the sea. Thus the alleyway passes between rows of innocent houses as if shielded by a bashful hand from the harbour. On this bashful, dripping hand, however, shines a signet ring on a fishwife's hard finger, the old Hôtel de Ville. Here, two hundred years ago, stood patricians' houses. The high-breasted nymphs, the snake-ringed Medusa's heads over their weather-beaten doorframes have only now

227

become unambiguously the signs of a professional guild. Unless, that is, signboards were hung over them as the midwife Bianchamori has hung hers, on which, leaning against a pillar, she turns a defiant face to all the brothel keepers of the quarter, and points unruffled to a sturdy baby in the act of emerging from an egg.

Noises. High in the empty streets of the harbour district they are as densely and loosely clustered as butterflies on a hot flower bed. Every step stirs a song, a quarrel, a flapping of wet linen, a rattling of boards, a baby's bawling, a clatter of buckets. Only you have to have strayed up here alone, if you are to pursue them with a net as they flutter away unsteadily into the stillness. For in these deserted corners all sounds and things still have their own silences, just as, at midday in the mountains, there is a silence of hens, of the axe of the cicadas. But the chase is dangerous, and the net is finally torn when, like a gigantic hornet, a grindstone impales it from behind with its whizzing sting.

Notre Dame de la Garde. The hill from which she looks down is the starry garment of the Mother of God, into which the houses of the Cité Chabas snuggle. At night, the lamps in its velvet lining form constellations that have not yet been named. It has a zipper: the cabin at the foot of the steel band of the rack railway is a jewel, from the coloured bull's-eyes of which the world shines back. A disused fortress is her holy footstool, and about her neck is an oval of waxen, glazed votive wreaths that look like relief profiles of her forebears. Little chains of streamers and sails are her earrings, and from the shady lips of the crypt issues jewellery of ruby-red and golden spheres on which swarms of pilgrims hang like flies.

Cathedral. On the least frequented, sunniest square stands the cathedral. This place is deserted, despite the proximity at its feet of La Joliette, the harbour, to the south, and a proletarian district to the north. As a reloading point for intangible, unfathomable goods, the bleak building stands between quay and warehouse. Nearly forty years were spent on it. But when all was complete, in 1893, place and time had conspired victoriously in this monument against its architects and sponsors, and the wealth of the clergy had given rise to a gigantic railway station that could never be opened to traffic. The façade gives an indication of the waiting rooms within, where passengers of the first to fourth classes (though before God they are all equal), wedged among their spiritual possessions as between cases, sit reading hymn-books that, with their concordances and cross-references, look very much like international timetables. Extracts from the railway traffic regulations in the form of pastoral letters hang on the walls, tariffs for the discount on special trips in Satan's luxury train are consulted, and cabinets where the long-distance traveller can discreetly wash are kept in readiness as confessionals. This is the Marseilles religion station. Sleeping cars to eternity depart from here at Mass times.

The light from greengroceries that is in the paintings of Monticelli comes from the inner streets of his city, the monotonous residential quarters of the long-standing inhabitants, who know something of the sadness of Marseilles. For childhood is the divining rod of melancholy, and to know the mourning of such radiant, glorious cities one must have been a child in them. The grey houses of the Boulevard de Longchamps, the barred windows of the Cours Puget, and the trees of the Allée de Meilhan give nothing away to the traveller if chance does not lead him to the cubiculum of the city, the Passage de Lorette, the narrow yard where, in the sleepy presence of a few women and men, the whole world shrinks to a single Sunday afternoon. A real-estate company has carved its name on the gateway. Does not this interior correspond exactly to the white mystery ship moored in the harbour, *Nautique*, which never puts to sea, but daily feeds foreigners at white tables with dishes that are much too clean and as if surgically rinsed?

Shellfish and oyster stalls. Unfathomable wetness that swills from the upper tier, in a dirty, cleansing flood over dirty planks and warty mountains of pink shellfish, bubbles between the thighs and bellies of glazed Buddhas, past yellow domes of lemons, into the marshland of cresses and through the woods of French pennants, finally to irrigate the palate as the best sauce for the quivering creatures. *Oursins de l'Estaque, Portugaises, Maremmes, Clovisses, Moules marinières*—all this is incessantly sieved, grouped, counted, cracked open, thrown away, prepared, tasted. And the slow, stupid agent of inland trade, paper, has no place in the unfettered element, the breakers of foaming lips that forever surge against the streaming steps. But over there, on the other quay, stretches the mountain range of "souvenirs," the mineral hereafter of sea shells. Seismic forces have thrown up this massif of paste jewellery, shell limestone, and enamel, where inkpots, steamers, anchors, mercury columns, and sirens commingle. The pressure of a thousand atmospheres under which this world of imagery writhes, rears, piles up, is the same force that is tested in the hard hands of seamen, after long voyages, on the thighs and breasts of women, and the lust that, on the shell-covered caskets, presses from the mineral world a red or blue velvet heart to be pierced with needles and brooches, is the same that sends tremors through these streets on paydays.

Walls. Admirable, the discipline to which they are subject in this city. The better ones, in the centre, wear livery and are in the pay of the ruling class. They are covered with gaudy patterns and have sold their whole length many hundreds of times to the latest brand of apéritif, to department stores, to the "Chocolat Menier," or Dolores del Rio. In the poorer quarters they are politically mobilized and post their spacious red letters as the forerunners of red guards in front of dockyards and arsenals.

The down-and-out who, after nightfall, sells his books on the corner of rue de la République and the Vieux Port, awakens bad instincts in the passers-by. They feel tempted to make use of so much fresh misery. And they long to learn more about such nameless misfortune than the mere image of catastrophe that it presents to us. For what extremity must have brought a man to tip such books as he has left on the asphalt before him, and to hope that a passer-by will be seized at this late hour by a desire to read? Or is it all quite different? And does a poor soul here keep vigil, mutely beseeching us to lift the treasure from the ruins? We hasten by. But we shall falter again at every corner, for everywhere the Southern peddler has so pulled his beggar's coat around him that fate looks at us from it with a thousand eyes. How far we are from the sad dignity of our poor, the war-disabled of competition, on whom tags and tins of boot blacking hang like braid and medals.

Suburbs. The farther we emerge from the inner city, the more political the atmosphere becomes. We reach the docks, the inland harbours, the warehouses, the quarters of poverty, the scattered refugees of wretchedness: the outskirts. Outskirts are the state of emergency of a city, the terrain on which incessantly rages the great decisive battle between town and country. It is nowhere more bitter than between Marseilles and the Provençal landscape. It is the hand-to-hand fight of telegraph poles against Agaves, barbed wire against thorny palms, the miasmas of stinking corridors against the damp gloom under the plane trees in brooding squares, short-winded outside staircases against the mighty hills. The long rue de Lyon is the powder conduit that Marseilles has dug in the landscape in order, in Saint-Lazare, Saint-Antoine, Arenc, Septèmes, to blow it up, burying it in the shell splinters of every national and commercial language. Alimentation Moderne, rue de Jamaïque, Comptoir de la Limite, Savon Abat-Jour, Minoterie de la Campagne, Bar du Gaz, Bar Facultatif— and over all this the dust that here conglomerates out of sea salt, chalk, and mica, and whose bitterness persists longer in the mouths of those who have pitted themselves against the city than the splendour of sun and sea in the eyes of its admirers.

1928

THE PANORAMA MESDAG

Mark Doty

A mile or so from the Mauritshaus, which is the serious museum in The Hague—or Den Haag, as the Netherlanders call it—is another museum, a startling and eccentric one.

The Mauritshaus is a seventeenth-century palace, full of Rembrandts, and two splendid Vermeers, and one of the only extant paintings of Carl Fabritius, a man who may have been Vermeer's teacher. He died at twenty-three, in Antwerp, when a powder keg exploded, and one of the few things he left behind is this small rectangle of canvas depicting a goldfinch chained by the ankle to an iron hoop embedded in a wall of yellowish plaster. Wall and bird are somehow palpably *there,* and distinctly paint as well, so they seem strangely fresh, as ambiguous and fragmentary as they must have the day they were painted, nearly four hundred years ago.

The day we visited the grand building was surrounded by scaffolding, all but the windows wrapped in billowing sheets of plastic. The cool, orderly rooms, their walls covered in dark damasks, look out onto a geometry of ponds and the orderly brick courtyards of public buildings, but that morning in each window a man in coveralls was scraping or painting, and out in the front courtyard two workers pursued the exacting task of goldleafing the spear-points of the wrought iron fence, one applying mastic, the other lifting thin, ragged sheets of metal into place. They stopped when the intermittent rain grew too heavy, and resumed again as soon as it cleared a little, sunlight breaking through onto the courtyard where the iron pickets they'd finished were gleaming with a startling brightness.

No gold, and no Vermeers, distinguish the Panorama Mesdag, which is found by following street signs from the great museum through some handsome downtown streets, turning onto a quiet edge of the commercial district. It's a curiosity, only to be visited by people with extra time, perhaps more a folly than a work of art exactly. Though what the guidebooks don't tell you is that Hendrik Willem Mesdag's circular extravaganza of a painting is also a parable, a meditation on limit, on what art might and might not achieve. And that, in the strange way that souvenirs of gone ambitions do, it gets under your skin.

If Carl Fabritius is the type of the artistic life truncated—vanished before his abilities could come to full bloom, the tiny goldfinch, alert and sad at once, looking off away from us the calling card of his genius—then Mesdag is the opposite, a man whose long artistic life was fulfilled, complete, conducted in public, attended by honors and professional recognitions that must have come to encase him like a very solid suit, an armor of reputation and regard. He was the very type of the successful nineteenth-century painter, the artist as businessman, his achievements held in high public regard, not open to doubt. Mesdag (pronounced Mes-dách, with that *ch* catching in the throat as in the Scottish *loch*) built his own museum, attached to his own house, in which he planned to display both his own work and the rather murky fin-de-siècle paintings he collected. Some of these aren't bad, and some of them are completely hilarious, especially a suite of Italian symbolist pictures representing fauns and nymphs caught in moments of candescent desire, leering out from messy swathes of paint. Mesdag had shaky taste, and he wasn't a good painter, either. He had his moments, in big horizontal landscapes that seem lit by a love for the Dutch countryside's peculiar horizontality: big flat fields, divided into bands of color, grainfields, bulb fields, bands of canal. Strips of color intricately fitted together, like marquetry, under wide, lively skies in which huge clouds move in from the North Sea, incandescent patches of blue opening between them.

But what made Mesdag famous, unfortunately, were seascapes. The dunes began just outside Den Haag in those days, and they rolled to the adjacent coastal town of Scheveningen, and the painter liked nothing better than portraying the swelling, roiling surface of the sea. He perfected a technique for this that seems to have more to do with an idea of the marine, or a feeling about it,

than with observation; my immediate response to his seascapes was to wonder how a painting of waves could be sentimental. Where does that quality reside? But sentimental they are; they make it very clear that Mr. Mesdag felt much more about his briny scene than we do. The paintings have everything to do with his desire to present the sea, or his own virtuosity in representing it, and nothing to do with the sea itself—the performance feels hollow, a quality doubtless enhanced by repetition. And repeat he did, generating for an eager market big, turbid seascapes in ponderous gilt frames.

But his Panorama is quite another thing. Unframed, continuous, borderless, the Panorama confounds the powers of description. In a wonderful book on Dutch painting and culture in the seventeenth century called *Still Life with Bridle,* the Polish poet Zbigniew Herbert points out that language must go to great lengths to accomplish a mere replica of what painting does in an instant; arranging sentences to describe a canvas, he writes, is like hauling heavy furniture around a room. And indeed Mesdag's Panorama makes me feel I must now muster a whole household of verbal furnishings—bottom to top, cellar to attic—and lug them about the page in order to give some sense of his project's peculiar presence.

It is housed in a building of its own, designed exclusively for this purpose—a fact that points to the collaborative nature of the thing, in which Sientje Mesdag-van Houten, Mesdag's wife, was also involved, as well as an architect and a number of other Den Haag painters. The Panorama isn't entirely anomalous; there was a bit of a fashion for them, in the late nineteenth century, when they were also called "cycloramas"—circular, sweeping paintings of large views. They were associated with exhibitions and large fairs; other examples represented Jerusalem and the awesome chasms of Niagara. In truth, the Panorama wasn't Mesdag's idea at all; he was commissioned to paint it by a panorama company, which must have intended to build an attraction rather than a work of art, though just at that moment the distinction between the two may not have been a firm one. It's odd to think of a painter taking on such an immense, flashy commission, agreeing to create a wonder, a tourist attraction. Did Mesdag know from the beginning he'd create something peculiar, enduring, ambiguous?

The building is of gray stone, big and square, and the door leads through entrance galleries full of bad Mesdags and antique Panorama souvenirs displayed in glass cases to the ticket counter, where two kind Dutch ladies and one pleasant, homosexual Dutch gentleman are waiting to take our guilders and provide us with brochures. The patrons trickling in don't seem your usual art museum consumers; mostly families with kids, mostly Dutch themselves; this place isn't high on the foreign traveler's list. Down a flight of stairs, around a narrow curving hallway, painted black, and soon we're on another, spiral stair, which is leading us up into the great chamber of the panorama itself.

Where to begin? The first impression is of light, cloudy daylight, which is not only coming from above but oddly ambient, in the way light really is at the seashore, reflecting from sand and water. And we *are* at the shore, or at least at a version of it, because the structure into which we have emerged from up the winding stair is a large beach pavilion, of wood, with a conical roof of thatch of some kind. Our pavilion—a simple round gazebo—is atop a hill of sand, and from it we look out, 360 degrees, as the sand descends, dotted with dry bits of beach grass and driftwood, to . . . what? A painting, a huge painting, which is wrapped all around us, and which represents the North Sea, reaching out to vast distances where light breaks through those towering clouds,

and the shore, where boats are clustered, and where people walk, and the dunes, and upon them the town of Scheveningen, with its summer houses and its chapels, its pleasure pavilion and hotels and music hall. A world, in other words, in which we are standing at the center. It smells like sand, dry old sand, and there is even a recording of seagulls and distant waves.

It is not a very good painting, it turns out, but it is a very good illusion. Because the bottom of the painting is obscured by sand and grass and bits of flotsam, and is some ways away from us as well, it seems to rise seamlessly out of the earth. Because the top is covered by the jutting vegetable roof of the pavilion in which we stand, the painting *has no edges*. It is unbroken, uninterruptible. And when you take a step forward or back, the experience is nothing like approaching or retreating from a painting hung on a wall; instead, weirdly, you realize instead you are *inside* of something. The "world" around you is a work of art, and you are its center.

That center is strangely, unnervingly unstable, because every way you step your perspective changes a little. Not in the effortless way it does in the world outside; within this strange hothouse of a theater there's a disorienting little adjustment every time Paul and I move. Our eyes readjust in relation to a new perspective on an illusion. The focus of our attention shifts: that woman with the white umbrella on the beach (who turns out to be Sientje Mesdag), those sailboats far out in the bluegreen shallows. And over it all sky and sky, endless, complicated by grand marine clouds, whole armadas of them. Where is all this light coming from, and why does it keep shifting in these swift and subtle ways?

There's an oculus in the ceiling, hidden by the pavilion's roof, that bathes this world in natural light, and because it's a day of rapidly shifting weather, the light inside pulses and changes as those clouds—prototypes of the billows forever frozen in here—hurry overhead, themselves like heavy, graceful ships.

And the effect of all this effort?

A weird sense of being transported into an illusory space, like the dicey three-dimensionality of a stereopticon slide, or the fuzzy depths of a hologram. Something inescapably false about it, and something endearing about that falsity. Something childlike? Quasi-scientific, in a sort of gee-whiz nineteenth-century way, something that would have earned the admiration of Jules Verne. A sense of a rather comical arrogance, the result of the artist's ambition to get closer and closer to reality? *I'll make a painting that seems as large as the world!* Walt Disney said that his "audio-animatronic" figures—the walking, talking Mr. Lincoln, for instance, a robotic Madame Tussaud manikin—were art's highest achievement, because they were the closest art had yet come to the real. There's something endearingly quaint about the notion, provincial as Scheveningen, doomed to failure.

And yet the Panorama Mesdag doesn't fail, not exactly, since it has this odd, unsettling power. Of what sort, exactly?

The Panorama denies the tyranny of the frame. We're used to art held in its place, contained, nailed to the wall, separated from the world by a golden boundary that enhances and imprisons it. What if art refused to stop there, on the museum wall? Wouldn't the result be revolution?

A great ambition, to take us inside, for art to subsume reality.

Fabritius vs. Mesdag; the former is tiny, bounded. We are in control, we walk away and turn our attention elsewhere. The painting has edges; the shadow of the finch is headless, jutting out of the frame to the right; the painting doesn't try to include everything. It occupies only its own space, contained, in some way indifferent to us. There it is, whether you look at it or not. It bears its signature proudly, as though it were inscribed in stone: *C Fabritius 1654.*

But even that bold signature seems modest in the face of Mesdag's hubris. Carl Fabritius is quite content to represent one bird, and to fill that little feathered vessel with feeling of a decidedly ambiguous, poetic sort. He is deeply concerned with light on a patch of plaster no larger than, say, the Yellow Pages. While Mr. Mesdag requires nothing less than a universe, his only limit the unbanishable edge of the horizon. If he could get rid of the horizon, one guesses, he would.

But how unpressurized art is without its frame! This big, encompassing gesture fails to move. Well, that's not entirely true; it seems that everyone mounting the dark stairs and stepping out into the filtered light of this grand theatrical space feels something: awe, amusement, surprise? But it couldn't make anyone weep, could it, except perhaps at the folly of human pride?

The brochure says after its first hundred years the Panorama was in sorry shape, and a team of experts came to restore it: cleaning, restretching the great canvas on its circle of poles, retouching where necessary. Queen Beatrix was here for the final brushstroke. "We would have lost our beautiful Panorama," the text says, touchingly including us all in the sad prospect that has been so fortunately averted.

But I confess: I would have loved the Panorama more in disarray; I'd have loved to have seen it with stains of mildew creeping through its skies, or a worry of unraveling the mice had done down in the sands beneath the high dunes of Scheveningen. Then, in the face of time's delicate ruination of human ambition, I would have been moved.

Could he have known his work would become history? At the moment of its conception, when he made his original sketch, then transferred it to a glass cylinder, and shone a strong light through it to project the rough sketch onto the huge suspended canvas, he was recording how Scheveningen looked—its actual present. It's the action of time, not of the painter, that's made it quaint, historical, an artifact. Look around you, right now, turning in a circle from where you sit. Suppose what you see in this circle, from your body to your horizon, were recorded, on canvas, or in a photograph: in a hundred years it would be a history of your moment, of the daily surround. It would have passed out of the realm of the ordinary, the familiar become not quite imaginable, unreal.

Later, I ask Paul what he thinks the Panorama is about. He says, "Instability, everything in flux. Everywhere you step it all seems to shift, the light looks different. And weather! That looming dark storm hurrying in."

"What storm?" I say. "I don't remember a storm."

"There's a storm," he says, "coming in over the village, and it's terrifically dark."

I find the brochure I've bought, a fold-out panorama of the Panorama that seems to flatten the whole thing out, darken it and place it more firmly in the nineteenth century. It looks like a big stage backdrop for an operetta. There's some shading in the clouds, over the buildings the brochure identifies as the Pavilion VonWied and the Hotel des Galeries, but hardly a storm. "In the original," Paul says, "those clouds are *much* darker."

I say I think the Panorama is about hubris, about the limitless ambitions of art, which here have become a kind of joke. But then I think, no. A beautiful and moving joke.

The sweeping novel that contains a world, the epic poem that entirely believes in itself,

the house in which every element bears the hallmark of its maker—those things all seem historical. We've lost such ambitions; no one believes in them quite. Either we don't live in a moment that allows for such coherence, or else we're terrified of the broader vision. Are we collectively holding at bay the awareness of a gathering apocalypse? And so prefer a poetry of interiority, a painting safely ironic and self-referential, a fiction of limited means? Should we try to be Mesdags?

On the evidence of this painting, no; the effort partakes too much of the city council, of civic pride, of public ceremonies, a kind of bourgeois boosterism. I imagine Mesdag and company being presented with medallions hung on ribbons while a brass band plays. One misses an art of intimacy, of privacy, of emotional urgency and connection. There's something hollow and flimsy about the grand gesture.

And yet. There is something I miss about the scale of the ambition, something lovely about the longing the project represents: *here is the world around me this minute, all of it.*

In fact, the Panorama isn't much like a painting. It's like a poem. It wishes to place you in the center of a moment, wishes to colonize your attention for a while, while time seems held in suspension. A ring whose center is everywhere and whose circumference is nowhere. Well, the painting's circumference is *there,* a fact in space, but it doesn't seem to be—these skyey horizons open on and on. It's an ancient figure for the divine, the circle whose rim we can't find, can't reach, which seems to have no outer limit.

We step outside. It's raining a little more energetically, people pulling out umbrellas or pulling jackets and anoraks up over their heads. I have a plastic bag full of postcards, including my pull-out brochure of the entire panorama in the form of an antique tinted photograph seen in the mode of early in this century. Also in the bag is the souvenir Paul's bought—a little plastic TV set with a tiny peephole on the back side; you hold it up to the light and—voila!—there's a little 3-D view of a portion of the Panorama. Click a button on top and another view slides into place. Like the Panorama itself, this little perspective box seems part and parcel of the Dutch love of illusion, a long-standing fascination with the intricacies of seeing. Trompe l'oeil, still life, the minute gestures of the painter rendering the silvery lip of an opened oyster, the translucent jelly of a ripe gooseberry. Anamorphosis, those peculiar paintings that are unreadable till reflected in a curving mirror. And the more pragmatic applications of this fascination: lenses, ground and set into microscopes and telescopes. Gifts of vision, without which the disposable contact lenses I wear, curved to the steep pitch of my cornea and weighted so as to correct, in each eye, a different degree of astigmatism, would not exist. Without them, the tricks and subtleties of Mesdag—or Fabritius or Vermeer for that matter—would be lost on me.

Paul's little aqua blue television set reminds me of Proust's magic lantern—wavery images, on the remembered walls, the stuff of legend and daydream. Now the Panorama Mesdag's filtered through another layer of nostalgia: these plastic TV sets were popular in America in the early sixties. I remember buying one at the Grand Canyon; Paul brought them home from junky tourist shops in Florida or the Jersey shore.

Did Mesdag intuit that his subject, no matter what he intended it to be, would become memory? Everyone who enters this pavilion returns to some original, interior-ized beach, memory's shoreline: crash and back-suck of wave, sunlight, sudden cool approach of a cloud's shadow, salt-scent and foam and bits of shell. Textures of sand, crook of an arm, curve of a shoulder. Layers of memory, narratives made out of the slip stream of impressions in time: this is the circle in which I stood. Sunflower petals rayed around the center's furled whorls. This is what seemed to radiate around me, this is the world I arranged merely by standing in the center of my life.

Each man or woman or child who mounts the curving stair into Mesdag's dream palace enters something in the collective memory—here was a beach town, just as it was, in 1881. And here is something of how we understood ourselves, in the last century's twilight, our pleasures and our ambitions. And we understand then, perhaps without saying it to ourselves, that our moment's just as fleeting, just as certain to seem antique and quaintly lit; that we become, in time, one of those figures on the shore, not very detailed, not particularly individual, a representative of our era, when seen from such a distancing perspective. Oddly paradoxical, and oddly moving—to be reminded that we stand at the center of our own lives, and that those lives are historical, and fleeting. What could the effect be, then, but tenderness?

Now we stand on the wet street, Paul and I, in the center of a realm of light and shadow—reflections off wet cars, a "walk" sign distorted in a puddle over cobblestone—and any way we step that world shifts around us, an optical paradox. Already I seem to be recognizing that the Panorama is better in memory—less quaint, more profound, more troubling, not a large bad painting but an accomplished chamber of recollection, a parable, something to keep. We're walking back toward the train station, carrying our souvenirs. Our shoulders keep touching as we walk along the sidewalk. I'm aware of our paired steps, this cool late afternoon, the physical fact of us, his body, mine, how even in motion we seem to stand in the center of circle after circle. Having been in a Panorama once, it seems we never entirely leave.

HOW DOES A WORK WORK WHERE?

Matthew Goulish

8.1 WHAT IS A WORK?

To answer the question, "How does a work work where?" we must first divide it into three subquestions: 1) What is a work? 2) What is work? and 3) What is where? Once we answer these, we may go on to the how.

Question #1: What is a work?

A work is an object which is infinite and singular. By infinite, I mean that the singularity of the work, which allows us in fact to refer to it as a work, is itself comprised of infinite events. We can divide those events into two kinds of infinities: first the infinity of microevents on a molecular, atomic, and subatomic level, because anything which is noticeable must be made up of parts which are not; and second the infinity of macroevents, that are happening in our present, and that have happened in our past, and that clearly define a work, and temper and shape our perceptions of it, and our responses to it.

Take for example a painting. Let us attempt to view *The Conversion of St Paul* by Caravaggio. First, we must travel to Rome.

Once there, we must find the Chiesa Santa Maria del Popolo. Upon entering the unlit cavernous church, we see the painting immediately, and see that we cannot see it. It hangs high on the wall obscured in shadow twenty feet away beyond an uncrossable boundary. We notice a small box to our right, labeled with the word *luce,* below which is a slot the size of a 100 lira coin. One of us volunteers to drop a coin in the slot, and suddenly a miraculous heavenly beam of electric light from the ceiling illuminates *The Conversion of St Paul* by Caravaggio. Before we can begin our contemplation, we realize that tourists from all corners of the church have swarmed to our position, it being the only illuminated area. Jostling to maintain our view of the painting, we focus our concentration on the cramped and colorful composition. We feel momentarily overwhelmed, not just by the startling structures and figures, but also by the textures. We see St Paul on his back on the ground, eyes closed and arms outstretched to an interior heaven, his horse beside him, one front hoof poised above Paul's chest, reined by a frightened steward. Above Paul's head, the horse's head; above the horse's head, the steward's head; above the steward's head just off the corner of the canvas, in the sky . . . With a click the light has gone out, plunging the painting back into darkness. The tourists hesitate, waiting for somebody to volunteer another coin. When no one does, they wander off again into the interior of the church.

What is *The Conversion of St Paul* by Caravaggio? We expected a painting, but found a series of events. Does the painting we expected exist? There is the painting, but there is also the coin box and the coin, ourselves and the crowd, the church of Santa Maria del Popolo and the city of Rome, the shadows and the light. Of course *The Conversion of St Paul* by Caravaggio exists, but this is not really the question. The question is where does *The Conversion of St Paul* by Caravaggio stop? What is a work? A work is an object overflowing its frame, converging into a series of other objects each overflowing their frames, not becoming one another, but becoming events, each moving in the direction of their own infinite singularity and difference. Somebody pulls another 100 lira coin from a pocket, holds it over the slot, and says, "Get ready."

8.2 WHAT IS WORK?

Question #2: What is work?

A human being is an organism that works; this man is a unit of labor. This is not a quote from Karl Marx, but rather what I thought growing up in Flint, Michigan, before I encountered people who don't work. My grandfather, my father's father, worked in the General Motors auto plant that gave birth, in 1927, to the United Auto Workers Union as a result of the massive sit-down strike that he participated in. At the outset of our performance *How Dear to Me the Hour When Daylight Dies,* when my grandfather was 92, I contributed what for me was a homage to his years on the assembly line—a

sequence in which I stood very still, lifted both arms to chest level, rubbed the back of my right hand in a circular motion with the fingers of my left hand, dropped both arms, took three breaths, and repeated the gesture. Under Lin's direction and with the input of the group, the homage took shape. After seven repetitions, I left my right hand raised, and lowered my left only. After nine repetitions of that, I left both hands raised. After twelve repetitions of that, I dropped both arms and began again. The performance of the action required considerable concentration, which I had not expected when I began devising it. As I performed it in front of an audience, in the stillness and the focus which ensued, I imagined the spirit of my grandfather descending on me, even though he was still living, and I imagined my gesture becoming a repetition of his countless gestures at work, my hands becoming his, my face becoming his. My work became the work of becoming my grandfather at work, and when his spirit joined me, it did not descend, but grew from micropoints inside me—in my hands, behind my eyes, in my arms and my chest, and in my feet. When I articulated my intentions at a work-in-progress discussion in Colorado Springs in the fall of 1995, an elderly woman in the audience volunteered the comment that she had once worked on an assembly line, and the experience was just like that gesture. When I called my mother from Glasgow in the spring of 1996 to tell her we had successfully premiered *How Dear to Me the Hour When Daylight Dies,* she told me my grandfather had died three days earlier. He had died on the day of the first performance.

What is work? Work is life.
A human being is an organism that works;
this man is a unit of labor.
This man is free,
not because he is determined from within,

238

but because every time
he constitutes the motive of the event that
he produces.
What he does, he does entirely,
that being what comprises his liberty.

8.3 WHAT IS WHERE?

Question #3: What is where?

Where is inside. What does inside mean? Inside means inside my car. What is my car doing? It is traveling along its own particular road. What is inside my car? I am inside my car, and since I am inside my car, I cannot perceive anything outside my car until it enters my point of view, which is inside. Thus we can say that not only am I inside my car, but in fact, everything is inside my car—the road is inside my car, *The Conversion of St Paul* by Caravaggio is inside my car, and my grandfather who built my car is inside my car. Does my car have windows? No, it is a windowless car, because how could it have windows when everything is already inside? In fact, there is no outside, there are only more windowless cars. Each one speeds along its own particular road. Each one contains everything else, including its own particular road and all the other windowless cars. But each everything inside has a certain pattern of emphasis, of clarity and obscurity, depending on the car's specific speed, direction, and point of view. In this way there are different everythings. Each car comprises a different everything. We are not speaking of closure, but of infinite convergences. The convergence of all the windowless cars of my body and mind comprise the windowless car of my self, in which everything happens. But not every everything, only my particular everything. So this is not to say that there is nothing outside of myself, but rather that every everything is inside of itself and every other everything, including me.

Question #4: How does a work work where?

A work is an object overflowing its frame. Work is an event in which the human participates; the human is an organism that works. A work works when it becomes an event of work. A work works when it becomes human. This becoming occurs when we realize it. Specifically, it occurs when we realize it where it occurs. It occurs inside. We do not need to find a way into a work, since the work is already inside. Instead we realize a work and its harmony with our point of view. Then it and we begin to work, and the play of work begins.

Design and Discipline: The Legend of an Urban Park

Blagovesta Momchedjikova

ABSTRACT

*L*ocated in the geographical center of the metropolis and covering 1,255 acres, Flushing Meadows Corona Park in Queens is the second largest recreation area in New York City. Once a dumping ground, it was redeveloped into a flat, public park by the controversial city planner Robert Moses for the two world's fairs (1939/40, 1964/65) he brought to the site. But to what end? Today certain immigrant communities engage in recreation activities (strolling, playing soccer, snacking) beyond the official perimeter of the park and its facilities. I would argue that the "flatness" of the park is not only ideological but also emblematic of Moses' ambition to oversee and control the whole city and the movement of its peoples. Thus for Moses public spaces are carefully constructed products and public life—a highly disciplined practice.

So this was the former site of the fairgrounds—grand tree-lined alleys, several strange-looking buildings, two space rockets, random statues, abandoned fountains, a disconnected electricity pole, and a gigantic hollow globe in the midst of it all. There was no one in sight, just the dull traffic noise from the surrounding highways. Chills ran down my spine. Maybe I shouldn't have come here alone.

It was the spring of 1999 and I had just strolled into the immense, flat, and desolate area of Flushing Meadows Corona Park in Queens, New York, determined to take pictures of it for my world's fair class final project. After all, it had hosted two world's fair events, *The World of Tomorrow* in 1939/40 and *Peace Through Understanding* in 1964/65, and was, as its entering sign proclaimed, "heritage" of the latter. I tried to imagine the glorious times of world expositions—crowds of visitors, colorful pavilions, many languages. Alas! Most of the remains of the fair were too decrepit to overlook: the spider webs spanning the New York State Pavilion, the decay of the NASA rockets, the dry fountain around the Unisphere. This site evoked sadness, even neglect, not popular entertainment and recreation.

Upon a second visit to the park, this time on rollerblades, I came across a curious phenomenon: on a vacant, no-man's patch of land on 111th street, just outside the official northwest side perimeter of the park, several generations of Latin Americans gathered together, playing sports, picnicking, people-watching, sitting on plastic crates, and socializing. Frequently, the elders would send the youngsters "back home," which was just across the street, to bring more food, more plastic crates to sit on, more music to listen to. The no-man's land was small and, therefore, rather crowded, but everybody knew each other and everybody was having fun. Why weren't these residents enjoying themselves within the boundaries of the grand public park nearby, strolling on its alleys, using its facilities, resting on its benches?

In the years that followed, I would talk to these users of the "unofficial" park as well as to the few I would encounter in the official one, and ponder their comments about the park being "too big," its facilities— "too far away," its benches— "too few." What they were all longing for was a neighborhood park for daily use: small, located in the midst of their communities, easily accessible on foot, equipped with benches, picnic tables, a children's playground, and a small, multi-purpose field. Flushing Meadows Corona Park offered these and other facilities but buried deep inside its epic size and at immense distances from each other. As a result, the communities appropriated the no-man's patch of land outside the park, the site they would pass by on their daily walks, for their immediate park needs. So, who was Flushing Meadows Corona Park for, if not for those who lived around it and could use it

regularly? How was it, to use a famous Jane Jacobs phrase, a "creature of its surroundings" (Jacobs, 98), that is, organic to, not imposed on, the neighborhoods around?

For several years now Queens has enjoyed the status of the most ethnically diverse county in the nation (US Census, 2000) but no one would have guessed that from the empty alleys in its largest park. Public parks, as we know them today, are free, green, outdoor spaces for recreational public use, such as promenading, sports, picnicking. They provide unique opportunities for people from different cultures, classes, and races to socialize with each other. Owned by city or park state agencies and run by conservancies, parks, when properly kept and used, often evoke a sense of civic pride in their users (Tate, 79), and are even considered among the top city attractions a tourist should visit. There is indeed an ongoing belief that "well-planned, well-designed and well-managed parks remain invaluable components of liveable and hospitable cities" (Tate, 3).

Descendants of the landscaped aristocratic gardens of Europe, urban parks inspired the allocation of large land for public use, the creation of "non-productive, vegetated scenery," and the rise of the profession of landscape architecture (Tate, 1–2). North American urban parks developed in several stages, as Galen Cranz suggests in her study: from *pleasure gardens* in the nineteenth century, through *reform parks* and *recreation facilities* in the first half of the twentieth century, to the *open space concept* in the last few decades of the twentieth century. Each of these periods points to people's evolving understanding of green spaces in the city, and, consequently, of cities themselves: from a necessary evil requiring an antidote (in the time of the *pleasure garden*), through a reformable entity and a carefully put together machine (in the time of the *reform park* and the *recreation facility*), to an artifact worthy of contemplation and appreciation (in the time of the *open space* concept) (Cranz, 119–122).

Although most neighborhood parks today combine elements from all four periods of park history, traditionally, the park's design (seating patterns, circulation system, recreation facilities) should be affected by whatever seems more important: getting together, picnics, games, and sports or simple people-watching. For instance, downtown parks used by office workers have a meandering circulation system, which allows for privacy and prevents one from getting into unwanted conversations with strangers; residential parks, on the contrary, have a direct circulation system, which encourages controlled interaction among regular visitors who know each other. Yet, while being arenas for public recreation where people of different classes relax and mix together, parks, just like other public open spaces in the city (marketplaces, squares, streets), continue to be instruments of "social control" (Marcus et al, 87–88), geared towards the monitoring of leisure. Indeed, in parks one learns how to behave appropriately in the presence of strangers— "in public"—by following the specific ground design, using the recreation facilities, and interacting with others responsibly, thus becoming a member of a modern, civilized group of people—"the public."

As a direct product from the two New York world's fairs of the twentieth century, Flushing Meadows Corona Park, however, is a confusing "instrument" of social control: the round-point ground design (circular plazas, radiating alleys, central axis) and the mechanically produced flatness of the terrain, both of which once served the purpose of popular entertainment (and thus, prominence of display, navigation of crowds, and amusement), have been light-heartedly appropriated to serve the purpose of recreation (and thus, wondering, respite, and

sports). Constructed for one specific type of audience, the fairgoers, and for one specific type of event, the world's fair, both of which have been gone from our cultural experience for a few decades now, Flushing Meadows Corona Park is what Jane Jacobs might call a "problem park." Ringed with highways and on the edge of the community, it is not a vital part of the community's life. "The worst problem parks are located precisely where people do not pass by and likely never will," confirms Jacobs (Jacobs, 103).

But Flushing Meadows has existed on the outskirts of community life and the imagination for quite some time, a fact that characterizes it, historically, as a typical heterotopic place (Foucault, 26). Prior to becoming the magical fairgrounds for the New York's World Fair of 1939/40, the site was known as Corona Dump—a prosaic yet gigantic dumping ground (3? miles long and 1 mile wide) of processed Brooklyn trash. Its biggest garbage hill, Mount Corona, reached 100 feet in height. F. Scott Fitzgerald described the area in his famous novel *The Great Gatsby* thus:

> *About halfway between West Egg and New York the motor road hastily joins the railroad and runs beside it for a quarter of a mile, so as to shrink away from a certain desolate area of land. This is a valley of ashes — a fantastic farm where ashes grow like wheat into ridges and hills and grotesque gardens; where ashes take the forms of houses and chimneys and rising smoke and, finally, with a transcendent effort, of men who move dimly and already crumbling through the powdery air (Fitzgerald, 23).*

But what Fitzgerald, with the eye of a keen observer and fiction writer, saw as "ridges," "hills," and "grotesque gardens" of ashes, Robert Moses, with the eye of a ruthless urban planner, saw as an ideal opportunity for a glorious urban park situated in the geographical center of the metropolis, that would rival Manhattan's Central Park by size, landscape, recreation facilities, and number of visitors.

To achieve his goal, Robert Moses decided to use the agency of the world's fair, which was not an unusual proposition. In fact, world's fairs were often used as urban redevelopment tools—because of them various transportation systems were expanded, neglected neighborhoods—beautified, new buildings—added to the urban landscape, and abandoned sites—transformed into green spaces. Chicago's Jackson Park, for instance, is legacy of Olmsted's special landscaping for the White City of the World's Columbian Exposition (1893). Moses thought that the world's fair would help finance his urban park project rather easily—the fair would generate funds for the redevelopment of the site, transform the ashen place into a popular destination, and provide the basic layout and vegetation for the future park. Little did he know that it would take him not one but two world's fairs and over thirty years to carry out that plan.

First popular for securing private land for public parkland on Long Island, Moses was a firm believer of rest through exercise and was thus major proponent of the *recreation facility* park. In the course of his long city career, he increased park land in New York from 14,000 to 34,673 acres (www.nycgovparks.org). Under Roosevelt's New Deal inaugurated in 1933, he built many major public works in the city, such as highways, bridges, beaches, and housing projects but ended up displacing thousands of minorities and poor people from their homes in the process. His accomplishments, to name just a few, include Jones Beach, the Central Park Zoo, Astoria Pool, the Long Island Expressway, the Cross-Bronx Expressway, the Triborough Bridge, the Verrazano Narrows

Bridge, Co-op City, and allowed his biographer, Robert Caro, to call him not only a "power broker" but also "America's greatest builder" (Caro, 10).

Influenced by Ebenezer Howard's ideas about a Garden City and Le Corbusier's about a Radiant City, both of which involved the usage of parks in the hope of making cities more habitable, Moses, as chairman of the Metropolitan Conference on Parks (at the New York Park Association) in 1930, helped issue a report "recommending the immediate acquisition of thousands of acres of the last natural areas in the city" and the construction of a system of parkways including the Belt, Grand Central, Cross Island, and Henry Hudson, to alleviate traffic congestion in the city. That report guided much of the park and parkway construction supervised by the Parks Department in the 1930s. When Mayor LaGuardia appointed him sole Parks Commissioner of a unified park system in New York City in 1934, a position he held for twenty six years, Moses summoned a staff of 1,800 designers and engineers to work on developing an integrated park system in New York, paid for by New Deal's federal money (www.nycgovparks.org). Around that time, he set his unforgiving eye on Corona Dump.

But neither was Moses the first urban park designer in North America nor was Flushing Meadows Corona Park the first man-made park in New York. Urban park design became popular in the United States with the name of Frederick Law Olmsted (1822–1903), who, together with Calvert Vaux (1824–95), created many urban parks in North America—New York's most beloved Central Park (1853) and Prospect Park (1868) among them—a whole century before Moses built Flushing Meadows Corona Park. Olmsted and Vaux constructed parks by shaping, designing, and building from scratch basic park features: lakes, promenades, bridges, trees, rocks (Tate, 1–2). Most prominent in their design of Central Park were the transverse roads, a feature Olmsted borrowed from Liverpool's Birkenhead Park (1847), which allowed for the separation of carriage from pedestrian roads and accommodated traffic passing from one side of the park to the other, without disturbing the meandering walks of visitors.

Although both Moses and Olmsted harbored ideas of urban parks for public use, their views on the necessity and functions of urban parks differed radically. While Olmsted insisted that "the beauty of the rural scenery," which he tried to recreate in his parks, "is a restorative antidote to the artificiality and oppression of urban conditions" (Tate, 148), Moses had no interest "in the natural qualities of urban parks," considering them strictly "places for active, wholesome play," which had socially restorative functions; he believed, for instance, that Central Park should be "neither English nor French, neither Romantic nor classical, but efficient, purposeful, and unapologetically American" (Tate, 152). Thus while Olmsted made varied and rich pastoral landscapes, Moses made uniform and boring flat terrains.

Moses' "flatness" was as much practical—to aid recreation and sports—as it was ideological—to impose his all-seeing self over a particular territory, and, by extension, over the whole city, and control the movement of its residents. To understand the nature of such total, totalizing, and totalitarian presence, one may consider the example of seventeenth century Versailles, where the Sun King used the mechanically produced flatness of the terrain to intensify his power over the city, country, and nation. There, the flat terrain suggested total visibility and the notion of the view as speed: "The view is all velocity," writes architectural critic Vincent Scully, "the evergreen hedges of the geometric parterres of Italy are cut down tight so as not to impede the rapid movement of the eye, and the broderie leaps out across the thin plane of the ground" (Scully, 15). It also promoted a new form of art, landscape portraiture—a "portrayal of the ideal order," "a pure drawing upon the surface, free of mass"—which presented the Sun King with a great possibility: to centralize his city and country via the carefully executed centralization of this garden: using "straight new roads and long canals," which extend " 'indefinitely' towards the horizon," he thus created the "portrait of his new France," with himself and his all-seeing eyes in the center of it (Scully, 16). His very being imprinted in the flat parterres, the Sun King, with his arms stretching like powerful diagonals through the etoiles, from the garden into the city, in fact, established the sovereignty of vision and helped shape the modern nation state. It is no secret that the fabric of the modern city of Paris is cut to the shapes of Versailles (Hunt, 22).

Moses was New York's Sun King and Flushing Meadows Corona Park—his laboratory where he was going to draw the portrait of "the ideal order" he strived to establish in the city. On June 29th, 1936, the major redevelopment of Corona Dump began: 7,000 000 cubic yards of ash-fill were removed, the course of Flushing River was diverted (the river itself was cleaned); two great tidal gates and a dam were built to prevent saltwater seepage into the great artificial freshwater lakes (Fountain Lake and Lagoon of Nations), 758 miles of piling were driven into the crust of the site as foundations for more than 200 structures for the fair, and 10 000 trees, 400 000 pansies, 500 000 hedge plants, 1,000 000 bulbs, and 1,500 000 bedding plants were put into the leveled ground. All in all, the improvement of the area cost $12 million and was completed by March of 1937, in nine months—way ahead of schedule. The 1,216 acres of park were now eagerly awaiting their fairgoers.

When the fair opened in 1939, the rond-point layout and flatness contributed to the strategic display of exhibits and crowd control: the Trylon and Perisphere, at the very center, symbolized America and its progress, the international pavilions, in remote areas, had a subordinate position to "dominant" America as did the amusement area—itself in a totally separate zone. But despite its strategies, technological wonders, and futuristic renderings, the fair ended as a financial disaster, which, for Moses, meant only one thing: it failed to generate the profits necessary for the further development of the fairgrounds into an urban park. The area remained idle until 1945, when, for five years, the United Nations met in the New York City Pavilion, one of the few permanent structures that remained after the fair. Then, for over a decade, the site was idle again until the early 1960s, when another fair, under the presidency of Moses, came to Flushing Meadows again. That fair used the same ground design from 1939/40, which architectural critic Scully stigmatized in a 1964 issue of *Life* as "the same zombie ground plan that was already dead for the 1939 World's Fair" (Rydell et al, 107).

Still, the uneventful layout at Flushing Meadows did not prevent Walt Disney, the famous animator and theme park pioneer, who had designed four pavilions for the fair ("It's a Small World," "The Carousel of Progress," "Great Moments with Mr. Lincoln," and "Magic Skyway") and had perfected his technique of audio-animatronics, from wanting to expand his empire there. Upon the closing of the 1964–65 fair, he approached Moses with the proposal to develop his own form of massive, safe, and clean family entertainment—the theme park—on the former fairgrounds. Disney, who had attended the New York World's Fair in 1939 and had gotten ideas about his future theme parks from it, had already opened Disneyland in Anaheim, California, in 1955, and was eager to expand his venture also on the East Coast. But Moses was not going to give up the idea of a large urban park, which had been brewing in his mind

for almost three decades, to an entertainment enterprise, which he had no interest in (in fact, he hated entertainment, which was obvious from the sanitized Amusement Zone at the fair of 1964). Although the fair was a financial fiasco, by now Moses could pull in sources from the Triborough Bridge and Tunnel Authority and invest in the park: he said "No" to Disney.

Yet these two visions about the future of the fairgrounds in Queens—Moses' of an urban park and Disney's of an amusement area—point to two concepts about how recreation should be achieved, through sports or through entertainment, and to two ideas about the nature of recreation—public and free or private and expensive, respectively. They also indicate the residents' changing relationship to leisure, one based not on restful recreation, quiet contemplation, and unproductive strolls, but on total entertainment, fast consumption, and the latest technology. Originally understood and practiced through the activity of walking or promenading—along the city's tree-lined boulevards or the pleasure garden's alleys—leisure, as a modern concept, gave residents of the industrial city the opportunity to take a break from their fast-paced, industrial lives, get some rest, and re-charge themselves for the upcoming weeks via the experience of nature, socializing, picnicking, and other idle activities.

By the mid-twentieth century that concept morphed into the idea that one rests best through exercise, and so leisure became about sports practiced in public parks equipped with recreation facilities; by the late twentieth century—it had morphed again, this time into leisure as a rather sedentary form—entertainment—during which one's senses are constantly bombarded by various stimulants. Walking is now considered slow, backward, and nonproductive, while rides, thrills, consumption, and "massively multiplayer games" (Kirsner, 2)—the best way to spend one's free time. That practice has left us immobilized and passive, having forgotten the thrill from a good old walk. To fulfill our needs, amusement parks, based on rides, have grown in numbers while gardens and parks, based on walks, have given way to real estate developments.

In 1967, two years after the closing of the fair, Robert Moses presented the Parks Commission of New York City, which he had left seven years earlier in order to preside over the 1964/65 Fair Corporation, with Flushing Meadows Corona Park. Accessible via several parkways and a subway, carefully laid out, and equipped with recreation facilities, it was, Moses thought, fully integrated into the city. But it stuck out like a sore, as it does now, after almost forty years, still struggling to find its unique park "identity." In spite of the highest number of sports and recreational facilities, cultural institutions, and ethnic festivals of any New York City park (i.e., The Unisphere, Shea Stadium, US Open, Theaterama, Queens Museum of Art, the New York Hall of Science, a golf course, an ice-skating rink, two lakes, the Queens Zoo, the Queens Botanical Gardens, many playgrounds, a carousel, the Latino Cultural Festival and the Dragon Boat Festival, etc.), Flushing Meadows Corona Park was and remains, sadly, empty.

To this day, the Park provides no small gathering areas where people could meet and interact and no benches on the periphery for those who do not want to participate in structured recreational activities, thus failing to address the needs of the street-walking, immigrant communities who live around it. Moreover, the flat terrain, which allows for total visibility is, in fact, "boring" (John Mattera, personal interview), and does not create a feeling of closeness and warmth; in fact, on cloudy, cold, dark days, the visibility of the park contributes, paradoxically, to the fear of park goers: yes, a possible attacker could be seen but how long before somebody could actually come to one's rescue at these immense distances? Not to mention that the "velocity" of the eye, our unobstructed vision, stimulated by the flat terrain, becomes easily numbed by that same flatness, thus skipping certain areas of the landscape.

Perhaps the construction plans for the New York Olympics bid brings some hope for Flushing Meadows Corona Park. After all ". . .parks, like cities," insists Alan Tate "are constantly developing and are never completed" (Tate, 1–2). But perhaps this temporary spectacle, just like the World's Fair, would leave lasting effects on the park, further opening the sore, under the pretext of "revitalizing" it.

Was Flushing Meadows Corona Park indeed Moses' laboratory for drawing the "ideal order," which he aimed to impose on the City of New York? At the fair of 1964/65 Moses commissioned a scale model exhibit of the whole metropolis, *The Panorama of the City of New York*. On permanent exhibit in the former New York City Pavilion, now Queens Museum of Art (since 1972), the model offers a bird's eye view of the whole city, which Moses helped interconnect with bridges, tunnels, and highways. A ride at the fair, the *Panorama* is now experienced from an ascending circumferential walkway and thus visitors own their agency of observation. Clean, clear-cut, quiet, and regularly updated, however, the model lacks representations of people and everything that comes with them: interaction, spontaneity, danger, dirt—all major components of the lived city—and is thus an eerie reminder of how Moses ignored and displaced a lot of these people to make room for his grand urban projects (Momchedjikova, 268–269).

It also reflects what Moses understood urban life to be all about—discipline. In order to discipline urban life, Moses needed to discipline the urban public and the places they occupied. Thus he contributed greatly not only to the development of public recreation and how it should be practiced but also to the understanding of public recreation itself as discipline. This is visible in the strictly geometric plan of Flushing Meadows Corona Park (and in the model), one of many public places he constructed in the city. In his miniaturized metropolis—testimony to his sweepingly destructive, "flattening" gestures through numerous vibrant city communities, where the Park is one of many public places—we see Moses' ultimate solution for an ideal city: the one devoid of any public.

REFERENCES

Caro, Robert. *The Power Broker: Robert Moses and the Fall of New York.* New York: Alfred A. Knopf, 1974.

Galen Cranz, "Four Models of Municipal Park Design in the US" in *Denatured Visions: Landscape and Culture in the 20th Century* (Oct. 1988 Symposium on Landscape Design), ed. Stuart Wrede and William Howard Adams, New York: Museum of Modem Art, Distr. by H. N. Abrams, 1991 and 1994, pp. 118–123.

Fitzgerald, F. Scott. *The Great Gatsby.* New York: Charles Scribner's Sons, 1925.

Hunt, John Dixon. "The Garden as Cultural Object," in *Denatured Visions: Landscape and Culture in the 20th Century* (Oct. 1988 Symposium on Landscape Design), ed. Stuart Wrede and William Howard Adams, New York: Museum of Modern Art, Distr. by H. N. Abrams, 1991 and 1994, pp. 19–32.

Jacobs, Jane. *The Death and Life of Great American Cities.* New York: Random House, 1961.

Kirsner, Scott. "Rebuilding Tomorrowland" in *Wired*, Issue 10.12 –December 2002, p. 2

Marcus, Clare Cooper and Carolyn Francis, ed. *People Places: Design Guidelines for Urban Open Space.* New York: Van Nostrand Reinhold, 1990.

Mattera, John. New York City Parks Librarian. Personal Interview, Spring 2004.

Momchedjikova, Blagovesta. "My Heart's in the Small Lands: Touring the MiniatureCity in the Museum" in *Tourist Studies*. London, Thousand Oaks and New Delhi: Sage Publications, 2002, pp. 267–280.

Rydell, Robert, John E. Findling, and Kimberly D. Pelle. *Fair America: World's Fairs in the United States..* Washington and London: Smithsonian Institution Press, 2000.

Scully, Vincent, "Architecture: the Natural and the Manmade" in *Denatured Visions: Landscape and Culture in the 20th Century,* (Oct. 1988 Symposium on Landscape Design). New York: Museum of Modem Art. Distr. By H. N. Abrams, 1991 and 1994. pp. 7–18.

Tate, Alan. *Great City Parks.* London and New York: Spon Press, 2001.

www.census.gov.

www.nycgovparks.org.

THE SYNTHETIC SUBLIME

from the *New Yorker*

Cynthia Ozick

More than any other metropolis of the Western world, New York disappears. It disappears and then it disappears again; or say that it metamorphoses between disappearances, so that every seventy-five years or so another city bursts out, as if against nature—new shapes, new pursuits, new immigrants with their unfamiliar tongues and worried uneasy bustle. In nature, the daffodil blooms, withers, vanishes, and in the spring returns—always a daffodil, always indistinguishable from its precursor. Not so New York, preternatural New York! Go to Twenty-third Street and Eighth Avenue: where is the Grand Opera House, with its statuary and carvings, its awnings and Roman-style cornices? Or reconnoitre Thirteenth Street and Broadway: who can find Wallack's Theatre, where the acclaimed Mrs. Jennings, Miss Plessy Mordaunt, and Mr. J. H. Stoddart once starred, and where, it was said, "even a mean play will be a success"? A hundred years ago, no one imagined the dissolution of these dazzling landmarks; they seemed as inevitable, and as permanent, as our Lincoln Center, with its opera and concerts and plays and its lively streaming crowds.

Yet catapult us forward another hundred years, and (though we won't recognize the place) it is certain to be, uninterruptedly, New York, populous, evolving, faithfully inconstant, magnetic, manmade, unnatural—the synthetic sublime. If you walk along Lexington Avenue, say, it isn't easy to be reminded that Manhattan is an island, or even that it lies, like everything else, under an infinitude of sky. New York's sky is jigsawed, cut into geometric pieces glimpsed between towers or caught slantwise across a granite-and-glass ravine. There is no horizon; the lucky penthouses and fifteenth-floor apartments and offices may have long views, but the streets have almost none. At night, the white glow that fizzes upward from the city—an inverted electric Niagara—obscures the stars, and except for the planetarium's windowless mimicry New York is oblivious of the cosmos. It is nearly as indifferent, by and large, to its marine surround.

Walt Whitman once sang of the "tall masts of Mannahatta" and of the "crested and scallop-edg'd waves," but the Staten Island ferry and the Circle Line beat on mastless, and the drumming ribbon of the West Side Highway bars us from the sound and smell of waters rushing or lapping. New York pretends that it is inland and keeps dry indoors and feels shoreless; New York water means faucets and hidden pipes and, now and then, a ceiling leak or the crisis of a burst main. Almost in spite of itself, Riverside Drive looks out on the Hudson and can, if it likes, remember water. On Manhattan's other flank, the FDR Drive swims alongside the East River like a heavy-chuffing landlubber crocodile, unmindful of the moving water nearby. New York domesticates whatever smacks of sea. And when the two rivers, the Hudson and the East, converge and swallow each other at the Battery's feet, it is the bays alone, the Upper and the Lower, that hurry out to meet the true deep. New York turns its back on the Atlantic. The power and the roar New York looks to are its own.

The Russian poet Joseph Brodsky—born in Leningrad, exiled to New York, buried in Venice—used to say that he wrote to please his predecessors, not his contemporaries. Often enough, New York works toward the opposite: it means to impress the here-andnow, which it autographs with an insouciant wrecking ball. For New Yorkers, a millennium's worth of difference can be encompassed in six months. Downtown lofts on spooky dark blocks that once creaked under the weight and thunder and grime of industrial machinery are suddenly filled with sofas upholstered in white linen and oak bars on wheels and paintings under track lighting and polyurethaned coffee tables heaped with European magazines. Bryant Park, notorious shady hangout, blossoms into a cherished noonday amenity. Or else the deserted tenements along the Metro-North line, staring out eyeless and shame-faced at the commuters' train down from Stamford, will, overnight, have had their burned-out hollows covered over with painted plywood—trompe l'oeil windows and flowerpots pretending, Potemkin-like, and by municipal decree, that human habitation has resumed.

Despite New York's sleight-of-hand transmutations and fool-the-eye pranks, the lady isn't really sawed in half: she leaps up, alive and smiling. If physical excision is the city's ongoing principle, there are, anyhow, certain surprising tenacities and keepsake intuitions. Wait, for instance, for the downtown No. 104 at the bus stop on Broadway at Seventy-second Street, look across the way, and be amazed—what Renaissance palazzo is this? A tall facade with draped female sculptures on either side, arched cornices, patterned polychrome bricks: ornamental flourish vying with ornamental flourish. And then gaze down the road to your right: one vast slab after another, the uncompromising severity of straight lines, brilliantly winking windows climbing and climbing, not a curve or entablature or parapet or embrasure ruffling the sleek skin of these new residential monoliths. In sharp winter light, a dazzling juxtaposition, filigreed cheek by modernist jowl. The paradox of New York is that its disappearances contain constancies—and not only because some buildings from an earlier generation survive to prod us toward historical self-consciousness. What is most steadfast in New York has the fleet look of the mercurial: the city's persistent daring, vivacity, enchantment, experiment; the marvel of new forms fired by old passions, the rekindling of the snuffed.

The Lower East Side, those tenement-and-pushcart streets of a century ago, once the venue of synagogues and sukkahs and religious-goods stores and a painful density of population, and later the habitat of creeps and druggies, is now the neighborhood of choice for the great-grandchildren of earlier tenants who were only too happy to escape to the Bronx. At the nearby Knitting Factory and in other clubs, you may catch up with Motel Girl, a band specializing in "Las Vegas stripper *noir*"—avant-garde jazz described as jarring, flashy, seedy, sexy, Movietone-violent, dark. Many of the singers and musicians live in the old tenement flats (toilet down the hall) on Avenue B, with rents as high as a thousand dollars. Broadway and Prince, where Dean & Deluca boasts three hundred varieties of cheese, was home to a notions shop two generations ago; not far away, on Orchard Street, the Tenement Museum stands as an emblem of nostalgic consecration, ignored by its trendy neighbors. You can still buy pickles out of the barrel at Guss's, but the cutting-edge young who come down to Ludlow and Stanton for the music or the glitz rarely find those legendary greenhorn warrens of much historic interest; their turf is the East Village. The Lower East Side's current inhabitants, despite their fascination with the louche, are educated and middle-class, with mothers back on Long Island wishing their guitar-playing daughters had gone to medical school. What these seekers on A, B, and C are after—like their aunts and uncles gyrating in the talismanic Rainbow Room, or like Scott and Zelda plunging into fountains to jump-start the Jazz Age—is New York's insuperable constant: the sense of belonging to the glamorous marrow of one's own time.

Uptown's glamour drive is more domestic. On the Upper West Side, the great style emporia dominate, behemoths of food, cooking devices, leather accessories, "natural" cosmetics, no-color cotton sheets, Mission furniture. Zabar's, the Fairway, Barney Green-grass, Citarella, H&H Bagels—dizzyingly flooded with epicurean getters and spenders—harbor prodigalities of dimpled breads, gourmet coffees, the right kind of polenta, the right kind of rice and salsa, the right kind of coffeemaker. Across town,

the Upper East Side seems, in contrast, staid, reserved, nearly quiet. The streets are less peopled. The wind is colder. A hauteur lurks in the limestone. If the West Side is a roiling marketplace, the East Side is a marble lobby presided over by a monarchical doorman. Fifth Avenue can be tacky here and there, but Madison, with its rows of elite European designers, grows more and more burnished, New York's version of the Rue du Faubourg-Saint-Honoré. On Park and Madison, affluence reigns, and with it a certain neighborhood serenity—a privacy, a regal intimacy. (Over on Lexington and Third, the city's rush begins again.)

Posh East and extravagant West dislike each other, with the ingrained antipathy of restraint and profusion, calm and bustle; nor are they likely, except for an audacious handful of crosstown adventurers, to rub elbows in the shops. A silent cold war chills Manhattan. Its weapons are Zabar's in the West, Versace in the East. There is no hot line between them.

Who lives in New York? E. B. White, mulling the question fifty years ago, imagined "a farmer arriving from Italy to set up a small grocery store in a slum, or a young girl arriving from a small town in Mississippi to escape the indignity of being observed by her neighbors, or a boy arriving from the Corn Belt with a manuscript in his suitcase and a pain in his heart." This has a musty if sweetish scent for us now—eau de Jimmy Stewart, perhaps. The circumstances of the arrivals were generally not so benign; neither was their reception. In a 1922 address before the New York-based American Academy of Arts and Letters, Owen Wister, the author of *The Virginian*, said of the newcomers, "Recent arrivals pollute the original spring. . . . It would be well for us if many recent arrivals would become departures." He meant the immigrants who were just then inundating Ellis Island; but the children of those immigrants would soon be sorting out the dilemmas of welcome and unwelcome by other means.

I remember a ferocious street game that was played in the northeast Bronx long ago, in the neighborhood known as Pelham Bay. It was called war, and it was exclusively a girls' game. With a piece of colored chalk you drew a small circle, in which you placed a pink rubber ball. Then you drew a second circle around it, concentric but far larger. This second circle you divided into as many pie slices as there were players. Each player was assigned a pie slice as her designated territory and wrote in it the name of a country she felt to be her own. So it went like this: Peggy Scanlon chose Ireland; Dorothy Wilson, Scotland; Hilda Weber, Germany; Carolyn Johnson, Sweden; Maria Viggiano (whose Sicilian grandmothers yearly wrapped their fig trees in winter canvas), Italy; Allegra Sadacca (of a Sephardic family recently from Turkey, a remnant of the Spanish Jews exiled by Ferdinand and Isabella in 1492), Spain; Madge Taylor (an immigrant from Iowa), America; and I (whose forebears had endured the despots of Russia for nearly a thousand years), Palestine. So much for the local demographics. Immediately after these self-defining allegiances were declared, someone would shriek "War!" and the asphalt mayhem of racing and tackling and rumbling would begin, with the pink rubber globe as prize. I don't suppose little girls anywhere in New York's boroughs nowadays play this disunited-nations game, but if they do, surely the pie slices are chalked up with preferences for Trinidad, Jamaica, Haiti, Puerto Rico, the Dominican Republic, Colombia, Mexico, Peru, Greece, Lebanon, Albania, Pakistan, India, China, and, of course—for antecedents who were never willing immigrants—Africa. In New York, origins still count, and not always benevolently.

* * *

Though proletarian and patrician may inhabit adjoining streets, it is the upper crust that runs the city. This stratum of the social order was once dubbed the Four Hundred, but New York's current patriciate, however it may have multiplied, escapes being counted—though it counts as heavily as ever and remains as conscientiously invisible. Elitism of this kind is rarely political; it almost never becomes mayor. In a democratic ambience, New York's potentates and nabobs have no easy handle; no one names them, not even in tabloid mockery. Then let us call them, collectively, by what they possess: Influence. Influence is financial, corporate, loftily and discreetly legal; Influence is power and planning and money. And money is the armature on which the mammoth superstructure that is New York is sculptured: architecture and philanthropy, art galleries and libraries and foundations, zoos and conservatories and museums, concert halls and universities and houses of worship. The tallest buildings—the Chrysler, the Empire State, the risen polyhedrons of Rockefeller Center, the Twin Towers, assorted old spires—all have their ankles in money. Influence *means* money, whether in the making of it, the spending, or the giving. Influence is usually private and guarded; it may shun celebrity; it needs no public face; its precincts are often reclusive. You are not likely to follow Influence in its daily maneuvers—though you can, all week long, observe the subway riders as they patiently swarm, intent on getting in and getting out and getting there. The jerky cars grind out their wild sawing clamor; locked inside the racket, the passengers display a Buddhist self-forgetfulness. Noiseless Influence, meanwhile, is driven in smoked-glass limousines, hidden, reserved, arcane. If all the rest of the citizenry were carted off and only Influence were left, the city would be silent. But if

Influence were spirited away in some grand and ghostly yacht, a kind of Flying Dutchman, say, the men in their dinner jackets, the women in their gowns, what would happen to New York? The mysterious and mazy coursings of money would dry up. The city would come to a halt.

Old money—New York's old muse—made the palaces; time impaired them. Grand Central Terminal, Cornelius Vanderbilt's embellished paragon of a transport temple, by the 1950s had declined into a routinely seedy train depot. But what old money brought into being, new money, along with civic determination, refurbishes. New York, the Eraser and the Renewer, with a sweep of its resuscitating will, has cleansed the temple's degradation. The gawky advertising signs are banished and the constellations on the vaulted horizon scrubbed until their stars glitter. The theme is artful mirroring: the existing grand stair engenders an answering grand stair on the opposite end of the great concourse. Grand Central has no fear of the ornamental; it revels in breadth and unstinting scale; it intends to inspire. The idea of the publicly palatial—unashamed lavishness—has returned.

And not only here. Follow Forty-second Street westward to Fifth Avenue and enter the most illustrious temple of all, the lion-sentried library, where the famed third-floor reading room has just undergone its own rebirth—both in homage to and in dissent from the modern. High-tech computers parade across vast polished tables under a gilded rococo ceiling, a beaux-arts confection frosted with floral arabesques. Whatever the mavens may say and however the critics may scowl, New York (in at least one of its multiple manifestations) thirsts for intimations of what the Victorians did not hesitate to invoke: Noble Beauty. New York has learned to value—though never to

venerate—its old robber-baron muses, not for their pre-income-tax devourings but for their appetite for the baronial: the Frick Collection, the Morgan Library, the Cooper-Hewitt (housed in Andrew Carnegie's sixty-four-room mansion). The vanished Pennsylvania Station, the original—razed a generation ago as an elaborate eyesore, now regretted, its bargain-basement replacement a daily discouragement—will soon rise again, in the nearby body of the superannuated General Post Office (Roman, kingly, columned). Fancy, then, a soaring apparition of the Metropolitan Museum of Art, that prototype of urban palace, and of its philosophical rival, the Museum of Modern Art, hovering over the city, scanning it for symptoms of majesty—the Met and MOMA, joined by spectral flights of the City Ballet, the serious little theaters, and Carnegie Hall, all whispering, "Aspire, aspire!"

But grandeur of this style is a neighborhood of the mind, and a narrow one at that. Real neighborhoods and psychological neighborhoods may in fact overlap—literary Greenwich Village being the most storied case in point. Nowadays, Village literariness (Hart Crane, Marianne Moore, and all the rest of the enshrined) hangs as a kind of tattered nimbus not over the old, mostly temporary residences of the celebrated but over the bars, cellars, and cafés they once frequented. Neighborhoods of the mind, though, are rarely so solidly placed in a single site. Of actual neighborhoods (or "sections," in moribund New Yorkese)—SoHo, Tribeca, Chinatown, Little Italy, Chelsea, Gramercy Park, Harlem, Murray Hill, South Street Seaport—only a few are as determinedly self-defined as the Village. But a denizen of any of them can venture out to a collectivity of taste and imagination and familiarity unconstrained by geography. Jazz and blues and nightlife aficionados, movie buffs, gays, rap artists, boxing and wrestling zealots, singles, esoteric-restaurant habitués, Central Park joggers, marathon runners, museum addicts, lovers of music or theater or dance, lonelyhearts, shoppers, hotel weekenders, barflies, churchgoers, Talmud enthusiasts, Bronx-born Tibetan Buddhists, students of Sufism, kabbalists, theosophists, voice or ski coaches, SAT and LSAT crammers, amateur painters, union members, members of boards and trustees, Internet devotees, fans of the Yankees or the Mets or the Jets or the Knicks, believers in psychics and tea-leaf readers, street-walkers and their pimps, antiques fanciers, art collectors, philanthropists, professors of linguistics, lexicographers, copy editors, librarians, kindergarten teachers, crossing guards, wine votaries, storefront chiropractors, Chinese or Hebrew or Arabic calligraphers—all these, and inconceivably more, can emerge from any locality to live, if only for a few hours, in a sympathetic neighborhood of affinity. Expertise and idiosyncrasy and bursting desire burn and burn in New York: a conflagration of manifold, insatiable, tumultuous will.

I was born in a brownstone on East Eighty-eighth Street, between First and York Avenues—but both the latter avenue and the area have since altered their designations and their character. York was once Avenue A, and the neighborhood, populated largely by German immigrants, was called Yorkville. It was here before my birth that my infant brother was kidnapped by a madwoman. The story as it was told to me is set in a certain year but not in any special weather; it seems to me that it must have been summer. I see my mother, hot, sleeveless, breathless, frantic, running through the night streets of Yorkville to find the kidnapper and snatch her baby back. He had been sleeping in his wicker carriage in a nook among rows of brown bottles and drawers filled with maple-

flavored rock candy on strings, not four yards from where my young father, in his pharmacist's jacket, a fountain pen always in its pocket, stood tending to his mortar and pestle, working up a medicinal paste. Into my parents' drugstore the madwoman flew, seizing baby and carriage and all, and out into the dark she fled, only to be discovered some hours later in nearby Carl Schurz Park, disheveled and undone by furious infantile howls, and grateful to relinquish the captive screamer.

In my half-dreaming recreation of this long-ago scene—the stolen child, the fleeing madwoman—why must it be summertime? I think I know why. New York in summer is another sort of city; in mood and weight it has nothing in common with wintry New York. A New York summer is frenetic, syncopated, blistered, frayed, dusty. There is a desperation in its heat, and a sense of letdown, despite relief, in its air-conditioned indoors. Melting squads of tourists, in shorts and open shirts or halters, sweat pooling under their camera straps, their heads swiveling from one gaudy carnival sight to the next, push through Times Square in anxious quick march. Smells of perspiring hot dogs under venders' grease-lined umbrellas mingle with the exhaust fumes of heaving buses. There is nothing relaxed about the summer city. New York's noise is louder, New York's toughness is brasher, New York's velocity is speedier. Everything—stores, offices, schedules, vacations, traffic—demands full steam ahead; no one can say the livin' is easy. New York in July is out of sync, not quite itself, hoping for ransom, kidnapped by midsummer frolicking: picnickers awaiting free twilight performances of Shakespeare in Central Park; street parades of nighttime swelterers along Museum Mile, where tappers and clappers gather before the Jewish Museum to salute the tootling klezmer players; break-dancers down from Harlem, twelve-year-olds effortless and expert and little and lithe, who spin on their heels across from the hive of Madison Square Garden. In the American heartland in summer, babies fall down wells and pipes, and that is news. In New York— fidgety, frittering, frenzied, boiling New York— summer itself is news.

The true city is the winter city. The woolly enchantment of a population swaddled and muffled, women and men in long coats, eccentric boots, winding scarves; steam sculptures forming out of human breath; hushed streets; tiny white electric points on skeletal trees! The icy air like a scratch across a sheet of silver, the smoky chestnut carts, the foggy odor of hot coffee when you open a door, a bakery's sweet mist swirling through its transom, a glimpse of rosy-nosed skaters in the well of the Rockefeller stelae, the rescuing warmth of public lobbies—New York in February is a city of grateful small shocks. And just as in an antiquated English novel of manners, New York has its "season"—lectures, readings, rallies, dinner parties, chamber music in someone's living room. While in summer you cannot rely on the taxis to turn on their air-conditioning, in winter each yellow capsule is a hot little bullet; the driver in his turban remembers his subcontinental home. There is no dusk like a New York winter dusk: the blurry gray of early evening, when the lone walker, ferried between day and night, jostled by strangers in packs, feels most desolate, and when the privacy of burrowing into a coat collar brings on a nameless loss. At such a moment, the forest of flowering lights (a brilliance suddenly apprehended) makes its cheering claim: that here, right here, is importance, achievement, delight in the work of the world; that here, right here, is the hope of connection, and life in its fulfillment. In a gregarious New York winter, especially in restaurants at eight o'clock, you will hear jokes, stories with amazing climaxes, futures plotted out, jealousies retailed, gossip above all: who's up, who's down, what's in, what's out. Central heating never abolished the theory and practice of the fireside.

What Manhattan talks about, obliquely or openly—what it thinks about, whatever the season—is ambition. Europeans always make much of this: how *hard* New Yorkers work, the long days, the paltry vacations, the single-minded avarice for status, the obsessiveness, the terrible drive. What? No *dolce far niente*? But only an outsider would remark on the city's striving; for New Yorkers it is ingrained, taken for granted, valued. Unlike Bartleby, downtown's most distinctive imaginary inhabitant, New York never prefers not to. New York prefers and prefers and prefers—it prefers power and scope to tranquillity and intimacy, it prefers crowds and tumult to gardens and ease, it prefers struggle and steel to acquiescence and cushions. New York is where you go to seize the day, to leave your mark, to live within the nerve of your generation. Some might say that there is nothing new in this—why else did Willa Cather begin in Red Cloud, Nebraska, and end on Bank Street? Why else did Jackson Pollock, born in Cody, Wyoming, land in New York?

Yet there is a difference. New York ambition has changed its face. Fifty years ago, when postal clerks and bank tellers wearing vests were what were still called "family men," the hankering young were on the lowest rung of any hierarchy. Their patience was commanded; their deference was expected. It was understood that power and position were the sovereign right of middle age, and that a twenty-three-year-old would have to wait and wait. Opportunity and recognition were light-years away. A few— writers mostly—broke out early: Mary McCarthy at twenty-two, Norman Mailer at twenty-five, Philip Roth and John Updike at twenty-six. Leonard Bernstein and Bobby Fischer were youthful stars. Still, these were all prodigies and exceptions. In the run-of-the-mill world of getting ahead, the young were at the bottom, and stayed there until judged—by their elders at the top—to be sufficiently ripe. The Information Age, with its ear to the ground, reverses all that. The old ways are undone. A twenty-something young woman in publishing keeps a television set on in her office all day, monitoring possible acquisitions: what sells, who's cool. The auditory and the visual, in whatever mode, belong almost exclusively to the newest generation. Everywhere in New York, the knowledgeable young are in charge of the sound, the image, the latest word; ambition need no longer stand in line and wait its graying turn. Fifty-somethings, their passion still unspent, and recalling the slower passages of long ago, may be a little wistful.

Now and then, heartstruck, I pass the crenellated quasi-Gothic building that once housed my high school, where latecomers, myself among them, would tremble before its great arched doorway, fearing reprimand; but the reprimanders are all dead. My Latin teacher is dead. My German teacher is dead. My biology teacher is dead. It is only the city itself that lives on, half amnesiac, hardly ever glancing back, reinventing its fabric, insisting on being noticed for what it is now. There is no grief for what precedes the common memory, and ultimately the fickle urban tide, as mutable as the Nile, accommodates every disappearance.

In May of 1860, when Frederick Law Olmsted's Central Park was just in the making, a forty-year-old Wall Street lawyer named George Templeton Strong recorded in his diary his own wistfulness:

The park below the reservoir begins to look intelligible. Unfinished still, and in process of manufacture, but shewing the outline now of what it is to be. Many points are already beautiful.

What will they be when their trees are grown and I'm dead and forgotten?

One thinks sometimes that one would like re-juvenescence, or a new birth. One would prefer, if he could, to annihilate his past and commence life, say in this a.d. 1860, and so enjoy longer acquaintance with this era of special development and material progress, watch the splendid march of science on earth, share the benefits of the steam engine and the electric telegraph, and grow up with this park— which is to be so great a fact for the young men and maidens of New York in 1880, if all goes well and we do not decompose into anarchy meanwhile. . . . Central Park and Astor Library and a developed Columbia University promise to make the city twenty years hence a real center of culture and civilization, furnishing privileges to youth far beyond what it gave me in my boyhood.

A century and a half on, Strong's "era of special development and material progress" may seem quaint to us, for whom fax and e-mail and jets and microwaves are everyday devices, and whose moonwalkers are already old men. By now, the park below the reservoir, the library on Fifth Avenue, and the university on Morning-side Heights are seasoned inheritances—established components of the city's culture and civilization. But even standing as we do on the lip of the next millennium, who can resist falling into George Templeton Strong's wishful dream of a new birth and a longer acquaintance? His New York of steam engine and telegraph, as ephemeral as the May clouds of 1860, has ceased to be. Our New York too will melt away, and a renewed and clarified city will lift out of the breathing breast of the one we know. New York, Enemy of the Merely Picturesque, Headquarters of Misery and Marvel, Eraser and Renewer, Brain and Capital of the Continent!

The immigrants will come—what language will they speak? The towers will climb to the sky—what shapes will they have? The crowds will stream in the streets—what thoughts will they think? Will they think our outworn thoughts, or imaginings we cannot imagine?

THE "ROCKY" DILEMMA

MUSEUMS, MONUMENTS, AND POPULAR CULTURE
IN THE POSTMODERN ERA

Danielle Rice

*I*n 1982 United Artists film studios installed a statue of Rocky Balboa, the celebrated boxer played by Sylvester Stallone, at the top of the steps of the Philadelphia Museum of Art for the making of *Rocky III.* In the film, the statue is ceremoniously dedicated in front of a cheering crowd and a humbly bashful Rocky. The actor-mayor thanks Rocky on behalf of the citizens of Philadelphia for his many accomplishments and his generous contributions to the city's charities. He lauds the monument as a "celebration of the indomitable spirit of man," and, as the sculpture is unveiled, Rocky's eyes open wide with surprise at the larger-than-life bronze posed in his characteristic victory gesture. While the band plays and the crowd applauds, Rocky turns bashfully to his wife, Adrian, who declares, "It's beautiful!" as she eyes the statue admiringly.

After the completion of *Rocky III,* Stallone donated the film prop to the city of Philadelphia, assuming that the statue would remain in its prominent and strategically significant position, overlooking the grand Benjamin Franklin Parkway, on axis with a monument to George Washington and the statue of William Penn located atop City Hall. But, after much controversy, the statue was removed to the Spectrum, the sports stadium in South Philadelphia where the fictional Rocky and the real Stallone have their roots.

In 1989 United Artists requested permission to reposition the statue for the filming of *Rocky V.* Having been burned the first time around, when they had to pay to have the statue removed from the museum steps, museum authorities negotiated to have the film studio remove the statue at their expense immediately after the shooting. But Stallone reopened the debate regarding the proper home for the Rocky statue at a press conference that generated much interest in his new film, supposedly the last in the series. In a conflation of fiction and reality characteristic of the Reagan era, Stallone claimed that he had done as

259

essay illuminates the conflict between the sculpture and museum

much for the museum as Walter Annenberg (who donated $5 million and recently loaned his art collection for exhibition at the museum) and that he had single-handedly done more for Philadelphia than Benjamin Franklin. Museum authorities were once again accused of elitism, and the media eagerly picked up the ball and stirred up the old controversy, casting it in the expected terms of authorities versus ordinary citizens, elite culture versus popular culture.

Although the museum does not actually have jurisdiction over the disposition of sculpture on its grounds—city property is supervised by the Fairmount Park Art Association—it clearly is the most visible and influential target. Museum authorities had to fend off the media attack. They began by arguing that the statue was not art because it had a specific function, that of movie prop. This line quickly became untenable given the nature of the museum's diverse collections, including the celebrated ready-mades of Marcel Duchamp. Stallone hired lawyers to keep the statue there. His lawyers began by arguing the legitimacy of the sculpture as art. It is the work of a Colorado-based artist, Thomas Schomberg (b. 1943), who was called by *Sports Illustrated* (March 23, 1987) "perhaps the best known sports sculptor working today." It is interesting that Schomberg's name is not actually mentioned in any of the numerous newspaper articles about the statue, a fact that would indicate that the piece was indeed conceived of more as a prop. That is, in fact, what Stallone's lawyers ultimately decided when they did an about-face and embraced the museum's initial position, claiming that indeed the sculpture was merely a movie prop and not art at all. This reversal was log-

ical in light of the fact that the Philadelphia Art Commission, and not the museum, has ultimate responsibility for the disposition of public art. In claiming that the statue was not art, Stallone's lawyers hoped to keep the decision on its ultimate disposition out of the hands of the Art Commission and in the hands of city officials eager to capitalize on the statue's popularity with tourists. In the end, the Art Commission considered a number of possible sites for the statue; however, because the piece had already been removed to the Spectrum, and substantial funds were required for the transfer of the 1,500-pound bronze, the Rocky monument remains at the sports arena at the time of this writing.[1]

It could be argued that the Rocky movies themselves constitute a popular monument more appropriate to today's culture than any other form of art, such as sculpture, because the movies more accurately reflect the tastes of a majority. But it is clear that these tastes have been rather consciously manipulated for the financial gain of a few individuals rather than for loftier ideals. The myth of the Rocky films is the wish-fulfillment fantasy of the hometown boy who achieves success through perseverance and hard work but maintains his humility despite a number of challenges and temptations. After confronting his own limitations and sometimes awesome foes, the hero always triumphs and generally savors the fruits of his success in the arms of the woman he loves. Rocky's rigorous training includes a symbolic run from the bowels of South Philadelphia, a neighborhood inhabited largely by a mixture of working-class Italian, African, and Asian Americans, down the imposing Benjamin Franklin Parkway. The run climaxes at the

Questions if sculpture is more connected than art

[1] Philadelphia Art Commission, "Report on the Rocky Statue," March 23, 1990. The commission's report evaluates four sites: the museum steps, the Philadelphia Visitors' and Convention Bureau, the current Spectrum site, and a location in South Philadelphia, the home of the fictional Rocky. The report concludes that the South Philadelphia site would be the most desirable.

top of the museum steps, that ultimate monument to ascendant, owning-class culture. The message of the working-class boy triumphing over the authority of the elite is thinly veiled, although it is never explicit in the movies. Inspired by the Rocky story, thousands of tourists and busloads of schoolchildren each year ascend the museum steps, now commonly referred to as "The Rocky Steps," in order to jump up and down with their hands in the air at the top, like their hero.

While situated at the top of the museum steps, the Rocky statue was acknowledged by city officials to be the second largest tourist attraction in the city after the Liberty Bell. State senator Vincent Fumo introduced a resolution to keep the statue at the museum, saying that it is "a symbol of the spirit of Philadelphia" much like the famed Liberty Bell itself.[2] Because tourism in modern industrial societies helps people define who they are and what matters in the world, it may be interesting to consider the significance of the Rocky monument as a tourist attraction. In his book entitled *The Great Museum,* Donald Horne deconstructs the symbolic language of European monuments, pointing out that "as tourists moving among Europe's sights, we are moving among symbols that explain the world in ways that justify the authority of the few over the many."[3] This symbolic discourse of monuments can probably also be applied to the United States. But there is a second rhetorical thread that is particular to the American tourist experience.

One of the powerful concepts sustained in the three primary nationalistic tourist sites in the United States—Boston, Philadelphia, and Washington, DC—is the peculiarly American notion of the rights of the individual, more broadly defined as the pursuit of liberty. In Boston one visits the places where the pursuit of liberty began in the American Revolution; in Philadelphia one pays homage to the cradle of the documents of liberty, the Declaration of Independence and the Constitution; in Washington, DC, one can be awed by the hallowed halls that safeguard liberty in the present time. The operative American definition of liberty is the opportunity to achieve enormous individual success and wealth through hard work and perseverance.

The Liberty Bell and the Rocky monument are not as dramatically different as they may at first appear. Rocky is perfectly suited to reinforcing the mythic vision of liberty as free enterprise, and thus it molds itself perfectly to the American dream. During the Reagan era, this myth of self-fulfillment through hard labor took on heroic proportions and became the prime justification for the free-market economic system that shaped the policies of the administration. Ronald Reagan himself, a movie star, had achieved the ultimate symbol of success, the presidency of the United States. The discourse of the Rocky movies is the perfect complement to the mythos of the Reagan years and may in part account for the great popularity of these redundant flicks. The "he-man" boxer, not much brains but lots of heart, is the perfect counterpart to Reagan's tough-man persona, the man who created "Star Wars" and the readiness to fight the "Evil Empire." Like Reagan, Rocky is a small-town boy who does good. And if a movie star can become president, why not a monument to the fictional hero himself who, as the real-life mayor of Philadelphia, Wilson Goode, argued, "represents the struggle of so many people."[4]

[2]Quoted by Steve Lopez, *Philadelphia Inquirer,* February 22, 1990, p. 1B.

[3]Donald Horne, *The Great Museum* (Sydney and London: Pluto Press, 1984), p. 1.

[4]Lopez, *Philadelphia Inquirer.*

As a number of analysts have pointed out, the Reagan era was characterized by a great conflation of illusion and reality. Barbara Goldsmith in "The Meaning of Celebrity" suggests how the long-term American preference for illusion has been given new meaning and power in the last twenty years, owing to the combination of technological expansion and the collective disillusionment following the destruction of the heroes of the 1960s—Martin Luther King and the Kennedys—and the Watergate-Vietnam crises.[5] In her book, *Selling Culture,* Debora Silverman traces the degradation of historical thinking in the Reagan era. She points out how during the 1980s museums also participated in this illusionism, celebrating the aristocracy of taste, often with little concern for historical issues. Her study focuses on a number of exhibitions organized by the Metropolitan Museum's Costume Institute and shows how these extravagant installations not only corresponded with marketing efforts at department stores such as Bloomingdale's and Neiman-Marcus but often were indistinguishable from displays in the stores. Silverman cites the exhibitions "Chinese Imperial Robes" (1980), "The Eighteenth-Century Woman" (1981), "La Belle Epoque" (1982), and "Twenty-five Years of Yves Saint Laurent" (1983) and describes how they both glorified aristocratic tastes and disregarded historical accuracy in favor of an approach that celebrated the cult of visible wealth and distinction as a new cultural style concordant with the politics born at the first Reagan inauguration.[6]

A *New Yorker* cartoon recently defined a hero as "a celebrity who has done something real." The confusion between real and manufactured heroism today is clear in the newspaper coverage of the Rocky statue controversy. One Philadelphia writer expressed her regrets that the Rocky statue had been removed as follows: "A hero: But to the museum administrators and their Main Line cohorts, Rocky belonged anywhere else. He was a boxer, after all, a hero of the masses: hardly one of the cultured elite."[7] Clearly this author's definition of hero does not require that he or she have done anything real at all.

Rocky probably comes closer to embodying a modern-day hero than any actual historic figure. He is more widely known than actual historic figures in this society, where curriculum in history varies considerably from school to school and district to district. Only television and the movies can now create such broadly known and revered figures as Rocky and the president of the United States. As a result, Rocky is in a sense more real to a large number of people than George Washington or William Penn, the subjects of the two monuments on axis with the Rocky statue when it was displayed at the top of the museum steps.

The popularity of the Rocky movies and their perfect fit with the myth of the day combined to give the debate over the placement of the Rocky statue, the flavor of political controversy. But, whereas in 1982 the controversy over the statue was cast primarily in terms of popular versus elite culture, in 1989 the public brouhaha was all the more poignant against the backdrop of the conservative backlash against the arts brought on by the censorship of the Robert Mapplethorpe and Andres Serrano exhibitions. The aggressive actions of conservative politicians such as Senator Jesse Helms, seeking to destroy government funding for the arts by limiting the powers of the National

---

[5]Barbara Goldsmith, "The Meaning of Celebrity," in *New York Times Magazine,* December 4, 1983, p. 80.

[6]Debora Silverman, *Selling Culture* (New York: Pantheon Books, 1986), p. 11.

[7]Paula Guzzetti, "Yo Adrian! Is This Art?" *Newsweek,* June 18, 1990.

Endowment for the Arts, also fueled a public outcry against the perceived esoteric nature of contemporary art. Although Helms and his supporters supposedly attacked obscenity in art, all art of an obscure and difficult nature became suspect.[8]

In the art world, the realm of expertise and specialization that is characteristic of all disciplines today has traditionally been more suspect than in other fields, such as math and science. The public institutions of the art world, especially art museums and art education, founded as they are on Enlightenment idealism, still celebrate the concept of art as a universal language. Ironically, this assumed universality of art, the principle that museums and art world institutions represent, can be inverted by outsiders to call into question any art practice that one does not understand or accept. In effect, this is what gave Senator Helms his self-righteous position against the judgment of art world experts.

The idealist theory of art as a universal language comes into direct and virtually daily conflict with the actual practices of the contemporary art world. Thomas Crow characterizes the art world as a village culture, with a localized dialect. This dialect, the language of high theory, he says, "has become part of the material of art-making."[9] Thus the meaning of art is not the concrete, perceptible substance of the art objects; rather it is everywhere extrinsic to them. In this kind of village culture, outsiders who fail to understand the local argot are doomed to remain outsiders. In contemporary museum culture, however, outsiders are all too aware of their outsider status, and resentful of it. The media further fuels the fire by creating the illusion of a universal culture.

Conservative politicians are easily able to capitalize on the ready resentment of people excluded from the high art hegemony. Although many people did not support the more restrictive of Senator Helms's attempts to limit artistic expression, large numbers registered their dissatisfaction with the practices of the art world. For example, a *Los Angeles Times* poll taken September 14–19, 1989, revealed that while two out of three Americans supported freedom of speech, on the issue of who should make decisions regarding government funding of the arts, an overwhelming majority thought the question should be put to public vote (as opposed to being decided by artists or government-picked experts as is currently still the procedure).[10]

The Rocky controversy coincided with this upsurge of hostility toward the "authority" of the art world, symbolized by the imposing structure of the museum itself. Rocky atop the steps of the Philadelphia Museum of Art stands for the victory of the disenfranchised outsiders of the art world over their snooty and elitist cousins. Hostility toward the hegemony of art world practices easily translates into a hostility toward oppressive authority in general, thus the self-righteous tone of many of the articles in the Rocky controversy.

It is not surprising that this same political environment nurtured another well-publicized controversy over the removal of a symbol of art world authority from a public space. Richard Serra's *Tilted Arc* was removed from Federal Plaza in New York

---

[8]A large number of art journals covered, with self-righteous indignation and a sense of impending doom, the developments on Capitol Hill. See, for example, the May 1990 issue of *Art in America* for a number of discussions regarding the conservative censorship crusade.

[9]"Versions of Pastoral in Some Recent American Art," in *The Binational: American Art of the Late 80s* (Boston: Institute of Contemporary Art and Museum of Fine Arts, 1988), p. 20.

[10]*The Polling Report*, December 4, 1989, pp. 6–8.

City during the summer of 1989, just a few months before the Rocky controversy. The destruction of Serra's piece resulted primarily from the efforts of a single individual, the politically appointed General Services Administration's regional administrator, who took office in 1984, three years after the piece had been commissioned and installed.[11]

Public art, specifically the contemporary practice of installing works of art in urban spaces, usually through a process that combines jurying by art world "experts" with consensus building among bureaucrats and city dwellers, has traditionally provided a forum for the airing of conflicting opinions about the nature and role of art. The controversies over the Rocky statue and *Tilted Arc* highlight the failure of communication between the practitioners and experts of the art world and the diverse publics of urban environments. But the controversies also reveal the active—and to a great degree unstudied—role of the media in mythifying and representing so-called public opinion. It is not coincidental that these media-supported and, in the case of Rocky, probably media-created controversies ensued in this particular political climate at this particular moment. Under a banner celebrating mass culture over elite culture, strong individuals have tried to bypass well-established, democratic review procedures either for reasons of personal aggrandizement, as in Stallone's case, or for political ones, as in the case of Helms and Diamond (the GSA administrator responsible for the demise of *Tilted Arc*). Much remains to be written about the pressure from conservative politicians to erode in the 1980s the due processes established in the 1970s for the facilitation of public art and the granting of public money for art.

Finally, the controversy over the Rocky statue raises questions about the nature of the monument in contemporary society. What does a monument of our age look like? Who gets to decide? Is an authentic artifact of a fictional hero the perfect answer? Could the Rocky monument have been transformed from self-aggrandizement and pop cult worship to a form of public art able seriously to engage people in questioning modes of authority? The difficulty of resolving such questions may make one wish for a simpler, gentler time, just like in the movies. Inspired by the Rocky controversy, David Boldt imagined the following scenario:

> Sylvester Stallone has stopped by the museum for a late afternoon glass of sherry with his new friends, museum president Robert Montgomery Scott and director d'Harnoncourt. After an hour or so of pleasant chat, Sly gets up to go, and with a smile playing on his face, starts talking in his Rocky voice as he hands an envelope to Scott.

> "Bob and Anne, diss is something I wanted youse to have," he says. "De only ting is dat I don't want youse to tell where youse got it. Unnerstan?"

> Scott glances at what's in the envelope, looks up and says, "Absolutely, Mr. Balboa."

A month or six weeks later a brief press release from the museum announces that thanks to a huge gift from a donor who desires to remain anonymous, the museum's current capital fund campaign goal has at last been reached. Maybe even exceeded.[12]

Ah, would that life were really just like in the movies!

---

[11]Harriet F. Senie, "Richard Serra's *Tilted Arc:* Art and Non-Art Issues," *Art Journal,* Winter 1989, p. 298.
[12]David Boldt, *Philadelphia Inquirer,* March 25, 1990.

A WALK WITH DAVID HAMMONS

Peter Schjeldahl

At a Starbucks in Cooper Square one recent evening, I waited in vain to meet David Hammons, the charismatic, elusive African-American artist whose much anticipated current solo show, at the Ace Gallery, is his first in New York in ten years. As the minutes went by and Hammons failed to appear (it would turn out that he was waiting for me at another Starbucks, across the square), I weighed the odds that I was being treated to a custom-designed work. Hammons's astonishing, strangely moving new installation, entitled *Concerto in Black and Blue*, consists entirely of empty, pitch-dark rooms which visitors are invited to explore with tiny flashlights in the company of other visitors whose presence is registered only by whisperings, footsteps, and firefly points of blue light. What, I thought, could be a more apt complement to an exhibition of nothing than a non-rendezvous with the artist himself?

Hammons, who is fifty-nine years old, has long flouted an art world eager to make him a star. Museums and collectors prize such racially charged objects as stones crowned with hair, which the artist collects from black barbershops, and drawings made by repeatedly bouncing a soiled basketball on ten-foot sheets of paper. He sells these works privately, often in Europe. His installations and performances tend to be ephemeral in the extreme. Perhaps his most famous work survives only in a droll photograph of the artist standing on a winter street in 1983, peddling snowballs. "I decided a long time ago that the less I do the more of an artist I am," Hammons had said to me on the phone. "Most of the time, I hang out on the street. I walk." He agreed to let me walk with him.

Apparently stood up at Starbucks, I took the walk myself, throughout the East and West Villages. I looked at things in what I fancied was a Hammonsy way: with an eye for the odd human touch. He is a connoisseur of the frowzy and the ad hoc. He once told an interviewer, "I really love to watch the way black people make things . . . just the way we use carpentry. Nothing fits, but everything works. . . . Everything is a thirty-second of an inch off." He makes both an aesthetic and

[handwritten margin note, left column, vertical:] about waiting for Hammon and an art piece that inspired Schjeldahl

[handwritten margin note, bottom:] scruffy and neglected in appearance.

an ethic of that spirit, with or without regard to its racial provenance. Back home, rather pleased with myself, I got a perplexed call from the artist, who, after waiting for me, had set out on his own.

The following evening, Hammons and I met at the St. Mark's Bookshop, of which there is only one. A pleasantly gaunt, soft-spoken, watchful man, he wore a voluminous overcoat and a colorful knit cap. He shrugged off a crack that I made about the proliferation of Starbucks. He reveres Starbucks, he let me know, for having made café culture universal and, not least, for providing toilets to walkers in the city. He takes walking seriously. In his company, I felt introduced to the East Village, which has been my neighborhood since 1973. Street people—or were they just people on the streets?—greeted him warmly like constituents of a popular politician. He responded with courtly deference, giving them his full attention.

During our stroll, Hammons paused to behold casual marvels: a peculiar arrangement of potted plants braving the chill air outside a Japanese barbershop—"I always check out this place," he said—or a swath of gleaming aluminum foil, held down with dirty bricks, set to block drafts under an unused door of a restaurant on St. Mark's Place. In shadowy Tompkins Square Park, we passed a woman walking a dog that wore a floppy plastic supermarket bag on an apparently injured foot. "Something like that is worth a whole night out," Hammons said, gazing after the gimpy animal.

Hammons was born and grew up in Springfield, Illinois, the youngest of ten children of a single mother who worked menial jobs. "I still don't know how we got by," he said. A poor student, he was shunted to vocational courses. He found drawing and other art activities so easy that he had disdain for them. In 1964 he moved to Los Angeles, where, after a halfhearted foray into commercial art, he attended the Chouinard Art Institute (later CalArts). He became excited by the antagonistic avant-gardism of such L.A.-based international artists as Bruce Nauman and Chris Burden. He joined a scene that was both laid back and irascible. "If you showed more often than every three years, no one took you seriously," he said. "Some people worked and worked and never showed at all. That's what I come from." He is friends with many jazz musicians, whose scornful attitudes toward commercial success he described with relish.

Hammons's brand of Dada isn't substantially original. Yves Klein exhibited a vacant gallery, entitled *The Void*, in 1958. Innumerable artists have exploited the poignance of shabby materials. Hammons freely admits to having been influenced by Arte Povera. (He told me that he was thrilled when that movement's master, Jannis Kounellis, agreed to a dual show with him in Rome in 1993.) But nothing in contemporary art matches his poetic compound of modesty, truculence, and wit. His radical independence stands out, to say the least, in today's scrabbling art world. It also distinguishes him from the itinerant artist-shamans who pop up regularly at international festivals. He regards that circuit as a trap. "The way I see it," he said, "the Whitney Biennial and Documenta need me, but I don't need them."

At one point in our meanderings, Hammons went into a bodega on First Avenue and bought a box of rice. A few minutes later, as we were passing a church, he said, "Watch this," and tossed a few handfuls of grains the steps. I said, "Who's getting married?" He said, "The wedding was earlier. We missed it." He added, "That's for somebody who'll come along and have to deal with it." I found the stunt hokey at the time, but now I can't shake a vision of that forlorn rice, pale on cold concrete, testifying to a wedding that never took place. Hammons married young, and he has two adult children. Divorced in

266

the early 1970s, he has never remarried. "As an artist, you have to keep reinventing yourself," he said. "In a marriage, you have to be consistent. It's difficult."

Hammons mentioned having once heard a tape of a rehearsal at which the late mystical jazzman, Sun Ra, instructed his musicians to play a standard—that is, an artifact of white culture—"incorrectly," Ra explained, "They don't need you to play their music correctly. If you do, they have you." Hammons commented, "That got to me. You know, you can play every note sharp or flat and still carry the tune." For him, violating norms and expectations seems to be a craft that demands painstaking attention to detail.

I didn't ask him what it's like being black in a profession that remains overwhelmingly white. But he volunteered, "It's like a white man in the jazz world, like Chet Baker or Jerry Mulligan. They had confidence. I feed off the confidence of jazz greats. It's a matter of confidence, nothing else." He disparaged the academic ironies of younger artists, including blacks, who pose as subversives. He said, "I'm the C.E.O. of the D.O.C.—the Duchamp Outpatient Clinic. We have a vaccine for that smartness virus that's been in the art world for the last fifty years." The cure may be expressive activity that is streetwise, heartfelt, and utterly matter-of fact.

We stopped for dinner at a Japanese restaurant on Avenue A. Under his overcoat, Hammons wore a lavender leather sportcoat and an orange pullover shirt. He likes Japan, he said as we ordered. He recently did a work in Yamaguchi: a huge boulder set in a miniature Japanese landscape (done by a local plant nursery) on a flatbed truck, which travelled from neighborhood to neighborhood. Hammons's experience in Japan helped inspire Concerto in Black and Blue. A visit to the Zen gardens in Kyoto made him realize, he said, that "there are so many different kinds of nothingness."

Ace, an immense gallery on Hudson Street near the Holland Tunnel, is run by Doug Christmas, a maverick dealer whose career has been almost as unpredictable as the artist's. "Doug was after me for six years to show with him," Hammons said. "I had to wait until I analyzed the space. If you try to dominate it, it will make a fool of you every time." He said that he dislikes the sterility of most New York galleries and museums, preferring European institutions, which are steeped in history. "The only place I really would like to show at in New York is the Metropolitan," he said. "It's full of spirit."

The nothingness of Concerto feels beautifully measured, as if a mountain of darkness had been carved to fit snugly into the gallery's echoey rooms. As I wielded my dim cone of soft blue light, I felt curious about the identities of my invisible fellow-explorers but somehow forbidden to approach them. If the experience was profoundly disorienting, it was also endearingly funny in its frugality—a quality that is always crucial to the artist. Hammons told me that he was aggrieved that many people had been stealing the flashlights, which, he said, cost seventy cents apiece. He added that the installation, whose only materials are the flashlights, can be bought for a lofty price that varies according to how much space the buyer wants to darken. Our laughter, he didn't need to point out, is free.

267

LAS VEGAS, OR THE LONGEST DISTANCE BETWEEN TWO POINTS

Rebecca Solnit

*T*would have preferred to step out into the Peak District. I had been looking for a last tour of the sites of walking's history, and that locale seemed to have everything. I had envisioned starting in the hedge maze at the magnificent estate of Chatsworth, then wandering through the surrounding formal gardens into the Capability Brown–landscaped later gardens. From there I could go into the wilder reaches of the Peak, toward Kinder Scout, where the great right-of-way battles were fought, and past the famous gritstone climbs where "the working-class revolution in climbing" took place, then head for bordering Manchester with its formative suburbs or Sheffield with its industrial ruins and climbing gym in a former forge. Or I could begin with the industrial cities and work my way into the country and then to the garden and the maze. But all these picturesque schemes came to an end with the sneaking suspicion that proving that it was still possible to walk in Britain didn't count for much at all. Even Britain's industrial wastelands signify the pale northern European past, and

it wasn't pedestrianism's past but its prognosis that I wanted to inspect. So one December morning I stepped out of Pat's van onto Fremont Street in downtown Las Vegas, and he set off to spend the day climbing the boulders and cliffs at Red Rocks.

Down most of Vegas's east-west avenues straight as latitude lines you can see the thirteen-mile-long escarpment of Red Rocks and, behind its ruddy sandstone domes and pillars, the ten-thousand-foot-high gray peaks of the Spring Range. One of the least celebrated aspects of this arid, amnesiac boomtown is its spectacular setting, with mountain ranges on three sides and glorious desert light, but Las Vegas has never been about nature appreciation. *Las vegas* means "the meadows" and makes it clear the Spanish got to this Southern Paiute oasis before the Anglos did, but the oasis didn't become a town until the twentieth century—until 1905, when the railroad from Los Angeles to Salt Lake City decided to put in a station here. Las Vegas remained a town for drifters and tourists long after the oasis was sucked dry. It lacked the mineral resources of much of the state and only began to flourish when gambling became legal in Nevada in 1931, while Hoover Dam was being built on the Colorado River, thirty miles to the southeast. In 1951 the Nevada Test Site was established sixty miles to the northwest, and in the decades since more than a thousand nuclear weapons have been detonated on its premises (until 1963, most of the tests were above ground, and there are some startling photographs of mushroom clouds rising up above the casinos' towering signs). Las Vegas is bracketed by these colossal monuments to the ambition to dominate rivers, atoms, wars, and to some extent, the world. It may be, however, a much smaller but more pervasive invention that most shaped this city in the Mojave Desert: air conditioning, which has much to do with the recent American mass migration south and west to places where many will spend all summer in climate-controlled interiors. Often portrayed as exceptional, Las Vegas is instead emblematic, an extreme version of new kinds of places being built around the United States and the world.

Las Vegas's downtown was built around the railroad station: visitors were expected to get off the train and walk to the casinos and hotels of downtown's compact Glitter Gulch area around Fremont Street. As cars came to supersede trains for American travelers, the focus shifted: in 1941 the first casino-hotel complex went in along what was then the highway to Los Angeles, Highway 91, and is now the Las Vegas Strip. Long ago, after falling asleep in a car headed for the annual antinuclear gathering at the Nevada Test Site, I woke up when we came to a halt at a traffic light on the Strip to see a jungle of neon vines and flowers and words dancing, bubbling, exploding. I still remember the shock of that spectacle after the blackness of the desert, heavenly and hellish in equal measure. In the 1950s, cultural geographer J. B. Jackson described the then-new phenomenon of roadside strips as another world, a world built for strangers and motorists. "The effectiveness of this architecture is finally a matter of what that other world is: whether it is one that you have been dreaming about or not. And it is here that you begin to discover the real vitality of this new other-directed architecture along our highways: it is creating a dream environment for our leisure that is totally unlike the dream environment of a generation ago. It is creating and at the same time reflecting a new public taste." That taste, he said, was for something wholly new, something that dismissed earlier Eurocentric aping-one's-betters notions of recreation and taste, something adapted to cars and to the new futuristic and tropical fantasies of those cars' inhabitants: "those streamlined facades, flamboyant entrances and deliberately bizarre color effects, those cheerfully self-assertive masses of color and light and movement that clash so roughly with the old and traditional." This vernacular architecture invented for automotive America was celebrated in the famous 1972 architectural manifesto *Learning from Las Vegas*.

In recent years, however, something wholly unexpected has happened on the Strip. Like those islands where an introduced species reproduces so successfully that its teeming hordes devastate their surroundings and starve en masse, the Strip has attracted so many cars that its eight lanes of traffic are in continual gridlock. Its fabulous neon signs were made to be seen while driving past at a good clip, as are big signs fronting mediocre buildings on every commercial strip, but this Strip of Strips has instead in the last several years become a brand-new outpost of pedestrian life. The once-scattered casinos on the Strip have grown together into a boulevard of fantasies and lures, and tourists can now stow their car in one casino's behemoth parking lot and wander the Strip on foot for days, and they do, by the millions—more than 30 million a year, upward of 200,000 at once on the busiest weekends. Even in August, when it was about 100 degrees Fahrenheit after dark, I have seen the throngs stream back and forth on the Strip, slowly—though not much more slowly than the cars. Casino architecture itself has undergone radical changes since the prescient 1966 Caesars Palace played up fantasy architecture over neon signage and the 1989 Mirage presented the first facade specifically designed as a pedestrian spectacle. It seemed to me that if walking could suddenly revive in this most inhospitable and unlikely place, it had some kind of a future, and that by walking the Strip myself I might find out what that future was.

Fremont Street's old-fashioned glitter has suffered by comparison with the Strip's new fantasy environments, so it has been redesigned as a sort of cyber-arcade. Its central blocks have been closed to cars so that pedestrians can mill around freely, and up above the resurfaced street is set a high, arched roof on which laser shows are beamed by night, so that what was once sky is now a kind of giant television screen. It's still a sad half-abandoned place in daylight, and it didn't take me long to tour it and wander south on Las Vegas Boulevard, which would eventually become the Strip. Before it becomes the Strip, the boulevard is a skid row of motels, shabby apartments, and sad souvenir, pornography, and pawn shops, the ugly backside of the gambling, tourism, and entertainment industries. A homeless black man huddled in a brown blanket at a bus stop looked at me walking by, and I looked at an Asian couple across the street coming out of one of the tiny wedding chapels, him in a dark suit, her in a chalk-white dress, so impersonally perfect they could have fallen off a colossal wedding cake. Here each enterprise seemed to stand on its own; the wedding chapel unintimidated by the sex shops, the fanciest casinos by the ruins and vacant lots around them. There weren't many people on the sidewalk with me in this sagging section between the two official versions of Vegas.

Farther on I came to the old El Rancho hotel, burned out and boarded up. The desert and the West had been romanticized by many of the earlier casinos: the Dunes, the Sands, the Sahara, and the Desert Inn on the Strip and the Pioneer Club, the Golden Nugget, the Frontier Club, and the Hotel Apache on Fremont Street, but more recent casinos have thrown regional pride to the winds and summoned up anyplace else, the less like the Mojave the better. The Sands is being replaced by the Venetian, complete with canals. I realized later that my walk was an attempt to find a continuity of experience here, the spatial continuity walking usually provides, but the place would defeat me with its discontinuities of light and fantasy. It defeated me another way too. Las Vegas, which had a population of 5 at the beginning of the twentieth century, 8,500 in 1940, and about half a million in the 1980s, when the casinos seemed to stand alone in the sweep of creosote bushes and yuccas, now has about 1.25 million residents and is the fastest growing city in the country. The glamorous Strip is surrounded by a colossal sprawl of trailer parks, golf courses, gated communities, and generic subdivisions—one of Vegas's abundant ironies is that it has a pedestrian oasis in the heart of the ultimate car suburb. I had wanted to walk from the Strip to the desert to connect the two, and I called the local cartographic company for recommendations about routes, since all my maps were long out of date. They told me that the city was growing so fast they put out a new map every month and recommended some of the shortest routes between the southern Strip and the city edge, but Pat and I drove along them and saw they were alarming places for a solitary walker—a mix of warehouses, light industrial sites, dusty lots, and walled homes from which an aura of abandonment emanated, only occasionally interrupted by a car or grimy hobo. So I stuck to the pedestrian oasis and found that I could mentally move the great casinos like chess pieces from the flat board of the desert: ten years back the fantasy casinos were gone; twenty years back the casinos were scattered and there were almost no pedestrians; fifty years back there were only a few isolated outposts; and a century ago only a tiny whiskey-saloon hamlet disturbed the pale earth spreading in every direction.

Under the tired pavilion in front of the Stardust, an old French couple asked me for directions to the Mirage. I watched them walk slowly away from the old vehicular American fantasyland of glittering futures and toward the new nostalgic fantasyland at the Strip's heart and followed them south myself. The scattered walkers began to become crowds as I traveled south. The bride and groom I had seen come out of the wedding chapel showed up again walking down the boulevard near me, she with a delicate quilted jacket over her wedding dress and spike heels. Tourists come here from around the affluent world (and employees from some of the less affluent ones, notably Central America). Another of Vegas's ironies is that it is one of the world's most visited cities, but few will notice the actual city. In, for example, Barcelona or Katmandu, tourists come to see the locals in their natural habitat, but in Vegas the locals appear largely as employees and entertainers in the anywhere-but-here habitat built for tourists. Tourism itself is one of the last major outposts of walking. It has always been an amateur activity, one not requiring special skills or equipment, one eating up free time and feeding visual curiosity. To satisfy curiosity you must be willing to seem naive, to engage, to explore, to stare and be stared at, and people nowadays seem more willing or able to enter that state elsewhere than at home. What is often taken as the pleasure of another place may be simply that of the different sense of time, space, and sensory stimulation available anywhere one goes slowly.

The Frontier was the first casino I went inside. For six and a half years visitors could watch an outdoor floor show there, a round-the-clock picket of workers—maids, cocktail waitresses, busboys—fighting the union-busting new owners, testifying with their feet and their signs day and night, in summer's withering heat and winter's storms. During those years 101 babies were born and 17 people died among the Frontier strikers, and none of them crossed the picket line. It became the great union battle of the decade, a national inspiration to labor activists. In 1992 the AFL-CIO organized a related event, the Desert Solidarity March. Union activists and strikers walked three hundred miles from the Frontier across the desert to the courthouse in Los Angeles in a show of their willingness to suffer and prove their commitment. Vegas filmmaker Amie Williams commented, while showing me rushes from her documentary on the Frontier strike, that the union is like an American religion of family and solidarity: it has a credo, "An injury to one is an injury to all"— and in the Desert Solidarity March it got its pilgrimage. In Amie's footage, people who looked like they didn't walk much at all straggled in a line alongside old Route 66, bared their feet for bandaging in the evenings, and got up and did it again the next day. A carpenter and union representative named Homer, a bearded man who looked like a biker, testified to the pilgrimage's miracle: in the middle of a rainstorm, a sunspot followed them, and they stayed dry, and he sounded as enthused as one of the children of Israel for whom the Red Sea parted. Finally the union-busting family that had bought the Frontier was forced to sell, and on January 31, 1997, the new owners invited the union back in. Those who had spent six exhilarating years walking the line went back to mixing drinks and making beds. There was nothing of that struggle to see inside the Frontier, just the usual supernova of dizzily patterned carpet, jingling slots, flashing lights, mirrors, staff moving briskly and visitors milling slowly in the twilight that suffuses every casino. They are modern mazes, made to get lost in, with their windowless expanses full of odd angles, view-obscuring banks of slot machines, and other distractions designed, like those in malls and department stores, to prolong visitors' encounters with the temptations that might make them open their wallets before they find the well-concealed exits. Many casinos have "people movers"— moving ramps like those in airports—but here they are all inward-bound. Finding the way out is up to you.

Wandering and gambling have some things in common; they are both activities in which anticipation can be more delicious than arrival, desire more reliable than satisfaction. To put one foot in front of one another or one's cards on the table is to entertain chance, but gambling has become a highly predictable science for the casinos, and they and the law enforcement of Las Vegas are trying to control the odds on walking down the Strip too. The Strip is a true boulevard. It is exposed to the weather, open to its surroundings, a public space in which those glorious freedoms granted by the First Amendment can be exercised, but a mighty effort is being made to take them away, so that the Strip will instead be a sort of amusement park or mall, a space in which we can be consumers but not citizens. Next to the Frontier is the Fashion Show Shopping Center, where leafletters hang out together, forming one of the Strip's many subcultures. Many are undocumented Central Americans, Amie Williams said, and the leaflets most often pertain to sex (though Vegas has a huge sex industry, customers are sought largely by advertisements, not by street hustling; the dozens of clusters of newsstands along the Strip contain very few newspapers and a veritable library of brochures, cards,

and leaflets with color photographs advertising an army of "private dancers" and "escort services"). Since the women themselves are largely invisible, the visibility of the ads has come under assault. The county passed an ordinance making "off-premises canvassing" in the "resort district" a misdemeanor. The director of the Nevada outpost of the American Civil Liberties Union, Gary Peck, spoke to me of "the almost transparent paradox that Vegas markets itself as anything goes—sex, alcohol, gambling—and on the other hand has this almost obsessive attempt at thorough control of public space, advertising on billboards, in the airport, panhandling, free speech." The ACLU's fight over the handbill ordinance had reached the Federal Court of Appeals, and other issues kept cropping up. Earlier that year, petition-gathers were harassed and a pastor and four companions were arrested for proselytizing in the Fremont Street Experience on charges of "blocking a sidewalk," though the now-pedestrian arcade is one vast sidewalk it would take dozens to obstruct.

The casinos and the county, Peck told me, are trying to privatize the very sidewalks, to give themselves more muscle for prosecuting or removing anyone engaging in First Amendment activities—speaking about religion, sex, politics, economics—or otherwise ruffling the smooth experience visitors are supposed to have (similarly, Tucson has recently looked into privatizing sidewalks by leasing them for one dollar to businesses, to allow them to drive out the homeless). Peck worries that if they succeed in taking away the ancient "freedom of the city" at the sidewalk level, it will set a precedent for the rest of the country, malling what were once genuine public spaces, making cities into theme parks. "The theme park," writes Michael Sorkin, "presents its happy regulated version of pleasure—all those artfully hoodwinking forms—as a substitute for the democratic urban realm, and it does so appealingly by stripping troubled urbanity of its sting, of the presence of the poor, of crime, of dirt, of work." The Mirage has already posted a little sign on one of its lawns: "This sidewalk is the private property of the Mirage Casino Hotel upon which an easement has been granted to facilitate pedestrian movement. Anyone found loitering or otherwise impeding pedestrian movement is subject to arrest for trespass," and signs up and down the strip say, "Resort District: No Obstructive Uses Permitted on Public Sidewalks." The signs are there not to protect the freedom of movement of pedestrians, but to restrict what those pedestrians can do or see.

I was hot and weary from the four miles or so I'd gone from Fremont Street, for it was a warm day and the air was stale with exhaust. Distance is deceptive on the Strip: the major intersections are about a mile apart, but the new casinos with their twenty-or-thirty-story hotel towers tend to look closer because their scale doesn't register. Treasure Island is the first of the new theme-park casinos one reaches from the north, and one of the most fantastic—named not after a place or period like the rest, but after a boys' book about pirate life in the South Seas. With a facade of fake rock and picturesque building fronts behind its lagoon of palm trees and pirate ships, it resembles a hotel-resort version of Disneyland's Pirates of the Caribbean ride. But it was the adjoining Mirage that invented the pedestrian spectacle in 1989, with its volcano that erupts every fifteen minutes after dark, to the delight of gathered crowds. When Treasure Island opened in 1993, it upstaged the volcano with a full-fledged pirate battle climaxing with the sinking of a ship—but the battle only takes place a few times a day.

The authors of *Learning from Las Vegas* long ago groused that "the Beautification Committee would continue to recommend turning the Strip into a western Champs-Elysées, obscuring the signs with trees and raising the humidity with giant fountains." The fountains have arrived, and the vast sheets of water fronting the Mirage and Treasure Island are dwarfed by the eight-acre lake at Bellagio, down where the Dunes used to be, across Flamingo Road from Caesars Palace. Together these four casinos make something altogether new and surprisingly old-fashioned, a wild hybrid of the formal garden and the pleasure garden spread out along a public thoroughfare. The Mirage's volcano buried the old Vegas as decisively as Vesuvius did Pompeii, changing architecture and audiences together. The fountains are everywhere, and it *is* a kind of western Champs-Élysées, in that walking to look at the architecture and the other walkers has become a pastime. The Strip is replacing its neon-go-go Americana futurama vision with Europe, a fun pop-culture version of Europe, a Europe of architectural greatest hits and boulevardiers in shorts and T-shirts. Is there anything less peculiar about setting miniature Italian and Roman temples and bridges in English gardens than in putting up gargantuan ones in the desert, in building volcanoes in eighteenth-century gardens such as Wörlitz in Germany than on boulevards in Nevada? Caesars Palace, with its dark green cypresses, fountains, and classical statuary out front, calls up many of the elements of the formal garden, which was itself an Italian extension of Roman practices adapted by the French, Dutch, and English. Bellagio, with its frontage of fountains, recalls Versailles, whose scale was a demonstration of wealth, power, and triumph over nature. These places are mutant reprises of the landscapes in which walking as scenic pleasure was developed. Vegas has become the successor to Vauxhall, Ranelagh, Tivoli, and all the other pleasure gardens of the past, a place where the unstructured pleasures of walking and looking mingle with highly organized shows (stages for music, theater, and pantomimes were an important part of pleasure gardens, as were areas to dance, eat, drink, and sit). As a Vegas promoter might say, the garden is making a comeback, crossbred with the boulevard, and with them comes pedestrian life.

All the efforts to control who strolls and how suggest that walking may in some way still be subversive. At least it subverts the ideals of entirely privatized space and controlled crowds, and it provides entertainment in which nothing is spent or consumed. Though walking may be an inadvertent side effect of gambling—after all, the casino facades weren't built out of public-spiritedness—the Strip is now a place to walk. And after all, Paris's Champs-Élysées also belongs to tourists and foreigners nowadays, strolling, shopping, eating, drinking, and enjoying the sights. New pedestrian overpasses eliminate the intersection of people and cars where Flamingo Road crosses the Strip, and they are handsome bridges giving some of the best views around. But these bridges are entered and exited from within the casinos, so there may come a time when only the well-dressed can cross the street safely here, and the rabble will have to take their chances with the cars or make a long detour. The Strip is not the Champs-Élysées reborn for other reasons too; it lacks the perfect straightness Le Nôtre gave the older road, the straightness that lets you see far into the distance. It bends and bulges, though there are always the cross-streets—and the bridge over Flamingo Road between Bellagio and Caesars provided the best view yet of the desert to the west and Red Rocks. From the other bridge, the one over the Strip from Bellagio to Bally's, I could see—Paris. I had forgotten that a Paris casino was under construction, but there rising out of the dusty soil of the Mojave like an urban mirage, a flâneur's apparition, was the Eiffel Tower, only half finished and half scale but already aggressively straddling what looked like a stumpy Louvre with the Arc de Triomphe jostling it in an antigeographic jumble of architectural greatest hits.

Of course Vegas is reinventing not only the garden, but the city: New York, New York is just down the road from Bellagio, the Tokyo-homage Imperial Palace is up the street, and a much older version of San Francisco—the Barbary Coast—faces Caesars. The 1996 New York, New York is, like the Paris casino, a cluster of famous features; inside is a funny little maze of streets made to look like various Manhattan neighborhoods, complete with street signs, shops (of which only the souvenir and food shops are real, as I found when I foolishly lunged for a bookstore), air conditioners jutting out third-floor windows, and even a graffiti corner—but, of course, without the variety, productive life, dangers, and possibilities of real urban life. Fronted by a Statue of Liberty welcoming gamblers rather than huddled masses yearning to be free, New York, New York is a walk-through souvenir of the city. No longer pocket-size and portable but a destination in itself, it performs a souvenir's function: recalling a few pleasant and reassuringly familiar aspects of a complicated place. I ate a late lunch in New York, New York and drank three pints of water to replenish what had evaporated from me in the desert aridity of my all-day walk.

Back on the boulevard, a young woman from Hong Kong asked me to take a picture of her with the Statue of Liberty behind her and then with the huge golden MGM lion across the street, and she looked ecstatic in both shots. Fat people and thin people, people in baggy shorts and in sleek dresses, a few children and a lot of old people streamed around us, and I handed the camera back and continued south with the crowd, to the last station on these stations of the odds, the Luxor, whose pyramid shape and sphinx say ancient Egypt, but whose shiny glass on which lasers play at night says technology. The newlyweds I had seen before were there in the entryway: she had laid aside her coat and purse to pose for his camera in front of one of the mock-Egyptian statues. I wondered about them, about why they had chosen to spend the first hours of their honeymoon strolling the Strip, about what past they brought to this encounter with global fantasy filtered through the Nevada desert's climate and gambling's economy. Who am I to say that because these people who streamed by to my right and my left were Las Vegas tourists they did not have other lives: that this English couple might not take their next vacation in the Lake District, that the old French couple might not live in Paris or near Plum Village where the Vietnamese Buddhist Thich Nhat Hanh teaches walking meditation, that the African-Americans might not have marched in Selma as children, that the beggar in a wheelchair could not have been hit by a car in New Orleans, that the bride and groom might not be Japanese climbers of Mount Fuji, Chinese descendants of mountain hermits, southern Californian executives with treadmills at home, that this Guatemalan handing out helicopter-ride coupons might not walk the stations of the cross in her church or once have promenaded the plaza in her hometown, that bartender going to work might not have gone on the AFL-CIO march across the desert? The history of walking is as expansive as human history, and the most attractive thing about this pedestrian oasis in the middle of suburban blight in the middle of a great desert expanse is that it hints at that history's breadth—not in its fake Rome and Tokyo, but in its Italian and Japanese tourists.

Las Vegas suggests that the thirst for places, for cities and gardens and wilderness, is unslaked, that people will still seek out the experience of wandering about in the open air to examine the architecture, the spectacles, and the stuff for sale, will still hanker after surprises and strangers. That the city as a whole is one of the most pedestrian-unfriendly places in the world suggests something of the problems to be faced, but that its attraction is a pedestrian oasis suggests the possibility of recovering the spaces in which walking is viable. That the space may be privatized to make the liberties of walking, speaking, and demonstrating illegal suggests that the United States is facing as serious a battle over rights-of-way as did English ramblers half a century ago, though this time the struggle is over urban, not rural, space. Equally scary is the widespread willingness to accept simulations of real places, for just as these simulations usually forbid the full exercise of civil liberties, so they banish the full spectrum of sights, encounters, experiences, that might provoke a poet, a cultural critic, a social reformer, a street photographer.

But the world gets better at the same time it gets worse. Vegas is not an anomaly but an intensification of mainstream culture, and walking will survive outside that mainstream and sometimes reenter it. When the automotive strip and suburb were being developed in the decades after World War II, Martin Luther King was studying Gandhi and reinventing Christian pilgrimage as something politically powerful at one edge of this continent, while at the other Gary Snyder was studying Taoist sages and walking meditation and rethinking the relationship between spirituality and environmentalism. At present, space in which to walk is being defended and sometimes enlarged by pedestrian activist groups springing up in cities across the United States, from Feet First in Seattle and Atlanta's PEDS to Philly Walks and Walk Austin, by the incendiary British-based Reclaim the Streets, by older organizations like the Ramblers' Association and other British insurrections for walking and access, and by pedestrian-favoring urban redesign from Amsterdam to Cambridge, Massachusetts. Walking traditions are maintained by the resurgence of the foot pilgrimage to Santiago de Compostela in Spain and the thriving one in Chimayó, New Mexico, the growing popularity of climbing and mountaineering, the artists working with walking as a medium and the writers with it as a means, the spread of Buddhism with its practices of walking meditation and circumambulating mountains, the newfound secular and religious enthusiasm for labyrinths and mazes. . . .

"This place is a *maze,*" grumbled Pat when he found me in Caesars Forum, the arcade attached to the casino. The Forum is the capstone of the arch, the crowning jewel of Vegas's recreation of the past. It is an arcade in exactly the sense Walter Benjamin described Parisian arcades—he quoted an 1852 guidebook that said, "Both sides of these passageways, which are lighted from above, are lined with the most elegant shops, so that such an arcade is a city, even a world, in miniature," and added, "The arcades were a cross between a street and an *interieur.*" With its arched roof painted to look like the sky and recessed lighting that changes from day to twilight and back every twenty minutes or so, this one is more so than Benjamin could have imagined. Its curving "streets" are disorienting and full of distractions: the stores full of clothes, perfumes, toys, knickknacks, a fountain whose backside is a huge tropical fish tank, the famous fountain of nubile gods and goddesses who periodically "come to life" during a simulated thunderstorm with laser lightning snaking across the skylike dome. I had visited the arcades of Paris only six months before, and they were beautiful dead places, like streambeds through which water no longer runs, with half their shops closed and few wanderers along their mosaic'd corridors, but Caesars Forum is constantly thronged (as are the arcades of Bellagio, modeled after Milan's famous Galleria). It is one of the most financially successful malls in the world, says the *Wall Street Journal,* adding that a new addition is planned, a recreation of a Roman hill town with occa-

sional appearances by horse-drawn chariots. An arcade was never much more than a mall, and though a flâneur was supposed to be more contemplative than the average mall rat, shallow gentlemen are as common as soulful shoppers. "Let's get out of here," I said to Pat, and we finished our drinks and headed for Red Rocks.

Red Rocks is as open, as public, as Las Vegas Boulevard, but nobody is promoting it, just as no one (unless they're selling gear) is promoting the free activity of walking in preference to the lucrative industry of cars. While tens of thousands of people wander the Strip, perhaps a hundred or so at most roam the larger terrain of Red Rocks, whose spires and buttresses are far taller and more spectacular than any casino. Many people only drive through or step out long enough to take a photograph, unwilling to surrender to the slower pace here, a twilight that comes only once a day, wildlife that does as it pleases, a place with no human trace to structure one's thoughts but a few trails, climbing bolts on the rocks, litter, and signs (and an entrenched tradition of nature-worship). Nothing happens here most of the time, except seasons, weather, light, and the workings of one's body and mind.

Musing takes place in a kind of meadowlands of the imagination, a part of the imagination that has not yet been plowed, developed, or put to any immediately practical use. Environmentalists are always arguing that those butterflies, those grasslands, those watershed woodlands, have an utterly necessary function in the grand scheme of things, even if they don't produce a market crop. The same is true of the meadowlands of imagination; time spent there is not work time, yet without that time the mind becomes sterile, dull, domesticated. The fight for free space—for wilderness and for public space—must be accompanied by a fight for free time to spend wandering in that space. Otherwise the individual imagination will be bulldozed over for the chain-store outlets of consumer appetite, true-crime titillations, and celebrity crises. Vegas has not yet decided whether to pave over or encourage that space.

That night we would sleep out near Red Rocks, in an unofficial campground with figures silhouetted against the small fires burning here and there under the starry sky and the glow of Vegas visible over the hill. In the morning we would rendezvous with Paul, a young guide who often drove out from Utah to climb here and who had invited Pat to climb with him. He would lead us along a trail snaking up and down across small arroyos and a dry streambed, past the gorgeous foliage I remembered from earlier trips, junipers with desert mistletoe, tiny-leafed desert oaks, yuccas, manzanitas, and an occasional barrel cactus, all stunted and spread sparsely by the rocky soil, aridity, and scattered boulders in a way that recalls Japanese gardens. Still limping from a fall six months earlier, Pat brought up the rear, while Paul and I talked as we went along about music, climbing, concentration, bicycles, anatomy, apes. When I turned back to look at Las Vegas as I had so often looked toward Red Rocks the day before, he would say, "Don't look back," but I would stare, amazed how thick the city's smog was. The place appeared to be a brown dome with a only few spires murkily visible within it. This state of things whereby the desert could be seen clearly from the city but not the other way round seemed as neat an allegory as I'd ever met. It was as though one could look back from the future to the past but not forward from this ancient place to the future shrouded in trouble, mystery, and fumes.

Paul would lead us off the trail into the brush that led up steep, narrow Juniper Canyon, and I would manage to heave myself up the various shelves where the rock grew more and more gorgeous, sometimes striped red and beige in thin layers, sometimes spotted with pink spots the size of coins, until we were at the foot of the climb. "Olive Oil: This route ascends obvious crack systems for 700 feet up the south side of the Rose Tower," I would read in Pat's battered *American Alpine Club Climber's Guide* for the region. I lounged and watched them climb with ease up the first few hundred feet and studied the mice, who were less glamorous than the white tigers and dolphins of the Mirage, but livelier. Afterward I would turn around and spend the afternoon wandering in flatter terrain, ambling along the few trails alongside the clear rushing water of Pine Creek, exploring another canyon, turning back to watch the shadows over the hills grow longer and the light thicker and more golden, as though air could turn to honey, honey that would dissolve into the returning night.

Walking has been one of the constellations in the starry sky of human culture, a constellation whose three stars are the body, the imagination, and the wide-open world, and though all three exist independently, it is the lines drawn between them—drawn by the act of walking for cultural purposes—that makes them a constellation. Constellations are not natural phenomena but cultural impositions; the lines drawn between stars are like paths worn by the imagination of those who have gone before. This constellation called walking has a history, the history trod out by all those poets and philosophers and insurrectionaries, by jaywalkers, streetwalkers, pilgrims, tourists, hikers, mountaineers, but whether it has a future depends on whether those connecting paths are traveled still.

THE SHAPE OF A WALK

Rebecca Solnit

The disembodiment of everyday life I have been tracing is a majority experience, part of automobilization and suburbanization. But walking has sometimes been, at least since the late eighteenth century, an act of resistance to the mainstream. It stood out when its pace was out of keeping with the time—which is why so much of this history of walking is a First World, after-the-industrial-revolution history, about when walking ceased to be part of the continuum of experience and instead became something consciously chosen. In many ways, walking culture was a reaction against the speed and alienation of the industrial revolution. It may be countercultures and subcultures that will continue to walk in resistance to the postindustrial, postmodern loss of space, time, and embodiment. Most of these cultures draw from ancient practices—of peripatetic philosophers, of poets composing afoot, of pilgrims and practitioners of Buddhist walking meditation—or old ones, such as hiking and flâneury. But one new realm of walking opened up in the 1960s, walking as art.

Artists, of course, have walked. In the nineteenth century the development of pho-tography and spread of plein-air painting made walking an important means for image makers—but once they found their view, they stopped traipsing around, and more importantly, their images stopped the view forever. There are countless wonderful paintings of walkers, from Chinese prints in which tiny hermits stray amid the heights to, for example, Thomas Gainsborough's *Morning Walk* or Gustave Caillebotte's *Paris Street, Rainy Day,* with its umbrella-carrying citizens going wherever they please on the Parisian cobblestones. But the aristocratic young couple in *The Morning Walk* are forever frozen with their best foot forward. Among all the works that come to mind, only the nineteenth-century Japanese printmaker Hiroshige's *Fifty-three Views on the Tokuida Road* seem to suggest walking rather than stopping; they are, like stations of the cross, sequenced to reprise a journey, this time a 312-mile journey from Edo (now Tokyo) to Kyoto, which most then made on foot, as they do in the prints. It is a road movie from when roads were for walkers and movies were woodblock prints.

Language is like a road; it cannot be perceived all at once because it unfolds in time, whether heard or read. This narrative or temporal element has made writing and walking resemble each other in ways art and walking do not—until the 1960s, when everything changed and anything became possible under the wide umbrella of visual art. Every revolution has many parents. One godfather for this one is the abstract expressionist painter Jackson Pollock, at least as one of his offspring portrayed him. Allan Kaprow, himself an important performance and interdisciplinary artist, wrote in 1958 that Pollock shifted the emphasis from the painting as an aesthetic object to a "diaristic gesture." The gesture was primary, the painting secondary, a mere souvenir of that gesture which was now its subject. Kaprow's analysis becomes an exuberant, prophetic manifesto as he weighs the consequences of what the older artist had done: "Pollock's near destruction of this tradition may well be a return to the point where art was more actively involved in ritual, magic, and life than we have known it in our recent past. . . . Pollock, as I see him, left us at the point where we must become preoccupied with and even dazzled by the space and object of our everyday life, either our bodies, clothes, rooms, or, if need be, the vastness of Forty-second Street. Not satisfied with the suggestion through paint of our other senses, we shall utilize the specific substances of sight, sound, movements, people, odors, touch."

For the artists who took up the invitation Kaprow outlined, art ceased to be a craft-based discipline of making objects and become a kind of unbounded investigation into the relationship between ideas, acts, and the material world. At a time when the institutions of galleries and museums and the objects made for them seemed moribund, this new conceptual and dematerialized art sought a new arena and a new immediacy for artmaking. Art objects might be only the evidence of such an investigation or props and prompts for the viewers' own

investigations, while artists could model themselves after scientists, shamans, detectives, or philosophers as they expanded the possible repertoire of gestures far beyond that of the painter at his canvas. Artists' bodies themselves became a medium for performances, and as art historian Kristine Stiles writes, "Emphasizing the body as art, these artists amplified the role of process over product and shifted from representational objects to presentational modes of action." In retrospect, it seems as though these artists were remaking the world, act by act, object by object, starting with the simplest substances, shapes, gestures. One such gesture—an ordinary one from which the extraordinary can be derived—is walking.

Lucy Lippard, who has been writing subversive histories of art for more than thirty years, traces the parentage for walking as a fine art to sculpture, not performance. She focuses on Carl Andre's 1966 sculpture *Lever* and his 1968 *Joint,* the former made of bricks lined up to extend from one room to another so that the viewer has to travel, the other a similar line but this time of hay bales in a meadow traversing a far greater distance. "My idea of a piece of sculpture is a road," Andre wrote then. "That is, a road doesn't reveal itself at any particular point or from any particular point. Roads appear and disappear. . . . We don't have a single point of view for a road at all, except a moving one, moving along it." Andre's minimal sculptures, like Chinese scrolls, reveal themselves over time in response to the movement of the looker; they incorporate travel into their form. "By incorporating an oriental notion of multiple viewpoints and both implied movement and direct intervention in the landscape, Andre set the scene for a subgenre of dematerialized sculpture which is simply, and not so simply, *walking,*" concludes Lippard.

Other artists had already built roads of sorts: Carolee Schneemann built a labyrinth for friends to walk through out of a fallen tree of heaven and other tornado debris in her Illinois backyard in the summer of 1960, before she moved to New York and became one of the most radical artists in the burgeoning field of performance art. Kaprow himself was building environments for audiences and performers to move through and participate in by the early 1960s. The same year Andre built *Joint,* Patricia Johanson built *Stephen Long.* As Lippard describes it, "A 1,600-foot wooden trail painted in gradated pastels and laid out along an abandoned railroad track in Buskirk, New York, it was intended to take color and light beyond traditional impressionism by adding the elements of distance and time taken to perceive it." In the American West, even longer lines were being drawn, though they were no longer necessarily related to walking: Michael Heizer made his "motorcycle drawings" by using said vehicle to draw in the desert; Walter de Maria commissioned a bulldozer to make similarly grandiose earth art on Nevada's arid surface, with lines that could be seen whole from a airplane or perceived over time and partially from the ground; but perhaps Robert Smithson's 1,500-foot-long *Spiral Jetty,* a rough but walkable path of rock and earth curling into the Great Salt Lake, was human in scale. Though its first inhabitants walked for millennia, the American West is often perceived as inimical to pedestrian scale; the earth art, as it came to be called, made there often seemed to echo the massive development projects of the conquest of the West, the railroads, dams, canals, mines.

England, on the other hand, has never ceased to be pedestrian in scale, and its landscape is not available for much further conquest, so artists there must use a lighter touch. The contemporary artist most dedicated to exploring walking as an artistic medium is the Englishman Richard Long. Much of what he has done since was already present in his early *Line Made by Walking* of 1967. The black-and-white photograph shows a path in grass running straight up the center to the trees at the far end of the meadow. As the title makes clear, Long had drawn the line with his feet. It was both more ambitious and more modest than conventional art: ambitious in scale, in making his mark upon the world itself; modest in that the gesture was such an ordinary one, and the resultant work was literally down to earth, underfoot. Like that of many other artists who emerged at the time, Long's work was ambiguous: was *A Line Made by Walking* a performance of which the line was a residual trace, or a sculpture—the line—of which the photograph was documentation, or was the photograph the work of art, or all of these?

Walking became Long's medium. His exhibited art since has consisted of works on paper documenting his walks, photographs of further marks in the landscape made in the course of those walks, and other sculptures made indoors that reference his outdoor activities. Sometimes the walk is represented by a photograph with text, or a map, or by text alone. On the maps the route of the walk is drawn in to suggest that walking is drawing on a grand scale, that his walking is to the land itself as his pen is to the map, and he often walks straight lines, circles, squares, spirals. Similarly, his sculptures in the landscape are usually made by rearranging (without relocating) rocks and sticks into lines and circles, a reductive geometry that evokes everything—cyclical and linear time, the finite and the infinite, roads and routines—and says nothing. Yet other works lay out those lines, circles, and labyrinths of sticks, stones, or mud on the gallery floor. But walking in the landscape is always primary to the work. One magnificent early sculpture uniting these approaches was titled *A Line the Length of a Straight Walk from the Bottom to the Top of Silbury Hill.* With boots dipped in mud he had walked the distance not as a straight line but as a spiral on the gallery floor, so that the muddy path both represented the route he had taken elsewhere and became a new route indoors, evidence of and an invitation to walk. It plays with the concreteness of experience—the walk and its location (Silbury Hill is an ancient earthwork of unknown religious significance in southern England)—and with the abstractions of language and measurement in which that walk is described. The experience cannot be reduced to a place name and a length, but even this scant information is enough to start the imagination going. "A walk expresses space and freedom and the knowledge of it can live in the imagination of anyone, and that is another space too," Long wrote years later.

In some ways Long's works resemble travel writing, but rather than tell us how he felt, what he ate, and other such details, his brief texts and uninhabited images leave most of the journey up to the viewer's imagination, and this is one of the things that distinguishes such contemporary art, that it asks the viewer to do a great deal of work, to interpret the ambiguous, imagine the unseen. It gives us not a walk nor even a representation of a walk, only the idea of a walk and an evocation of its location (the map) or one of its views (the photograph). Formal and quantifiable aspects are emphasized: geometry, measurement, number, duration. There is, for example, Long's piece—a drawing of a squared-off spiral—captioned "A Thousand Miles A Thousand Hours A Clockwise Walk in England Summer 1974." It plays with correlations between time and space without showing or telling us anything further of the walk but the nation and the year, plays with what can be measured and what cannot. Yet it is enough to know that in 1974, as life seemed to get more complicated, crowded, and cynical, someone found the time and space to engage in such an arduous and apparently satisfying encounter with the land in quest of alignments between geography, body, and time. Then there was the map with inset text, "A Six Day Walk Over All Roads, Lanes and Double Tracks Inside a Six-Mile Wide Circle Centred on the Giant of Cerne Abbas," with the routes he had walked radiating like arteries out from the figure Long had placed at the heart of his walk. Another inset portrayed that figure—a 2,000-year-old chalk outline of a 180-foot-tall figure with a club and an erect penis on a Dorset hillside.

Long likes places where nothing seems to have broken the connection to the ancient past, so buildings, people, and other traces of the present or recent past rarely appear. His work revises the British tradition of country walks while representing its most enchanting and problematic faces. He has gone to Australia, the Himalayas, and the Bolivian Andes to make his work, and the idea that all these places can be assimilated into a thoroughly English experience smacks of colonialism or at least high-handed tourism. It raises once again the perils of forgetting that the rural walk is a culturally specific practice, and though it may be a civil, gentle thing in itself, imposing its values elsewhere is not. But while the literary art of the rural walk bogged down in convention, sentimentality, and autobiographical chatter, Long's art is austere, almost silent, and entirely new in its emphasis on the walk itself as having shape, and this is less a cultural legacy than a creative reassessment. His work is breathtakingly beautiful at times, and its insistence that the simple gesture of walking can tie the walker to the surface of the earth, can measure the route as the route measures the walker, can draw on a grand scale almost without leaving a trace, can be art, is profound and elegant. Long's friend and contemporary Hamish Fulton has also made walking his art, and his photographs-with-text pieces are almost indistinguishable from the other peripatetic Englishman's. But Fulton emphasizes a more spiritual-emotional side to his walking, more often choosing sacred sites and pilgrimage routes, and he makes no sculptures in the gallery or marks in the land.

There have been other kinds of walking artists. Probably the first artist to have made walking into performance art is a little-known emigré from Dutch Surinam, Stanley Brouwn. In 1960 he asked strangers on the street to draw him directions to locations around town and exhibited the results as a vernacular art of encounters or a collection of drawings; later he held a conceptual exhibition of "all the shoe-shops in Amsterdam" which would've called for viewers to take a walking tour; installed in a gallery signposts pointing out cities around the world and inviting viewers to take the first few steps toward Khartoum or Ottawa; spent a whole day in 1972 counting his steps; and otherwise explored the everyday world of urban walking. The magisterial German performance artist and sculptor Joseph Beuys, who often imbued simple acts with profound meaning, did one performance where he simply swept up after a political parade and another where he walked through one of the bogs he loved. This 1971 *Bog Action* was documented in photographs that show him walking, sometimes with only his head and trademark fedora visible above water.

The New York performance artist Vito Acconci did his *Following Piece* over twenty-three days in 1969; like much conceptual art of the time, it played with the intersection between arbitrary rules and random phenomena by choosing a stranger and following him or her until he or she entered a building. Sophie Calle, a French photographer whose works arise from interactions and encounters, later revised Acconci's performance with two of her own, documented in photographs and text. *Suite Venitienne* recounts how she met a man at a party in Paris and surreptitiously followed him to Venice, where she tailed him like a detective until he confronted her; years later she had her mother hire an actual detective to do the same to her in Paris, and incorporated the detective's photographs of her into her own artwork as a kind of commissioned portraiture. These pieces explored the city's potential for suspicion, curiosity, and surveillance arising from the connections and disconnections between strangers on the street. In 1985 and 1986, the Palestinian-British artist Mona Hatoum used the street as a performance space, stenciling footprints containing the word *unemployed* down streets in Sheffield, as if to make visible the sad secrets of passersby in that economically devastated city, and performing two different walking acts in Brixton, a working-class outpost of London.

Of all the performances involving walking, the most dramatic, ambitious, and extreme was Marina Abramović and Ulay's 1988 *Great Wall Walk*. Radical performance artists from the Communist east—she from Yugoslavia, he from East Germany—they began to collaborate in 1976 on a series of what they called "relation works." They were interested in testing both their own and the audiences' physical and psychic boundaries with performances that threatened danger, pain, transgression, boredom; they were also interested in symbolically uniting the genders into an ideal whole; and they were increasingly influenced by shamanistic, alchemical, Tibetan Buddhist, and other esoteric traditions. Their work calls to mind what Gary Snyder described as the Chinese tradition of the " 'four dignities'—Standing, Lying, Sitting, and Walking. They are 'dignities' in that they are ways of being fully ourselves, at home in our bodies, in their fundamental modes," or Vipassana Buddhism's similar emphasis on meditating in these four postures. In their first piece, *Relation in Space,* they walked rapidly from opposite walls of a room toward each other until they collided, again and again. In 1977's *Imponderabilia* they stood nude and motionless in the doorway of a museum so that visitors had to decide who to face as they slipped sideways between them. In 1980's *Rest Energy,* they stood together while she held a bow and he held the arrow notched on the taut bow-string, pointing at her heart; their balanced tension and stillness prolonged this moment and stabilized its danger. That same year, they went to the Australian outback hoping to communicate with aboriginal people, who ignored them. They stayed and spent months of a scorching desert summer practicing sitting without moving, learning "immobility, silence and watchfulness" from the desert. Afterward, they found the locals more communicative. From this experience came their *Nightsea Crossing* performance in Sydney, Toronto, Berlin, and other cities: while remaining silent and fasting twenty-four hours a day, they spent several hours each day on successive days in a museum or public space sitting motionless, facing each other across a table, living sculptures displaying a kind of ferocious commitment.

"When I went to Tibet and the Aborigines I was also introduced to some Sufi rituals. I saw that all these cultures pushed the body to the physical extreme in order to make a mental jump, to eliminate the fear of death, the fear of pain, and of all the bodily limitations we live with," Abramović later said. "Performance was the form enabling me to jump to that other space and dimension." The *Great Wall Walk* was planned at the height of her collaboration with Ulay. They intended to walk toward each other from opposite ends of the 4,000-kilometer wall, meet, and marry. Years afterward, when they had finally cleared the bureaucratic hurdles set up by the Chinese government, their relationship had so changed that the walk became instead the end of their collaboration and relationship. In 1988 they spent three months walking toward each other from 2,400 miles away, embraced at the center, and went their separate ways.

The Great Wall, built to keep marauding nomads out of China, is one of the world's great emblems of the desire to define and secure self or nation by sealing its bound-

aries. For these two raised behind the Iron Curtain, this transformation of a wall separating north from south into a road linking east to west is full of political ironies and symbolic meanings. After all, walls divide and roads connect. Their performance could be read as a symbolic meeting of East and West, male and female, the architecture of sequestration and of connection. Too, the artists believed the wall had been, in the words of Thomas McEvilley, the critic who has most closely followed their work, "mapped out over the millennia by feng shui experts, so if you followed the wall exactly you would be touching the serpent-power lines that bind together the surface of the earth." The book on the project records, "On March 30, 1988 Marina Abramović and Ulay began their walk over the Great Wall from opposite ends. Marina embarked from the east, by the sea. Ulay started far to the west, in the Gobi desert. On June 27, to the blare of horns, they met up in a mountain pass near Shenmu in Shaanxi Province, in the midst of Buddhist, Confucian and Taoist temples." McEvilley points out that this last performance also expanded upon their first, in which they strode toward each other until they collided.

Both artists have a section in this book in which sparse words and evocative photographs give a sense of their experience, functioning like Richard Long's photograph-and-text pieces to evoke carefully chosen fragments of a complex experience. In between the two texts McEvilley's essay revealed another face of the walk: its entanglement with endless layers of bureaucracy throughout the journey. Like Tolstoy's Princess Marya wishing to be a pilgrim on the road, Abramović and Ulay seem to have set out with an image of themselves walking alone in a clear, uncluttered space and state of mind, but McEvilley describes the minivans that took them to lodgings every night, the handlers, translators, and officials that bustled around them, ensuring they met the government's requirements and attempting to slow them down so they would spend more time and thus money in each province, the quarrel Ulay got into at a dance hall, the way schedules, rules, and geography had fragmented Ulay's walk (while Abramović made sure she started each morning where she stopped the night before, declaring, "I walk every fucking centimeter of the wall."). The wall was crumbling in many sections, calling for climbing as much as walking, and atop it the wind was often overwhelming. The walk had, in McEvilley's version, become another kind of performance, like a record-seeking one, in which the official goal is realized only at the cost of countless unofficial distractions and annoyances. But perhaps the two artists who had worked so long on their powers of concentration were able to shut out the surrounding clutter from their time on the wall. Their texts and images speak of the essence of walking, of the basic simplicity of the act amplified by the ancient emptiness of the desert around them. Like Long's pieces, theirs seem a gift to viewers of the assurance that a primeval purity of bodily encounter with the earth is still possible and that the human presence so crowded and dominating elsewhere is still small when measured against the immensity of lonely places. "It took a great number of days before, for the first time, I felt the right pace," Ulay wrote. "When mind and body harmonized in the rhythmical sway of walking."

Afterward, Abramović began to make sculptures that invited viewers to participate in the basic acts her performances had explored. She set geodes, chunks of crystal, and polished stones into wooden chairs or on pedestals and mounts where they could be sat with or stood under—furniture for contemplation and for encounters with the elemental forces she believes the stones hold. The most spectacular of the sculptures were several pairs of amethyst shoes included in a big survey of her work at the Irish Museum of Modern Art in 1995. I had arrived there at the end of a long walk from downtown Dublin to find that the museum was housed in an elegant old military hospital, and the walk and the building's history seemed preparation for the shoes—great rough chunks of translucent mottled purple that had been hollowed out and polished inside, like a fairy-tale version of the wooden shoes European peasants once wore. Viewers were invited to put them on and close their eyes, and with them on I realized my feet were, in a sense, inside the earth itself, and though it was possible to walk, it was difficult to do so. I closed my eyes and saw strange colors, and the shoes seemed like fixed points around which the hospital, Dublin, Ireland, Europe, revolved; shoes not to travel in but to realize you might already be there. Later I read that they were made for walking meditation, to heighten awareness of every step. They were titled *Shoes for Departure.*

Kaprow's 1958 prophesy is fulfilled by all these walking artists: "They will discover out of ordinary things the meaning of ordinariness. They will not try to make them extraordinary but will only state their real meaning. But out of this they will devise the extraordinary." Walking as art calls attention to the simplest aspects of the act: the way rural walking measures the body and the earth against each other, the way urban walking elicits unpredictable social encounters. And to the most complex: the rich potential relations between thinking and the body; the way one person's act can be an invitation to another's imagination; the way every gesture can be imagined as a brief and invisible sculpture; the way walking reshapes the world by mapping it, treading paths into it, encountering it; the way each act reflects and reinvents the culture in which it takes place.

TRADITION AND THE INDIVIDUAL TALENT

T. S. Eliot

basically saying when things are inventive we barely focus on what is actually traditional

I

In English writing we seldom speak of tradition, though we occasionally apply its name in deploring its absence. We cannot refer to "the tradition" or to "a tradition"; at most, we employ the adjective in saying that the poetry of So-and-so is "traditional" or even "too traditional." Seldom, perhaps, does the word appear except in a phrase of censure. If otherwise, it is vaguely approbative, with the implication, as to the work approved, of some pleasing archæological reconstruction. You can hardly make the word agreeable to English ears without this comfortable reference to the reassuring science of archæology.

Certainly the word is not likely to appear in our appreciations of living or dead writers. Every nation, every race, has not only its own creative, but its own critical turn of mind; and is even more oblivious of the shortcomings and limitations of its critical habits than of those of its creative genius. We know, or think we know, from the enormous mass of critical writing that has appeared in the French language the critical method or habit of the French; we only conclude (we are such unconscious people) that the French are "more critical" than we, and sometimes even plume ourselves a little with the fact, as if the French were the less spontaneous. Perhaps they are; but we might remind ourselves that criticism is as inevitable as breathing, and that we should be none the worse for articulating what passes in our minds when we read a book and feel an emotion about it, for criticizing our own minds in their work of criticism. One of the facts that might come to light in this process is our tendency to insist, when we praise a poet, upon those aspects of his work in which he least resembles anyone else. In these aspects or parts of his work we pretend to find what is individual, what is the peculiar essence of the man. We dwell with satisfaction upon the poet's difference from his predecessors, especially his immediate predecessors; we endeavour to find something that can be isolated in order to be enjoyed. Whereas if we approach a poet without this prejudice we shall often find that not only the best, but the most individual parts of his work may be those in which the dead poets, his ancestors, assert their immortality most vigorously. And I do not mean the impressionable period of adolescence, but the period of full maturity.

Yet if the only form of tradition, of handing down, consisted in following the ways of the immediate generation before us in a blind or timid adherence to its successes, "tradition" should positively be discouraged. We have seen many such simple currents soon lost in the sand; and novelty is better than repetition. Tradition is a matter of much wider significance. It cannot be inherited, and if you want it you must obtain it by great labour. It involves, in the first place, the historical sense, which we may call nearly indispensable to anyone who would continue to be a poet beyond his twenty-fifth year; and the historical sense involves a perception, not only of the pastness of the past, but of its presence; the historical sense compels a man to write not merely with his own generation in his bones, but with a feeling that the whole of the literature of Europe from Homer and within it the whole of the literature of his own country has a simultaneous existence and composes a simultaneous order. This historical sense, which is a sense of the timeless as well as of the temporal and of the timeless and of the temporal together, is what makes a writer traditional. And it is at the same time what makes a writer most acutely conscious of his place in time, of his contemporaneity.

No poet, no artist of any art, has his complete meaning alone. His significance, his appreciation is the appreciation of his relation to the dead poets and artists. You cannot value him alone; you must set him, for contrast and comparison, among the dead. I mean this as a principle of æsthetic, not merely historical, criticism. The necessity that he shall conform, that he shall cohere, is not one-sided; what happens when a new work of art is created is something that hap-

pens simultaneously to all the works of art which preceded it. The existing monuments form an ideal order among themselves, which is modified by the introduction of the new (the really new) work of art among them. The existing order is complete before the new work arrives; for order to persist after the supervention of novelty, the *whole* existing order must be, if ever so slightly, altered; and so the relations, proportions, values of each work of art toward the whole are readjusted; and this is conformity between the old and the new. Whoever has approved this idea of order, of the form of European, of English literature, will not find it preposterous that the past should be altered by the present as much as the present is directed by the past. And the poet who is aware of this will be aware of great difficulties and responsibilities.

In a peculiar sense he will be aware also that he must inevitably be judged by the standards of the past. I say judged, not amputated, by them; not judged to be as good as, or worse or better than, the dead; and certainly not judged by the canons of dead critics. It is a judgment, a comparison, in which two things are measured by each other. To conform merely would be for the new work not really to conform at all; it would not be new, and would therefore not be a work of art. And we do not quite say that the new is more valuable because it fits in; but its fitting in is a test of its value—a test, it is true, which can only be slowly and cautiously applied, for we are none of us infallible judges of conformity. We say: it appears to conform, and is perhaps individual, or it appears individual, and may conform; but we are hardly likely to find that it is one and not the other.

To proceed to a more intelligible exposition of the relation of the poet to the past: he can neither take the past as a lump, an indiscriminate bolus, nor can he form himself wholly on one or two private admirations, nor can he form himself wholly upon one

288

preferred period. The first course is inadmissible, the second is an important experience of youth, and the third is a pleasant and highly desirable supplement. The poet must be very conscious of the main current, which does not at all flow invariably through the most distinguished reputations. He must be quite aware of the obvious fact that art never improves, but that the material of art is never quite the same. He must be aware that the mind of Europe—the mind of his own country—a mind which he learns in time to be much more important than his own private mind—is a mind which changes, and that this change is a development which abandons nothing *en route,* which does not superannuate either Shakespeare, or Homer, or the rock drawing of the Magdalenian draughtsmen. That this development, refinement perhaps, complication certainly, is not, from the point of view of the artist, any improvement. Perhaps not even an improvement from the point of view of the psychologist or not to the extent which we imagine; perhaps only in the end based upon a complication in economics and machinery. But the difference between the present and the past is that the conscious present is an awareness of the past in a way and to an extent which the past's awareness of itself cannot show.

Some one said: "The dead writers are remote from us because we *know* so much more than they did." Precisely, and they are that which we know.

I am alive to a usual objection to what is clearly part of my programme for the *métier* of poetry. The objection is that the doctrine requires a ridiculous amount of erudition (pedantry), a claim which can be rejected by appeal to the lives of poets in any pantheon. It will even be affirmed that much learning deadens or perverts poetic sensibility. While, however, we persist in believing that a poet ought to know as much as will not encroach upon his necessary receptivity and necessary laziness, it is not desirable to confine knowledge to whatever can be put into a useful shape for examinations, drawing rooms, or the still more pretentious modes of publicity. Some can absorb knowledge, the more tardy must sweat for it. Shakespeare acquired more essential history from Plutarch than most men could from the whole British Museum. What is to be insisted upon is that the poet must develop or procure the consciousness of the past and that he should continue to develop this consciousness throughout his career.

What happens is a continual surrender of himself as he is at the moment to something which is more valuable. The progress of an artist is a continual self-sacrifice, a continual extinction of personality.

There remains to define this process of depersonalization and its relation to the sense of tradition. It is in this depersonalization that art may be said to approach the condition of science. I shall, therefore, invite you to consider, as a suggestive analogy, the action which takes place when a bit of finely filiated platinum is introduced into a chamber containing oxygen and sulphur dioxide.

II

Honest criticism and sensitive appreciation is directed not upon the poet but upon the poetry. If we attend to the confused cries of the newspaper critics and the susurrus of popular repetition that follows, we shall hear the names of poets in great numbers; if we seek not Blue-book knowledge but the enjoyment of poetry, and ask for a poem, we shall seldom find it. In the last article I tried to point out the importance of the relation of the poem to other poems by other authors, and suggested the conception of poetry as a living whole of all the poetry that has ever been written. The other aspect of this Impersonal theory of poetry is the relation of the poem to its author. And I hinted, by an analogy, that the mind of the mature poet differs from that of the immature one not precisely in any valuation of "personality," not being

289

necessarily more interesting, or having "more to say," but rather by being a more finely perfected medium in which special, or very varied, feelings are at liberty to enter into new combinations.

The analogy was that of the catalyst. When the two gases previously mentioned are mixed in the presence of a filament of platinum, they form sulphurous acid. This combination takes place only if the platinum is present; nevertheless the newly formed acid contains no trace of platinum, and the platinum itself is apparently unaffected; has remained inert, neutral, and unchanged. The mind of the poet is the shred of platinum. It may partly or exclusively operate upon the experience of the man himself; but, the more perfect the artist, the more completely separate in him will be the man who suffers and the mind which creates; the more perfectly will the mind digest and transmute the passions which are its material.

The experience, you will notice, the elements which enter the presence of the transforming catalyst, are of two kinds: emotions and feelings. The effect of a work of art upon the person who enjoys it is an experience different in kind from any experience not of art. It may be formed out of one emotion, or may be a combination of several; and various feelings, inhering for the writer in particular words or phrases or images, may be added to compose the final result. Or great poetry may be made without the direct use of any emotion whatever: composed out of feelings solely. Canto XV of the *Inferno* (Brunetto Latini) is a working up of the emotion evident in the situation; but the effect, though single as that of any work of art, is obtained by considerable complexity of detail. The last quatrain gives an image, a feeling attaching to an image, which "came," which did not develop simply out of what precedes, but which was probably in suspension in the poet's mind until the proper combination arrived for it to add itself to.

The poet's mind is in fact a receptacle for seizing and storing up numberless feelings, phrases, images, which remain there until all the particles which can unite to form a new compound are present together.

If you compare several representative passages of the greatest poetry you see how great is the variety of types of combination, and also how completely any semi-ethical criterion of "sublimity" misses the mark. For it is not the "greatness," the intensity, of the emotions, the components, but the intensity of the artistic process, the pressure, so to speak, under which the fusion takes place, that counts. The episode of Paolo and Francesca employs a definite emotion, but the intensity of the poetry is something quite different from whatever intensity in the supposed experience it may give the impression of. It is no more intense, furthermore, than Canto XXVI, the voyage of Ulysses, which has not the direct dependence upon an emotion. Great variety is possible in the process of transmution of emotion: the murder of Agamemnon, or the agony of Othello, gives an artistic effect apparently closer to a possible original than the scenes from Dante. In the *Agamemnon*, the artistic emotion approximates to the emotion of an actual spectator; in *Othello* to the emotion of the protagonist himself. But the difference between art and the event is always absolute; the combination which is the murder of Agamemnon is probably as complex as that which is the voyage of Ulysses. In either case there has been a fusion of elements. The ode of Keats contains a number of feelings which have nothing particular to do with the nightingale, but which the nightingale, partly, perhaps, because of its attractive name, and partly because of its reputation, served to bring together.

The point of view which I am struggling to attack is perhaps related to the metaphysical theory of the substantial unity of the soul: for my meaning is, that the poet has, not a "personality" to express, but a particular medium, which is only a medium and not a personality, in which impressions and experiences combine in peculiar and unexpected ways. Impressions and experiences which are important for the man may take no place in the poetry, and those which become important in the poetry may play quite a negligible part in the man, the personality.

I will quote a passage which is unfamiliar enough to be regarded with fresh attention in the light—or darkness—of these observations:

> *And now me thinks I could e'en chide myself*
> *For doating on her beauty, though her death*
> *Shall be revenged after no common action.*
> *Does the silkworm expend her yellow labours*
> *For thee? For thee does she undo herself?*
> *Are lordships sold to maintain ladyships For the poor benefit of a bewildering minute?*
> *Why does yon fellow falsify highways, And put his life between the judge's lips. To refine such a thing—keeps horse and men To beat their valours for her?. . .*

In this passage (as is evident if it is taken in its context) there is a combination of positive and negative emotions: an intensely strong attraction toward beauty and an equally intense fascination by the ugliness which is contrasted with it and which destroys it. This balance of contrasted emotion is in the dramatic situation to which the speech is pertinent, but that situation alone is inadequate to it. This is, so to speak, the structural emotion, provided by the drama. But the whole effect, the dominant tone, is due to the fact that a number of floating feelings, having an affinity to this emotion by no means superficially evident, have combined with it to give us a new art emotion.

It is not in his personal emotions, the emotions provoked by particular events in his life, that the poet is in any way remarkable or interesting. His particular emotions may be simple, or crude, or flat. The emotion in his poetry will be a very complex thing, but not with the complexity of the emotions of people who have very complex or unusual emotions in life. One error, in fact, of eccentricity in poetry is to seek for new human emotions to express; and in this search for novelty in the wrong place it discovers the perverse. The business of the poet is not to find new emotions, but to use the ordinary ones and, in working them up into poetry, to express feelings which are not in actual emotions at all. And emotions which he has never experienced will serve his turn as well as those familiar to him. Consequently, we must believe that "emotion recollected in tranquillity" is an inexact formula. For it is neither emotion, nor recollection, nor, without distortion of meaning, tranquillity. It is a concentration, and a new thing resulting from the concentration, of a very great number of experiences which to the practical and active person would not seem to be experiences at all; it is a concentration which does not happen consciously or of deliberation. These experiences are not "recollected," and they finally unite in an atmosphere which is "tranquil" only in that it is a passive attending upon the event. Of course this is not quite the whole story. There is a great deal, in the writing of poetry, which must be conscious and deliberate. In fact, the bad poet is usually unconscious where he ought to be conscious, and conscious where he ought to be unconscious. Both errors tend to make him "personal." Poetry is not a turning loose of emotion, but an escape from emotion; it is not the expression of personality, but an escape from personality. But, of course, only those who have personality and emotions know what it means to want to escape from these things.

III

ὁ δὲ νοῦς ἴσως θεωτεςόν τι χαὶ ἀπαθές
ἐότιν

This essay proposes to halt at the frontier of metaphysics or mysticism, and confine itself to such practical conclusions as can be applied by the responsible person interested in poetry. To divert interest from the poet to the poetry is a laudable aim: for it would conduce to a juster estimation of actual poetry, good and bad. There are many people who appreciate the expression of sincere emotion in verse, and there is a smaller number of people who can appreciate technical excellence. But very few know when there is expression of *significant* emotion, emotion which has its life in the poem and not in the history of the poet. The emotion of art is impersonal. And the poet cannot reach this impersonality without surrendering himself wholly to the work to be done. And he is not likely to know what is to be done unless he lives in what is not merely the present, but the present moment of the past, unless he is conscious, not of what is dead, but of what is already living.

Reaction #1

↳ Emotions aren't the thing the poet creates. It is the craft of it all.

How my reaction changed
Elliot's piece is full of contradictions but as I reread it started to make sense especially the stuff about needing to use old works and the stuff about new knowing more than old.

3 Things I Looked Up

1) What is a "simultaneous order"?
   ↳ It's timelessness / a fusion of past and present but has a sense of now.
   page 288

2) censure: express severe disapproval of
   kind of got this out of context clues but it reaffirmed that tradition is locked on as negative when its actually necessary.

3) approbative: approving.
   talks about how is sometimes seen that tradition adds on

STEREOTYPE

Anne Bogart

The problem with clichés is not that they contain false ideas, but rather that they are superficial articulations of very good ones. They insulate us from expressing our real emotions. As Proust himself put it, we are all in the habit of 'giving to what we feel a form of expression which differs so much from, and which we nevertheless after a little time take to be reality itself'. This leads to the substitution of conventional feelings for real ones.

(Christopher Lehman-Haupt)

In this chapter, I examine our assumptions about the meaning and uses of stereotype, cliché and inherited cultural memory. I am interested in these issues both from the point of view of the artist's interaction with them and the audience's reception of them.

In conversation with the Japanese director Tadashi Suzuki in a living room in San Diego, I started to suspect my deeply ingrained assumptions about stereotypes and clichés. We were discussing actors and acting when he mentioned the dread word,

'stereotype'. Suzuki is renowned for his iconoclastic productions of Western classics done in a distinctly Japanese fashion. For many years he worked with the extraordinary world-class performer Kayoko Shiraishi. Some claim that she is the best actor in the world. With Suzuki, she created the central roles around which he built many landmark productions. In 1990 she left his company to pursue an independent career.

Through a translator, Suzuki intimated his chagrin that Shiraishi had been invited by Mark Lamos, then Artistic Director of Hartford Stage in Connecticut, to play Medea in a production at his theatre. Unhappy about the prospect of Shiraishi appearing in Lamos's production, Suzuki complained that the results would be unfortunate. At first I protested. What a wonderful idea for an actor of her skill and calibre to appear in a play at an American regional theatre. Suzuki still looked unhappy and I assumed a kind of *hubris* on his part; I thought that he was troubled by the notion of another director having a success with 'his' actor. Finally I began to understand that the reason was far more complex and fascinating.

Hartford audiences, Suzuki explained, would be charmed by Shiraishi's distinctly

Japanese approach to acting because to them it would seem exotic. They would be enchanted with the Kabuki and Noh influences and by the remarkable way she spoke and moved. But, he continued, Lamos would not see the necessity of driving Shiraishi through these Japanese stereotypes towards genuine expression. Audiences would be satisfied with the exoticism but would go home without the real goods.

Intrigued by Suzuki's mention of stereotype and by the dilemma that international exchange presents in the light of codified cultural behaviour, I wanted to pursue the subject.

In rehearsal, Suzuki went on, Shiraishi always started out as the weakest actor in the room. Everything she did was an unfocused cliché. While all the other actors managed to rehearse well, she would struggle crudely with the material. Eventually, 'fuelled by the fire he lit under her,' as Suzuki described it, the clichés and stereotypes would transform into authentic, personal, expressive moments and finally, with the proper prodding, she would ignite and eclipse everyone around her with her brilliance and size.

The notion of putting a fire under a stereotype stopped me in my tracks. I started to wonder about the negative connotations around the word stereotype and about my persistent efforts to avoid them.

In my own rehearsals, I had always mistrusted clichés and stereotypes. I was afraid of settling on any solution that wasn't completely unique and original. I thought that the point of a rehearsal was to find the most inventive and novel staging possible. Suzuki's dilemma started me wondering about the meaning of the word stereotype and about how we handle the many cultural stereotypes we inherit. Should we assume that our task is to avoid them in the service of creating something brand-new, or do we embrace the stereotypes; push through

them, put a fire under them until, in the heat of the interaction, they transform?

Perhaps stereotype might be considered an ally rather than an enemy. Perhaps the obsession with novelty and innovation is misguided. I decided to study this phenomenon and my assumptions around innovation and inherited tradition.

In his essay 'Tradition and the Individual Talent', T. S. Eliot suggests that an artist's work should be judged not by its novelty or newness, but rather by how the artist handles the tradition he or she inherits. Historically, he wrote, the concept of originality referred to the transformation of tradition through an interaction with it as opposed to the creation of something brand-new. More recently, the art world became obsessed with innovation.

Actually, the word stereotype stems from the Greek *stere,* solid or solid body; having or dealing with three dimensions of space. *Type* comes from the word pressure or pounding, such as the action of typing on a typewriter. In the original French, stereotypes were the first printing machines. A stereotype was a plate cast from a printing surface. The French verb *stereotype* means to print from stereotyped plates. The word cliché came from the sound of metal jumping when the ink dye is struck during the printing process.

The negative connotations first arose in the nineteenth century in England when stereotype began to refer to authenticity in art: 'The standardized figurative sense of an image, formula, or phrase cast in a rigid mould.' During the twentieth century, stereotype continued to accrue disparaging definitions: 'An oversimplified opinion, prejudiced attitude or uncritical judgement; a set of wide generalizations about the psychological characteristics of a group or class of people; a rigid, biased perception of an object, animal, individual or group; a uniform, inflexible mode of behaviour; a standardized mental picture that's held in common by members of a group; to reproduce or perpetuate in an unchanging or standardized form; cause to conform to a fixed or preconceived type'.

I like that the etymology of stereotype refers to solidity. These inherited solid shapes, images and even prejudices can be entered and embodied, remembered and reawoken. If we think of a stereotype as three-dimensional, as a container, isn't it encouraging to interact with substantial shapes in the hyper-ephemeral art of the theatre? Isn't 'putting a fire' under inherited stereotypes a very clear and specific action in a field which is so much about remembering? The task is suddenly so concrete, so definite. A stereotype is a container of memory. If these culturally transmuted containers are entered, heated up and awakened, perhaps we might, in the heat of the interaction, reaccess the original messages, meanings and histories they embody.

Perhaps we can stop trying so hard to be innovative and original; rather, our charge is to receive tradition and utilize the containers we inherit by filling them with our own wakefulness. The boundaries of these containers, their limits, can serve to magnify the experience of entering them.

Because we can walk and talk, we assume that we can act. But an actor actually has to reinvent walking and talking to be able to perform those actions effectively upon the stage. In fact, the most familiar actions are perhaps the most difficult to inhabit either with fresh life or a straight face. When asked to walk downstage carrying a gun while saying the words 'You've ruined my life for the last time', an actor senses the danger that all of these sounds and movements might be hackneyed and predictable. The concern is real and concrete. If the actor has preconceived assumptions about how to perform the actions and words, the event has no chance to come to

life. The actor must 'put a fire' under these clichés in order to bring them to life.

In life and in representations of life, so much has been done before and said before that they have lost their original meanings and have been transmuted into stereotype. Representations of life are containers for meaning which embody the memory of all the other times they have been done.

In 1984 I directed a production of the Rodgers and Hammerstein musical *South Pacific* with undergraduate acting students at New York University. I wanted to channel the sizzling energy of the original 1949 production, so we set our show in a clinic for war-damaged young people who had undergone stressful experiences in the then-current political crises in Grenada and Beirut. The clinic was a fictional invention which offered a contemporary context in which the musical could be performed intact. Each actor played a 'client' whose therapy for their particular trauma was to play various roles in *South Pacific* as part of the graduation ceremony from the clinic.

The rehearsals began with an investigation of the underlying sexual and racial tensions inherent in the musical. I asked the actors to create compositions around specific themes. At one rehearsal I asked the men and the women to divide into male/female pairs. Each couple was to compose seven physical 'snapshots' illustrating archetypical patterns found in male/female relationships. The women were to portray men and the men women. I asked the men to guide the women in selecting and portraying the male archetypes, and the women were each to show their male partners how to embody the archetypes of women. I never anticipated the ensuing fireworks. The energy in the room as the actors created the snapshots accelerated until I thought that the roof would lift off the studio. Because of the gender switch, the actors felt the freedom to enter and embody certain taboo stereotypes with pleasure, zeal and intimacy. The interaction between the men and women was so intense that it affected our entire rehearsal process and galvanized the performances. Fire had been placed under the stereotypes of male/female behaviour.

Although sexual and behavioural stereotypes abounded in commercials, songs and movies, it was socially taboo during the 1980s for these young men and women to enact them. Exaggerated macho behaviour and stereotypical expressions of feminine acquiescence were politically incorrect and the issue was a particularly heated one because it was considered exploitive of women and insensitive to men. But in the context of the rehearsal where the roles were reversed, the permission to recreate the clichés, to put the fire under the stereotypes, released a volatile and priceless energy within the stereotypical snapshots. The staging became a container for released energy. The result was sexy, vital and powerful performances by the young actors. The stereotypes became meaningful because they were presented to the audience outside a commercial context. We were not trying to sell goods; rather, within the context of theatre, audiences and actors alike dealt in a fresh and critical way with the sexual stereotypes we live with daily.

It is natural to want to avoid stereotypes because they can be oppressive and dangerous to certain people. For example, racial stereotypes make fun of and degrade people in a way that is hurtful and insulting. Stereotypes *can* be oppressive if they are blindly accepted rather than challenged. They *can* be dangerous because without 'putting the fire under them', they will reduce rather than expand. They can be negative because historically people have been reduced to the bias of stereotype.

The decision to position a minstrel show at the very heart of my production *American Vaudeville* required that everyone involved in it confront history and stereotype in a very personal and immediate way. Performed by the entire cast of eighteen actors, the minstrel show was to be the centrepiece of our production.

American Vaudeville was one of a trilogy of plays I created about the roots of American popular entertainment. I wrote the play with Tina Landau and directed it at the Alley Theater in Houston, Texas, in 1991. A composite of rich American performance traditions, vaudeville flourished in the United States between 1870 and 1930. Within this populist entertainment empire, many cultures performed under the same roof with audiences from numerous immigrant backgrounds who gathered to enjoy the display of wit and spectacle. The acts, chock-full of stereotypes, were highly entertaining to a country of immigrants getting to know one another. Irish and German humour, family acts and minstrel shows were featured alongside Shakespeare, operatic renditions and new dance forms.

Handling ethnic stereotype in contemporary society presents certain ethical problems. For example, it would have been a misrepresentation not to include a minstrel show in our production because it was one of vaudeville's most popular components. But today, minstrelsy is rightly considered abhorrent; an insult to the African American community. And yet it represents a significant part of our cultural history. Minstrel shows were not only performed all over the United States but also as the first exported American entertainment, they toured the capitals of Europe to great acclaim. In minstrelsy it was common for white performers to put on blackface and enact the stereotypical behaviour of lazy black slaves. Black performers, in separate companies, also put on black make-up with white lips and performed the exaggerated stereotypes to enthusiastic houses worldwide.

This historical paradox provided us with a very specific challenge. We did not want to comment upon the material, or put a spin on it, or put quotation marks around the event. But we did want to light a fire under the enactment of the minstrel show with our own wakefulness and empathy. We encountered and channelled the issues by performing the stereotypes.

The most traumatic and emotional moments happened the first time the actors put on blackface make-up. This action was particularly macabre for the three African Americans in the cast. In front of long mirrors we watched each actor transform into a black-face/white-mouth archetype. To apply the make-up, wear the costumes and enact the jokes, songs and dances, we faced and felt a piece of history. The audiences encountered a documentary embodiment, shapes of history filled with the reverberation of our actual engagement, sorrow and freedom. The result was powerful and reminded us in a living way of our own history. Through the embodiment of severe stereotypes, a small exorcism was performed.

Another approach to stereotype requires a purer use of the body as a conduit to the past. Certain traditions around the world developed prescribed physical techniques to channel authentic experience through time. These formulas must be enacted without attempting to interpret them. The interaction with these forms is purer than the distortion necessary with culturally abused stereotypes and the result is a feeling of rapture as emotions are channelled.

Lisa Wolford's remarkable book *Grotowski's Objective Drama Research,* about the work Polish director Jerzy Grotowski conducted at the University of California at Irvine, describes Grotowski's investigation of the American Shaker tradition. If the indigenous songs and dances of the Shakers are embodied properly, he proposed, the performers would channel authentic experience from the elusive tradition of the Shaker community. The relatively simple Shaker movements and tunes had to be performed without embellishment or interpretation, simply concentrating on the steps and melodies in order to allow the actor access to authentic Shaker experience.

The Japanese use the word *kata* to describe a prescribed set of movements that are repeatable. *Katas* can be found in acting, in cooking, in martial arts as well as in flower arranging. The translation for the word *kata* in English is 'stamp', 'pattern' or 'mould'. In executing a *kata,* it is essential never to question its meaning but through the endless repetition the meaning starts to vibrate and acquire substance.

Americans are obsessed with freedom and often resent restrictions. I wonder if we have thought enough about the meaning of freedom? Do we mean the freedom to do or the freedom to be? Is it better to have the freedom to do anything we want any time we want, or to experience freedom as an internal liberty? Can you have both at the same time?

Perhaps we spend too much time concentrating on having the freedom to *do* what we want and proving that it is worthwhile. Perhaps we spend too much time avoiding *katas,* containers, clichés and stereotypes. If it is true that creativity occurs in the heat of spontaneous interaction with set forms, perhaps what is interesting is the quality of the heat you put under inherited containers, codes, and patterns of behaviour.

Many American actors are obsessed with the freedom to do whatever occurs to them in the moment. The notion of *kata* is abhorrent because, at first glance, it limits freedom. But everyone knows that in rehearsal you have to set *something;* you can either set *what* you are going to do or you can set *how* you will do it. To predetermine both *how* and *what* is tyranny and allows the actor no freedom. To fix neither makes it nearly impossible to intensify moments onstage through repetition. In other words, if you set too much, the results are lifeless. If you set too little, the results are unfocused.

So—if it is necessary to set something and also to leave something open, then the question arises, Do you set *what* is done or *how* it is done? Do you set the form or the content? Do you set the action or the emotion? Due to the pervasive American misunderstanding of the Stanislavsky system, rehearsals often become about eliciting strong emotions and then fixing those emotions. But human emotion is evanescent and ephemeral and setting the emotions cheapens the emotions. Therefore I believe that it is better to set the exterior (the form, the action) and allow the interior (the quality of being, the ever-altering emotional landscape) freedom to move and change in every repetition.

If you allow the emotions free rein to respond to the heat of the moment, then what you set is the form, the container, the *kata*. You work this way, not because you are ultimately most interested in form but, paradoxically, because you are most interested in the human experience. You move away from something in order to come closer to it. To allow for emotional freedom, you pay attention to form. If you embrace the notion of containers or *katas,* then your task is to set a fire, a human fire, inside these containers and start to burn.

Is it possible to meet one another fresh within the constraints of set form? Is it possible to burn through the inherited meanings of stereotype and unleash something fresh and share that with others?

A friend once described an incident in a crowded bus in San Francisco. She noticed two wildly disparate individuals pushed up close to each other on a narrow seat across from her: one a fragile elderly lady, and the second a flashy transvestite. Suddenly the bus lurched and the elderly lady's hair-net caught on to a ring on the transvestite's hand.

The moment the elderly lady's hair-net caught on to the transvestite's ring, the two were caught up in an exquisite mutual crisis. Forced by circumstances to deal with each other, the boundaries that normally defined and separated them dissolved instantly. Suddenly the potential for something new and fresh sprang into being. Perhaps one might express outrage, or possibly they would both burst out laughing. The boundaries evaporated and they found themselves without the cushion of definitions that had formerly sufficed to keep them separate.

When I heard this story, I jumped. It embodies an unmistakable lesson about what is possible between actors onstage and between actors and audience in a theatre.

The Japanese have a word to describe the quality of space and time between people: *ma'ai.* In the martial arts, the *ma'ai* is vital because of the danger of mortal attack. On the stage, the space between actors should also be continually endowed with quality, attention, potential and even danger. The *ma'ai* must be cultivated, respected and sharpened. The lines between actors on the stage should never go slack.

I spoke once with an actor who played Nick in *Who's Afraid of Virginia Woolf* with Glenda Jackson as Martha. He said that she never, ever, let the line between her and the other three actors go slack. The tendency with a lesser actor, playing a dissipated alcoholic character sliding into entropy, would be to loosen the tension and sink into the sofa. But with Jackson, the lines between her and the others had to be taut in every moment. Only when she left the stage did those lines loosen.

When approaching stereotype as an ally, you do not embrace a stereotype in order to hold it rigid; rather, you burn through it, undefining it and allowing human experience to perform its alchemy. You meet one another in an arena of potential transcendence of customary definitions. You awaken opposition and disagreement. If the character you are playing is dissipated and alcoholic you intensify the outward-directed energy. When you walk downstage you do not think about walking downstage; rather you think about not walking upstage. You wake up what is not. You mistrust assumed boundaries and definitions. You take care of the quality of space and time between yourself and others. And you keep the channels open in order to embody the living history of inherited stereotypes.

Stereotypes are containers for memory, history and assumption. I once heard a theory about how culture infiltrates the human imagination. It starts with the notion that the average American's mental pictures of the French Revolution are the images from the musical *Les Miserables,* even for those who have never seen *Les Mis.* Culture is invasive and fluid. It moves through the air and saturates human experience.

To play Stanley Kowalski in *A Streetcar Named Desire,* do you pretend that Marlon Brando never played the character? What do you do with the stereotypes of the T-shirt and posturing? Do you avoid thinking about Brando or do you study his performance and use it? Do you try to arrive at a completely novel Kowalski? What do you do with the audience's memory?

When staging classics such as *Romeo and Juliet, Oedipus Rex* or *Singin' in the Rain,* how do you handle the public's shared memory? Can you include the baggage of a play's history in the *mise-en-scène?* What is our responsibility to the audience's own shared history of stereotype and cliché? What is supposed to happen on the receiving end?

It is very easy to make me cry. A boy running across a field towards his lost pet collie named Lassie can be a trigger mechanism for me. I'm like Pavlov's dog; I burst into tears. As an audience member, my big emotional triggers are loss and transformation.

It is actually not difficult to make everyone in any audience feel and think the same thing at the same time. It is not difficult to lock down meaning and manipulate

response. What is trickier is to generate an event or a moment which will trigger many different possible meanings and associations. It takes craft to set up the circumstances that are simple and yet contain the ambiguities and the incongruity of human experience.

Should the whole audience feel and think the same thing at the same time or should each audience member feel and think something different at a different time? This is the fundamental issue that lies at the heart of the creative act: the artist's intentions vis-à-vis the audience.

Between the towns of Amherst and Northampton in western Massachusetts, two malls are situated right next to each other. Locally they are labelled the 'dead' mall and the 'live' mall. Both huge, one mall functions successfully, always full of activity and crowded stores, and the other, right next door, the dead one, is mostly empty and ghostlike, a visible failure. Both malls do have functioning multi-screen cineplexes, and film-goers are pretty much the only traffic the dead mall sees.

One summer afternoon during the summer that Stephen Spielberg released both *E.T.* and *Poltergeist,* I went to see *E.T.* at the dead mall. Because of the wild popularity of Spielberg's two films, it seemed that both malls, both cineplexes were showing either *E.T.* or *Poltergeist* in all their mini-theatres. As I watched the film I dutifully cried at the moments I was supposed to cry and walked out of the theatre at the end of the movie feeling small and insignificant and used. As I walked towards the parking lot, I could see thousands of other people exiting the theatres in both the dead mall and the live mall, all making a procession to their cars. The sun was setting, and as far as I could see there were cars full of Spielberg audiences making their way out towards the main highway. As I got into my car it was beginning to rain so I turned on the windshield wipers and headlights and saw thousands of other cars turning on their windshield wipers and headlights. Suddenly, watching this spectacle through the batting of the windshield wipers, I had the appalling sensation that each one of us, isolated in our separate cars and just having seen a Spielberg film, were feeling the same thing—not in a glorious communal sense that raises our hearts and spirits but rather, I felt, the film had made us smaller. We had been treated as mass consumers. We had been manipulated.

It is not difficult to trigger the same emotion in everyone. What is difficult is to trigger complex associations so that everyone has a different experience. Umberto Eco in his seminal book *The Open Text,* analyses the difference between closed and open text. In a closed text, there is one possible interpretation. In an open text, there can be many.

In the theatre we can choose to create moments in which everyone watching has a similar experience or moments which trigger different associations in everyone. Is our intention to impress the audience or to creatively empower them?

Susan Sontag, in her essay 'Fascinating Fascism', explores the aesthetics of fascism through the life and work of Hitler's filmmaker Leni Riefenstahl. She proposes that fascist aesthetics flow from a preoccupation with situations of control, submissive behaviour, the manipulation of emotions and the repudiation of the intellect. Fascist art glorifies surrender and exalts mindlessness.

Several years ago I visited two places in Germany during the course of one week and experienced two completely different kinds of architecture. Both were built for masses of people but the intentions motivating the design were so different as to be revelatory when thinking about the audience's experience of an artist's work. One was the site of the Nuremberg rallies where Hitler held forth to the masses and the other was the vast complex in Munich that hosted the 1980 Winter Olympics.

In Nuremberg the architecture is huge and impressive and as I walked around the grounds I felt small and insignificant. The architecture was definitely preoccupied with control, submissive behaviour, manipulation of emotions and the repudiation of the intellect. The opposite experience awaited me in Munich at the Olympic Stadium. Despite the magnitude of the gigantic complex, everywhere I walked, I felt present and large. The architecture invited diverse responses and hypertextual wandering.

The Nazi Party's rally ground is a huge complex of assembly halls and stadiums on a site that conformed to what Hitler's architect Albert Speer called *Versammlungsarchitektur* (assembly architecture). Related in function to Hitler's interest in mass psychology and how best to influence people en masse, Speer described the architecture as 'a means for stabilizing the mechanism of his domination'. The architecture induced servitude by putting everyone in their place. The intention behind the design of this site was to make people feel small and for them to be impressed.

In Munich, by contrast, the grounds and buildings of the 1980 Winter Olympics, designed by the noted architect Frei Otto, is an open playful environment. One of his most beautiful achievements is the roof of the Olympic Stadium, astonishing in its grace and fluidity. Otto specializes in tensile architecture. Structures designed as tensile architecture are created by tension, or pulling apart, in contrast to the more familiar, conventional architecture which is forged by compression. The buildings look like huge spidery tents. They are generous and asymmetrical and as you walk around them, the views constantly shift. The buildings and stadium lie gracefully over several hills and invite wandering and contemplation. Quite different from the fascist intention to control and subdue, these structures encourage people to move and think freely and creatively.

After the physical experience of these two contradictory expressions in architecture—one which unleashes the imagination and another which closes it down—I knew that I had to apply the lesson to my work as a director in the theatre. Do I want to create work in which everyone feels the same or everyone feels differently? Do I want the audience to feel small and manipulated or do I work towards something in which there is room for the audience to move around, imagine and make associations?

The paradox in an artist's relationship to an audience is that, in order to talk to many people, you must speak only to one, what Umberto Eco calls 'the model reader'. I learned about the model reader in the theatre after directing a play entitled *No Plays, No Poetry* . . . in 1988, based on the theoretical writings of Bertolt Brecht.

In New York City, around that time, a joke was circulating among the downtown theatre scene that downtown theatre people only made work for other downtown theatre people. In reaction to that bothersome notion, I always tried to throw as wide a net as I could in order to speak to the biggest, most diverse audience I could imagine. But with *No Plays, No Poetry* . . . I decided to go ahead and make a play for my friends. I wanted the play to serve as a love letter to the theatre community. At the end of the process, I always imagined an artist in the downtown theatre community as the receiver. I had no expectations of a wider public. Paradoxically, *No Plays, No Poetry* . . . became one of the most accessible works of theatre that I have ever directed. It spoke to many people because I chose one person to speak to. Since then, I have always pictured my model reader while preparing and rehearsing a play.

In the theatre we reach out and touch the past through literature, history and memory so that we might receive and relive significant and relevant human questions in the present and then pass them on to future generations. This is our function; this is our task. In light of that purpose, I want to think more positively about the usefulness of stereotypes and challenge my assumptions about originality. If we embrace rather than avoid stereotype, if we enter the container and push against its limits, we are testing our humanity and our wakefulness. The containers are powerful visual and audio stimuli for audiences and, if handled with great vigilance by the artist, can connect us with time.

CULTURE

Stephen Greenblatt

The term "culture" has not always been used in literary studies, and indeed the very concept denoted by the term is fairly recent. "Culture or Civilization," wrote the influential anthropologist Edward B. Tylor in 1871, "taken in its wide ethnographic sense, is that complex whole which includes knowledge, belief, art, morals, law, custom, and any other capabilities and habits acquired by man as a member of society." Why should such a concept be useful to students of literature?

The answer may be that it is not. After all, the term as Tylor uses it is almost impossibly vague and encompassing, and the few things that seem excluded from it are almost immediately reincorporated in the actual use of the word. Hence we may think with a certain relief that at least "culture" does not refer to material objects—tables, or gold, or grain, or spinning wheels—but of course those objects, as used by men and women, are close to the center of any particular society, and we may accordingly speak of such a society's "material culture." Like "ideology" (to which, as a concept, it is closely allied), "culture" is a term that is repeatedly used without meaning much of anything at all, a vague gesture toward a dimly perceived ethos: aristocratic culture,

youth culture, human culture. There is nothing especially wrong with such gestures—without them we wouldn't ordinarily be able to get through three consecutive sentences—but they are scarcely the backbone of an innovative critical practice.

How can we get the concept of culture to do more work for us? We might begin by reflecting on the fact that the concept gestures toward what appear to be opposite things: *constraint* and *mobility.* The ensemble of beliefs and practices that form a given culture function as a pervasive technology of control, a set of limits within which social behavior must be contained, a repertoire of models to which individuals must conform. The limits need not be narrow—in certain societies, such as that of the United States, they can seem quite vast—but they are not infinite, and the consequences for straying beyond them can be severe. The most effective disciplinary techniques practiced against those who stray beyond the limits of a given culture are probably not the spectacular punishments reserved for serious offenders—exile, imprisonment in an insane asylum, penal servitude, or execution—but seemingly innocuous responses: a condescending smile, laughter poised between the genial and the sarcastic, a small dose of indulgent pity laced with contempt, cool silence. And we should add that cultural boundaries are enforced more positively as well: through the system of rewards that range again from the spectacular (grand public honors, glittering prizes) to the apparently modest (a gaze of admiration, a respectful nod, a few words of gratitude).

Here we can make our first tentative move toward the use of culture for the study of literature, for Western literature over a very long period of time has been one of the great institutions for the enforcement of cultural boundaries through praise and blame. This is most obvious in the kinds of literature that are explicitly engaged in attack and celebration: satire and panegyric. Works in these genres often seem immensely important when they first appear, but their power begins quickly to fade when the individuals to whom the works refer begin to fade, and the evaporation of literary power continues when the models and limits that the works articulated and enforced have themselves substantially changed. The footnotes in modern editions of these works can give us the names and dates that have been lost, but they cannot in themselves enable us to recover a sense of the stakes that once gave readers pleasure and pain. An awareness of culture as a complex whole can help us to recover that sense by leading us to reconstruct the boundaries upon whose existence the works were predicated.

We can begin to do so simply by a heightened attention to the beliefs and practices implicitly enforced by particular literary acts of praising or blaming. That is, we can ask ourselves a set of cultural questions about the work before us:

What kinds of behavior, what models of practice, does this work seem to enforce?

Why might readers at a particular time and place find this work compelling?

Are there differences between my values and the values implicit in the work I am reading?

Upon what social understandings does the work depend?

Whose freedom of thought or movement might be constrained implicitly or explicitly by this work?

What are the larger social structures with which these particular acts of praise or blame might be connected?

Such questions heighten our attention to features of the literary work that we might not have noticed, and, above all, to connections among elements within the work. Eventually, a full cultural analysis will need to push beyond the boundaries of the text, to establish links between the text and values, institutions, and practices elsewhere in the culture. But these links cannot be a substitute for close reading. Cultural analysis has much to learn from scrupulous formal analysis of literary texts because those texts are not merely cultural by virtue of reference to the world beyond themselves; they are cultural by virtue of social values and contexts that they have themselves successfully absorbed. The world is full of texts, most of which are virtually incomprehensible when they are removed from their immediate surroundings. To recover the meaning of such texts, to make any sense of them at all, we need to reconstruct the situation in which they were produced. Works of art by contrast contain directly or by implication much of this situation within themselves, and it is this sustained absorption that enables many literary works to survive the collapse of the conditions that led to their production.

Cultural analysis then is not by definition an extrinsic analysis, as opposed to an internal formal analysis of works of art. At the same time, cultural analysis must be opposed on principle to the rigid distinction between that which is within a text and that which lies outside. It is necessary to use whatever is available to construct a vision of the "complex whole" to which Tylor referred. And if an exploration of a particular culture will lead to a heightened understanding of a work of literature produced within that culture, so too a careful reading of a work of literature will lead to a heightened understanding of the culture within which it was produced. The organization of this volume makes it appear that the analysis of culture is the servant of literary study, but in a liberal education broadly conceived it is literary study that is the servant of cultural understanding.

I will return to the question of extrinsic as opposed to intrinsic analysis, but first we must continue to pursue the idea of culture as a system of constraints. The functioning of such a system is obvious in poems like Pope's "Epistle to Doctor Arbuthnot" or Marvell's "Horatian Ode" on Cromwell, works that undertake to excoriate dullness as embodied in certain hated individuals and celebrate civic or military virtue as embodied in certain admired individuals. Indeed culture here is close to its earlier sense of "cultivation"—the internalization and practice of a code of manners. And this sense extends well beyond the limits of satire and panegyric, particularly for those periods in which manners were a crucial sign of status difference.

Consider, for example, Shakespeare's *As You Like It*, where Orlando's bitter complaint is not that he has been excluded from his patrimony—Orlando accepts the custom of primogeniture by which his brother, as the eldest son, inherits virtually all the family property—but rather that he is being prevented from learning the manners of his class: "My father charged you in his will to give me a good education: you have train'd me like a peasant, obscuring and hiding from me all gentleman-like qualities." Shakespeare characteristically suggests that Orlando has within him an innate gentility that enables him to rise naturally above his boorish upbringing, but he equally characteristically suggests that Orlando's gentility needs to be shaped and brought to fruition through a series of difficult trials. When in the Forest of Arden the young man roughly demands food for his aged servant Adam, he receives a lesson in courtesy: "Your gentleness shall force/More than your force move us to gentleness." The lesson has a special authority conferred upon it by the fact that it is delivered by the exiled Duke, the figure at the pinnacle of the play's social order. But the entire world of *As You Like It* is engaged in articulating cultural codes of behavior, from the elaborate, ironic training in courtship presided over by Rosalind to the humble but dignified social order by which the shepherds live. Even the simple country wench Audrey receives a lesson in manners from the sophisticated down Touchstone: "bear your body more seeming, Audrey." This instruction in the management of the body, played no doubt for comic effect, is an enactment in miniature of a process of acculturation occurring everywhere in the play, and occurring most powerfully perhaps on an almost subliminal level, such as the distance we automatically keep from others or the way we position our legs when we sit down. Shakespeare wittily parodies this process—for example, in Touchstone's elaborate rule-book for insults—but he also participates in it, for even as his plays represent characters engaged in negotiating the boundaries of their culture, the plays also help to establish and maintain those boundaries for their audiences.

Art is an important agent then in the transmission of culture. It is one of the ways in which the roles by which men and women are expected to pattern their lives are communicated and passed from generation to generation. Certain artists have been highly self-conscious about this function. The purpose of his vast romance epic, *The Faerie Queene,* writes the Renaissance poet Edmund Spenser, is "to fashion a gentleman or noble person in virtuous and gentle discipline." The depth of our understanding of such a project, extended over a complex plot involving hundreds of allegorical figures, depends upon the extent of our grasp of Spenser's entire culture, from its nuanced Aristotelian conception of moral hierarchies to its apocalyptic fantasies, from exquisite refinement at court to colonial violence in Ireland. More precisely, we need to grasp the way in which this culture of mixed motives and conflicting desires seemed to Spenser to generate an interlocking series of models, a moral order, a set of ethical constraints ranged against the threat of anarchy, rebellion, and chaos.

To speak of *The Faerie Queene* only in terms of the constraints imposed by culture is obviously inadequate, since the poem itself, with its knights and ladies endlessly roaming an imaginary landscape, is so insistent upon mobility. We return to the paradox with which we started: if culture functions as a structure of limits, it also functions as the regulator and guarantor of movement. Indeed the limits are virtually meaningless without movement; it is only through improvisation, experiment, and exchange that cultural boundaries can be established. Obviously, among different cultures there will be a great diversity in the ratio between mobility and constraint. Some cultures dream of imposing an absolute order, a perfect stasis, but even these, if they are to reproduce themselves from one generation to the next, will have to commit themselves, however tentatively or unwillingly, to some minimal measure of movement; conversely, some cultures dream of an absolute mobility, a perfect freedom, but these too have always been compelled, in the interest of survival, to accept some limits.

What is set up, under wildly varying circumstances and with radically divergent consequences, is a structure of improvisation, a set of patterns that have enough elasticity, enough scope for variation, to accommodate most of the participants in a given culture. A life that fails to conform at all, that violates absolutely all the available patterns, will have to be dealt with as an emergency—hence exiled, or killed, or declared a god. But most individuals are content to improvise, and, in the West at least, a great many works of art are centrally concerned with these improvisations. The novel has been particularly sensitive to the diverse ways in which individuals come to terms with the governing patterns of culture; works like Dickens' *Great Expectations* and Eliot's *Middlemarch* brilliantly explore the ironies and pain, as well as the inventiveness, of particular adjustments.

In representing this adjustment as a social, emotional, and intellectual education, these novels in effect thematize their own place in culture, for works of art are themselves educational tools. They do not merely passively reflect the prevailing ratio of mobility and constraint; they help to shape, articulate, and reproduce it through their own improvisatory intelligence. This means that, despite our romantic cult of originality, most artists are themselves gifted creators of variations upon received themes. Even those great writers whom we regard with special awe, and whom we celebrate for their refusal to parrot the clichés of their culture, tend to be particularly brilliant improvisers rather than absolute violaters or pure inventors. Thus Dickens crafted cunning adaptations of the melodramatic potboilers of his times;

306

Shakespeare borrowed most of his plots, and many of his characters, from familiar tales or well-rehearsed historical narratives; and Spenser revised for his own culture stories first told, and told wonderfully, by the Italian poets Ariosto and Tasso.

Such borrowing is not evidence of imaginative parsimony, still less a symptom of creative exhaustion—I am using Dickens, Shakespeare, and Spenser precisely because they are among the most exuberant, generous, and creative literary imaginations in our language. It signals rather a further aspect of the cultural mobility to which I have already pointed. This mobility is not the expression of random motion but of *exchange*. A culture is a particular network of negotiations for the exchange of material goods, ideas, and—through institutions like enslavement, adoption, or marriage—people. Anthropologists are centrally concerned with a culture's kinship system—its conception of family relationships, its prohibitions of certain couplings, its marriage rules—and with its narratives—its myths, folktales, and sacred stories. The two concerns are linked, for a culture's narratives, like its kinship arrangements, are crucial indices of the prevailing codes governing human mobility and constraint. Great writers are precisely masters of these codes, specialists in cultural exchange. The works they create are structures for the accumulation, transformation, representation, and communication of social energies and practices.

In any culture there is a general symbolic economy made up of the myriad signs that excite human desire, fear, and aggression. Through their ability to construct resonant stories, their command of effective imagery, and above all their sensitivity to the greatest collective creation of any culture—language—literary artists are skilled at manipulating this economy. They take symbolic materials from one zone of the culture and move them to another, augmenting their emotional force,

altering their significance, linking them with other materials taken from a different zone, changing their place in a larger social design. Take, for example, Shakespeare's *King Lear:* the dramatist borrows an often-told pseudo-historical account of an ancient British king, associates with it his society's most severe anxieties about kinship relations on the one hand and civil strife on the other, infuses a measure of apocalyptic religious expectation mingled paradoxically with an acute skepticism, and returns these materials to his audience, transformed into what is perhaps the most intense experience of tragic pleasure ever created. A nuanced cultural analysis will be concerned with the various matrices from which Shakespeare derives his materials, and hence will be drawn outside the formal boundary of the play—toward the legal arrangements, for example, that elderly parents in the Renaissance made with their children, or toward child-rearing practices in the period, or toward political debates about when, if ever, disobeying a legitimate ruler was justified, or toward predictions of the imminent end of the world.

The current structure of liberal arts education often places obstacles in the way of such an analysis by separating the study of history from the study of literature, as if the two were entirely distinct enterprises, but historians have become increasingly sensitive to the symbolic dimensions of social practice, while literary critics have in recent years turned with growing interest to the social and historical dimensions of symbolic practice. Hence it is more possible, both in terms of individual courses and of overall programs of study, for students to reach toward a sense of the complex whole of a particular culture. But there is much to be done in the way of cultural analysis even without an integrated structure of courses, much that depends primarily on asking fresh questions about the possible social functions of works of art. Indeed even if one begins to achieve a sophisticated historical sense of the cultural materials out of which a literary text is constructed, it remains essential to study the ways in which these materials are formally put together and articulated in order to understand the cultural work that the text accomplishes.

For great works of art are not neutral relay stations in the circulation of cultural materials. Something happens to objects, beliefs, and practices when they are represented, reimagined, and performed in literary texts, something often unpredictable and disturbing. That "something" is the sign both of the power of art and of the embeddedness of culture in the contingencies of history. I have written at moments as if art always reinforces the dominant beliefs and social structures of its culture, as if culture is always harmonious rather than shifting and conflict-ridden, and as if there necessarily is a mutually affirmative relation between artistic production and the other modes of production and reproduction that make up a society. At times there is precisely such an easy and comfortable conjunction, but it is by no means necessary. The ability of artists to assemble and shape the forces of their culture in novel ways so that elements powerfully interact that rarely have commerce with one another in the general economy has the potential to unsettle this affirmative relation. Indeed in our own time most students of literature reserve their highest admiration for those works that situate themselves on the very edges of what can be said at a particular place and time, that batter against the boundaries of their own culture.

Near the end of his career Shakespeare decided to take advantage of his contemporaries' lively interest in New World exploration. His play *The Tempest* contains many details drawn from the writings of adventurers and colonists, details that are skillfully displaced onto a mysterious Mediterranean island and interwoven with echoes from Virgil's *Aeneid,* from other art forms such as the court masque and pastoral tragicomedy, and from the lore of white magic. The play reiterates the arguments that Europeans made about the legitimacy and civilizing force of their presence in the newly discovered lands; indeed it intensifies those arguments by conferring upon Prospero the power not only of a great prince who has the right to command the forces of this world but of a wizard who has the ability—the "Art" as the play terms it—to command supernatural forces as well. But the intensification has an oddly discordant effect: the magical power is clearly impressive but its legitimacy is less clear.

As magician Prospero resembles no one in the play so much as Sycorax, the hated witch who had preceded him as the island's ruler. The play, to be sure, does not endorse a challenge to Prospero's rule, any more than Shakespeare's culture ever encouraged challenges to legitimate monarchs. And yet out of the uneasy matrix formed by the skillful interweaving of cultural materials comes an odd, discordant voice, the voice of the "savage and deformed slave" Caliban:

This island's mine, by Sycorax my mother,
Which thou tak'st from me. When thou cam'st first
Thou strok'st me, and made much of me;
wouldst give me
Water with berries in't; and teach me how
To name the bigger light, and how the less,
That burn by day and night: and then I lov'd thee,
And show'd thee all the qualities o'th'isle,
The fresh springs, brine-pits, barren place and fertile:
Curs'd be I that did so! All the charms
Of Sycorax, toads, beetles, bats, light on you!
For I am all the subjects that you have,
Which first was mine own King: and here you sty me

In this hard rock, whiles you do keep from me
The rest o'th'island.

Caliban, of course, does not triumph: it would take different artists from different cultures—the postcolonial Caribbean and African cultures of our own times—to rewrite Shakespeare's play and make good on Caliban's claim. But even within the powerful constraints of Shakespeare's Jacobean culture, the artist's imaginative mobility enables him to display cracks in the glacial front of princely power and to record a voice, the voice of the displaced and oppressed, that is heard scarcely anywhere else in his own time. If it is the task of cultural criticism to decipher the power of Prospero, it is equally its task to hear the accents of Caliban.

SUGGESTED READINGS

Bakhtin, Mikhail. 1968. *Rabelais and His World.*

Benjamin, Walter. 1968. *Illuminations.*

Elias, Norbert. 1978. *The Civilizing Process.*

Geertz, Clifford. 1973. *The Interpretation of Cultures.*

Williams, Raymond. 1958. *Culture and Society, 1780–1950.*

LOOK WHAT WE DID

Jonathan Jones

*P*oor Goya. In his lifetime he had to put up with deafness, the Spanish Inquisition and the Duke of Wellington. Now he has Jake and Dinos Chapman to contend with. The brothers called one of their earliest tributes to the great Spanish painter, printmaker and visionary Great Deeds Against the Dead—quoting Goya—in which they reproduced one of his horrific images of cruelty as a lifesize tableau featuring a dismembered mannequin impaled on a tree. Their latest work is another great deed against the dead—a desecration of the memory of Goya.

Two years ago, the Chapmans bought a complete set of what has become the most revered series of prints in existence, Goya's *Disasters of War*. It is a first-rate, mint condition set of 80 etchings printed from the artist's plates. In terms of print connoisseurship, in terms of art history, in any terms, this is a treasure—and they have vandalised it.

"We had it sitting around for a couple of years, every so often taking it out and having a look at it," says Dinos, until they were quite sure what they wanted to do. "We always had the intention of rectifying it, to take that nice word from The Shining, when the butler's trying to encourage Jack

Nicholson to kill his family—to rectify the situation," interrupts Jake.

"So we've gone very systematically through the entire 80 etchings," continues Dinos, "and changed all the visible victims' heads to clowns' heads and puppies' heads."

The "new" work is called Insult to Injury. The exhibition in which it will be shown for the first time, at Modern Art Oxford, is called The Rape of Creativity.

Goya's *Disasters of War* is a precocious modern masterpiece, a work left by its creator as his final savage bequest to the 19th, 20th and 21st centuries—it was far too anti-clerical and unpatriotic to be published in his lifetime, and the first ever edition came out in 1863, three and a half decades after his death in 1828. From the very start of its public existence, it has been experienced not as a historic but as a contemporary work, its images so urgent and truthful that they function as living, new art.

And it is this colossus whose masterpiece the Chapman brothers have chosen to defile.

"He's the artist who represents that kind of expressionistic struggle of the Enlightenment with the ancién regime," says Jake, "so it's kind of nice to kick its underbelly. Because he has a predilection for violence under the aegis of a moral framework. There's so much pleasure in his work. To produce the law, one has to transgress it. Not to be too glib in the current conditions, but there's something quite interesting in the fact that the war of the Peninsula saw Napoleonic forces bringing rationality and enlightenment to a region that was presumed Catholic and marked by superstition and irrationality. And here's Goya, who's very cut free from the Church, who embodies this autonomous enlightened being, embodied as a gelatinous dead mass without redemption—then you hear George Bush and Tony Blair talking about democracy as though it has some kind of natural harmony with nature, as though it's not an ideology."

Whoah, step back a minute. Defacing a work of art is, perhaps, the last taboo of the liberal, Britart-loving, Tate Modern-going public. The crime novelist Patricia Cornwell's purchase and destruction of works by the British artist Walter Sickert in pursuit of her theory that the disturbing early-20th century painter of music hall audiences and seedy interiors was Jack the Ripper nauseated many, me included. To destroy a work of art is a genuinely nasty, insane, deviant thing to do.

The Chapmans have recently found it remarkably difficult to offend people. While their early works—the lifesize girl mannequins with penises for noses—were routinely dismissed as emblematically egregious grotesqueries of '90s British art, in the past few years they have received massive acclaim, in language they profess to find baffling and hilarious. They made Hell, a tableau in which thousands of toy second world war German soldiers mutilate and kill each other and themselves in a psychotic Nazi orgy, and had it interpreted as a profound comment on the Holocaust and its representations: "The idea of making 5,000 little toy soldiers all running round mutilat-

ing each other, and then find pathos in that—it's alarming that people are prepared to cathartically reappropriate these things which are so redundant and void," says Jake. "It took us three years to make 5,000 people. It took the Germans three hours to kill 15,000 Russian prisoners of war."

Then last autumn, they unveiled Works from the Chapman Family Collection, displayed at the White Cube gallery in sombre, museum-like conditions with the works picked out in spots of light amid the darkness; you wandered among astonishingly powerful examples of tribal art: huge carved wooden masks with raffia hair and fetish nails; then realised these were parodies, carved by the Chapmans, with McDonald's logos, scary clown faces, or features composed of burger buns.

It was, I thought, genuinely on the edge of racism and fascism—"primitive" art has been consumed by western modernism for more than 100 years, and here was an exhibition that seemed deliberately to associate African tribal artifacts with darkness and evil. And this spectacle was reviewed and hailed as a devastating moral critique of fast food, America and so on. "The 'best' reviews were the ones that pointed up this incredibly dumb and vulgar binary opposition between McDonald's bad and ecology good, as though the work was some sort of attack on globalisation," says Jake. In fact, they claim: "We want to make McDonald's into a religion."

So one reason for altering 80 original Goya prints is that it may finally offend the people the Chapmans see as their target—an audience in which they include themselves; the liberal, humanist, gallery-going chattering classes. (When asked whom he sees as the enemy, Jake says "Dinos".) It worked on me, when I first heard about it. After all, Goya's Disasters of War is not some dry old relic no one cares about—it is a work that has never lost its power to shock.

In 1863, the very year the Academy of San Fernando in Madrid published the first edition of *Los Desastres de la Guerra*, French modern artists watched appalled as the cynical regime of Napoleon III installed and then betrayed a puppet government in Mexico; the great modern painter Edouard Manet's painting of the end of this squalid imperial episode, *The Execution of Maximilian* (1867–8), emulates Goya's cynical delineation of war atrocities in its icy, close-up depiction of a firing squad killing at embarrassingly close range.

Because Goya was the first artist to reveal the gross face of war stripped of all chivalry, romance and idealism, because he captured something quintessential about modern war, all succeeding generations of artists have seen war through his eyes: they have recognised in the *Disasters of War* a template for their own nightmares.

During the Spanish civil war, Picasso turned back to Goya's etchings—and his paintings in the Prado, the *Second* and *Third of May 1808*—as he planned his own anti-war masterpiece, *Guernica*. If *Guernica* mimics Goya's twin history paintings of the popular Madrid uprising against the French on May 2 1808 and its bloody suppression, his etched cartoon strip, *The Dream and Lie of Franco* (1937), uses the same form as the *Disasters* to denounce fascism. Perhaps, though, it is Salvador Dali in his paintings *Soft Construction with Boiled Beans: Premonition of Civil War* (1936) and *Autumn Cannibalism* (1936) who captures the madness and total ambivalence of Goya's etchings—because Goya, like Dali, had no faith in the forces of progress.

What we see in Goya's prints is the death throes of an idealist. Goya started as the artist of the Enlightenment, in so far as there was an Enlightenment in Spain. Brilliantly colourful and relishing the empiricism he learned from the British modern portraiture of Gainsborough and Reynolds, Goya's early paintings subtly endorse liberal-minded politicians and secular values; when Napoleon, the self-styled champion of Enlightened values, who was so progressive

that he took archaeologists with him to invade Egypt, occupied the Iberian peninsula in 1807 and manoeuvred his brother Joseph on to the Spanish throne, middle-class intellectuals might have been expected to side with this alien moderniser. Instead, the popular rising commemorated by Goya's *Second of May 1808* began a savage, chaotic struggle in which—it is clear from his *Disasters of War*—Goya found it hard to take sides: his images depict peasants torturing and desecrating the corpses of French soldiers; French barbarities against the Spanish; and the irrationality of the neoconservative return to Catholic order that followed the Duke of Wellington's driving Napoleon out of Spain (Goya's great portrait of the Iron Duke is in London's National Gallery).

It is the disabused nature of Goya's *Disasters of War* that makes them so compelling; other artists saw the Napoleonic wars in romantic and, indeed, Romantic terms—Antoine-Jean Gros's astonishing picture, *Napoleon Visiting the Plague Victims at Jaffa*, in the Louvre, gives the emperor Christ-like powers and clearly makes him a quasi-religious figure; the British claimed that he in fact ordered the slaughter of 3,000 Turkish prisoners when he captured Jaffa.

Goya's modernity has never exhausted itself; he was as immediate to Picasso and Dali as he was to Manet; of all pre-modern artists, he is the one who most resembles a modernist. This is who the Chapmans have victimised.

But, of course, it's not quite as it seems.

Apart from Goya's surviving proofs—above all, a unique album with his handwritten captions in the British Museum's prints and drawings collection—there are no entirely "original" sets of the *Disasters*; published posthumously, it does not even have Goya's original title—he called the etchings "Fatal consequences of the Bloody War in Spain against Buonaparte and other Emphatic Caprichos."

The Chapmans' series is from a— historically very significant—edition published directly from Goya's plates in 1937, as a protest against fascist atrocities in the Spanish civil war; its frontispiece is a photograph of bomb damage to the Goya Foundation. Given how important the *Disasters of War* were to Picasso, Dali and the image of the civil war, this is clearly an important, evocative, emotionally raw thing, and they have scribbled all over it.

Yet the antecedent they themselves claim puts the gesture in a different light. In the 1950s, points out Jake, the American artist Robert Rauschenberg erased a drawing by Willem de Kooning, the great abstract expressionist painter. On the face of it, Rauschenberg was being aggressive—as a younger artist, a founder of pop and conceptual art, he was erasing the work of the older, dominant generation in a flamboyantly oedipal gesture. Yet he said he chose de Kooning for this fate specifically because he admired him; and he sought the older artist's permission. Destruction can be an act of love.

And whatever you think of the Chapmans, you can't deny the systematic and consistent nature of their interest in Goya. They have been reworking him since the early 90s; as well as their lifesize *Great Deeds Against the Dead*, there was a miniature tableau of all the atrocities in the etchings, and then, at the same time as they were working on Hell, they produced their own series of etchings inspired by Goya's *Disasters*—combining motifs from Goya with Nazis, volcanos and cartoon horror.

For some critics, this is all a callow waste of energy. It seems pathetic to take the most powerful of all artist-moralists, an artist who needs no apology or explanation and for whom the deadening phrase "old master" seems utterly inappropriate, and make these sterile simulacra, these crass copies. The critic Robert Hughes, who is writing a book on Goya, has dismissed the

Chapmans' translations of his images as superficial exercises.

But we live in ahistoric, depthless times, not least in art, and it's getting hard to be unimpressed by the sheer dedication of the Chapmans. The artists themselves claim they prefer to be despised as banal anti-humanists than praised piously as humanists. The language of praise we use for art is amazingly limited; if we like a work of art, we feel compelled to find depth, anger, moral fervour, spiritual truth—all the things the Chapmans claim to reject.

The new works are not in the studio when we talk about them. I feel I have a pretty good idea of the Chapmans' approach to Goya, so I don't worry too much about this. We talk about criticism and the way it resorts, always, to the humanist rhetoric of moral, emotional and political meaning. We laugh at the pious things the art critic of the Sunday Times said about them.

It's all very sophisticated. The next day I see the images. I think they are brilliant and profound. Oh dear. Somehow, they do not destroy, but find something new in the *Disasters of War*. The Chapmans use the word "evil" to describe the atmosphere that pervaded their recent ethnographic show; there is a wild sense of evil in what they've done to Goya. The altered prints make you think a serial killer with an addiction to drawing psychotic clown faces has got into the British Museum's prints and drawings room—like the killer in *Red Dragon* who eats an original Blake.

Violet and white bursts of colour, the clown heads and puppy faces are astonishingly horrible. They are given life, personality, by some very acute drawing, and so it's not a collision but a collaboration, an assimilation, as they really do seem to belong in the pictures—one art historical antecedent is Max Ernst's collages in which 19th-century lithographs are reorganised into a convincing dream world. What the Chapmans have released is something nasty, psychotic and value-free; not so much a travesty of Goya as an extension of his despair. What they share with him is the most primitive and archaic and Catholic pessimism of his art—the sense not just of irrationality but something more tangible and diabolic.

The Chapmans have remade Goya's masterpiece for a century which has rediscovered evil. And I have fallen into their trap.
March 31, 2003

article available at:
http://www.guardian.co.uk/arts/features/story/0,11710,926134,00.html

pictures:
http://www.guardian.co.uk/arts/gallery/0,8542,926340,00.html

ON THE RELATION OF ANALYTICAL PSYCHOLOGY TO POETRY[1]

C. G. Jung

In spite of its difficulty, the task of discussing the relation of analytical psychology to poetry affords me a welcome opportunity to define my views on the much debated question of the relations between psychology and art in general. Although the two things cannot be compared, the close connections which undoubtedly exist between them call for investigation. These connections arise from the fact that the practice of art is a psychological activity and, as such, can be approached from a psychological angle. Considered in this light, art, like any other human activity deriving from psychic motives, is a proper subject for psychology. This statement, however, involves a very definite limitation of the psychological viewpoint when we come to apply it in practice. Only that aspect of art which consists in the process of artistic creation can be a subject for psychological study, but not that which constitutes its essential nature. The question of what art is in itself can never be answered by the psychologist, but must be approached from the side of aesthetics.

A similar distinction must be made in the realm of religion. A psychological approach is permissible only in regard to the emotions and symbols which constitute the phenomenology of religion, but which do not touch upon its essential nature. If the essence of religion and art could be explained, then both of them would become mere subdivisions of psychology. This is not to say that such violations of their nature have not been attempted. But those who are guilty of them obviously forget that a similar fate might easily befall psychology, since its intrinsic value and specific quality would be destroyed if it were regarded as a mere activity of the brain,

[1][A lecture delivered to the Society for German Language and Literature, Zurich, May, 1922. First published as "Über die Beziehungen der analytischen Psychologie zum dichterischen Kunstwerk," *Wissen und Leben* (Zurich). XV:19–20 (Sept., 1922); reprinted in *Seelenprobleme der Gegenwart* (Zurich, 1931); translated by H. G. Baynes, as "On the Relation of Analytical Psychology to Poetic Art," *British Journal of Psychology* (Medical Section) (Cambridge), III:3 (1923), reprinted in *Contributions to Analytical Psychology* (London and New York, 1928).—EDITORS.]

and were relegated along with the endocrine functions to a subdivision of physiology. This too, as we know, has been attempted.

Art by its very nature is not science, and science by its very nature is not art; both these spheres of the mind have something in reserve that is peculiar to them and can be explained only in its own terms. Hence when we speak of the relation of psychology to art, we shall treat only of that aspect of art which can be submitted to psychological scrutiny without violating its nature. Whatever the psychologist has to say about art will be confined to the process of artistic creation and has nothing to do with its innermost essence. He can no more explain this than the intellect can describe or even understand the nature of feeling. Indeed, art and science would not exist as separate entities at all if the fundamental difference between them had not long since forced itself on the mind. The fact that artistic, scientific, and religious propensities still slumber peacefully together in the small child, or that with primitives the beginnings of art, science, and religion coalesce in the undifferentiated chaos of the magical mentality, or that no trace of "mind" can be found in the natural instincts of animals—all this does nothing to prove the existence of a unifying principle which alone would justify a reduction of the one to the other. For if we go so far back into the history of the mind that the distinctions between its various fields of activity become altogether invisible, we do not reach an underlying principle of their unity, but merely an earlier, undifferentiated state in which no separate activities yet exist. But the elementary state is not an explanatory principle that would allow us to draw conclusions as to the nature of later, more highly developed states, even though they must necessarily derive from it. A scientific attitude will always tend to overlook the peculiar nature of these more differentiated states in favour of their causal derivation, and will endeav-

our to subordinate them to a general but more elementary principle.

These theoretical reflections seem to me very much in place today, when we so often find that works of art, and particularly poetry, are interpreted precisely in this manner, by reducing them to more elementary states. Though the material he works with and its individual treatment can easily be traced back to the poet's personal relations with his parents, this does not enable us to understand his poetry. The same reduction can be made in all sorts of other fields, and not least in the case of pathological disturbances. Neuroses and psychoses are likewise reducible to infantile relations with the parents, and so are a man's good and bad habits, his beliefs, peculiarities, passions, interests, and so forth. It can hardly be supposed that all these very different things must have exactly the same explanation, for otherwise we would be driven to the conclusion that they actually are the same thing. If a work of art is explained in the same way as a neurosis, then either the work of art is a neurosis or a neurosis is a work of art. This explanation is all very well as a play on words, but sound common sense rebels against putting a work of art on the same level as a neurosis. An analyst might, in an extreme case, view a neurosis as a work of art through the lens of his professional bias, but it would never occur to an intelligent layman to mistake a pathological phenomenon for art, in spite of the undeniable fact that a work of art arises from much the same psychological conditions as a neurosis. This is only natural, because certain of these conditions are present in every individual and, owing to the relative constancy of the human environment, are constantly the same, whether in the case of a nervous intellectual, a poet, or a normal human being. All have had parents, all have a father- or a mother-complex, all know about sex and therefore have certain common and typical human difficulties. One poet may be influenced more by his relation to his father, another by the tie to his mother, while a third shows unmistakable traces of sexual repression in his poetry. Since all this can be said equally well not only of every neurotic but of every normal human being, nothing specific is gained for the judgment of a work of art. At most our knowledge of its psychological antecedents will have been broadened and deepened.

The school of medical psychology inaugurated by Freud has undoubtedly encouraged the literary historian to bring certain peculiarities of a work of art into relation with the intimate, personal life of the poet. But this is nothing new in principle, for it has long been known that the scientific treatment of art will reveal the personal threads that the artist, intentionally or unintentionally, has woven into his work. The Freudian approach may, however, make possible a more exhaustive demonstration of the influences that reach back into earliest childhood and play their part in artistic creation. To this extent the psychoanalysis of art differs in no essential from the subtle psychological nuances of a penetrating literary analysis. The difference is at most a question of degree, though we may occasionally be surprised by indiscreet references to things which a rather more delicate touch might have passed over if only for reasons of tact. This lack of delicacy seems to be a professional peculiarity of the medical psychologist, and the temptation to draw daring conclusions easily leads to flagrant abuses. A slight whiff of scandal often leads spice to a biography, but a little more becomes a nasty inquisitiveness—bad taste masquerading as science. Our interest is insidiously deflected from the work of art and gets lost in the labyrinth of psychic determinants, the poet becomes a clinical case and, very likely, yet another addition to the curiosa of *psychopathia sexualis*. But this means that the psychoanalysis of art has turned aside from its proper objective and strayed into a province that is as broad as mankind, that is not in the least specific of the artist and has even less relevance to his art.

This kind of analysis brings the work of art into the sphere of general human psychology, where many other things besides art have their origin. To explain art in these terms is just as great a platitude as the statement that "every artist is a narcissist." Every man who pursues his own goal is a "narcissist"—though one wonders how permissible it is to give such wide currency to a term specifically coined for the pathology of neurosis. The statement therefore amounts to nothing; it merely elicits the faint surprise of a *bon mot*. Since this kind of analysis is in no way concerned with the work of art itself, but strives like a mole to bury itself in the dirt as speedily as possible, it always ends up in the common earth that unites all mankind. Hence its explanations have the same tedious monotony as the recitals which one daily hears in the consulting-room.

The reductive method of Freud is a purely medical one, and the treatment is directed at a pathological or otherwise unsuitable formation which has taken the place of the normal functioning. It must therefore be broken down, and the way cleared for healthy adaptation. In this case, reduction to the common human foundation is altogether appropriate. But when applied to a work of art it leads to the results I have described. It strips the work of art of its shimmering robes and exposes the nakedness and drabness of *Homo sapiens,* to which species the poet and artist also belong. The golden gleam of artistic creation—the original object of discussion—is extinguished as soon as we apply to it the same corrosive method which we use in analysing the fantasies of hysteria. The results are no doubt very interesting and may perhaps have the same kind of scientific value as, for instance, a post-mortem examination of the brain of

Nietzsche, which might conceivably show us the particular atypical form of paralysis from which he died. But what would this have to do with *Zarathustra?* Whatever its subterranean background may have been, is it not a whole world in itself, beyond the human, all-too-human imperfections, beyond the world of migraine and cerebral atrophy?

I have spoken of Freud's reductive method but have not stated in what that method consists. It is essentially a medical technique for investigating morbid psychic phenomena, and it is solely concerned with the ways and means of getting round or peering through the foreground of consciousness in order to reach the psychic background, or the unconscious. It is based on the assumption that the neurotic patient represses certain psychic contents because they are morally incompatible with his conscious values. It follows that the repressed contents must have correspondingly negative traits—infantile-sexual, obscene, or even criminal—which make them unacceptable to consciousness. Since no man is perfect, everyone must possess such a background whether he admits it or not. Hence it can always be exposed if only one uses the technique of interpretation worked out by Freud.

In the short space of a lecture I cannot, of course, enter into the details of the technique. A few hints must suffice. The unconscious background does not remain inactive, but betrays itself by its characteristic effects on the contents of consciousness. For example, it produces fantasies of a peculiar nature, which can easily be interpreted as sexual images. Or it produces characteristic disturbances of the conscious processes, which again can be reduced to repressed contents. A very important source for knowledge of the unconscious contents is provided by dreams, since these are direct products of the activity of the unconscious. The essential thing in Freud's reductive method is to collect all the clues pointing to

the unconscious background, and then, through the analysis and interpretation of this material, to reconstruct the elementary instinctual processes. Those conscious contents which give us a clue to the unconscious background are incorrectly called *symbols* by Freud. They are not true symbols, however, since according to his theory they have merely the role of *signs* or *symptoms* of the subliminal processes. The true symbol differs essentially from this, and should be understood as an expression of an intuitive idea that cannot yet be formulated in any other or better way. When Plato, for instance, puts the whole problem of the theory of knowledge in his parable of the cave, or when Christ expresses the idea of the Kingdom of Heaven in parables, these are genuine and true symbols, that is, attempts to express something for which no verbal concept yet exists. If we were to interpret Plato's metaphor in Freudian terms we would naturally arrive at the uterus, and would have proved that even a mind like Plato's was still struck on a primitive level of infantile sexuality. But we would have completely overlooked what Plato actually created out of the primitive determinants of his philosophical ideas; we would have missed the essential point and merely discovered that he had infantile-sexual fantasies like any other mortal. Such a discovery could be of value only for a man who regarded Plato as superhuman, and who can now state with satisfaction that Plato too was an ordinary human being. But who would want to regard Plato as a god? Surely only one who is dominated by infantile fantasies and therefore possesses a neurotic mentality. For him the reduction to common human truths is salutary on medical grounds, but this would have nothing whatever to do with the meaning of Plato's parable.

I have purposely dwelt on the application of medical psychoanalysis to works of art because I want to emphasize that the psychoanalytic method is at the same time an essential part of the Freudian doctrine. Freud himself by his rigid dogmatism has ensured that the method and the doctrine—in themselves two very different things—are regarded by the public as identical. Yet the method may be employed with beneficial results in medical cases without at the same time exalting it into a doctrine. And against this doctrine we are bound to raise vigorous objections. The assumptions it rests on are quite arbitrary. For example, neuroses are by no means exclusively caused by sexual repression, and the same holds true for psychoses. There is no foundation for saying that dreams merely contain repressed wishes whose moral incompatibility requires them to be disguised by a hypothetical dream-censor. The Freudian technique of interpretation, so far as it remains under the influence of its own one-sided and therefore erroneous hypotheses, displays a quite obvious bias.

In order to do justice to a work of art, analytical psychology must rid itself entirely of medical prejudice; for a work of art is not a disease, and consequently requires a different approach from the medical one. A doctor naturally has to seek out the causes of a disease in order to pull it up by the roots, but just as naturally the psychologist must adopt exactly the opposite attitude towards a work of art. Instead of investigating its typically human determinants, he will inquire first of all into its meaning, and will concern himself with its determinants only in so far as they enable him to understand it more fully. Personal causes have as much or as little to do with a work of art as the soil with the plant that springs from it. We can certainly learn to understand some of the plant's peculiarities by getting to know its habitat, and for the botanist this is an important part of his equipment. But nobody will maintain that everything essential has then been discovered about the plant itself. The personal orientation which the doctor needs when confronted with the question of aetiol-

ogy in medicine is quite out of place in dealing with a work of art, just because a work of art is not a human being, but is something supra-personal. It is a thing and not a personality; hence it cannot be judged by personal criteria. Indeed, the special significance of a true work of art resides in the fact that it has escaped from the limitations of the personal and has soared beyond the personal concerns of its creator.

I must confess from my own experience that it is not at all easy for a doctor to lay aside his professional bias when considering a work of art and look at it with a mind cleared of the current biological causality. But I have come to learn that although a psychology with a purely biological orientation can explain a good deal about man in general, it cannot be applied to a work of art and still less to man as creator. A purely causalistic psychology is only able to reduce every human individual to a member of the species *Homo sapiens,* since its range is limited to what is transmitted by heredity or derived from other sources. But a work of art is not transmitted or derived—it is a creative reorganization of those very conditions to which a causalistic psychology must always reduce it. The plant is not a mere product of the soil; it is a living, self-contained process which in essence has nothing to do with the character of the soil. In the same way, the meaning and individual quality of a work of art inhere within it and not in its extrinsic determinants. One might almost describe it as a living being that uses man only as a nutrient medium, employing his capacities according to its own laws and shaping itself to the fulfilment of its own creative purpose.

But here I am anticipating somewhat, for I have in mind a particular type of art which I still have to introduce. Not every work of art originates in the way I have just described. There are literary works, prose as well as poetry, that spring wholly from the author's intention to produce a particular result. He submits his material to a definite treatment with a definite aim in view; he adds to it and subtracts from it, emphasizing one effect, toning down another, laying on a touch of colour here, another there, all the time carefully considering the over-all result and paying strict attention to the laws of form and style. He exercises the keenest judgment and chooses his words with complete freedom. His material is entirely subordinated to his artistic purpose; he wants to express this and nothing else. He is wholly at one with the creative process, no matter whether he has deliberately made himself its spearhead, as it were, or whether it has made him its instrument so completely that he has lost all consciousness of this fact. In either case, the artist is so identified with his work that his intentions and his faculties are indistinguishable from the act of creation itself. There is no need, I think, to give examples of this from the history of literature or from the testimony of the artists themselves.

Nor need I cite examples of the other class of works which flow more or less complete and perfect from the author's pen. They come as it were fully arrayed into the world, as Pallas Athene sprang from the head of Zeus. These works positively force themselves upon the author; his hand is seized, his pen writes things that his mind contemplates with amazement. The work brings with it its own form; anything he wants to add is rejected, and what he himself would like to reject is thrust back at him. While his conscious mind stands amazed and empty before this phenomenon, he is overwhelmed by a flood of thoughts and images which he never intended to create and which his own will could never have brought into being. Yet in spite of himself he is forced to admit that it is his own self speaking, his own inner nature revealing itself and uttering things which he would never have entrusted to his tongue. He can only obey the apparently alien impulse within him and follow where it leads, sensing that his work is greater than himself, and wields a power which is not his and which he cannot command. Here the artist is not identical with the process of creation; he is aware that he is subordinate to his work or stands outside it, as though he were a second person; or as though a person other than himself had fallen within the magic circle of an alien will.

So when we discuss the psychology of art, we must bear in mind these two entirely different modes of creation, for much that is of the greatest importance in judging a work of art depends on this distinction. It is one that had been sensed earlier by Schiller, who as we know attempted to classify it in his concept of the *sentimental* and the *naïve*. The psychologist would call "sentimental" art *introverted* and the "naïve" kind *extraverted*. The introverted attitude is characterized by the subject's assertion of his conscious intentions and aims against the demands of the object, whereas the extraverted attitude is characterized by the subject's subordination to the demands which the object makes upon him. In my view, Schiller's plays and most of his poems give one a good idea of the introverted attitude: the material is mastered by the conscious intentions of the poet. The extraverted attitude is illustrated by the second part of *Faust:* here the material is distinguished by its refractoriness. A still more striking example is Nietzsche's *Zarathustra,* where the author himself observed how "one became two."

From what I have said, it will be apparent that a shift of psychological standpoint has taken place as soon as one speaks not of the poet as a person but of the creative process that moves him. When the focus of interest shifts to the latter, the poet comes into the picture only as a reacting subject. This is immediately evident in our second category of works, where the consciousness of the poet is not identical with the creative process. But in works of the first category the opposite appears to hold true. Here the poet appears to be the creative process itself, and to create of his own free will without the slightest feeling of compulsion. He may even be fully convinced of his freedom of action and refuse to admit that his work could be anything else than the expression of his will and ability.

Here we are faced with a question which we cannot answer from the testimony of the poets themselves. It is really a scientific problem that psychology alone can solve. As I hinted earlier, it might well be that the poet, while apparently creating out of himself and producing what he consciously intends, is nevertheless so carried away by the creative impulse that he is no longer aware of an "alien" will, just as the other type of poet is no longer aware of his own will speaking to him in the apparently "alien" inspiration, although this is manifestly the voice of his own self. The poet's conviction that he is creating in absolute freedom would then be an illusion: he fancies he is swimming, but in reality an unseen current sweeps him along.

This is not by any means an academic question, but is supported by the evidence of analytical psychology. Researches have shown that there are all sorts of ways in which the conscious mind is not only influenced by the unconscious but actually guided by it. Yet is there any evidence for the supposition that a poet, despite his self-awareness, may be taken captive by his work? The proof may be of two kinds, direct or indirect. Direct proof would be afforded by a poet who thinks he knows what he is saying but actually says more than he is aware of. Such cases are not uncommon. Indirect proof would be found in cases where behind the apparent free will of the poet there stands a higher imperative that renews its peremptory demands as soon as the poet voluntarily gives up his creative activity, or that produces psychic complications whenever his work has to be broken off against his will.

Analysis of artists consistently shows not only the strength of the creative impulse arising from the unconscious, but also its capricious and wilful character. The biographies of great artists make it abundantly clear that the creative urge is often so imperious that it battens on their humanity and yokes everything to the service of the work, even at the cost of health and ordinary human happiness. The unborn work in the psyche of the artist is a force of nature that achieves its end either with tyrannical might or with the subtle cunning of nature herself, quite regardless of the personal fate of the man who is its vehicle. The creative urge lives and grows in him like a tree in the earth from which it draws its nourishment. We would do well, therefore, to think of the creative process as a living thing implanted in the human psyche. In the language of analytical psychology this living thing is an *autonomous complex*. It is a split-off portion of the psyche, which leads a life of its own outside the hierarchy of consciousness. Depending on its energy charge, it may appear either as a mere disturbance of conscious activities or as a supraordinate authority which can harness the ego to its purpose. Accordingly, the poet who identifies with the creative process would be one who acquiesces from the start when the unconscious imperative begins to function. But the other poet, who feels the creative force as something alien, is one who for various reasons cannot acquiesce and is thus caught unawares.

It might be expected that this difference in its origins would be perceptible in a work of art. For in the one case it is a conscious product shaped and designed to have the effect intended. But in the other we are dealing with an event originating in unconscious nature; with something that achieves its aim without the assistance of human consciousness, and often defies it by wilfully insisting on its own form and effect. We would therefore expect that works belonging to the first class would nowhere overstep the limits of comprehension, that their effect would be bounded by the author's intention and would not extend beyond it. But with works of the other class we would have to be prepared for something suprapersonal that transcends our understanding to the same degree that the author's consciousness was in abeyance during the process of creation. We would expect a strangeness of form and content, thoughts that can only be apprehended intuitively, a language pregnant with meanings, and images that are true symbols because they are the best possible expressions for something unknown—bridges thrown out towards an unseen shore.

These criteria are, by and large, corroborated in practice. Whenever we are confronted with a work that was consciously planned and with material that was consciously selected, we find that it agrees with the first class of qualities, and in the other case with the second. The example we gave of Schiller's plays, on the one hand, and *Faust II* on the other, or better still *Zarathustra,* is an illustration of this. But I would not undertake to place the work of an unknown poet in either of these categories without first having examined rather closely his personal relations with his work. It is not enough to know whether the poet belongs to the introverted or to the extraverted type, since it is possible for either type to work with an introverted attitude at one time, and an extraverted attitude at another. This is particularly noticeable in the difference between Schiller's plays and his philosophical writings, between Goethe's perfectly formed poems and the obvious struggle with his material in *Faust II,* and between Nietzsche's well-turned aphorisms and the rushing torrent of *Zarathustra.* The same poet can adopt different attitudes to his work at different times, and on this depends the standard we have to apply.

The question, as we now see, is exceedingly complicated, and the complication grows even worse when we consider the case of the poet who identifies with the creative process. For should it turn out that the apparently conscious and purposeful manner of composition is a subjective illusion of the poet, then his work would possess symbolic qualities that are outside the range of his consciousness. They would only be more difficult to detect, because the reader as well would be unable to get beyond the bounds of the poet's consciousness which are fixed by the spirit of the time. There is no Archimedean point outside his world by which he could lift his time-bound consciousness off its hinges and recognize the symbols hidden in the poet's work. For a symbol is the intimation of a meaning beyond the level of our present powers of comprehension.

I raise this question only because I do not want my typological classification to limit the possible significance of works of art which apparently mean no more than what they say. But we have often found that a poet who has gone out of fashion is suddenly rediscovered. This happens when our conscious development has reached a higher level from which the poet can tell us something new. It was always present in his work but was hidden in a symbol, and only a renewal of the spirit of the time permits us to read its meaning. It needed to be looked at with fresher eyes, for the old ones could see in it only what they were accustomed to see. Experiences of this kind should make us cautious, as they bear out my earlier argument. But works that are openly symbolic do not require this subtle approach; their pregnant language cries out at us that they mean more than they say. We can put our finger on the symbol at once, even though we may not be able to unriddle its meaning to our entire satisfaction. A symbol remains a perpetual challenge to our thoughts and feelings. That probably explains why a symbolic work is so stimulating, why it grips us so intensely, but also why it seldom affords us a purely aesthetic enjoyment. A work that is manifestly not symbolic appeals much more to our aesthetic sensibility because it is complete in itself and fulfils its purpose.

What then, you may ask, can analytical psychology contribute to our fundamental problem, which is the mystery of artistic creation? All that we have said so far has to do only with the psychological phenomenology of art. Since nobody can penetrate to the heart of nature, you will not expect psychology to do the impossible and offer a valid explanation of the secret of creativity. Like every other science, psychology has only a modest contribution to make towards a deeper understanding of the phenomena of life, and is no nearer than its sister sciences to absolute knowledge.

We have talked so much about the meaning of works of art that one can hardly suppress a doubt as to whether art really "means" anything at all. Perhaps art has no "meaning," at least not as we understand meaning. Perhaps it is like nature, which simply *is* and "means" nothing beyond that. Is "meaning" necessarily more than mere interpretation—an interpretation secreted into something by an intellect hungry for meaning? Art, it has been said, is beauty, and "a thing of beauty is a joy for ever." It needs no meaning, for meaning has nothing to do with art. Within the sphere of art, I must accept the truth of this statement. But when I speak of the relation of psychology to art we are outside its sphere, and it is impossible for us not to speculate. We must interpret, we must find meanings in things, otherwise we would be quite unable to think about them. We have to break down life and events, which are self-contained processes, into meanings, images, concepts, well knowing that in doing so we are getting further away from the living mystery. As long as we ourselves are caught up in the process of creation, we neither see nor understand;

indeed we ought not to understand, for nothing is more injurious to immediate experience than cognition. But for the purpose of cognitive understanding we must detach ourselves from the creative process and look at it from the outside; only then does it become an image that expresses what we are bound to call "meaning." What was a mere phenomenon before becomes something that in association with other phenomena has meaning, that has a definite role to play, serves certain ends, and exerts meaningful effects. And when we have seen all this we get the feeling of having understood and explained something. In this way we meet the demands of science.

When, a little earlier, we spoke of a work of art as a tree growing out of the nourishing soil, we might equally well have compared it to a child growing in the womb. But as all comparisons are lame, let us stick to the more precise terminology of science. You will remember that I described the nascent work in the psyche of the artist as an autonomous complex. By this we mean a psychic formation that remains subliminal until its energy-charge is sufficient to carry it over the threshold into consciousness. Its association with consciousness does not mean that it is assimilated, only that it is perceived; but it is not subject to conscious control, and can be neither inhibited nor voluntarily reproduced. Therein lies the autonomy of the complex: it appears and disappears in accordance with its own inherent tendencies, independently of the conscious will. The creative complex shares this peculiarity with every other autonomous complex. In this respect it offers an analogy with pathological processes, since these too are characterized by the presence of autonomous complexes, particularly in the case of mental disturbances. The divine frenzy of the artist comes perilously close to a pathological state, though the two things are not identical. The *tertium comparationis* is the autonomous complex. But the presence of autonomous complexes is not in itself pathological, since normal people, too, fall temporarily or permanently under their domination. This fact is simply one of the normal peculiarities of the psyche, and for a man to be unaware of the existence of an autonomous complex merely betrays a high degree of unconsciousness. Every typical attitude that is to some extent differentiated shows a tendency to become an autonomous complex, and in most cases it actually does. Again, every instinct has more or less the character of an autonomous complex. In itself, therefore, an autonomous complex has nothing morbid about it; only when its manifestations are frequent and disturbing is it a symptom of illness.

How does an autonomous complex arise? For reasons which we cannot go into here, a hitherto unconscious portion of the psyche is thrown into activity, and gains ground by activating the adjacent areas of association. The energy needed for this is naturally drawn from consciousness—unless the latter happens to identify with the complex. But where this does not occur, the drain of energy produces what Janet calls an *abaissement du niveau mental*. The intensity of conscious interests and activities gradually diminishes, leading either to apathy—a condition very common with artists—or to a regressive development of the conscious functions, that is, they revert to an infantile and archaic level and undergo something like a degeneration. The "inferior parts of the functions," as Janet calls them, push to the fore; the instinctual side of the personality prevails over the ethical, the infantile over the mature, and the unadapted over the adapted. This too is something we see in the lives of many artists. The autonomous complex thus develops by using the energy that has been withdrawn from the conscious control of the personality.

But in what does an autonomous *creative* complex consist? Of this we can know next to nothing so long as the artist's work affords us no insight into its foundations. The work presents us with a finished picture, and this picture is amenable to analysis only to the extent that we can recognize it as a symbol. But if we are unable to discover any symbolic value in it, we have merely established that, so far as we are concerned, it means no more than what it says, or to put it another way, that it *is* no more than what it *seems* to be. I use the word "seems" because our own bias may prevent a deeper appreciation of it. At any rate we can find no incentive and no starting-point for an analysis. But in the case of a symbolic work we should remember the dictum of Gerhard Hauptmann: "Poetry evokes out of words the resonance of the primordial word." The question we should ask, therefore, is: "What primordial image lies behind the imagery of art?"

This question needs a little elucidation. I am assuming that the work of art we propose to analyse, as well as being symbolic, has its source not in the *personal unconscious* of the poet, but in a sphere of unconscious mythology whose primordial images are the common heritage of mankind. I have called this sphere the *collective unconscious,* to distinguish it from the personal unconscious. The latter I regard as the sum total of all those psychic processes and contents which are capable of becoming conscious and often do, but are then suppressed because of their incompatibility and kept subliminal. Art receives tributaries from this sphere too, but muddy ones; and their predominance, far from making a work of art a symbol, merely turns it into a symptom. We can leave this kind of art without injury and without regret to the purgative methods employed by Freud.

In contrast to the personal unconscious, which is a relatively thin layer immediately below the threshold of consciousness, the collective unconscious shows no tendency to become conscious under normal conditions, nor can it be brought back to recollec-

326

tion by any analytical technique,[2] since it was never repressed or forgotten. The collective unconscious is not to be thought of as a self-subsistent entity; it is no more than a potentiality handed down to us from primordial times in the specific form of mnemonic images[3] or inherited in the anatomical structure of the brain. There are no inborn ideas, but there are inborn possibilities of ideas that set bounds to even the boldest fantasy and keep our fantasy activity within certain categories: *a priori* ideas, as it were, the existence of which cannot be ascertained except from their effects. They appear only in the shaped material of art as the regulative principles that shape it; that is to say, only by inferences drawn from the finished work can we reconstruct the age-old original[4] of the primordial image.

The primordial image, or archetype, is a figure—be it a daemon, a human being, or a process—that constantly recurs in the course of history and appears wherever creative fantasy is freely expressed. Essentially, therefore, it is a mythological figure. When we examine these images more closely, we find that they give form to countless typical experiences of our ancestors. They are, so to speak, the psychic residua of innumerable experiences of the same type. They present a picture of psychic life in the average, divided up and projected into the manifold figures of the mythological pantheon. But the mythological figures are themselves products of creative fantasy and still have to be translated into conceptual language. Only the beginnings of such a language exist, but once the necessary concepts are created they could give us an abstract, scientific understanding of the unconscious processes that lie at the roots of the primordial images. In each of these images there is a little piece of human psychology and human fate, a remnant of the joys and sorrows that have been repeated countless times in out ancestral history, and on the average follow ever the same course. It is like a deeply graven river-bed in the psyche, in which the waters of life, instead of flowing along as before in a broad but shallow stream, suddenly swell into a mighty river. This happens whenever that particular set of circumstances is encountered which over long periods of time has helped to lay down the primordial image.

The moment when this mythological situation reappears is always characterized by a peculiar emotional intensity; it is as though chords in us were struck that had never resounded before, or as though forces whose existence we never suspected were unloosed. What makes the struggle for adaptation so laborious is the fact that we have constantly to be dealing with individual and atypical situations. So it is not surprising that when an archetypal situation occurs we suddenly feel an extraordinary sense of release, as though transported, or caught up by an

---

[2][By this Jung probably meant the analytical techniques that were in use at the time (1922), and more particularly the Freudian. Whether he had by then developed his own technique for constellating the collective unconscious is an open question. Cf. "The Transcendent Function" (orig. 1916), pp. 67ff., and ch. VI of Jung's *Memories, Dreams, Reflections.*—EDITORS.]

[3][Here Jung defines the *collective unconscious* in much the same way as a year earlier (*Psychological Types,* pars. 624, 747) he had defined the *archetype.* Still earlier, in 1919, using the term "archetype" for the first time, he had stated: "The instincts and the archetypes together form the 'collective unconscious' " ("Instinct and the Unconscious," par. 270). This is in better agreement with his later formulations. The subject of the above sentence should therefore be understood as the archetype.—EDITORS.]

[4][Lit., "primitive Vorlage." In the light of Jung's later formulations, this would mean the "archetype *per se*" as distinct from the "archetypal image." Cf. particularly "On the Nature of the Psyche," par. 417.—EDITORS.]

overwhelming power. At such moments we are no longer individuals, but the race; the voice of all mankind resounds in us. The individual man cannot use his powers to the full unless he is aided by one of those collective representations we call ideals, which releases all the hidden forces of instinct that are inaccessible to his conscious will. The most effective ideals are always fairly obvious variants of an archetype, as is evident from the fact that they lend themselves to allegory. The ideal of the "mother country," for instance, is an obvious allegory of the mother, as is the "fatherland" of the father. Its power to stir us does not derive from the allegory, but from the symbolical value of our native land. The archetype here is the *participation mystique* of primitive man with the soil on which he dwells, and which contains the spirits of his ancestors.

The impact of an archetype, whether it takes the form of immediate experience or is expressed through the spoken word, stirs us because it summons up a voice that is stronger than our own. Whoever speaks in primordial images speaks with a thousand voices; he enthrals and overpowers, while at the same time he lifts the idea he is seeking to express out of the occasional and the transitory into the realm of the ever-enduring. He transmutes our personal destiny into the destiny of mankind, and evokes in us all those beneficent forces that ever and anon have enabled humanity to find a refuge from every peril and to outlive the longest night.

That is the secret of great art, and of its effect upon us. The creative process, so far as we are able to follow it at all, consists in the unconscious activation of an archetypal image, and in elaborating and shaping this image into the finished work. By giving it shape, the artist translates it into the language of the present, and so makes it possible for us to find our way back to the deepest springs of life. Therein lies the social significance of art: it is constantly at work educating the spirit of the age, conjuring up the forms in which the age is most lacking. The unsatisfied yearning of the artist reaches back to the primordial image in the unconscious which is best fitted to compensate the inadequacy and one-sidedness of the present. The artist seizes on this image, and in raising it from deepest unconsciousness he brings it into relation with conscious values, thereby transforming it until it can be accepted by the minds of his contemporaries according to their powers.

People and times, like individuals, have their own characteristic tendencies and attitudes. The very word "attitude" betrays the necessary bias that every marked tendency entails. Direction implies exclusion, and exclusion means that very many psychic elements that could play their part in life are denied the right to exist because they are incompatible with the general attitude. The normal man can follow the general trend without injury to himself; but the man who takes to the back streets and alleys because he cannot endure the broad highway will be the first to discover the psychic elements that are waiting to play their part in the life of the collective. Here the artist's relative lack of adaptation turns out to his advantage; it enables him to follow his own yearnings far from the beaten path, and to discover what it is that would meet the unconscious needs of his age. Thus, just as the one-sidedness of the individual's conscious attitude is corrected by reactions from the unconscious, so art represents a process of self-regulation in the life of nations and epochs.

I am aware that in this lecture I have only been able to sketch out my views in the barest outline. But I hope that what I have been obliged to omit, that is to say their practical application to poetic works of art, has been furnished by your own thoughts, thus giving flesh and blood to my abstract intellectual frame.

REPRESENTATION

W. J. T. Mitchell

Probably the most common and naive intuition about literature is that it is a "representation of life." Unlike many of the terms in this collection, "representation" has always played a central role in the understanding of literature. Indeed, one might say that it has played the definitive role insofar as the founding fathers of literary theory, Plato and Aristotle, regarded literature as simply one form of representation. Aristotle defined all the arts—verbal, visual, and musical—as modes of representation, and went even further to make representation the definitively human activity:

> From childhood men have an instinct for representation, and in this respect man differs from the other animals that he is far more imitative and learns his first lessons by representing things.

Man, for many philosophers both ancient and modern, is the "representational animal," *homo symbolicum,* the creature whose distinctive character is the creation and manipulation of signs—things that "stand for" or "take the place of" something else.

Since antiquity, then, representation has been the foundational concept in aesthetics (the general theory of the arts) and semiotics (the general theory of signs). In the modern era (i.e., in the last three hundred years) it has also become a crucial concept in political theory, forming the cornerstone of representational theories of sovereignty, legislative authority, and relations of individuals to the state. We now think of "representative government" and the accountability of representatives to their constituents as fundamental postulates of modern government. One obvious question that comes up in contemporary theories of representation, consequently, is the relationship between aesthetic or semiotic representation (things that "stand for" other things) and political representation (persons who "act for" other persons). And one obvious place where these two forms of representation come together is the theater, where persons (actors) stand for or "impersonate" other (usually fictional) persons. There are vast differences, of course, between Laurence Olivier playing Hamlet and Ronald Reagan playing the role of the president—the difference, say, between playing and real life; between a rigid script and an open, improvised performance; or between an aesthetic contract and a legal one—but these should

329

not blind us to the structural similarities of the two forms of representation or to the complex interaction between playful fantasy and serious reality in all forms of representation. The fact that Ronald Reagan began his career as an actor and has continually exploited the symbolic, theatrical character of the presidency only makes the links between aesthetic/semiotic and political forms of representation more unavoidable.

What is the "structure" that is common to both the political and semiotic forms of representation? One way to think of it is as a triangular relationship: representation is always *of* something or someone, *by* something or someone, *to* someone. It seems that only the third angle of representation need be a person: we can represent stones with dabs of paint or letters or sounds, but we can represent things only *to* people. The other two angles can be occupied by people but need not be: I can represent a man with a stone, or a stone with a man; but it would seem very odd to speak of representing either a stone or a man *to* a stone. There also may be a fourth dimension to representation not captured by our triangle, and that would be the "intender" or "maker" of the representation, the one who says, "let this dab of paint stand for this stone to someone." This more complete picture of representation might be mapped as a quadrilateral with two diagonal axes, one connecting the representational object to that which it represents, the other connecting the maker of the representation to the beholder:

We might call these connecting lines the "axis of representation" (linking the dab of paint to the stone) and the "axis of communication" (linking the persons who understand the relation of paint to stone), respectively. The crossing of these axes suggests, I hope, one of the potential problems that comes up with representations: they present a barrier that "cuts across," as it were, our lines of communication with others, presenting the possibility of misunderstanding, error, or downright falsehood. As soon as we begin to *use* representations in any social situation—to claim, for instance, that this dab of paint represents *the fact that* this stone is in that place and looks like this— then representation begins to play a double role, as a means of communication which is also a potential obstacle to it.

So far I am speaking of simple, almost "atomistic" cases of representation, in which one thing stands for one other thing. But clearly the business of representation is much more complex than this. Representation is an extremely elastic notion which extends all the way from a stone representing a man to a novel representing a day in the life of several Dubliners. Sometimes one thing can stand for a whole group of things, as when the word "tree" stands for a concept that "covers" a multitude of individual things, or a political representative stands for a people, or a stick figure stands for the general concept of man, or a narrative represents a whole series of events. And the representational sign never seems to occur in

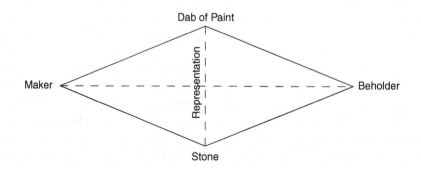

isolation from a whole network of other signs: the dab of paint that stands for a stone will probably do so only in the context of a whole field of dabs of paint that represent other things adjacent to the stone—grass, earth, trees, sky, other stones. Take the dab of paint out of that context, and it ceases to represent, becomes merely a dab of paint. In a similar way, the word "tree" represents a certain class of objects only in the context of a language, just as a note or a musical phrase has meaning only in relation to a larger piece and familiar systems of tonality. These "systems" (tonality, language, representational schemes in painting) may be called "codes," by which I simply mean a body of rules for combining and deciphering representational signs. When something stands for something to somebody, it does so by virtue of a kind of social agreement—"let us agree that this will stand for that"—which, once understood, need not be restated on every occasion. In fact, the decision to let A stand for B may (and usually does) open up a whole new realm of possibilities for representation: B becomes a likely candidate to stand for C, and so on.

Aristotle says that representations differ from one another in three ways: in object, manner, and means. The "object" is that which is represented; the "manner" is the way in which it is represented; the "means" is the material that is used. What I am calling "codes" here are basically the same thing as Aristotle's "means"—that is, language, musical forms, paint. But the "manner" suggests yet another feature of representation, and that is the particular way a representational code is employed. The "means" of literary representation is language, but there are many ways of employing that means (dramatic recitation, narration, description) to achieve all sorts of effects (pity, admiration, laughter, scorn) and represent all sorts of things. Similarly, all paintings may employ shapes, shades, and colors on a two-dimensional surface

(and this may be called the painter's "code"), but there are many ways of depicting a tree, many ways of applying paint to a surface. Some of them may become institutionalized as styles or genres, and these, like codes, are social agreements ("let us agree to represent this with that used in *this way*"), only of a more specialized nature. These "mini-codes" associated with styles of representation are usually called "conventions." The difference between a code and a convention may be illustrated by thinking of the difference between a medium and a genre: film is a medium, a material means of representation with a complex set of rules for combining and deciphering its signs; whereas the Hollywood Western is a particular kind of film, a genre that is recognized by the persistence of certain conventional elements (shootouts, wide open spaces, cowboys, Indians) from one example to another. In a similar way, we might think of language as one medium of representation, "literature" as the name of the aesthetic use of that medium, and things like poetry, the novel, and drama as very large genres within that medium.

One crucial consideration that enters into any analysis of representation is the *relationship* between the representational material and that which it represents. A stone may stand for a man, but how? By virtue of *what* "agreement" or understanding does representation occur? Semioticians generally differentiate three types of representational relationships under the names of icon, symbol, and index. An iconic account of the relation "stone-represents-man" would stress *resemblance:* a certain stone might stand for a man because it is upright, or because it is hard, or because its shape resembles that of a man. ("Mimesis" and "imitation" are thus iconic forms of representation that transcend the differences between media: I can imitate—i.e., mimic or produce a resemblance of—a sound, speech act, gesture, or facial expression and, thus, iconically reproduce it; icons are not just pictures.) Symbolic representations, by contrast, are not based on the resemblance of the sign to what it signifies but on arbitrary stipulation: the stone stands for a man because "we say so," because we have agreed to regard it this way. Representation in language is "symbolic," in that letters, words, and whole texts represent sounds and states of affairs without in the least resembling what they represent. Indexical representation, finally, explains "standing for" in terms of cause and effect or some "existential" relation like physical proximity or connectedness: the stone represents a man because a man set it up as a marker, to indicate (like a trace or footprint) the fact that he was here; a glove, a strand of hair, or a fingerprint are, to the skillful detective, all representations by "indication" of the person who left them behind. There is nothing, of course, to prevent any particular representation from employing more than one of these relationships: a written text may symbolically represent (describe or narrate or dramatize) an action, and it may also indexically represent (indicate the presence of) its author as the "cause" of which it is an "effect." Photographs are commonly thought to combine iconic and indexical representation, standing for visual objects by virtue of both resemblance and cause and effect.

Now it is important to realize that the long tradition of explaining literature and the other arts in terms of representation is matched by an equally long tradition of discomfort with this notion. Plato accepted the common view that literature is a representation of life, but for that very reason he thought it should be banished from the ideal state. Representations, Plato reasoned, are mere substitutes for the things themselves; even worse, they may be false or illusory substitutes that stir up antisocial emotions (violence or weakness), and they may represent bad persons and actions, encouraging imitation of evil. Only certain kinds of representations, carefully controlled by the state,

were to be permitted into Plato's republic of rational virtue.

Although Plato's hostility to representation may seem extreme, we should recognize that some prohibitions or restrictions on representations have been practiced by every society that has produced them. Taboos against graven images, against writing or uttering the name of God, against the representation of the human form, against the representation of evil or ugly objects, against sex or violence, are an equally important part of the "social agreements" that constitute representation. The formula "let this stand for that to them" is regularly subjected to restrictions on subject matter ("let this stand for *anything but* that") or on the audience/spectator ("let this stand for that, but *not* to them"). Sometimes the prohibition may be directed at particular types of representational relationships: iconic representations, especially pictures and statues, are generally subjected to more stringent restrictions than symbolic or verbal representations. Greek dramatic conventions allowed the narrative, descriptive representation of violence but not its direct, visual portrayal on the stage. Pornography provides the most interesting examples of all these attempts to limit the triangle of representation, either by specifying the kind of persons who may witness the representation ("adults"; "18 and over"; "men only") or by restricting the kind of things that may be represented (no frontal nudity; no genitals; no actual sex acts), or by restricting the kind of representational signs that may be employed (dirty pictures and movies are usually subjected to more stringent prohibitions than dirty books).

It should be clear that representation, even purely "aesthetic" representation of fictional persons and events, can never be completely divorced from political and ideological questions; one might argue, in fact, that representation is precisely the point where these questions are most likely to enter the literary work. If literature is a "representation of life," then representation is exactly the place where "life," in all its social and subjective complexity, gets into the literary work.

There have been many other challenges to the notion of literary representation. Most of them, like prohibitions against idolatry or pornography, accept the basic model of the representational triangle but try to restrict or modify it in the service of some set of values. Thus, "idealist" theories of the arts will often posit some "higher nature" as the preferred object of representation and consign the representation of ordinary life to "lower" genres, such as caricature or satire, or some nonaesthetic genre, like "documentary" or "history." Realist theories of the arts tend to consign the idealist genres to the realm of "romance" and to see them as merely imaginary, fanciful representations. Both theories adopt the representational model of art: they simply disagree about what is to be represented (what Aristotle called the "object").

More strenuous challenges to representation come from the traditions of expressionism and formalism. Expressionism generally posits an unrepresentable essence (God, the soul, the author's intention) that is somehow manifested in a work. The "somehow" is the key: the unrepresentable is often construed as the invisible, the unpicturable, even the unspeakable—but not, generally, as the unwritable. Writing, arbitrary marks, hieroglyphics, and allegory are the signs that "encrypt" representation in a secret code. Thus, the cult of the artistic genius and the aura-laden artifact often accompany the expressive aesthetic. The aesthetic object does not "represent" something, except incidentally; it "is" something, an object with an indwelling spirit, a trace in matter of the activity of the immaterial. The anthropological model for the expressive aesthetic is fetishism, which does not treat its sacred objects as icons (i.e., representations by resemblance; pictures) or, in a

sense, as representations at all (though they are frequently describable as indexes). The mimetic aesthetic, by contrast, finds its anthropological counterpart in the notion of idolatry, the worship of graven images that represent by resemblance.

Formalist or "abstract" theories of art have provided the most fundamental challenges to representational models in the modern era. Many of these theories take music (which, for obvious reasons, is hard to describe in representational terms) as the paradigm for all the arts. Formalism emphasizes the representational means and manner—the materiality and organization of the "signifier" or representational object—and de-emphasizes the other two angles of the representational triangle. The represented object may even disappear when the medium turns itself back on its own codes, engaging in self-reflexive play. The potential witnesses to the representational act are reduced finally to an elite of technical experts and connoisseurs who appreciate the ostensibly nonrepresentational object. Modernism frequently presents itself as having "grown out of" representational models of art, language, and mind, and it has, in the modern era, been very unfashionable to talk about literature or the other arts as representations of life. To the formalist, literature is about itself: novels are made out of other novels; all poems are about language. If representation sneaks back in, it is likely to be turned backward: life imitates art, reality (nature, society, the unconscious) is a text, and there is nothing outside the text.

Once this turn is made, then the opposition between "life" and "literature" which animates the traditional notion of literary representation begins to fall apart. But the structure of representation itself, as a relation of standing for, seems to come back with a vengeance. Postmodern culture is often characterized as an era of "hyper-representation," in which abstract, formalist painting has been replaced by experiments like photorealism,

333

and reality itself begins to be experienced as an endless network of representations. The paradigm for the arts shifts from the pure nonrepresentational formalism of abstract painting and music to mass media and advertising, in which everything is indefinitely reproducible and representable as a commodity. Categories such as "the thing itself," the "authentic," and "the real" which were formerly considered the objects of representation (or as the presence achieved by formal purity) now become themselves representations, endlessly reduplicated and distributed.

A survey of postmodern experiments in literary representation would be outside the scope of this essay, which in any case is intended to raise the issue of representation as a problem that runs throughout the history of literary production. Suffice it to say that concepts such as the identity of the text, the determinacy of meaning, the integrity of the author, and the validity of interpretation all play a role in the representational (or antirepresentational) character of literary texts. The highly self-conscious fictive "labyrinths" of Jorge Luis Borges, with their pastiches of scholarly and historical documentation, deadpan realism, and bizarre fantasy, are often cited as paradigms of postmodern literary representation.

But it may be more useful to take as an example of literary representation a more traditional text, one that initiates a historic shift in conventions of literary representation and that takes the activity of representation itself as a theme. Robert Browning's "My Last Duchess" provides an especially interesting case study because it draws together so many different conventions of literary representation (lyric, dramatic, and narrative), and because it reflects as well on other modes of representation, including the pictorial and the political. Browning's text, to begin with, is a representation of a speech act, and thus of a speaker, a listener, and a specific setting. The Duke of Ferrara is "pre-

sented" to us (represented, that is, as if he were immediately present to us), describing a painting of his late wife ("my last duchess") to the agent of a certain count whose daughter is engaged to be married to the duke.

MY LAST DUCHESS

FERRARA

That's my last duchess painted on the wall,
Looking as if she were alive. I call
That piece a wonder, now: Frà Pandolf's hands
Worked busily a day, and there she stands.
Will't please you sit and look at her? I said
"Frà Pandolf" by design, for never read
Strangers like you that pictured countenance,
The depth and passion of its earnest glance,
But to myself they turned (since none puts by
The curtain I have drawn for you, but I)
And seemed as they would ask me, if they durst,
How such a glance came there; so, not the first
Are you to turn and ask thus. Sir, 'twas not
Her husband's presence only, called that spot
Of joy into the Duchess' cheek: perhaps
Frà Pandolf chanced to say "Her mantle laps
"Over my lady's wrist too much," or "Paint
"Must never hope to reproduce the faint
"Half-flush that dies along her throat": such stuff
Was courtesy, she thought, and cause enough

334

For calling up that spot of joy. She had
A heart—how shall I say?—too soon
    made glad,
Too easily impressed; she liked
    whate'er
She looked on, and her looks went
    everywhere.
Sir, 'twas all one! My favor at her
    breast,
The dropping of the daylight in the
    West,
The bough of cherries some officious
    fool
Broke in the orchard for her, the white
    mule
She rode with round the terrace—all
    and each
Would draw from her alike the approv-
    ing speech,
Or blush, at least. She thanked men—
    good! but thanked
Somehow—I know not how—as if she
    ranked
My gift of a nine-hundred-years-old
    name
With anybody's gift. Who'd stoop to
    blame
This sort of trifling? Even had you skill
In speech—which I have not—to make
    your will
Quite clear to such an one, and say,
    "Just this
"Or that in you disgusts me; here you
    miss,
"Or there exceed the mark"—and if
    she let
Herself be lessoned so, nor plainly set
Her wits to yours, forsooth, and made
    excuse,
—E'en then would be some stooping;
    and I choose
Never to stoop. Oh sir, she smiled, no
    doubt,
Whene'er I passed her; but who passed
    without
Much the same smile? This grew; I
    gave commands;

Then all smiles stopped together.
    There she stands
As if alive. Will't please you rise? We'll
    meet
The company below, then. I repeat,
The Count your master's known
    munificence
Is ample warrant that no just pretense
Of mine for dowry will be disallowed;
Though his fair daughter's self, as I
    avowed
At starting, is my object. Nay, we'll go
Together down, sir. Notice Neptune,
    though,
Taming a sea-horse, thought a rarity,
Which Claus of Innsbruck cast in
    bronze for me!

The first thing that may strike us about this poem is the way that Browning renounces any direct representation of his own views: the poet does not lyrically describe the painting, or narrate any events in his own voice; he lets his invented character, the duke, do all the talking, as if he were a character in a play. The second thing that may strike us is that this is not a play but something like a fragment or extract—a single speech or "monologue"—presented, however, as a whole poem. Browning has, in other words, deliberately collapsed the distinction between two kinds of literary representation—the brief, self-sufficient lyric utterance of the poet, and the dramatic speech that would conventionally belong in a more extended representation—in order to create a new hybrid genre, the dramatic monologue. This "collapse" of lyric and dramatic conventions is itself an act of representation in which what would have been a part or fragment (a dramatic speech) is allowed to "stand for" or take the place of the whole. And, indeed, one of the pleasures of reading this brief monologue is the unfolding of the whole drama that it represents in miniature. We quickly surmise that the duke is an obsessively jealous husband who had his last duchess killed because she was too free with her affections and approval—"she liked whate'er / She looked on, and her looks went everywhere."

The truly tantalizing mystery, however, is the meaning of the drama that this speech represents in little. Why is the duke telling this story to the agent of his bride-to-be's father? Is he trying to impress the emissary with his power and ruthlessness? Is he indirectly doing what he was unable to do with his last duchess, "stooping" to warn his next duchess that she had better be more discreet in her behavior? Is his speech better understood as a calculated threat in which signs of spontaneity are disguises for a deep plot or as an unwitting confession of the duke's inability to control the affections of women? What state of affairs (including "state of mind") does the duke's speech really represent? And (a rather different but related problem) what authorial intention or meaning is conveyed by Browning's *presentation* of the duke in just this way? What judgment are we being invited to make about the speaker and his words? It would seem clear enough that we are meant to disapprove, but what specific form does this disapproval take?

One way of getting at these questions is to reflect on the role of yet another character in the poem, that of the auditor, whose reactions are represented to us by the duke. The auditor is, of course, a representative of his "master" the count, a go-between who presumably is working out details about the dowry (the duke is evidently confident that the count's "known munificence" guarantees that he will make money on the marriage: "no just pretense / Of mine for dowry will be disallowed"), though the duke protests that he is really marrying for love ("his fair daughter's self, as I avowed / At starting, is my object"). But if the emissary represents the count to the duke in the implied drama of Browning's poem, he also represents the *reader* in its implied lyric address: like us, he is the auditor of the speech. What does this mean? What role are we, as readers, being coerced into by having ourselves represented within the poem?

One possibility is that Browning wants to place his reader in a position of weakness and servitude, forced to hear a repugnant, menacing speech but deprived of any voice or power to counteract it. The count's representative, presumably, has the responsibility for seeing that negotiations go smoothly in a marriage that will raise the count's daughter in the sociopolitical order (the difference between a duke and a count, exemplary representatives of feudal hierarchy, is crucial here). Should he warn the count that he's marrying his daughter to a Bluebeard? Should he warn the daughter to watch her step? Neither of these actions really opposes the duke's will; on the contrary, they are ways of carrying out his will, of "stooping" on the duke's behalf to convey warnings the duke would never "stoop" to make in person. If the duke represents the aristocratic, feudal social order, understood here principally as a system giving some men absolute power over others, and particularly over women in a system of exchange, the emissary represents a servant class or (as a representative of the reader) the new bourgeois class of nineteenth-century readers who may hear this speech as the echo of a bygone era, the "bad old days" of absolute power—a power which may be deplored, but which still has a power to fascinate, and which lies beyond our intervention.

The only representation in this poem that seems to have some power to intervene is the portrait of the duchess, which seems still to mock the duke with its free looks from the wall. He may control who can see her by drawing aside or closing the curtain that veils the painting, but he cannot control the way the painting looks. He could, of course, destroy it, just as he destroyed its original, the duchess herself; but he chooses not to. Is that because he wants it as a reminder that now he has her under his power? Or because he is, in some sense, no more capable of destroying the duchess's smiling image than he is of destroying those galling, disgusting memories of her behavior that he pours out on the envoy? If the painting functions as a representation of the duke's power, it also seems to be a continual reminder of his weakness, his inability to "make [his] will / Quite clear" to his wife. In a similar way, the duke's whole performance, his boasting speech to the envoy, is an expression of a wish for absolute power that has just the opposite effect, revealing the duke as someone who is so lacking in confidence about his power that he needs constant reassurance. His final appeal to the envoy to "notice" his statue of Neptune "taming a sea horse" is a transparent invitation to see the duke as a god "taming" nature, much as he "tamed" his duchess by having her painted on his wall. The duke thinks of his power as something that is certified by his control of representations—by his painting of the duchess hidden behind a curtain that only he can draw, by the statue of Neptune "cast in bronze for me," by his control over the envoy's attention (and those whom the envoy represents) with a strategic display of his gallery of representations. What Browning shows us, however, is the uncontrollability of representations, the way they take on a life of their own that escapes and defies the will to determine their meaning. If the duke truly has his last duchess (or himself) under control, why does he need to veil her image with a curtain? If he is so sure of his choosing "never to stoop" to make his will clear, why is he so conspicuously "stooping" to an underling, seducing a mere representative with this odd mixture of boasting and self-betrayal?

These, at any rate, are some of the questions that arise with respect to the duke's manipulation of representations within the mini-drama that makes up the poem. But what if we raised similar sorts of questions about the poem *as itself* a representation? Suppose, for instance, we think of this poem as itself a kind of dramatic portrait, a "speaking picture" in the gallery of Robert Browning's poetry? To what extent is Browning himself—or the commentator who claims to speak for Browning's intentions—playing a role like that of the duke, showing off his own power by displaying his mastery over representation? Should we think of Browning's poem, and the readings it evokes, as something we might call "My Last Duke"? Most readers of this poem have registered some version of Robert Langbaum's insight that "condemnation" is "the least interesting response" to the duke's outrageous display of evil. Just as the duke seems to hypnotize the envoy, Browning seems to paralyze the reader's normal moral judgment by his virtuosic representation of villainy. His poem holds us in its grip, condemning in advance all our attempts to control it by interpretation as mere repetitions of the duke's attempt to control his gallery of representations.

Browning's poem should make it clear why there would be a strong impulse in literature, and in literary criticism, to escape from representation and why such an escape can never succeed. Representation is that by which we make our will known and, simultaneously, that which alienates our will from ourselves in both the aesthetic and political spheres. The problem with representation might be summarized by reversing the traditional slogan of the American Revolution: instead of "No taxation without representation," no representation without taxation. Every representation exacts some cost, in the form of lost immediacy, presence, or truth, in the form of a gap between intention and realization, original and copy

("Paint / Must never hope to reproduce the faint / Half-flush that dies along her throat"). Sometimes the tax imposed by representation is so slight that we scarcely notice, as in the perfect copy provided by a laser disk recording ("Is it real or is it Memorex?"). Sometimes it is as ample as the gap between life and death: "That's my last Duchess painted on the wall, / Looking as if she were alive." But representation does give us something in return for the tax it demands, the gap it opens. One of the things it gives us is literature.

SUGGESTED READINGS

Aristotle. *Poetics.*

Auerbach, Erich. [1946]. 1953. *Mimesis: The Representation of Reality in Western Literature.*

Baudrillard, Jean. 1981. *For a Critique of the Political Economy of the Sign.*

Cavell, Stanley. 1979. *The World Viewed: Reflections on the Ontology of Film.*

Derrida, Jacques. 1978. "The Theater of Cruelty and the Closure of Representation." In *Writing and Difference.*

Eco, Umberto. 1976. *A Theory of Semiotics.*

Goodman, Nelson. 1976. *The Languages of Art.*

Langbaum, Robert. 1957. *The Poetry of Experience.*

Meltzer, Françoise. 1987. *Salome and the Dance of Writing.*

Mitchell, W. J. T. 1986. *Iconology: Image, Text, Ideology.*

Peirce, Charles Sanders. 1931–58. "The Icon, Index, and Symbol." In *Collected Works.*

Pitkin, Hanna. 1967. *The Concept of Representation.*

Plato. *Republic*, Book 10.

ACKNOWLEDGMENTS

Aciman, Andre. "Underground" from *False Papers,* pp 115–120, published by Farrar, Straus and Giroux, LLC.

Barthes, Roland. Excerpt from *Camera Lucida,* translated by Richard Howard. Translation copyright © 1981 by Farrar, Straus & Giroux, Inc. Reprinted by permission of Hill & Wang, a division of Farrar, Straus and Giroux, LLC.

——. "Leaving the Movie Theatre," reprinted by permission of Farrar, Straus & Giroux, LLC.

Bateson, Gregory. "Metalogue: About Games and Being Serious" from *Steps to an Ecology of Mind.* University of Chicago Press. 2000, pp. 3–8.

Benjamin, Walter. "Marseilles" from *One Way Street and Other Writings,* pp. 209–214. Copyright © 1985 by Verso Books NLB. Reprinted by permission of Verso Books NLB.

Berger, John. "Steps Toward a Small Theory of the Visible" from *The Shape of a Pocket*, copyright © 2001 by John Berger. Used by permission of Pantheon Books, a division of Random House, Inc.

Berger, John. "The White Bird" from *The Sense of Sight.* Vintage; 1st Vintage International edition 1993, pp. 5–11.

Berger, John. "Hiroshima" from *The Sense of Sight* by John Berger, copyright © 1985 by John Berger. Used by permission of Pantheon Books, a division of Random House, Inc.

Blume, Harvey. "Hammer." *Agni* 60, 2004, pp. 150–157. Published at Boston University. ISSN: 0191-3352.

Bogart, Anne. "Stereotype." *A Director Prepares: Seven Essays on Art and Theatre,* pp. 91–111. Copyright © 2000 Routledge, a division of the Taylor and Francis Group.

Carroll, Noël. "Art and Friendship" from *Philosophy and Literature*, Volume 26, Number 1, April 2002, pp. 199–206.

Doty, Mark. "Souls on Ice" from *Introspections: Contemporary American Poets on One of Their Own Poems,* edited by Robert Pack and Jay Parini, published by Middlebury College Press. Copyright © 1997 by Mark Doty. Used with permission. All rights reserved.

——. "The Panorama Mesdag" from *Drawing Us in: Writers on Visual Art.* Boston: Beacon Press. Copyright © 2000 by Mark Doty. Reprinted by permission. All rights reserved.

——. Excerpt from *Still Life with Oysters and Lemon.* Copyright © 2001 by Mark Doty. Reprinted by permission of Beacon Press, Boston.

"Joyas Voladoras" by Brian Doyle. First published in *The American Scholar*, Autumn 2004. Copyright © 2004 by Brian Doyle. Reprinted by permission of the author.

Eliot, T. S. "Tradition and Individual Talent" from *The Sacred Wood: Essays on Poetry and Criticism.* Alfred A Knopf, 1921.

Forster, E. M. "Art for Art's Sake" from *Two Cheers for Democracy,* copyright © 1949 by E. M. Forster and renewed 1977 by Donald Parry, reprinted by permission of Harcourt, Inc.

——. "Not Looking at Pictures" from *Two Cheers for Democracy,* copyright © 1951 by E. M. Forster and renewed 1979 by Donald Parry, reprinted by permission of Harcourt, Inc.

Goulish, Matthew. "Criticism" from *39 Microtechniques in Proximity of Performance.* Taylor & Francis Books, Ltd. Copyright © 2000 by Matthew Goulish. Reprinted by permission of publisher and author.

——. "How Does a Work Work Where?" from *39 Microtechniques in Proximity of Performance.* Taylor & Francis Books, Ltd. Copyright © 2000 by Matthew Goulish. Reprinted by permission of publisher and author.

Greenblatt, Stephen. "Culture," edited by Frank Lentricchia and Thomas McLaughlin, published by University of Chicago Press. Copyright © 1995.

Hillman, James. "The Poetic Basis of Mind," as appeared in *Blue Fire,* HarperCollins Publishers. Copyright © 1989 by James Hillman. Reprinted with permission of the author.

hooks, bell. "An Aesthetic of Blackness," *Yearning: Race, Gender, and Cultural Politics,* pp. 103–114. Copyright © 1990 South End Press. Reprinted by permission.

——. "Transgression and Transformation: Leaving Las Vegas" from *Reel to Real: Race, Sex, and Class at the Movies,* pp. 20–26. Copyright © 1996. Reproduced by permission of Routledge/Taylor & Francis Books, Inc.

Jones, Jonathan. "Look What We Did," from *Guardian Unlimited,* March 31, 2003. Copyright © 2003 Jonathan Jones. Reprinted by permission of the author. *http://www.guardian.co.uk/arts/features/story/0,11710,926134,00.html*

Jung, Carl G. "On the Relation of Analytical Psychology to Poetry." *The Spirit of Man, Art, and Literature,* Princeton University Press. Copyright © 1996 Bollingen, 1994 renewed. Reprinted by permission of Princeton University Press.

Sontag, Susan. "Against Interpretation" from *Against Interpretation.* Copyright © 1964, 1966, renewed 1994 by Susan Sontag. Reprinted by permission of Farrar, Straus and Giroux, LLC.

Sontag, Susan. "Looking At War," *The New Yorker.* December 2002, pp. 82–98.

Staples, Brent. "Just Walk on By: A Black Man Ponders His Ability to Alter Public Space." *Ms. Magazine.* September 1986.

——. "Vermeer in Bosnia" from *Vermeer in Bosnia: Cultural Comedies and Political Tragedies.* Copyright © 2004 by Lawrence Weschler. Used by permission of Pantheon Books, a division of Random House, Inc.

Wallace, David Foster. "Laughing with Kafka" from *Harper's Magazine*, July 1998, pp. 23–27.

Weschler, Lawrence. "We Join Spokes Together in a Wheel" from *Everything that Rises* by Lawrence Weschler, 2005. Copyright © 2005 by Lawrence Weschler. Reprinted by permission of the author.

Wilson, E.O. From *In Search of Nature* by Edward O. Wilson. Copyright © 1996 Edward O. Wilson. Reproduced by permission of Island Press, Washington, DC.

Winterson, Jeanette. "Art Objects" from *Art Objects: Essays on Ecstasy and Effrontery,* copyright © 1996 by Jeanette Winterson. Used by permission of Alfred A. Knopf, a division of Random House, Inc.

——. "The Semiotics of Sex" from *Art Objects: Essays on Ecstasy and Effrontery,* copyright © 1996 by Jeanette Winterson. Used by permission of Alfred A. Knopf, a division of Random House, Inc.

Woolf, Virginia. "The Cinema" from *The Captain's Death Bed and Other Essays;* copyright 1950 and renewed 1978 by Houghton Mifflin Harcourt Publishing Company, reprinted by permission of the publisher.

Woolf, Virginia. "The Death of the Moth" from *The Death of the Moth and Other Essays.* Harcourt Brace Jovanovich 1942, 1970, pp. 3–6.